SATIRE AND THE NOVEL

IN EIGHTEENTH-CENTURY ENGLAND

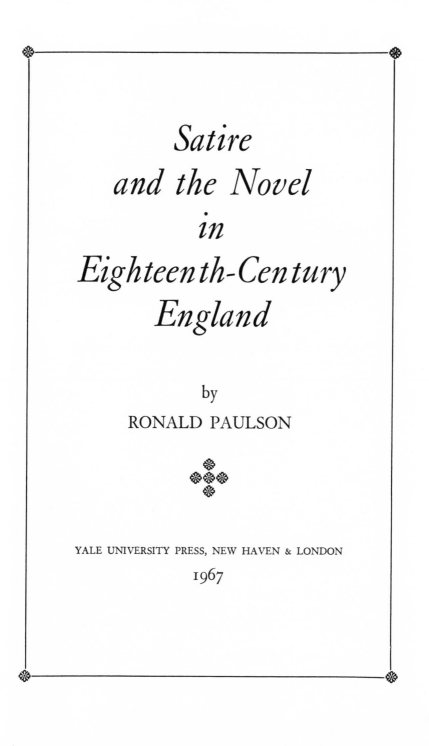

Satire
and the Novel
in
Eighteenth-Century
England

by
RONALD PAULSON

YALE UNIVERSITY PRESS, NEW HAVEN & LONDON

1967

❀ *Prefatory Note* ❀

My starting point is well summed up by Martin Price when he describes the novel as a derivative of two tendencies: "The mock heroic of Cervantes and his followers subjects the heroic image to the punishing presence of the commonplace. And the marvelous is naturalized as the saint's life, the rogue's picaresque career, the pilgrimage of the individual soul, are all enmeshed in the business of daily existence" (*To the Palace of Wisdom* [New York, Doubleday, 1964], p. 262). My intention is to pursue the first of these tendencies, tracing particularly the satiric strain that went into the making of the novel in eighteenth-century England. The subject, however, is dual: what happened to the novel when satire entered, and what happened to satire.

I treat in greater detail the specifically satiric phenomena of the Augustan Age in *The Fictions of Satire* (Baltimore, Johns Hopkins Press, 1967). A few sentences and several of the basic conclusions of that study appear in the present one, in which, however, my primary concern is with satire as it shades off into other modes of dealing with experience. Parts of Chapter 5 first appeared as "Satire in the Early Novels of Smollett," in the *Journal of English and Germanic Philology, 59* (1960), 381–402. Several paragraphs of Chapters 3 and 4 first appeared in a review in the same periodical (*61* [1962], 146–51) and subsequently, in revised form, in my introduction to *Fielding: A Collection of Critical Essays,* © 1962, reprinted by permission of Prentice-Hall, Inc., Englewood Cliffs, N.J. Thanks are due to the University of Illinois for a summer grant under which I began to think about satire and the novel; to Rice University for supplying me with a typist for the final draft; and to Mrs. Kathleen Roberts of the Yale Press for her careful copy-editing.

R. P.

Houston, Texas
December 1966

❀ Contents ❀

SATIRE AND THE NOVEL

IN EIGHTEENTH-CENTURY ENGLAND

Chapter 1

SATIRE

AND THE CONVENTIONS OF REALISM

The first half of the eighteenth century concluded the Augustan Age—the great age—of English satire. But in the same decade that saw the death of Swift and Pope, the novel, an ostensibly new genre but one with roots deep in the Grub Street writing attacked in *A Tale of a Tub* and *The Dunciad,* began to produce a series of masterpieces that contributed importantly to the eclipse of satire for the greater part of the next one hundred and fifty years.

This new kind of writing embodied many values abhorrent to the Augustan satirists; a form interested in human experience for its own sake replaced one that advocated strict moral judgment. Indeed, the novel and satire are convenient poles from which to chart the patterns of change in eighteenth-century literature and criticism. The novel, as the name implies, represents new values, and satire, usually a conservative genre, represents old. By the middle of the century the climate of opinion in England was Lockean, Latitudinarian, Shaftesburyian, benevolist, even deist, reacting against exclusive and extreme systems like Puritanism and High Church Anglicanism; it was middle class, matter-of-fact, and realistic in the sense of being interested in real people in real-life situations.

Justice vs. Law. The new age required a literary form that would express a more just, "more historical" interpretation of man's actions,[1] one that considered motives and extenuating circumstances before passing judgment. The organic conception of character defines character as a personality that endures in time, gradually developing,

---

1. See Stuart Tave, *The Amiable Humorist* (Chicago, University of Chicago Press, 1960), pp. 24–25.

maturing, decaying, and dying. Character is a man's life, a sequence of events. A second, opposing conception of character is essentially legalistic. The law defines character not as a personality developing in time but as an identity which exists in terms of a certain action—a crime—committed at a particular time. As Harold Rosenberg puts it, "Only information relevant and material to the legal 'cause of action' may be introduced as bearing on the parties and their transactions."[2] In literature satire is the genre most preoccupied with the moment of action rather than with the developing personality of the agent; it is legalistic to a fault, even more determined than the drama to judge and place the action, and almost wholly unconcerned with the culprit's past. It judges the man not for what he is but for what he did and, indeed, makes the ultimate error (according to the Age of Enlightenment) of equating the two. As Basil Willey has written of Swift,

> [the satirist] must, whether deliberately or not, miss precisely those aspects of the ignoble thing which in fact make it endurable to the non-satiric eye: that is to say, he must ignore the explanation of the thing satirized—how it came to be, its history. It is a fact of experience that *tout comprendre c'est tout pardonner,* and the satirist *ex officio* cannot pardon, so he must decline to understand all and explain all.[3]

The satirist shoots satiric rays out in space, catching as many aspects of folly and/or knavery as possible; but in time he touches only the past that was better and the future that will be worse, the ideal from which the fool or knave has fallen away and the greater depths of degradation or infamy to which he will sink (or the worse consequences which will follow). Change is often desired by the subject of satire, but it always remains false aspiration or attempted impersonation. Especially in the English Augustan Age, seen from the

2. See Harold Rosenberg, "Character Change and the Drama," in *The Tradition of the New* (New York, Horizon Press, 1959), pp. 135–53. I use Rosenberg's terminology although his point concerns the drama rather than satire.

3. *Eighteenth-Century Background* (New York, Columbia University Press, 1946), p. 107.

security of a conservative, order-conscious society, the typical satiric subject was the man who pretended, appeared, or even believed himself to be part of society, to be pious or rich, a doctor or a poet, while actually being an interloper from beyond the pale.

The distinction between organic and legal conceptions of character depends largely on whether the writer's primary concern is with the private individual or with society, with personal or public welfare. The impulses—and also the forms—that contributed most obviously to the novel were biography and other modes of private expression, often self-justificatory. The idea of organic character followed from the growing acceptance of the assumption (with which the satirist could never agree) that man is basically good and from the belief in progress. These led to, or demanded, a fiction that emphasized the growth of the individual. The hero of the new age—and par excellence of the novel—was the man "immediately oriented toward what he is not, toward what he desires to be"[4]—the Don Quixote who is no longer mad but who grows and changes before our eyes into what he wants to be. The villain of Augustan satire became the hero of the new age.

Subjectivity vs. Objectivity. More subtly dangerous to satire was the view of experience that followed the transition from the old epistemology to the new. Locke's doctrine that one can know only the impressions left on the individual consciousness by the hard particulars of the external world did not include such abstractions as truth. These objects, though certainly real enough, lost their objectivity and existed (or could be reached) only in the consciousness of the observer.

And so the eighteenth century heralds a change from a literature concerned with "the actions of a character in a situation with primary interest in the moral consequences and values of those actions"[5]—as in classical satire—to a literature concerned with the responses of a character's consciousness. Hume, who carries the concept to its logi-

4. Georges Poulet, *The Interior Distance,* trans. Elliott Coleman (Baltimore, Johns Hopkins Press, 1959; reprinted, Ann Arbor, University of Michigan Press, 1964), p. 97.

5. Ernest Tuveson, *The Imagination as a Means of Grace* (Berkeley and Los Angeles, University of California Press, 1960), p. 30.

cal extreme, argues that nothing can finally be established about an evil act; its quality cannot be ascertained by reason, only by the feeling of the observer:

> The vice entirely escapes you, as long as you consider the object. You never find it, till you turn your reflection into your own breast, and find a sentiment of disapprobation, which arises in you, towards this action. Here is a matter of fact; but 'tis the object of feeling, not of reason. It lies in yourself, not in the object. So that when you pronounce any action or character to be vicious, you mean nothing, but that from the constitution of your nature you have a feeling or sentiment of blame from the contemplation of it.

He concludes that "Vice and virtue, therefore, may be compar'd to sounds, colour, heat and cold, which, according to modern philosophy, are not qualities in objects, but perceptions in the mind."[6] In order to conform to this conception of mind, the satirist must shift his interest away from the satiric object—the culprit—to the satiric observer, either to the observer as observer or to the observer as a satiric object himself.

The distinction between old and new epistemologies applies to the object as well as to the observer. If the culprit is no longer identified with his action—no longer frozen in that symbolic pose—he becomes a walking consciousness, "nothing but a bundle or collection of different perceptions, which succeed each other with inconceivable rapidity, and are in a perpetual flux and movement."[7] Locke himself, arguing from the assumption that consciousness is identity, concludes that if the same awareness of the same sensations appears in Socrates and the "present mayor of Queensborough," they are the same person. Moreover,

> if the same Socrates waking and sleeping do not partake of the same consciousness, Socrates waking and sleeping is not the same person. And to punish Socrates waking for what sleeping

6. *Treatise of Human Nature* (1739–40), ed. L. A. Selby-Bigge (Oxford, Clarendon Press, 1888), Bk. III, Pt. i, Sec. i, pp. 468–69.

7. Ibid., Bk. I, Pt. 4, Sec. vi, p. 252.

Socrates thought, and waking Socrates was never conscious of, would be no more of right, than to punish one twin for what his brother-twin did, whereof he knew nothing.[8]

Whether the satirist deals with the observer or the object, he can no longer count on the emblematic character, a sitting duck in whom clear-cut patterns of right and wrong are evident to a reasonable, unprejudiced mind.

Immersion vs. Detachment. With the shift of interest from the objective action to the consciousness of it, and from the objective character to the dissolution of objective identity in consciousness, the reader finds himself no longer willing or able to step back and judge with detachment. José Ortega y Gasset remarks that in the novel both the narrative and didactic lines are lost in the piling up of descriptive detail, and what remains are a few characters and their world, with whom the reader becomes intimate:

> soon adventures by themselves lose attraction, and what then pleases is not so much the fortunes of the personages as their self-presence. We enjoy seeing those people before us and being admitted to their inner life, understanding them, and living immersed in their world of atmosphere.[9]

This is a world which, by means of its closeness to the particular character's mind, sucks the reader in and holds him there. "Immerse" is Ortega's key word to describe the effect of the novel, "a precinct, hermetically closed to all actual reality" into which the reader can sink.[10] Any doctrinal intention therefore destroys the hermetic quality of the work by directing the reader back into the real world, to the imperative Thou shalt not, or to the self-question, Am I a hypocrite? Am I self-centered? In the novel described by Ortega we "care" only "about the imaginary destinies of [the novelist's] personages" and their world, while in a moralizing form like satire we

8. *Essay Concerning the Human Understanding* (1690), Bk. II, Chap. 17, Sec. xix; cited, Tuveson, p. 28.

9. "Notes on the Novel," in *The Dehumanization of Art and Other Writings on Art and Culture* (Princeton, Princeton University Press, 1948; reprinted, New York, Doubleday Anchor Books, 1956), p. 57.

10. Ibid., p. 87.

must "face the acute problem of our own political or metaphysical destiny."[11]

In spite of these antinomies, however, the novel that emerged—at least the novel that leads from Fielding and Smollett to Austen and Dickens—was by no means uninfluenced by satire, and yet was no longer what a critic could safely call satire. It was not born in vacuo but appeared with telltale signs of its forebears. As one critic has put it, "There is hardly a function peculiar to other literary genres which [the novel] has not, partially at least, absorbed. The epic, history, tragedy, comedy, satire—all have contributed to feed this insatiable, growing organism."[12] In the eighteenth century, even as Richardson and Fielding and Smollett wrote, the novel was as yet undefined; this century helped to create its definition. In 1769 a novelist could insist that she knew "not whether the novel, like the epopée, has any rules, peculiar to itself"; and in 1771 another novelist could still exclaim:

How fortunate it is for us Historians, or, to take it a Peg lower, for us Life-writers, that no modern *Aristotle* has stept forth, and laid down Rules for the Conduct of History, like the Unities of Action, Time, and Place, prescribed by the Ancients to all dramatic Writers. (I hug myself when I think of it:).[13]

"Historian" and "Life-writer" give us this novelist's basic belief as to where he was going, and the repudiation of dramatic unities supports this belief. But one cannot dismiss his sense of joy at the freedom to make the novel whatever he wanted: he could call himself a biographer or a historian or an epic poet or a satirist.

On the other hand, satire itself, with only the most general kind of form of its own, infiltrates all other forms. The relationship between satire and the novel in the eighteenth century is in a general way analogous to the relationship between satire and the drama in the early seventeenth century. The tragic dramatist found uses for

---

11. Ibid., pp. 85–86.

12. F. C. Green, *French Novelists: Manners & Ideas* (New York, D. Appleton, 1931), p. 128.

13. Elizabeth Griffith, preface to *The Delicate Distress;* H. Lawrence, *The Contemplative Man, 1,* 213–14.

satiric conventions when he wished to expose reality beneath appearances or motives behind actions. Satire entered in various ways, touching the tragic hero and, through him, his fallen world, appearing as subtle undercutting and analysis as well as the vituperation of his disillusionment. In Shakespeare's mature tragedies, for example, the hero's pride, delusions, and mixed motivations have to be laid bare as well as his greatness established, which is the true tragic subject. The hero himself is given satire to utter and may, like Hamlet, Lear, Coriolanus, and Timon, partake of current conventions of satire such as the satyr-satirist and the satirist-satirized.

Alternatively satire was poured into an essentially nonsatiric genre, with a minimal attempt to subordinate the satire and a maximal one to subordinate the nonsatiric form. At the turn of the sixteenth century Jonson and Marston mechanically transferred formal verse satire to the stage, producing a scene that merely showed a railing satirist encountering a series of fools and knaves. But *Every Man Out of His Humour* was followed by *Volpone* and *The Alchemist,* and a new form evolved.[14]

The use of the play as a satiric form by the Elizabethan satirists in many ways parallels some of the attempts in the eighteenth century to use the form of the novel. The group of young Juvenalian satirists that included Jonson and Marston found itself without an outlet for its satire when the Bishop of London condemned its work, along with some Ovidian erotic poems, as obscene and consigned copies to the bonfire. By the middle of the eighteenth century the satirist was left without an adequate vehicle for his satire. Pope had carried formal verse satire and the satiric couplet beyond imitation, and the stage—which served as the testing ground for new satiric forms—was closed to satirists by Walpole's Licensing Act of 1737. After 1730 Fielding, Smollett, and Sterne were the only first-rate satiric temperaments to emerge in England, and all three turned to the novel. In the process they transformed satire beyond recognition and left the mark of satire upon the novel. Thanks largely to them, we now have other kinds of novel besides the one described by Ortega y Gasset.

But if Augustan satire infiltrated the novel at the relatively late date of Fielding's experiments, it was also one of the genres—with

14. See Alvin P. Kernan, *The Cankered Muse: Satire of the English Renaissance* (New Haven, Yale University Press, 1959).

the conduct book, the biography, the comedy of manners, and many more—from which the novels of Defoe and Richardson, as well as those of Fielding, gradually evolved. Once the romance came under attack, satire infiltrated so many of the long prose forms that any realistic form the novelist turned to for support had satire as an ingredient.

The English novel did not, of course, grow out of satire; they are two discontinuous forms. Throughout the ensuing chapters the reader should remember that satire is not *the* key to the meaning or essence of the major novels examined. It is only a partial answer, often accounting for means rather than ends, explaining *how* a novel got to be the way it is rather than *what* it is, illuminating rather than dogmatically fixing. Radically or subtly different novels resulted as the satiric intention continued or failed to exert its influence; thus Fielding clearly did not intend to write a satire when he introduced satiric conventions into *Joseph Andrews,* and Smollett as clearly did when he wrote *Roderick Random.* The satiric conventions used by both accordingly assume very different roles in the overall pattern of the works. A study of them may explain why certain effects appear in *Joseph Andrews* and others in *Tom Jones,* why others run through all of Smollett's novels, and even why some curious features remain in the novels of Austen.

The word "convention," which has appeared more than once in the last paragraph, refers to a rule, schema, or stereotype that formalizes experience to some artistic or generic end. What starts as a technique (e.g. stream of consciousness) may end as a convention, repetitiously and automatically used in certain situations, with or without its original aim. As time passes it becomes evident that the breakthrough to a new, more immediate effect is in fact the substitution of one convention for another, and it is advisable to consider no representation of experience as more than a particular kind of formalization. As art historians have shown, a painter, if he wants to paint a tree, goes to other paintings: "art is born of art, not of nature."[15]

In literature a new and original impulse may have to be expressed through old conventions which may, in turn, carry antithetic assump-

---

15. Ernst Gombrich, *Art and Illusion* (New York, Pantheon, 1960), pp. 24, 70–71; André Malraux, *The Voices of Silence,* trans. Stuart Gilbert (New York, Doubleday, 1953), p. 281.

tions. To complicate the picture further, the new impulse itself will not be pure but inevitably influenced to some degree by older generic aims, as well as by social, moral, and other contemporary conventions. Furthermore, the traditional aims of older genres will often be at odds with their currently popular conventions. The possibilities of relationship, influence, and effect are almost infinite. The particular conventions in which our two genres, satire and the novel, found their common ground were those of realism.

Satiric Realism

If the novel as it emerged in the seventeenth and eighteenth centuries has any generic aim at all, it is a commitment to the presentation of reality—not moral truth but the truth of actual experience—and the avoidance of convention and artifice. We can distinguish two main senses of "reality" to the early novelist. The more profound is the search for exactly what is real—whether it is matter or essence, manners or natural impulses, the poetic or the unpoetic. The more naïve but more pervasive sense of reality is expressed by Mary Mc-Carthy when she defines the novel as "A prose book of a certain thickness that tells a story of real life" and goes on to argue that "the distinctive mark of the novel is its concern with the actual world, the world of fact, of the verifiable, of figures, even, and statistics." This can mean the novelist's "passion for fact in a raw state,"[16] or it can include his wish to create the illusion of actuality—"that 'willing suspension of disbelief' that will render fiction . . . not *fictum*—wrought by appreciable artistry, but *fictum*—deceptive, illusory, something that blinds the reader to its existence as a medium intervening between him and his immediate perception of reality."[17] Out of this conception has grown what Claude Mauriac calls our modern "a-literature"—the literary work that attempts from the outset not to be literature.[18] *Paradise Lost,* for example, consciously sets out to be an

16. "The Fact in Fiction," in *On the Contrary* (New York, Farrar, Straus & Cudahy, 1961), pp. 250, 257.

17. A. Mendilow, *Time and the Novel* (London and New York, P. Nevill, 1952), p. 33. Mendilow's conclusion about the novelist's search is that his work "first tries to reflect reality as faithfully as it can, and then, despairing of the attempt, tries to evoke the feeling of a new reality of its own" (p. 38).

18. *The New Literature,* trans. Samuel I. Stone (New York, George Braziller, 1959), e.g. pp. 11–12.

epic, an exalted work of art; but *Robinson Crusoe* and *Pamela* pretend to be not literature at all but life—real documents written by persons named Crusoe and Pamela.

William Congreve, in his preface to *Incognita* (1692), expresses a remote precedent for this view, making the distinction between the romance and the novel that was generally accepted throughout the eighteenth century. The romance, he asserts, by its very nature deals with the wonderful, while the novel deals with the familiar and probable. Novels "represent to us Intrigues in practice, delight us with Accidents and Odd Events, but not such as are wholly unusual or unpresidented, such which not being so distant from our Belief bring also the pleasure nearer us."[19] Clara Reeve restates these assumptions —from the need for probability to the "pleasure" brought "nearer us"—at the end of the century in her *Progress of Romance* (1785):

> The Novel is a picture of real life and manners, and of the times in which it is written. The Romance in lofty and elevated language, describes what never happened nor is likely to happen. —The Novel gives a familiar relation of such things, as pass every day before our eyes, such as may happen to our friend, or to ourselves; and the perfection of it, is to represent every scene, in so easy and natural a manner, and to make them appear so probable, as to deceive us into a persuasion (at least while we are reading) that all is real, until we are affected by the joys or distresses, of the persons in the story, as if they were our own.[20]

Realism has come a long way from the permissive probability of Congreve to the immersion in a character's experience until one loses contact with the outside world—which is, in one sense, an unconscious return to romance. Both of the above statements—as well as the most famous of all such manifestos, Fielding's preface to *Joseph Andrews* (1742)—define the novel in terms of its opposition to the romance; and long before Congreve wrote, strongly satiric forms—

---

19. *Incognita: or, Love and Duty Reconcil'd. A Novel*, Percy Reprints, ed. H. F. B. Brett-Smith (Oxford, Blackwell, 1922), p. 6. Segrais, among others, had made the same distinction between romance and novel (*roman* and *nouvelle*) in his preface to *Les Divertisements de la Princesse Aurélie* (also called *Les Nouvelles françaises*, 1656).

20. *The Progress of Romance* (London, 1785), *I*, 111.

the picaresque novel and the burlesque or anti-romance—had developed various conventions of realism that played an important part in the eighteenth-century English novel. These forms arose in the sixteenth and seventeenth centuries as responses to the chivalric and pastoral romances and helped to revitalize prose fiction and make Congreve's dictum, by the time it appeared, a commonplace.

In the seventeenth century any work that we can now call an ancestor of the novel, and many that we cannot, maintained two essential elements: morality and some degree of realism. As Charles Sorel points out in his *Bibliothèque françoise* (1664), there were three paths toward a more lifelike presentation of experience in fiction: the romance itself, the *nouvelle*, and the *roman satirique*.[21] Even the romance writers were by this time insisting on a respect for probability in fiction, reflected in the successive modifications of the romance from chivalric to pastoral to historical. However, by realism they meant truth to historical fact or general probability *within* the old conventions of romance. While paying greater attention to psychological probability and/or historical accuracy, the romancers retained "the conventional poetic disguise"[22] of character (king, queen, knight, lady, squire, giant, dwarf, hermit, fairy, and savage man), oratory (set speeches, soliloquies, laments, and stylized conversations), and situation (love remains eternal). The *nouvelle*, which derived from the works of Boccaccio and Bandello, presented a less idealized love, with an urban setting, a much terser style, a shorter form, and—so far as it lived up to its name—a greater immediacy and topicality.

21. *Bibliothèque françoise*, 2d ed., pp. 177–81. See also A. J. Tieje, "The Expressed Aim of the Long Prose Fiction from 1597 to 1700," *Journal of English and Germanic Philology*, 11 (1912), 402–32; for the later period, see J. B. Heidler, *The History, from 1700 to 1800, of English Criticism of Prose Fiction*, University of Illinois Studies in Language and Literature, 13 (Urbana, University of Illinois Press, 1928). Also useful are Tieje's "The Expressed Critical Theory of European Prose Fiction before 1740 Exclusive of Problems of Characterization, Setting, and Style," Unpublished Doctoral Dissertation (University of Illinois, 1912), and *The Theory of Characterization in Prose Fiction Prior to 1740*, University of Minnesota Studies in Language and Literature, 5 (Minneapolis, University of Minnesota Press, 1916).

22. F. C. Green, "The Critic of the Seventeenth Century and His Attitude Toward the French Novel," *Modern Philology*, 24 (1927), 286. I am indebted to this article (pp. 285–95) for my quotations from Sorel. See also Gustave Reynier, *Le Roman réaliste au XVIIe siècle* (Paris, Hachette, 1914); F. Bar, "Le Roman réaliste en France au XVIIe siècle: problèmes de style," in *Stil-und Formprobleme in der Literatur* (Heidelberg, 1959), pp. 215–23.

But, Sorel objects, the *nouvelles* were immoral, wallowing in vice for its own sake; because of their brevity they had too limited a range; in fact, they really tended to be (or degenerate into) short, intense, more realistic romances. Congreve's *Incognita* itself was essentially a *nouvelle,* and its stylization removed it far from the realism sought by the eighteenth-century novelists. In the first half of the century, however, this remained the form generally meant by the term "novel."

The kind of fiction that gave the truest picture of life, according to Sorel, was the *roman satirique, burlesque,* or *comique.* First, "les actions communes de la vie étant leur objet"; they could show the particular manners, costumes, and details of living that were excluded from the romances. By their nature the burlesque novels stripped away the poetic disguise wrapped around the romance characters; as Sorel says in one of his own *romans satiriques, Francion* (1623), he adopts "le style comique et satirique" because "toutes les actions y paraissent sans dissimulation." Finally, this form, unlike the *nouvelle,* could present vices without lapsing into immorality because, being satire, it attacked them.[23]

Sorel's conclusion that comic novels give the most natural pictures of life is reflected in the titles of the most clearly realistic fiction of his time—*Histoire comique de Francion, Roman satirique, Roman comique,* and *Roman bourgeois, ouvrage comique.* Writing near the end of the seventeenth century, he sums up a tradition that goes back to the early sixteenth century. The writer of the period who wished to express the ordinary experience of day-to-day life, as opposed to the high aristocratic world of romance or the religious world of spiritual combat, had to go for his models to comedy or satire. He could not find such an account in the tragic, epic, or romantic genres, where it would have broken the rules of decorum as well as the assumptions of the genre; once Aristotle had made the distinction that comedy dealt with an imitation of man as less than he is and tragedy with man as more than he is, few attempted to violate it.[24] The real was the low and the low was the comic. Thus comedy in one form or another was a transitional force that did much to determine the

---

23. *Bibliothèque françoise*, p. 188; *De la Connaissance des bons livres* (1672), Chap. 4; and *Francion, 2, 217.*
24. *Poetics,* II.4.

shape of realistic fiction and the modern novel. To see why these writers turned to satire first and only with time modulated satire into comedy, we need to make an essential, followed by a historical, distinction between the two genres.

Comedy can be said to take two radically dissociated objects and by bringing them suddenly together produce an incongruous relationship. Two of the most incongruous categories from which objects are taken are the ideal and the real. James Feibleman's theory of comedy finds these the principal categories made to clash by the comic artist; comedy, he writes, is "the failure of things as they are to approximate to things as they ought to be." As he develops his theory, however, it emerges as a theory of satire. When he writes that comedy's aim is "the indirect affirmation of the ideal logical order by means of the derogation of the limited orders of actuality," he is revealing a distinction between comedy and satire.[25] We can illustrate this distinction with a very simple example of the comic. Groucho Marx as Captain Spaulding has just returned from a safari in darkest Africa and is regaling the guests at a party:

"We shot two bucks, and lost. That was all I had in my pocket. . . . We took some pictures of the native girls. Of course they were underdeveloped. But we hope to be back next year. . . . One morning I woke up and found a big rhinoceros staring right into my tent."
"And what did you do?"
"What could I do? I had to marry his daughter."[26]

Structurally these puns offer the simplest but most pervasive of comic patterns. The idea of big-game hunting ("bucks," "rhinoceros") or of anthropological research ("underdeveloped" photographs) with all of its connotations suddenly collides with an altogether different line of meaning (crap games or sex). The defeat of expectation is a contributing factor, but the comic effect depends mostly on the contrast between the romanticized African safari (established in Holly-

25. *In Praise of Comedy: A Study in Its Theory and Practice* (London, George Allen & Unwin Ltd., 1939), pp. 23, 178–79.
26. Ibid., p. 228. The analysis is mine.

wood movies of the 1930s) and the low-life realism of gambling and lechery. Depending upon the actor's emphasis, the passage can be comic or satiric. To the extent that the two areas of value and experience are simply put side by side, it is comic. However, as one side becomes normative and so causes a judgment to be made of the other, it tends toward satire; as the normative strengthens into the ideal, and the contrast sharpens to one between good and evil, the satire becomes more severe.

I suspect that we have here a small anti-romance, that the comic structure is being used to satirize the romanticism of travelers' tales, the tedium of lectures on strange lands, and the pomposity of the descriptions of scientific expeditions. As this analysis suggests, the satiric juxtaposition of ideal and real need not always find judgment in favor of the ideal. The ideal—here the world of the romance—is being attacked, at least as inappropriate for such as Groucho, the natural man who explodes its fraudulence. But satire, that thrifty genre, often uses the ideal-real opposition to catch aspects of both, the inappropriate conventions of romance and the man who uses them to mask his natural drives—all the talk of hunting and anthropology, we see, is a camouflage for the real reason that Groucho goes to Africa. Here we might say that a shred of idealism remains in the romance to criticize Groucho's lechery, and a shred of vitality remains in Groucho's lechery to criticize the romance. Comedy, on the other hand, makes no judgment, merely balancing the two orders of experience as equally acceptable.

Feibleman's use of "comedy" to cover a basically satiric intention is not without illustrious precedents and raises a curious point to which we shall return from time to time. Almost all theories of comedy before the eighteenth century equate comedy and satire, and most theories since then rigorously distinguish, as we have, ridicule (satiric laughter) from the risible or ludicrous (comic laughter). The significant fact is that apologists of comedy from the beginning have tried to make it respectable by emphasizing its moral aim, and the only way to do this was to turn it into ridicule of the morally or socially offensive. D. H. Monro cites the case of a little girl who explained why she laughed when a boy fell down and tore his trousers: "I saw a boy chasing a poor cat. He fell, and burst the seat of his trousers, so instead of hurting the cat he'll get hurt himself when he sees his mother."[27] There is something inherently comic about the small misfortunes of others, but in order to make human nature seem less cruel, one superimposes a moral order. Until the discovery of sympathetic laughter by theorists in the mid-eighteenth century, the only critical formula was for a laughter of censure.

Although it is possible to interpret Aristotle's dictum that comedy imitates the ugly as an incongruity theory, the critics who followed him transmitted it as a moral degradation theory. We laugh, they imply, from feeling superior to people less perfect than we. Through Cicero the theory reached the Renaissance: "The seat or province, so to speak, of the laughable [*ridiculum*] lies in a certain ugliness [*turpitudo*] and deformity [*deformitas*]; for those sayings are laughed at solely or chiefly which point out and designate something ugly in a manner that is not ugly."[28] And thence to Sidney: "Comedy is an imitation of the common errors of our life, which [it] representeth, in the most rediculous and scornefull sort that may be. So as it is impossible, that any beholder can be content to be such a one."[29] At the beginning of the eighteenth century, John Dennis still echoes the same didactic view:

> How little do they know of the Nature of true Comedy, who believe that its proper Business is to set us Patterns for Imitation. For all such Patterns are serious Things, and Laughter is the Life, and the very Soul of Comedy. 'Tis its proper Business to expose Persons to our View, whose Views we may shun, and whose Follies we may despise; and by shewing us what is done upon the Comick Stage, to shew us what ought never to be done upon the Stage of the Comick World.[30]

Thomas Hobbes, in the seventeenth century, is only looking with a colder eye than the Aristotelian when he defines laughter as "sudden glory," a grimace "caused either by some sudden act of their own,

---

27. *The Argument of Laughter* (Melbourne, Melbourne University Press, 1951), p. 76.

28. *De Oratore*, II.58, 236; cf. Aristotle, *Poetics*, V.I.

29. *Apologie for Poetrie* (1585), in *The Great Critics*, eds. J. H. Smith and E. W. Parks (New York, W. W. Norton & Co., 1951), p. 210.

30. *Defense of Sir Fopling Flutter* (1722), in *Critical Works*, ed. E. N. Hooker (Baltimore, Johns Hopkins Press, 1939–43), 2, 245.

that pleaseth them; or by the apprehension of some deformed thing in another, by comparison whereof they suddenly applaud themselves."[31] But Hobbes' correlation seems to have been the straw that broke the camel's back; through the eighteenth century the history of comic theory is the history of one attempt after another to refute Hobbes. The result was a series of distinctions proving what everyone (especially writers) already knew, that much that had been justified on the grounds of a general satiric intent was simply comic.

The transition from comedy-satire to comedy and satire, which to a large extent parallels the transition from satire to the novel, will be important for a later part of our study (Chap. 2), but at present the confusion of these two genres brings us back to the question of why satire was usually preferred as a means to realism. Although we may find an author calling his book interchangeably comedy and satire, he almost always defines it with a satiric vocabulary and, either crudely or with subtlety, satirizes his subject. As Sorel's comment on the immorality of the *nouvelle* suggests, the early novel was created in an age when moral justification was still necessary and the description of everyday life for its own sake was considered frivolous; therefore the "real" had to be attacked in order to be presented. Similarly, in aesthetic theory, decorum allowed for the treatment of the low but only as an object of ridicule, and so realistically conceived characters had to be foolish or knavish types.[32]

Although the novel may be ultimately concerned with understanding rather than judging, with comedy rather than satire, the situation was very different in the beginning. Satire was naturally most useful during the insurgent phase of a realistic movement, when manifestos were being issued and the strong walls of convention had to be broken through. Satire offered a militancy in the presentation of reality far beyond the reach of comedy.

The satirist customarily regards reality as something that the ordinary person can see only if he takes off the glasses of convention (the conventions of romance, pastoral, epic). He says, in effect: I am

---

31. *Leviathan* (1651), I.vi, ed. Michael Oakshott (Oxford, Blackwell, 1960), p. 36. For Hobbes' connection with Renaissance theories of comedy, see J. E. Spingarn, *A History of Literary Criticism in the Renaissance* (2d ed. New York, Columbia University Press, 1908), p. 103 n.

32. For a study of realism from this point of view, see Erich Auerbach, *Mimesis*, trans. Willard R. Trask (Princeton, Princeton University Press, 1953).

going to show you things as they really are. See how simple—all of this that appeared complex can be reduced to lust and greed; or else, See how complex—all of this that appeared to be simple is less easily formulable than you think. Surprising exposure is a basic satiric aim, and satirists have developed many ingenious ways of revealing truth under appearance. They have accordingly tended to adopt the pose of convention-destroyers and anti-romanticists. Beginning with Horace and Juvenal, satirists have established their "true" picture of life by contrasting it with the imaginary world of tragedy and romance.

If one satiric aim is exposure, another is to convince, at least momentarily, that its world is real and that the evil it shows really does exist. Satire's careful imitation of certain kinds of experiential reality is presumably what Gilbert Highet refers to when he says that the best satire has "the minimum of convention, the maximum of reality."[33] The classic models of satire—Horace and Juvenal—offered a much greater sense of formal realism than their comic equivalents —Plautus and Terence. Though realistic in its generosity of attitude, comedy was convention-ridden in form, trapped in the Terentian plot, and, in fact, closely connected with romance. As Shakespeare's comedies show, the genres of comedy and romance, with their common emphasis on the hero and his success, have as much in common as the genres of comedy and satire. Satire habitually turns its attention from the hero to the villain, even reducing the villain to one of a gang and eliminating the romance convention of a hero altogether.

Satura, or formal verse satire, Rome's contribution to satire, which made Quintilian claim that "Satura . . . tota nostra est,"[34] is the most influential of all satiric fictions. Its main aim is to expose a succession of different aspects of a single vice, a catalog or rogues' gallery, reserving a small niche somewhere for an indication of the good. The first-person speaker, however, is as important an element as the rogues described. The fiction constructed around him suggests a thoughtful or an outraged man describing what he sees or recalls, whether sitting in the solitude of his study or standing on a crowded Roman street. The object seen varies from recollected exempla to the looming presence of the bore in Horace's *Satire* I.9 or the garrulous Naevolus of Juvenal's ninth satire. Sometimes a third figure appears

33. *The Anatomy of Satire* (Princeton, Princeton University Press, 1962), p. 231.
34. *Institutio Oratoria,* X.93.

(or rather emerges) as the satire progresses: an adversary who questions the satirist or takes the contrary view. He is a vague figure who only serves to draw the satirist out, but he contributes to the illusion of a man talking and receiving occasional responses from a companion.[35]

Although it admits of many variations, *satura* is basically an imitation of a realistic situation. The speaker's perception is fragmentary, only that which one individual can see and remember, filtered through a sensibility; *satura* depends upon the immediacy of concern felt at something just seen or heard, and its end is the reader's empathy with the satirist. A real man, whose character has been carefully established, describes real events without, as Horace emphasizes, the ringing tones of epic or even the heightening of poetry; they are merely true. If Juvenal introduces the sublime style it is to match his outrage and, with the prolixity and confusion of his exposition, to establish the reality (and so the truth) of his indictment. In short, the fiction of Roman *satura* is that there is no fiction, that the vice in action and the exposure of the vice is actually happening.

The rambling speech—motivated by outrage or nonchalance—gives plausibility to the catalog form of *satura* at the same time that it disguises the careful climactic order, the thematic repetition, parallel, and contrast. The result is the exposition of a particular folly or knavery, seen from all angles in all its aspects.

The persistence of this general fiction (a speaker, the immediate apprehension of vice, and its castigation) in subsequent satire of all kinds is remarkable. Whenever a major satirist develops a new fiction, his imitators very soon reduce it to its conventional skeleton of *satura*—a phenomenon which serves to indicate both the academicism of most satirists and the conventionality of almost all satiric fictions. There is always a sense of inertia in satire that tends to draw the satirist away from fiction, plot, and imaginative realization to plain discourse, argument, and railing vituperation.

Confusion and prolonged critical battles over the etymology of satire have not helped matters. Those satirists who wished to rail supported the derivation from the Greek *satyra*—lecherous and satyr-

---

35. See Mary Claire Randolph, "The Structural Design of the Formal Verse Satire," *Philological Quarterly*, 21 (1942), 368–84, and "The Neo-Classic Theory of the Formal Verse Satire in England, 1700–1750," Unpublished Doctoral Dissertation (Chapel Hill, University of North Carolina, 1939).

ish—and those who felt cramped by the austere aims of satire supported the derivation from the Roman *satura,* which designated a form. *Satura* is the feminine of *satur,* meaning filled with food, cognate with the English "satisfaction" or "satiety." *Satura lanx* was a festival platter, filled to overflowing with meats finely chopped and heavily seasoned. In dramatic usage it designated a wild, plotless play derived from the Fescennine verses and not unlike the Old Comedy in its effect; legally, it was a catchall law. Thus from the Roman etymology, *satura* implies a form at least roughly dramatic into which almost anything can be poured, a form with a sociolegalistic content and even (it is impossible not to conclude) a preoccupation with food as symbol. As Highet puts it, "The essence of the original name therefore was variety—plus a certain down-to-earth naturalness, or coarseness, or unsophisticated heartiness."[36] Both derivations tell us something about Roman satire, but over the years they have sanctioned much nonsatiric writing under the banner of satire. The *satura* derivation led writers to produce works that contained much besides satire or that lacked an overall satiric action, with perfect confidence that they were satires. The *satyra* derivation led to the vast predominance of railing protagonists who, like Juvenal's first-person speaker, are separate from and personally unstained by contact with all the vice they witness. One of the vexing problems of later satirists—and more especially of those who attempted to write novels—was how to treat the spotless Juvenalian protagonist. Once he is a participating character in the action, his denunciation of the evil around him must be explained, either by making him a persecuted figure, as Juvenal usually does, or by admitting that his response is excessive and involving him in the satire, as Swift does with Gulliver in the Voyage to Houyhnhnmland.

The narrative equivalent of the catalog or anatomy of *satura* is the journey. The only difference is that in the narrative the series of encounters on the road are stretched out in time instead of being heaped together in a kaleidoscopic few moments. The chief problem of the narrative satirist is to decide what beginning and end to give his narrative. Satire is essentially the middle of the story, which Northrop Frye has described as the world of "complications" and "blocking characters" without hope of resolution in a happy or tragic

36. *The Anatomy of Satire,* p. 231.

ending, the time when "heroism and effective action are absent, disorganized or foredoomed to defeat, and . . . confusion and anarchy reign over the world."[37] And so a resolution, happy or otherwise, is antithetical to the general aim of satire, which can move only toward an intensification of the folly or evil already established, as Juvenal's women in *Satire* VI move from adultery to the poisoning of their husbands.

There is an interesting coincidence of effect here between the realist and the satirist. The realist seeks to convey the disorganized, truncated quality of experience, while the narrative satirist of necessity lavishes all his skill on the middle—on the individual episodes—and is sometimes very perfunctory about the containing action. He often writes works in which the middle bears very little relation to the beginning and end; or in which the beginning and end take up the very minimal space, suggesting that "one got through this time" but that the dragons and giants are still healthy and dangerous; or in which the conventional containing action is a parody and the happy ending only the crowning irony.

The satirist almost invariably begins with a concrete, historical particular, although he never stops there if he is more than a writer of lampoons; his subject is always the present, and by the quantity of particulars he dramatizes the multiplicity and disorder of the present, its lack of perspective and final judgment. Part of the pleasure of reading satire derives from its microscopic imitation of the topically and immediately commonplace. Even names of unknown people or places scattered in profusion on a page contribute to the realistic effect that is sought by the satirist; they suggest the actuality of a newspaper or the half-grasped reality one experiences in an overheard conversation on a street corner. Satire thus shares some of the thinginess that Mary McCarthy notes as a distinguishing characteristic of the modern novel and that Diderot called "petites Circonstances" and "petites choses."[38]

The novelist remains something of an anti-romanticist, and al-

---

37. *The Anatomy of Criticism* (Princeton, Princeton University Press, 1957), p. 192. Cf. Kernan, *Cankered Muse*, pp. 30–34, and *The Plot of Satire* (New Haven, Yale University Press, 1965).

38. See Denis Diderot, *Oeuvres*, Pleiade ed. (Paris, 1951), pp. 757, 1094; he is probably echoing Prosper Jolyot de Crébillon fils' "mille petites circonstances," *Oeuvres* (London, 1779), 7, iv.

though sometimes, unlike the satirist, he merely confirms the reader's own impression, invoking familiar reality, he just as often shows the reality that is hidden by manners or a lifetime of daily contact. The most essential difference is that he searches for an ultimate truth or reality, whereas the satirist seeks at best a provisional truth, in fact attacks the seeker of ultimate truths. As soon as the search for reality becomes a quest for its own sake, the search and/or the reality become subject matter for satire. The satirist may use reality as a way of knocking down the enemy's pretensions, or he may attack it as evil, or he may give it a moral significance of its own, but he always subordinates it as a means to a preordained end. It also follows that however realistic satire is formally—concealed in a travel book or an almanac—it must clearly get across the terms of its condemnation or ridicule, or, like Defoe's *Shortest Way with the Dissenters,* it fails.

We may also conclude that there is no such thing as experiential reality in a work of fiction, only different conventions for suggesting it. Satire's apparent realism is actually violent exaggeration; its slice-of-life is constructed of extremely stylized fictions; and its form-lessness conceals a conventional form that is symmetrical, discursive, and expository. Satire is as convention-ridden as comedy, the difference lying in its basic interest in exposure of *un*reality and in the present, which led to conventions intended to convey an appearance of the real. Satire, in spite of its conventionality, appears somewhat less conventional than other genres, and one of its conventions, at least in the works of its greatest artists, is the appearance of unconventionality.

Of course, the novel too conceals a variety of conventional expository forms under its apparent realism. In some instances these are satiric forms that have left their imprint, maintaining their original satiric meaning or merely persisting after the satiric intention of the anti-romance is gone.

The Evolution of Anti-Romance

In the sixteenth and seventeenth centuries, the aims of the satirist and the writer who wished to write realistic fiction coincided when both reacted against the chivalric and pastoral romances. Satire offered the first and perhaps the crudest kind of realism that contributed to the novel—a militant realism that establishes itself by destroying an illusion, by turning over a stone to expose the crawling things underneath. It attacks idealization by means of a counter-reality based on exaggerated probability, producing a travesty of the idealized world. Thus the ugly and gross, the sensual and fecal, are real in contrast to the beautiful and harmonious; the middling and commonplace, the urban and local, are real in contrast to the heroic and extraordinary, even to the ugly and gross as they approach melodrama.

The continental picaresque—from *Lazarillo de Tormes* to *Le Diable boiteux*—produces such realism in that it focuses on society at its most degraded. The picaro is everything that the hero of romance is not; he is of low birth, self-centered, mercenary, realistic, and adaptable to his surroundings, however mean. His illegitimate birth parodies the mysterious birth of the knightly hero, and his travels in search of food offer a mocking parallel to the knight's disinterested quest. The knight meeting dragons, beautiful maidens, and wicked magicians becomes the picaro meeting robbers, whores, and charlatans. The picaro's adventures with his masters are conflicts, ending in the defeat of one party (usually the picaro), just as the knight's adventures are conflicts with giants and monsters. Even the absolute contrast of good and evil in the romance is toned down until we can scarcely choose between hero and villain.

The fiction adopted by the picaresque novelist is usually that of a man recalling his misspent life, and the action begins with his family background, early childhood, and homelife before his connection with his first master. The emphasis, however, is not on his development but on the middle as middle—the series of relationships with masters as he moves up or down, backward or forward, in the world. The picaresque novelist most often stops with the middle, as his protagonist sails for a new life in South America or departs for a stint in the galleys. This abrupt end allows for a sequel, but it also supports the illusion of formal realism, implying that life has no pat denouement. When there is an ending, it is an ironic one, like that of *Lazarillo de Tormes* (1554), where the picaro at last finds the security he has persistently sought—in a life as husband of the local priest's whore.

What appears to be a man's life then is in fact a series of discrete relationships that serve as devices of satiric exposition. The basic fiction of picaresque satire involves the relationship between a fool and a knave or an innocent and a knave. The helpless, naïve, innocent picaro travels the road and meets men whose knavery is dramatized by their brutal treatment of him; or he meets men whose folly he himself can exploit, thereby demonstrating both his own knavery and their folly; or he is corruptible, a willing pupil for the scoundrel he meets and so a fool to the other's knave. The result is a spectrum of satiric subject matter presented through one of the most conventional of satiric fictions, traceable back at least as far as Horace and Juvenal.[39]

The relationships Juvenal employed—between patron and dependent, father and child, wife and husband, emperor and adviser, all essentially analogous to that of servant and master—were based on the subordination of one party and the benevolence and authority of the other. The most significant people the picaro encounters on his journey are his masters. With them he engages in a compact which involves a reciprocal responsibility that is lacking in his more casual encounters along the road. The master is responsible for his servant's education and welfare, and the servant owes loyalty and duty to his master. Every such relationship in the picaresque begins with the assumption of this norm and then deviates from it in various ways. One or both of the parties fail to live up to the contract (and the ideal).

In *Lazarillo de Tormes* the satiric effect of the relationship of the blind beggar with the servant Lazaro comes from the changes we observe in the latter, who reacts like a chameleon or, better, a thermometer to his environment. He must either assume the role of fool to his master's knave or starve. In this sense the picaro is anything but a rebel; he is, in fact, aspiring to become part of the social order with its security, comfort, and privileges. However, this is not enough; in the conflict over food he must, if he is to survive, become the aggressor, exchanging roles with his brutal master. He has to use against his master the very techniques of cheating and bullying that this same master has taught him. Lazaro finally repays his master

39. See my essay, "The Fool-Knave Relation in Picaresque Satire," *Rice University Studies in English, 51* (1965), 59–81.

for his stinginess and cruelty by sending him flying into a stone post. He has learned his lesson; in order to live he must become a knave.

If satiric realism in *Lazarillo* and its successors acts as a comment on the idealized figures of the romance and their improbable actions, it presents much more emphatically a fallen world in which no romance ideal can exist any longer. The Spanish picaresque may have begun as a comment on romance, but it is more significantly a comment on the world that is not the ideal. It resembles romance and differs from what is ordinarily thought of as realistic fiction, in that the realistic fictionalist takes joy in contemporary reality, while the satirist sees it as an ugly, repugnant alternative. To the latter it represents present corruptions as opposed to vanished ideals. As F. W. Chandler succinctly puts it, "The world of actualities, although a fresh interest in it had been discovered, was depicted in order to be attacked."[40] The reaction against romance became in the picaresque an attack on the world that rejected those romantic ideals.

A second, perhaps purer strain of anti-romance can be traced back to Erasmus and Rabelais and the early satires supporting the humanist revival. Their main purpose was to throw open windows, destroy the illusions, rigidities, and stupidities of the Scholastic categories, and return to an apostolic simplicity. There was no question with Rabelais as to whether reality—gross, imbibing, fornicating, defecating reality—was to be preferred to the dry and over-codified ideals by which men guided their every action. This satire utilized a peculiar figure, very different from the picaro seeking security whatever the cost. Reynard the Fox and Tyll Eulenspiegel were two such figures, but Panurge (in Rabelais' *Pantagruel,* 1532) was the most striking, with his abundant coat full of instruments, powders, and vials for use in discomfiting the pompous and self-assured. His satiric function is brought out in his debate with Thaumast (Chap. 18), in which the world of logic and reason (so refined that it cannot be put into words) is utterly defeated by the vulgar but real world of Panurge's gestures. His gestures extend as far as his shocking treatment of the lady of Paris and ultimately to the literal destruction of Dindinault and all his sheep. Each sheep dumbly following the leader and plunging to his death, followed by Dindinault and

40. *Romances of Roguery* (London, Macmillan, 1899), *1, 17.*

his shepherds, is the perfect symbol of the rigidity of behavior which Rabelais attacks. A Panurge is also necessary to cast overboard the first ram that starts the procession and to stand (as Urquhart translates) "on the gunnel of the ship, with an oar in his hand, not to help them, you may swear, but to keep them from swimming to the ship, and saving themselves from drowning" (Bk. IV, Chap. 8). Rabelais' purpose is in effect to cast his readers out into the sea with Dindinault to experience the real disorder and complexity of experience.

In the tradition of Rabelais the real, as the unpredictable, disorderly, and unformulable, is a corrective if not a good used to destroy the unreal romance of man-made conventions and stock responses. *Lazarillo de Tormes,* as it reacts against the clichés of romance, reflects to some extent the drift of the Rabelaisian anti-romance. Within the evil, fallen world Lazaro's openness, naïveté, limberness, and joy in deceit are brought into contact with the closefisted shrewdness of his masters, their blindness, miserliness, tight-shut knapsacks and locked chests. Generosity clashes with its opposite, and Lazaro goes around ripping and then sewing up a seam in the blind beggar's knapsack much as Panurge used to cut purses: "I would bleed that stingy sack, taking out not the usual nibble of bread he allowed me, but good big pieces, and also bacon and sausage."[41] The emphasis, however, falls on Lazaro's adjustment rather than on his rebellion, and so on his masters' knavery. Lazaro, unlike Panurge, never does anything except in self-defense. When he and the blind beggar eat grapes he keeps to their agreement and only when he sees that his master is taking two at a time does he eat as many as he can; then the clever master has the last word: "Do you know how I realized that you had eaten them three at a time? Because I ate them two at a time and you did not complain."[42]

Although the emphasis in *Lazarillo de Tormes* is conservative, the potential for celebration was recognized by later writers. They saw Lazaro's complete and appalling self-reliance as both a commentary on the world that forces him to this and a statement of man's essential independence from social restraint. It is an easy step from attacking this forced independence to using it as a weapon against the

41. *Lazarillo de Tormes,* trans. J. Gerald Markley (New York, Liberal Arts Press, 1954), p. 6.
42. Ibid., p. 14.

blind officialdom of secular and religious masters. Moreover, Lazaro is distinguished from his masters (whom we see only in their maturity) by the fact that he is not naturally evil but is forced by society to become a rogue. As Robert Alter puts it, "Though his scruples of conscience are few and faint, he demonstrates some strength in the virtues of the heart."[43] From the outset, the picaro is to some extent a representative of feeling against form. He is characteristically outside society but constantly reaffirms, by his fond memories of the beggar and his affection (however foolish) for the hidalgo, that he is part of the *condition humaine*. He cannot trust his masters or other authority figures in any form and must survive by cheating; however, this very knowledge about man in society tends to give him a greater brother-feeling with outcasts like himself, the unacceptable, the failures.

This hint of a duality in the picaresque is most evident in the function of physical suffering and the pervading motif of punishment. Punishment, especially in the later, more conventionalized picaresque novels, becomes the central action of individual episodes and is ordinarily used as a device of satiric exposition. When the victim is innocent, it serves to illuminate the punisher; when he is guilty, it illuminates the victim himself (the punishment becomes an emblem of his guilt), but, most often, it catches both parties.

With each encounter between the picaro and the characters he meets, the proportion of innocence and guilt shifts into a new ratio. The appearance of either a purely innocent victim or a completely just chastiser is rare, at least in the Spanish and continental picaresque. When the picaro is punished he usually has been caught cheating or stealing; when he is a punisher of wickedness it is usually to exploit someone's folly. *Lazarillo de Tormes* shows how closely the punisher-punished relation is bound up with the master-servant relation. When the blind beggar smashes Lazaro's head against the stone bull, he is punishing the innocent and reflecting his own evil, but he is also (as Lazaro himself recognizes) vividly demonstrating Lazaro's blockheadedness. And when Lazaro smashes the beggar's head against a post at the end of their association, he is perhaps unconsciously revealing a connection between the beggar's physical and moral blindness, but the action also reflects the wickedness of the servant. Even in the most abject hack writing that capitalized on the popularity and flexibility of the picaresque genre, one detects in the flaying fingernails and the stones that shatter teeth both a crude means of exposing illusions and a general comment on a brutal world. This double action, which is implicit in the world of *Lazarillo de Tormes,* finds its most perfect and influential embodiment in *Don Quixote.*

It is Cervantes' juxtaposition of the commonplace and the romantic that first brings us to something that we can claim is one kind of novel.[44] If Panurge is an antithetical, unidealized man put into a world of romance-deluded people, and Lazaro is a real man put into a real world, which still carries enough shreds of romance to remind the reader of the contrast, then Don Quixote is the final possibility, a romance-deluded man put into a real, unidealized, Panurgic world.

Beginning with the assumption that all literature instructs, Cervantes demonstrates that if a contemporary were seriously to imitate the courtly and ethereal ideals of the romances he read so avidly he would become not only ridiculous but dangerous; he would abandon his business and family to go in search of dragonish evils to slay, or he would challenge anyone who spoke slightingly of his "lady." The romance itself escaped being ridiculous only because its world was synchronized with the idealized code of manners it presented. This world was one in which love was the source of all actions; lovers were always faithful to the death; and dragons and giants did indeed lie in wait. The Cervantean anti-romance reproduced the ideal code of conduct, but placed it in a different world, real and unsynchronized.

44. Ortega y Gasset sees the novel as essentially an unresolved conflict between the romantic and realistic in which both are to some extent transformed; romance is absorbed and given perspective in a realistic context, and reality, an inert and desolate substance which cannot interest us by itself, is made poetic (*Meditations on Quixote* [1914], trans. E. Rugg and D. Márin [New York, W. W. Norton, 1961], p. 139). Following from Ortega's germinal essay, other critics have argued that the novel involves by definition some sort of confrontation of romance and a critical, militant, perhaps cynical realism, from which either or neither or both may emerge victorious. In this sense, the novel is born out of an act of satire. See Harry Levin, "The Example of Cervantes," in *Contexts of Criticism* (Cambridge, Harvard University Press, 1957), pp. 95–96; Lionel Trilling, "Manners, Morals, and the Novel," in *The Liberal Imagination* (New York, Macmillan, 1948), p. 203; Frye, *Anatomy of Criticism,* p. 306; Martin Price, *To the Palace of Wisdom* (Garden City, N.Y., Doubleday, 1964), p. 262.

Cervantes satirized the romances in *Don Quixote* by giving the romance code to an ordinary man living in seventeenth-century Spain. Quixote is a person who takes seriously the teachings of the romances he reads; his head is full of chivalric ideals and his mouth spouts vows of duty, succor, and poverty, as well as descriptions of his matchless Dulcinea. Moreover, he puts these words and ideas into disastrous practice, for he is totally unlike the romantic hero; he is old, poor, with creaky horse and shabby equipment, knighted in an innyard, even cowardly in the face of the commonplace sounds made at night by a mill. In one sense Cervantes has produced a travesty of the romance hero. He has bestowed on the real man the real physical hunger and exhaustion withheld from romance knights and the real shepherds and windmills of the Spanish countryside; he has shown the absurd and unhappy consequences of the conventions of knightly behavior in this realistic setting—prisoners loosed on an innocent populace, an extra whipping for a servant boy, broken heads for some, lost flocks of sheep for others, and many unpaid inn-reckonings besides the knight's own bruises.

But if Quixote is a travesty of the romance hero, the situation in which Cervantes places him is mock-heroic. He is an ordinary Spanish hidalgo of a decayed family who gets the idea that he, like his ancestors, is a knight-errant. The romance code is embodied in his delusion or insanity. The mock-heroic contrast is not between the ideal and the petty reality but between the man's mistaken idea of himself and the real man.

As contemporary satire, Cervantes' comment was that Spaniards were attempting to live by a code that was no less antiquated and self-deluding than Quixote's. However, as he develops his theme, it becomes apparent that the romance's lack of *vraisemblance* calls for attack on more than one count. The less serious is that the romance distorts experience while literature should tell the truth; the more serious is that in a sense the romance bespeaks an ideal world and code which, alas, real man does not measure up to. The following passage is typical:

> raising his fist high above his head, he came down with so fearful a blow on the gaunt jaws of the enamored knight as to fill the poor man's mouth with blood. Not satisfied with this, the mule driver jumped on his ribs and at a pace somewhat faster

than a trot gave them a thorough going-over from one end to the other.[45]

Here Quixote is being punished by the mule driver for seizing and manhandling his whore Maritornes, whom the deluded knight-errant took for a fair maiden come to test his chastity. Quixote's folly tries to make Maritornes into something she is not. The discrepancy emphasizes the squalor of the real Maritornes; but her squalor is nevertheless real, and Quixote's embraces would violate that reality, so nature punishes him. The mule driver's blows say: Look, this is real, you can feel it. A beating is a reminder of the supremacy of the real world over madmen's dreams and villains' attempts to confuse *meum* and *tuum*. The purgings and pummelings meted out to Don Quixote are tastes of reality opposed to his romantic illusions. His ribs are cracked, his teeth knocked out, and his fingers mashed as physical reminders that herds of sheep are not armies of giants.

But the punishment of Quixote at the hands of Maritornes' lover involves a double action. Cervantes presents one man being punished for his crime against reality (the emphasis is decidedly here), but also a second man, whose only standard is reality, beating him. *Don Quixote* becomes both an attack on a false ideal which, if practiced, would lead men to attack innocent folk with lances, and an attack on the real world in which the true ideal is unattainable. The unreal is attacked because it is unreal—and delusive, misleading, or capable of manipulation by hypocrites; the real is attacked because it is real and has usurped the place of the now unreal ideal.

I have stated this Cervantean balancing of romance against reality in moral and social terms, whereas the final effect of *Don Quixote* may suggest an epistemological problem. Again and again in the modern novel we encounter a protagonist who aspires to the idealized life of romance (literary, historical, heroic, aristocratic) and thereupon sees reality distorted through those aspirations; this life, with its code, aspirations, and way of thinking is contrasted to the protagonist's real world and true self. Cervantes shows that the romance world is an evil insofar as it represents a cramping of one's own nature, a madness that sees giants where there are only windmills, or a code of manners that is inappropriate to the particular

45. Cervantes, *Don Quixote*, Pt. I, Chap. 16; trans. Samuel Putnam (New York, Viking Press, 1949), *I*, 119.

man who aspires toward it or the particular time in which he lives. It can also be a good, however, insofar as it represents a corrective to the petty forms of the present, man's natural instincts that have been fettered by the customs of society, a higher reality revealed by some divine madness, the world of imagination and poetry, or even (by extension) the true reality beneath the deceiving appearances of the world, and the ideal world we fall short of. Quixote's point of view can therefore be used as a two-sided satiric device: on one side is the pattern of the unreal, unnatural, and immoral; on the other is an ideal world of dedication and eternal fidelity against which to measure the behavior of fallen, self-centered man.

That the double-edged satire of *Don Quixote* was not altogether overlooked by contemporaries is suggested by an early imitation, Charles Sorel's *L'Anti-roman, ou le Berger extravagant* (1627). Sorel's anti-romance attacks the recent French pastoral romances such as the *Bergeries de Juliette* (1588) and D'Urfé's *L'Astrée* (1607) and even accuses *Don Quixote* itself of falling into the errors it attacks. Sorel's protagonist, Lysis, is the young ward of a Parisian silk merchant. He refuses to be apprenticed and neglects his law studies but reads every romance he can get his hands on; accordingly, he falls in love with Charité, an ugly waiting-maid. "For her sake" he leaves home and becomes a shepherd, wandering at first near St. Cloud and later in the Lignon region familiar to readers of *L'Astrée*. He has a Sancho Panza, Carmelin, and at the end regains his sanity and marries the unprepossessing Charité.

The mock-heroic structure embodied within this character no doubt contributes to the double-edged quality of Sorel's satire; Lysis' isolation in his psychosis almost inevitably leads to the reader's partial sympathy. Like Quixote, Lysis is alone against a crowd of boorish villagers. Anselme, the courtly observer who follows Lysis about observing his symptoms, states the case: "For persons of greater understanding than the people of a Country-village might be deceiv'd, if they were soberly entertained with the extravagances of *Poetry*."[46] He contrasts Lysis with the city of Paris: he is going through his shepherd routine "not far enough from *ambition* and *avarice* to lead such an *innocent* life,"[47] and to prove it, the villagers

46. *The Extravagant Shepherd* (1633 ed.), p. 18.
47. Ibid., p. 20.

throw stones at Lysis. The question that begins to emerge is what to do with the irrational, the poetic element in life? Adrian, Lysis' guardian, a respectable Parisian silk merchant, follows the line of Quixote's canon and has Lysis' sheep sold and slaughtered and would "clap him in prison at *St. Martins,* where he should be whipt every day; or else send him to the Almshouse, to keep company with such fools as they dispose thither." Anselme, the gentlemanly dilettante who comes across Lysis as he would a butterfly or a curious stone, hopes to humor him and perhaps get him further away from Paris and the danger of a cure. He desires not to "deprive the world of the most excellent Fool that ever was; believing that if he should restore him to his understanding, it would have been a hard matter to reduce him to his folly." To him Lysis is "his Entertainer."[48]

The balancing of illusion against reality, whether in a character or a situation, is the most important quality of the Cervantean anti-romance. Our sympathy totters back and forth from Quixote's poetic imagination to Sancho's common sense, and inevitably the illusion and the reality become satiric comments on each other. After so much attention is given to the *dévot*'s delusion, the attention is shifted to the characters surrounding him, and his kind of reality becomes a test of theirs. The effect would be comic if a judgment were not being made at each stage.

The Quixote syndrome, when it appears whole, involves a partial recantation. It says that Quixote is totally wrong, that he is mad and the world is real; and yet in a sense he is right and the world is unreal or at least wicked and unimportant. *Don Quixote* is by all odds the most seminal narrative satire of the seventeenth and eighteenth centuries; in the majority of works influenced by it these contrary interpretations appear separately, with the emphasis at first on his error and then, in the later eighteenth century, increasingly on his innocence. Only in a significant few do they join.

Paul Scarron's Quixote is a yet more ordinary man than Sorel's. Anti-romance to Scarron means specifically travesty, the form most associated with his name (his *Virgile travesti* was translated into English as *The Scarronides*). In his *Roman comique* (1651) Quix-

---

48. Ibid., pp 21, 26.

ote's heroic imagination disappears and the Quixote-Lysis figure is reduced, by Scarronesque travesty, to the wretched and insignificant dwarf named Ragotin, who himself has written a heroic romance, *The Deeds and Achievements of Charlemagne,* in twenty-four books. Forsaking normal bourgeois pursuits, Ragotin desires—rather than aspires to—the romantic life of poets and actors and the love of a prima donna; thus Scarron's subject, a more plausible counterpart to Quixote's life of knight-errantry, is the squalid, unromantic life of an actor in seventeenth-century France.

The punishment motif of *Don Quixote* has become insistent by this time, and Ragotin, in consequence of his aspirations, is beaten, humiliated, tortured, and finally drowned. But whereas in *Don Quixote* the beatings point out the supremacy of hard reality over the hero's dream, in the *Roman comique* they represent an externalization of Ragotin's essentially mean and unheroic being. To begin with, he is a tiny man who is too proud. He lacks the heroic quality of a Quixote. While Quixote in his madness tries to change the world, Ragotin merely presumes to change his own status. His being purged, stripped, and whipped are steps in a return to the real Ragotin (not, as in Quixote's case, to the real world).

Ragotin's ordeal is part of the picaresque world in that it seems very likely that *anyone* who had imbibed, passed out, and been abandoned on that same road would have been treated as hostilely by nature and man. Scarron's emphasis, however, being on Ragotin's pride rather than his delusion, is also on humiliation rather than pain. In most of his punishments Ragotin is surrounded by the same group of people—the players whom he wishes to join and who act as a social context for his failures. In short, Ragotin represents the beginning of a transition from the metaphysical to the social, from punishment to embarrassment. Moreover, he is no longer even the central character of the book. Scarron uses him to point up the idea that a hero is contrary to reality: "for one will not serve our turn," he says, "and since there is nothing more perfect than a hero of a book, half a dozen heroes *or such as would be thought so,* will do more credit to mine than a single one."[49] So he populates his book with minor characters who think themselves heroes—from La Rappinière to La Rancune and Mme. Bouvillon.

49. Paul Scarron, *The Comical Romance, and Other Tales,* trans. Tom Brown and others (1700; London, 1892), *1,* 16; italics mine.

Although Scarron introduces his mock-heroes as grotesques, he is unique among anti-romanticists in including among all of his pseudo-heroes and aspirers to romance status a real hero and heroine—Destin and Etoile. Perhaps he has only taken one of the pairs of lovers from the interpolated tales of *Don Quixote,* but the effect is to combine romance and anti-romance and so suggest a larger, more generous grasp of reality. He admits romance to be one part of the larger complex of reality. Destin and Etoile, however, are carefully distinguished from the too idealized heroes and heroines of the inset stories and even from themselves as recounted in their romanticized histories.

Scarron's strategy is to play romance off against anti-romance—never letting romance in the present get out of hand, but also restraining and qualifying the world of anti-romance. In this way he expresses something similar to the ambiguous feelings toward reality and romance that Cervantes embodied in his protagonist. Three levels of reality are played off against each other—the romantic, idealized world of the characters' "histories" and digressions; the farcical adventures of Ragotin and his friends, which distort reality as much in their way as the romances do in an opposite direction; and between these two extremes the reality of Destin and Etoile, who, though their heroic and romantic potentials are never realized, are never mocked. Their actions are often prosaic, unexciting, and anticlimactic, but as characters they are regarded seriously and end as the norm of reality. Thus the persecution of Destin and Etoile is paralleled by the heightened stories of maidens and ravishers in the inset stories and also by the ridiculous antics of Ragotin and his painful persecution. Ragotin's end is one extreme, the romance ending another, with the fates of the ordinary people following a middle course.

The *Roman comique* casts a long shadow on the eighteenth-century English novel, a much longer one than on the French. We can detect in it the general plan of Fielding's *Joseph Andrews* and the novels of Smollett—a Quixotic fool and a pair of lovers, both parties pursued and persecuted, with one at least partly guilty and with ridiculous reactions to his persecution, the other innocent and dignified in adversity. In the second place, the *Roman comique* produces a satire set off by the romantic story of Etoile and Destin and shading off from the folly of Ragotin to the roguery of La Rancune, to the foolish knavery of La Rapinière, and to the quite different and more melodramatic evil of Saint Far and Saldagne and the heroes and villains of the interpolated stories. The pseudo-heroes, La Rapinière, Ragotin, La Rancune, and Mme. Bouvillon (a source for Fielding's Lady Booby-Slipslop), are shown to be merely part of the whole world that includes romantic heroes and villains embodied in story and the past and real heroes and villains in the present. The *Roman comique* shows that the picaresque structure can be given a semblance of unity by introducing a romance beginning and (however modified) ending—a pair of lovers pursued, separated, reunited, and married.

Early anti-romance questioned the romance assumptions as basically unreal and therefore wrong. The Quixotic anti-romance went a step further and questioned the reality that was opposed to the romance. By the later seventeenth century, French satirists—from Furetière to Molière and Boileau—were using the Quixote situation as a way to defend the romance (or the ideal, or the status quo). They transformed Quixote from an ambiguous symbol of the interdependence of illusion and reality into a symbol of the low masquerading as the ideal—a situation that altered neither the high nor the low, the romance nor the real, but attacked only the social climber or the bourgeois who tried to pass for a gentleman.

The first indication of a shift in emphasis can be seen in Sorel's changing his hero from a crazy old gentleman to the mixed-up young ward of a silk merchant. A new element, the social inappropriateness of pastoralism outside the circle of les précieuses, has been introduced. Quixote was a representative of the class that should, under certain circumstances, read romances; Sorel's hero should be learning his bourgeois trade instead. The later French anti-romances tend to follow *Lysis,* indeed going so far as to shift their emphasis from the conflict between illusion and reality, or the poetic and the actual, to the conflict between two codes of manners. The element of the fantastic in *Don Quixote* has disappeared: now there actually are peasants who act like knights and knights who behave as if they were peasants. In the *Roman comique* knight-errantry has become the life of actors and Quixote a bourgeois who sets out to imitate this inappropriate way of life.

In Antoine Furetière's *Roman bourgeois* (1666) the emphasis has moved decisively from the protagonist's ambiguous insanity to a more naturalistic explanation, his aspirations for a higher or more romantic social status than he actually enjoys and thus his adoption of a ludicrously inappropriate code of conduct. While Cervantes attacked the false conception of life the romance offered, the later satirists focused on this conception as it specifically affected the bourgeoisie. Presumably there might have been some point to the romance code's being accepted by the idle aristocracy, but there was something pernicious, unwholesome, and ridiculous about the bourgeois patterning his life on a romance. Yet, as Furetière tells it, the bourgeois is in fact defined by his snobbish aspirations. And so he traces the history of the busy bourgeois who assumes the ill-fitting armor, the actor's or shepherd's costume, and the stereotyped manners of the leisured aristocrat. That the aristocratic manners are not themselves questioned is made clear by the presence of Destin and Etoile as well as Ragotin in the *Roman comique;* it is only Ragotin's assumption of them that is comic, as in the Restoration fop's aping the externals of the rake's character.[50] Illusion and reality become aspiration and one's real status, and the result is the satiric entry into the novel or comedy of manners.

As its name suggests, the *Roman bourgeois* deals with middle-class characters who try to live by a romance code. Furetière opens with a mock-heroic invocation: "Je chante les amours et les avantures de plusieurs bourgeois de Paris, de l'un et de l'autre sexe." Javotte, a lawyer's daughter, becomes involved with a coterie of les précieuses, reads *L'Astrée,* and thereafter fancies herself another Astrée and will have nothing more to do with the elderly miser, Bedout, to whom she is affianced. Put into a convent by her disobliged parents, she elopes with her Celadon, Pancrace, one of the précieuses. She is, however, solidly bourgeois and, far from possessing wit, is tongue tied and stupid; her intoxication with preciosity loosens her tongue, but the resulting jargon is not happy. Javotte's aspiration to the manners of the précieuses is paralleled by the other heroine Lucrèce's indiscreet and unlucky admiration for the nobility. The consequence of

50. Aspiration itself was not frowned upon in the second half of the seventeenth century. M. Jourdain's error in *Le Bourgeois Gentilhomme* is in being presumptuous and pretending to be a gentleman when he is only a bourgeois; this is opposed to becoming an educated *honnête homme* of the upper bourgeoisie, like Jourdain's prospective son-in-law Cléonte (Auerbach, *Mimesis,* p. 368).

Lucrèce's aspiration to move above her station is seduction and the lover's theft of the written promise he had given her as security. An earlier suitor of Javotte's, Nicodème, a young Parisian advocate, has also read *L'Astrée* and *Le Grand Cyrus* and takes to grandiloquent speeches and gestures. One such gesture, proferring a guarantee of marriage to Lucrèce, who is in need of a father for her imminent child, causes him to lose his fiancée on the eve of their marriage. There is no mitigating sweetness or light of the Quixote kind in the *Roman bourgeois,* which is a single-minded analysis of middle-class pretensions.

As these later interpretations show, Quixote can also be transformed into a man who is not completely committed to one class or code of manners and who must define himself in terms of one or the other. Quixote has the education of the aristocrat without wealth and the poverty of the peasant without the possibility of doing manual labor. He can be taken as the representative of the lower class who tries to pass himself off as a denizen of the higher. Thus one line of development juxtaposes two sets of manners—those of an aristocratic coterie and those of the middle class—and introduces Quixotic figures who attempt to effect a transition from the lower to the higher. The development we have traced is from Quixotism to Bovarism, from Quixote's altruistic aspirations to Ragotin's and Javotte's egocentric daydreams. In relation to themselves and their own class the manners to which these figures aspire are both outdated and inappropriate. From this point on, in the France of Louis XIV, the anti-romance is less critical of the Quixotic manners—which are increasingly associated with the aristocracy—than of the bourgeois Quixote who makes a fool of himself, who ruins his prospects by mimicking the manners of his social superiors. This mimicry takes the form of preoccupation with the intricacies of fashion, the writing of elegant verse, and *l'amour précieu.* In England too the fop of Restoration comedy is never a comment on the manners of the court to which he aspires; he is only another Ragotin who, lacking wit and social poise, copies the externals of courtly manners while ignoring the spirit.

The development we have traced from *Don Quixote* to the *Roman bourgeois* shows the satirist and/or the realist moving from one area of subject matter to another which he considered more "real," from satiric realism as a gross antithesis of romance—the painful, fecal, and sexual—to realism as the commonplace. The transition is apparent in the difference between two statements of intention, one written in 1626, the other in 1648:

> If I dig in the ordures of the world, if I represent evil actions and even unchaste ones (although very rarely) in order to make them detested, and through bloody invectives which I make against vice purge the world of its corrupt manners, why will any one blame this labor?

> the true comic history according to the precepts of the best authors ought to be only a lively painting of all the diverse humours of man, with the lively censuring of a greater part of their faults under the simple appearance of joyous things . . . it is also said that it is ravishing to see there [in romance] only the deeds of kings and emperors, of princes and princesses . . . but there are other people who prefer to see the little adventures of a trip about Paris or of a promenade, such as could happen to them or to persons of their acquaintance, because that seems to them more natural and credible. . . . You will see them in this place under the names of diverse men the folly of some poets and senseless *amoureux,* the fanfarronades of some gentlemen of the sword, the gluttonies of spongers and flies of the court, the divers caprices of some women, the tricks of empyrics, alchemists, and false magicians. . . . What is still more to be observed is that in place of describing, as these kinds of books ordinarily do, only one way of life, e.g. that of a debauchee, a thief, or a *Chevalier hypochondriaque,* this book describes several.[51]

While the first of these statements harks back to the conventional Juvenalian pose of the satirist, the second has adjusted itself to its century. It makes the point that romance treats great, melodramatic, impossible evils, while the *histoire comique* treats the follies that escape the romancer as they escape the magistrate. The form assumed will be a series of satiric portraits whose subject will be the middle

51. Camus, *Cléoreste* (3d ed., 1626), 2, 720–21; Sorel's "Advertisement aux Lecteurs," *Polyandre, histoire comique* (1648), my translation.

class with its everyday doings—a variety of human social activities besides the lovemaking of the romances. Of its very nature this satire is a middle flight, both a corrective to romance and a more realistic form on its own terms. Furetière sums up the genre in his preface to *Le Roman bourgeois:*

> there have been very few who censure ordinary faults, which are so much more dangerous as being more common than great vices. . . . Does one not see every day an infinity of drunkards, bores, misers, pettifoggers, braggarts, flirts male and female? However, has there been any who dares to advise them of their faults and of their follies, if it has not been comedy or satire? They, leaving to the learned and the magistrates the care of combatting crimes, stop at the correcting of indecencies and of ridiculousness, if it is permissible to use that word.[52]

Furetière, we recall, supplies a middle-class subject in his novel, not the low or high life of *Don Quixote* or the actors and criminal types that are outside the social structure in the *Roman comique*. His aim is to render the middle area of experience which is neither melodramatic nor overtly symbolic, and, although he still treats his characters satirically—and they usually emerge as grotesques—they are shown to be neither very good nor very evil.

One of the most important aims of the later anti-romances was to correct the conventions of romance. Thus the hero and heroine were thrown out as the center of interest or at least reduced to an equal status with the minor characters. Furetière, claiming that he would not "make visible a hero dominant in all the piece," produced a series of related episodes with different leading characters; he reduced the second part of *Le Roman bourgeois* to little more than a series of portraits of nonheroes (not anti-heroes); even the symmetry of a conclusion in marriage is avoided. Although these principles were never completely adhered to even by Furetière, they do project a novel without the conventional romance form—a slice-of-life that finds its model in the catalog of satire, that restricts its portrayal to contemporary conditions, and that rejects the focus of interest upon

---

52. Paris ed., 1868, *1*, 1, 2 (my translation).

a central pair of characters and makes the minor characters as important as the romantic leads.

Furetière also shows—perhaps more importantly—that the meaning of reality is changing not merely from a more to a less extreme
materiality but from material objects to perceptions. At the outset of
our survey, reality was abstract; the ideal (ultimately God) was the
most real of all, compared to which men, tables, and chairs were
shadows. In the period of the anti-romance realism was materialis-
tically defined, though the anti-romanticist as satirist often saw the
materialistic real as less good than the ideal. But by the end of the
seventeenth century—even before the advent of Locke's *Essay Concerning the Human Understanding* (1690)—reality was being pushed
away from the hard external objects like tables and chairs to the
mind that perceives them. *Don Quixote* probably represents the most
influential sign of the change: Cervantes combines the apparent
reality of external objects with the apparent unreality of Quixote's
imagination and suggests that the true real is a combination of the
two. Furetière attacks the Quixotic figure and thus attacks false perception rather than, with the earlier anti-romanticists, the external
world. It is Javotte's idea of herself as an aristocrat that is wrong,
not the reality of herself or of the aristocrat. The emphasis on a mental state is very different indeed from the servant's relations with his
master, which remain purely physical in the picaresque; by turning
to the social scene, Furetière also substitutes for the brute reality of
drubbings the inward pain of embarrassment and social unease.

England: The Mixing of Conventions

The other, nonsatiric branch of the picaresque novel flourished in
England during these years and, in the works of Defoe, brought
forth the first blossom of the English novel. This genuinely English
picaresque is decidely centripetal, interested in the hero's life rather
than in the society through which he passes. A typical example is
the anonymous *Don Tomaso, or the Juvenile Rambles of Thomas
Dangerfield* (1680), which asks to be compared with *Lazarillo de
Tormes* and *Guzman de Alfarache,* even giving its hero's name a
Spanish form. The initial episodes closely follow these models:
Tomaso runs away from home with his rascally servant Jemmy, is

discomfited and exploited by Jemmy and his family in Scotland, and is subsequently robbed and stripped by a highwayman. However, "Fortune" steps forward and explains to the reader that "this young Guzman will be the better for these two robberies and this damned walk over the cursed rocks, as long as he lives. This is the way to try whether he have courage, whether he have patience, whether he have ingenuity."[53] These episodes, as Fortune explains, are not shown to test society on the touchstone of the hungry picaro, as in *Lazarillo* or *Guzman,* but rather "on purpose to put him upon trials of skill."[54] They are part of an initiation and education. Thereafter any resemblance between Tomaso and Guzman disappears, and the anonymous author makes the difference explicit when he comments on his hero's aim to appropriate "the whole Guinea trade":

> See here the difference between a Spanish and an English Guzman, the one pursuing a poor hungry plot upon his penurious master's bread and cheese, the other designing to grasp the riches of the fourth part of the world by the ruin of a national commerce.[55]

Another characteristic of the English picaresque is present in *Don-Tomaso:* the hero is from a higher sphere than the Spanish picaros, and when he sets out it is as master with Jemmy his servant. The English picaresque tends to deemphasize the servant-master relation. Nashe's *Unfortunate Traveller* (1594) was one authority for the writer of picaresque fiction in England, and Jack Wilton, though a servant of the Earl of Surrey, is most of the time virtually an independent agent; the choice of the criminal instead of the rogue shows a predisposition for the lone operator whose relationships, though still economic, are fleeting and, being robberies, one-sided.

Directly or indirectly the English picaresque takes its particular tone from the Protestant-Puritan heritage in which a man's life is

53. My text is Spiro Peterson's in *The Counterfeit Lady Unveiled and Other Criminal Fiction of Seventeenth Century England* (New York, Doubleday, 1961), p. 200. Peterson makes essentially the same point concerning Tomaso's Guzmanry in his introduction, p. 184. I have used his examples of English criminal biography because they are representative and easily accessible.

54. Ibid., p. 201.

55. Ibid., pp. 228–29.

more important than society—in which Christian flees his uncomprehending family and the city of Destruction to save his own soul. In the Spanish and French picaresque, where the Roman Catholic tradition remained strong, the protagonist's progress is not moral at all but prudential; at best he is allowed a progress toward self-knowledge. The irony of the Spanish picaresque is based on the amorality of the pilgrimage (or quest), which points up the secularized quality of the world through which the protagonist passes. In England, the Protestant strain of Christianity taught that every man, even the least, lives a life full of symbolic significance; thus the biography is the basic literary unit, not the episode as in the works of the classical writers (the whole life, not the Aristotelian action). The emphasis is on the individual whose life is followed; the life is no longer merely a pretext which accommodates or interacts with a picture of society. A man goes on the journey or the voyage of his life (a common metaphor in such works) and his encounters with people are conflicts, like the picaresque servant-master struggles, but these conflicts serve to define the traveler and not the people encountered; in fact they are usually his battering attempts to win through to his true destiny. His encounters become stages in his development toward good or evil, failure or completeness. His progression is a series of choices between good and bad alternatives of action. The ending, whether of a saint's life or a criminal's biography, is his conversion.

English realistic fiction is, in a sense, a secularizing of this tradition of spiritual biography. But certain serious difficulties are involved in the secularization. When Defoe reduces Christian to the ordinary man or woman, he retains both the suggestiveness of each situation in which his hero finds himself and (for partly conscious, partly unconscious reasons) the religious level of pious commentary, which no longer exactly fits the situation. In short, genres and intentions are mixed, and the reader is never very certain whether Moll or Jacque is struggling through the streets of the city of Destruction and Vanity Fair or through the various allegorical valleys and sloughs of his own character.

More to the point, the lives of both Christian and Mr. Badman offer room for incidental satire. The one puts an ordinary man on a road that is overtly symbolic of his life and puts in his way various dangers—Apollyon, Worldly Wiseman, Vain-hope. The other makes the traveler himself the danger, an evil type whose progress down-hill is marked by the villainies he perpetrates on the innocents (family, friends, neighbors) he meets; he is both a threat against which to be warned and a bad example whose behavior as well as his fate should make the reader sit up, take notice, and mend his ways.

Defoe stands out from the professional writers of his time because he gave a unifying core to his work; he wanted to show what it is like to struggle for survival in a marginal situation. His sense of the struggle as a reality was so great that he seldom relied on the clichés and conventions that served as experience for lesser writers. Only the conventional moral commentary remains, and this is so firmly embedded in the character's consciousness that it has often been accepted on a psychological level. When, as in *Captain Singleton* (1720), Defoe introduces the sentimental motifs of the faithful dog, the widow's mite, and the good sister, he recounts them no more emphatically than the other events that proceed and follow them; they are mere happenings and do not stand out as conventions. In his criminal biographies he is interested in some aspect of the life itself and so hardly transforms his story at all. If he must have a moral he adds it perfunctorily, often at the end. But all his interest goes into the criminal's profession—the skills through which he copes with his surroundings—and so he chooses criminals who are escape artists (Jack Sheppard) or pickpockets (Moll Flanders) or organizers (Jonathan Wild). As he says of Wild's life (preface), he does not present it "in a style of mockery and ridicule, but in a method agreeable to the fact."

The ordinary criminal biographer, however, seeing the world through a haze of conventions, simply reverted to the forms that he knew or that were popular and so produced cony-catching pamphlets, joke books, lives of Mr. Badman, and the like, all disguised as criminal biographies. Where we have contemporary newspaper accounts of a criminal, upon which the author could obviously have drawn, we can trace his conventionalizing and formalizing of the raw materials beyond recognition.[56] These works offer an excellent example of how the popular fiction of the time developed in practice.

56. E.g. ibid., p. 107.

We can start with the mere recounting of a life and see how such raw experience was shaped into a book. The primary tendency, of course, was to make the sensational facts respectable and turn the life into a moral exemplum, which involved introducing bits of commentary here and there and including a repentance and death at the end. The latter, a convention of life as well as literature, was usually supplied by the criminal himself. Richard Head turned *Jackson's Recantation* (1674) into a manual on highwaymen—how to be one and how to guard against one. The authors who wrote with a genuinely moral or didactic intention were, however, few. Many were interested in the crimes themselves, but unlike Defoe they could see them only through the eyes of Greene and Dekker, and the crimes were transformed into "pranks," "japes," and "mad frolics."

One tendency was to shape the story according to the conventions of picaresque satire, often underlined by calling the protagonist an English Guzman, Lazarillo de Tormes, or Quixote, without really producing satire or losing the centripetal movement of biography. The criminal served as an obvious translation of the picaro, and he ranged from the highwayman to the fugitive who must always keep moving to stay one step ahead of the law. However—the part that Defoe plays down in his criminal lives—the picaresque episode pits a servant against his avaricious master, and the result is a situation involving punishment or cheating. When the master becomes the robber's victim he loses the fairly complex personal relationship he had with his servant, but he is still the character who has authority on his side and, unlike some of Lazaro's masters, respectability. The picaresque's comparison of the two kinds of criminal, the unrespectable (robber) and the respectable (politician, merchant), allowed for ironic intensification in the British criminal biography, as in Will Morrell's so-called exploits and achievements.[57]

It is important to notice that most often the crimes described are not those that Defoe recounts, involving physical dexterity or a knowledge of the London streets, but confidence tricks which require victims who, though respectable, are themselves dishonest or greedy and criminals who disguise themselves. The confidence game serves these writers better than a simple robbery, where the separation of

57. *The Complete Memoirs of the Life of That Notorious Impostor Will. Morrell* (1694), in Peterson, p. 303.

guilt from innocence is clear-cut. These narratives most closely approach the spirit of their continental models in their emphasis on the satiric diffusion of guilt. Punishment—though much less violent and less symbolic than is suffered in the picaresque—is central to each episode, and no sympathy is wasted on the dupes of such swindlers as Will Morrell and Mary Carleton. Morrell, the country doctor who poses as a nobleman, fleeces women who want to marry for monetary advantage or social prestige; they all think they are taking advantage of his love, whereas he is taking advantage of their avarice or snobbery. Mary Carleton begins her career by outwitting fortune hunters who, thinking she is a German princess, want to marry her and make off with her money; "the bird usually came into the net of its own accord."[58] The ancestry of these scenes can be traced back to satires like Jonson's *Volpone,* where bad as Volpone and Mosca are they are never quite as bad as Corbaccio, Voltore, and Corvino, the rich and respectable merchants and lawyers who come to them to obtain easy money (and are relieved of their own). The important difference between the cheater-cheated relation in the English criminal biographies before us and in *Volpone* or the continental picaresque is that in the latter it is a device for assigning guilt and is accompanied by a sense of indignation. In the former it is simply part of the world, one of life's little ironies like Mary's duping of the very men who were so joyful when she won acquittal at her trial. The cheater-cheated form has been drained of its satiric meaning; without this, it amounts to a relationship between two different professions and two different social classes. The emphasis falls not on the folly or greed of the dupes but either on the cleverness of the confidence man (as in Defoe's lives) or on the battle of wits between the insider and the outsider.

The confidence game also connects with one of the continental picaro's standard devices, disguise—Quevedo's Don Pablos, for example, dressed as a king in school, later disguised as a gentleman to seek a rich and beautiful bride, as a beggar, a hidalgo, and finally, doubly disguised, as an actor playing a character in a play. The criminal biographer tends to seek out criminals whose acts are indirect and involve deception. Words like "counterfeit," "unveiled," and

58. *Counterfeit Lady* (1673), in Peterson, p. 75.

"imposter" appear in the titles; even those criminal biographies not directly concerned with confidence tricksters show this preoccupation, as when a highwayman disguised as a traveler is planted among travelers or when a robbed seaman deceives the robbers into thinking that he wants to join them and then steals back his money (*Jackson's Recantation*). All of the episodes in *The Counterfeit Lady* and *Will Morrell* have this in common—a man or woman pretending to be rich and upper class deceives the middle-class, respectably acquisitive shopkeeper (or his daughter) and makes off with his money.

In the anti-romance a Quixote figure fancied himself of a higher class and went out to act upon this assumption, willfully seeing everything he encountered as conforming to his delusion. At first the allusions to Quixote in *The Counterfeit Lady* and *Will Morrell* appear ironic. Mary Carleton reads too many romances ("believing all she read to be true") and sets out to dupe other people into thinking that she really is a German princess; Will Morrell is a doctor whose "industry honestly got him by his practice a comfortable subsistence, with which he maintained himself, his wife and family very handsomely, until about twenty years ago he began to be very lazy and much addicted to hanker after the conversation of the gentry thereabouts." Morrell, though called "our new Guzman," is also compared to Hudibras and to Don Quixote himself, and his abandonment of his family is called "knight-errantry."[59] However, Morrell and Carleton set out to delude the people they meet, as if Quixote were to convince the innkeeper that he *was* a knight. Nevertheless, there is something genuinely Quixotic about these two criminals. In almost every case the author takes time to explain why the protagonist behaves the way he does, and the answer is usually the same— a restless acquisitiveness that is finally irrational. Mary Carleton, we are told, goes to her death claiming that she *is* the German princess. She was not sexually profligate: "No, it was her other tricks of cheating and its attendants, lying and wheedling; at these she was her arts mistress, and these were so innate and natural with her that they were part of herself. You might as well expect to have a fish live out of the water as to expect her to be without acting some of these falsities."[60] When her lying propensity is compared to kleptomania, we

59. *Memoirs of Will. Morrell*, in Peterson, pp. 302, 303, 304, 359.
60. *Counterfeit Lady*, in Peterson, p. 55.

begin to see that she is, in her own way, as self-deluded and obsessed as Quixote.

Thus England in the early eighteenth century purveyed a large body of writing in which satiric conventions and forms from the picaresque survived in nonsatiric works. Even Defoe was not entirely immune. When Moll Flanders encounters the London marriage mart, she cannot refrain from describing it in satiric terms and arranging it into a satiric anatomy. These conventions again appear infused with satiric meaning in the works of Fielding and Smollett, but the effect is inevitably not quite the same; some of the satiric sting has gone out of them and some of the sense that this is simply "the way of the world" remains. The structure persists, however; the action is a mere container—birth, adventures, death (or conversion, transportation, imprisonment)—for episodes and situations such as the relations of punisher and punished, master and servant, or cheater and cheated. The same juxtaposition of classes and different manners remains, as well as the theme of appearance and/or illusion and reality that informs this social juxtaposition.

The other great strain of literature that comes to bear on the English novel in the eighteenth century—and which in general still carried the name "novel" at the beginning of the period—derives from the romance; instead of following the chronology of a man's life, it begins in medias res, lopping off birth and death and concentrating on one important episode in that life. Moreover, it does not limit itself to one protagonist but uses a couple, a pair of lovers, and the unit is usually a courtship. The general plot has the boy and girl separated, go their different ways, and be reunited at the end. The middle—the adventures—is superficially similar to the adventures of a picaro: often in dire straits, in danger, the hero and heroine struggle to survive. However, certain basic differences appear. The picaro has only his hunger to worry about, whereas the lover has a definite goal and his every act is determined by his love for his mistress; the nature of the danger is usually sexual, particularly in the case of the heroine, whose one object is not to obtain food (heroes and heroines of romance never eat) but to preserve her chastity for her lover. The conventional motifs that appear in almost every case are the remote setting, the lustful captain, the seizure by pirates, the sale into slavery, the seraglio, and plentiful disguises (whose effects are quite different

when used by a hero or heroine than when used by a criminal) leading up to the recognition scene and the reunion of the lovers.

The use of these elements by English writers in the early eighteenth century is exactly analogous to their use of satiric conventions.
Mrs. Mary Davys' *Accomplished Rake or Modern Fine Gentleman*
(1727),[61] for example, employs the plot of the boy and girl in love,
separated (his rape of the girl serves as the misunderstanding), and
eventually reunited; this plot is supported by an outright romance
plot involving the secondary characters, as well as a recognition scene
between the hero and his sister in a brothel, and various disguises.
However, as the use of scenes and dialogue (taken bodily from Restoration comedies) shows, Mrs. Davys also has in mind the plot of
the rake who wants a maidenhead without marriage and the lady
who wants to marry and domesticate the rake, with the ensuing
witty battle of the sexes. Both the romance and the Restoration comedy plots, however, turn out to be incidental to the real emphasis,
which falls upon the biography (the novel begins with the hero's
birth) and the progress of a rake, ending in his repentance. Again
the English novelist gravitates toward the exemplary life, however
much it is concealed and confused by the intrusion of complicating
conventions. Such complication can be a virtue, but in *The Accomplished Rake* the conventional stage-comedy plot of witty seduction
jostles the Mr. Badman plot, and both of these cancel out the most
interesting aspect of the novel as novel—the relationship that is partly
developed between the protagonist and his mother.

We have here a problem that seems to have been particularly in-
digenous to the eighteenth-century novel in England. As Arnold
Kettle has said, speaking of a nineteenth-century example, the novel
seems to be a kind of fiction in which "the centre of interest, the essential pattern of the novel, is not its plot, and it is the fault of the
plot that it does not correspond with this central interest."[62] There
is very often a lack of congruence between stated intention and the
total book, between logical and psychological progressions, between
plot and symbolism, and between differing conventions.

61. See *Four Before Richardson, Selected English Novels, 1720–1727*, ed. W. H.
McBurney (Lincoln, University of Nebraska Press, 1963).
62. *An Introduction to the English Novel* (London, Hutchinson & Co., 1951; reprinted, Harper Torchbooks, 1960), *1*, 130.

These faltering novelists of the 1720s mark the end of the first phase of satire's relationship with the novel. During the seventeenth and early eighteenth centuries a number of interactions can be traced between satire and nonsatiric forms. In most cases the common denominator is satiric realism, extending from the militant realism of anti-romance to the typical writer's unwearying effort to make the reader believe his story and to render his fiction morally acceptable.

We have therefore a wide range of essentially nonsatiric works that either employ satire or at least invoke it. Some writers, like Sorel and Furetière, wishing to write realistically about their contemporaries, needed to reveal the real under what people had complacently accepted as the real. Even if the writer's ultimate aim was descriptive, he required satire to open the door, and he still regarded with disapproval the pretensions of the bourgeois. Since satiric realism and the kind of realism that he appreciated were nearly synonymous, the realistic tone was characterized by its satiric bite.

At the other limit were works that wished to examine the psychology of passion, that were interested in the seamy and scandalous, or that were simply lubricious and regarded satire as a safe label. They are summed up by Bandello when he explains why he introduces indecency into his narratives (*epistre* to Vol. III): "I speak here of love, entirely as does a good surgeon of some putrefaction or abscess." The criminal biographer's typical explanation of why he described the lurid and wicked can be culled from Defoe's preface to *Roxana* (1724): "When vice is painted in its low-prized colours, it is not to make people in love with it, but to expose it." And so these writers pay lip service to satire or actually make the passion or the bourgeois citizen the object of a railing attack. Often the result is a strong assertion of works as satire when the author lacks the slightest competence as a satirist.

However, most serious realists before Richardson are able to see the subjects that interest them only through the eyes of the satirist. The tendency to see certain aspects of nature through the satirist's conventions was so difficult to overcome that even Defoe occasionally slips into the habit, and Richardson more than occasionally.

England has now become the main center of our attention. Although French realistic fiction of the seventeenth century shows a strong satiric bias and contributed to the English satiric novel, the

French novel of the eighteenth century—while tinctured by the works of Sorel, Scarron, and Furetière—went its own way. The accomplishment of the French was to break away early from the realism-satire partnership in works like Mme. de La Fayette's *Princesse de Clevès* (1678) and De Préschac's *Illustre Parisienne* (1679), and in the eighteenth century to develop the novel of psychological analysis through Marivaux, Crébillon fils, and Choderlos de Laclos. French satire, as written by Voltaire and others, turned from realistic forms to the completely unrealistic (oriental tales, *conte des fées,* etc.). Even for Crébillon fils, who used the sexual relationship in the manner of a satirist, satire is only incidental to a study of the play of social attitudes against the individual's mind. Le Sage, the exception that proves the rule, wrote self-consciously in the Spanish, not the French tradition.

In general, the English novel developed in two directions in the eighteenth century, neither profoundly influenced by the French. One was concerned with psychological processes and states of consciousness, but with their presentation rather than their analysis. Defoe and Richardson, the characteristic figures in this respect, were satisfied to create the reality and the complexity and made no conscious attempt to understand or dissect it. As one eighteenth-century French critic noted, the English novelists (particularly Richardson) "catch passion in the act" while the French express it analytically, looking backward or downward. Their triumph is their concern with detail, with fact. The other branch of the English novel was devoted to ordered exposition, sometimes bordering on—and in Fielding becoming—subtle analysis; but it analyzed a moral problem (for example, the rightness or wrongness of Tom Jones' actions), not the psychology of a character.

Chapter 2

FIELDING THE SATIRIST

Augustan Satire—and Comedy

Henry Fielding began his career consciously and ostentatiously grasping the coattails of the great English Augustan satirists. His first play was presented four years after the appearance of Hogarth's *Masquerades and Operas,* two years after *Gulliver's Travels,* and at almost exactly the time when Pope's *Dunciad* and Gay's *Beggar's Opera* seized the imagination of literary London. In *The Author's Farce* (1729) and *Pasquin* (1736) Fielding literally translated *The Dunciad* into the idiom of the stage. He merely restated Pope's epic action when he had the Poet in "The Pleasures of the Town" (the puppet show that makes up the second part of *The Author's Farce*) explain that "My lord mayor has shortened the time of Bartholomew Fair in Smithfield, and so they are resolved to keep it all the year round at the other end of the town."[1] The reference is to the popularity of pantomimes, harlequinades, and puppet shows in the west-end playhouses that was driving legitimate theater off the boards. "The Pleasures of the Town" presents Pope's allegorical kingdom where Queen Dulness (Fielding uses the name Nonsense, drawn from Pope's model, Dryden's *Mac Flecknoe*) is shown choosing a consort and awarding a prize, the contestants being Signor Opera, Monsieur Pantomime, Mrs. Novel, and Dr. Orator (cf. *Dunciad,* Bk. II). Seven years later, in the second half of *Pasquin,* Fielding transforms Dulness' conquest of London into Queen Ignorance's invasion of the kingdom of Queen Common-Sense. To emphasize the extension of literary transgressions to larger moral ones, he gives Queen Common-Sense as her chief ministers Law, Religion, and Medicine and shows

1. III.1, in *The Complete Works of Henry Fielding, Esq.,* ed. W. E. Henley and others (London, William Heinemann, 1903), *8,* 235. Subsequent parenthetical references are to this edition.

them betraying and then murdering her in order to turn the realm over to the usurping Queen Ignorance, under whose rule they will be able to carry on in greater safety.

It is a significant indication of the centrality of these plays in the satiric literature of the 1730s that Pope himself seems to have taken hints from them—including the stage-like setting and the introduction of nonliterary vices—for the fourth book he added to his *Dunciad* in 1742.[2] Fielding drew on Pope, Swift, and Gay as freely as he did on Homer and Virgil, and he perpetuated the war against dullness as a contemporary, making his association with the Augustans unmistakable by the pseudonym Scriblerus Secundus and by many complimentary references to their works. The target he aimed at in satire after satire for the next ten years was the same as theirs—the shoddy literary and artistic world of England from which could be intimated the larger political and moral malaise.

The Edmund Curllish bookseller, Bookweight, in *The Author's Farce* demonstrates the Augustan analogy between literary and other kinds of immorality when he recalls that one of his translators is "in Newgate for shop-lifting. The rogue had a trick of translating out of the shops, as well as the languages" (II.5; *8*, 222). Fielding sums up the satiric picture in Witmore's advice to Luckless:

> 'Sdeath! in an age of learning and true politeness, where a man might succeed by his merit, there would be some encouragement. But now, when party and prejudice carry all before them; when learning is decried, wit not understood; when the theatres are puppet-shows, and comedians ballad-singers; when fools lead the town, would a man think to thrive by his wit? If thou must write, write nonsense, write operas, write Hurlothrumbos, set up an oratory and preach nonsense, and you may meet with encouragement enough. Be profane, be scurrilous, be immodest; if you would receive applause, deserve to receive sentences at the Old Bailey; and if you would ride in a coach, deserve to ride in a cart. (I.5; *8*, 204)

Here in short are the devices and motifs of Augustan satire adopted by Fielding: the hint of an ideal ("an age of learning and true po-

2. See George Sherburn, "*The Dunciad*, Book IV," *Studies in English, 1944* (Austin, University of Texas Press, 1945), pp. 174–90.

liteness") against which to judge the present, the heavy admonitory irony, the links drawn between the sensational shows of Rich or Orator Henley and the shows of Sir Robert Walpole the prime minister, the analogy between the successful writer or politician and the common robber, and the general tone which pretends to herald chaos and doom. Twenty-five years later Fielding was still fighting his "paper war" with dullness (along the lines of Swift's *Battle of the Books*) in *The Covent-Garden Journal* and recalling the favorite imagery of Swift and Pope.

The Augustan tendency to embody a man's vice or folly in his literary offshoots in order to expose at once debased men and debased attitudes contributed to a particular image of evil that dominated Augustan, or Augustan Tory, satire. In the Grub Street writings parodied and ridiculed by Swift and the Scriblerians, which might be regarded as the ultimate extension of the reaction against romance, reality had come to mean, first, mere chaos and disorder— the reductio ad absurdum of Tristan le Hermite's argument before *Le Page disgracie* (1643) that "truth will present itself so badly apparelled that one will be able to say that it is entirely naked"— and, second, the personal and subjective. These erratic books, and the pride their authors took in their eccentricity (making claims for "the universal benefit of mankind"), point to an image of the evil man as a humor-character who lets one part of himself get out of control and dominate the rest—equally illustrated in the productions of Grub Street and the rebel Achitophel, both unbalanced, deformed, and ultimately useless, and yet proud of their deformity and eager to impose their imbalance on all other men, but of course doomed to failure.

The historical images of the religious fanatic, the economic individualist, and the political opportunist rebelling against his anointed king all found their appropriate analogue (the satirist argued) in the religious image of Satan rebelling against God. Once Dryden embodied the figure in *Absalom and Achitophel* (1681), he became specifically Milton's Satan, and his chief characteristics were hatred of the social body and established order, the intention of erecting an alternative world of his own and seducing as many others as possible to his plan, and impotence to do any lasting harm. This last element is of special interest; not only was the universe-changer trying to accomplish the impossible, to change God's creation and natural law, but he also demonstrated that it is in the very nature of evil to be self-deceiving, self-tormenting, and self-destructive. As Achitophel allows his reason (his capacity for plotting the overthrow of constituted authority) to grow, his body withers, and his disease and decrepitude give some suggestion of the weakness and inevitable failure of evil, while emphasizing its wastefulness. Another consequence of his imbalance is that although he is a force to be reckoned with in the body politic, Achitophel is comically ineffective in the commonest matters of life. King David's conception of Absalom is pointedly contrasted with that of Achitophel's "unfeather'd two-legged thing, a son" (l. 170). Absalom was presumably "inspir'd by some diviner lust, / His father got him with a greater gust" (ll. 19–20), while the son of Achitophel suffers the misfortune of Tristram Shandy's homunculus when Mrs. Shandy reminded her husband that he had forgotten to wind the clock. Achitophel conceives his son "while his soul did huddled notions try," and the result is naturally "a shapeless lump, like anarchy" (ll. 171–72). The result is also indicative of the end of all his plans and reminiscent of Satan's conceptions of Sin and Death, which were concrete embodiments of the idea of rebellion.

In Swift's satire the universe-changer, without losing his Satanic overtones, became a Quixote, a more comic and ineffectual analogue, who was brought back to reality by the commonplace world of windmills and sheep. Pope's image of duncical evil, though he made it clear that his subject was on a much lower level than Dryden's, was still much the same. Answering the objection that the scribblers he attacked were too obscure to merit his lash, too poor and dull and foolish, he replies that most criminals are poor: "But Poverty here is the accident, not the subject; he who describes malice and villany to be pale and meagre, expresses not the least anger against paleness or leanness, but against malice and villany." In fact, he concludes, "poverty itself becomes a just subject of satyre, when it is the consequence of vice, prodigality, or neglect of one's lawful calling. . . . For men are not bunglers because they are poor, but they are poor because they are bunglers."[3] Poverty is part of the trappings of folly,

---

3. "Letter to the Publisher," *Dunciad Variorum,* in *The Poems of Alexander Pope,* Twickenham Edition, ed. John Butt and others (London, Methuen; New Haven, Yale University Press, 1939—), 5, 15. Subsequent citations are to this edition. The subject of Tory and Whig satiric fictions is treated in greater detail in my *Fictions of Satire* (Baltimore, Johns Hopkins Press, 1967).

and Pope's duces are dangerous precisely because, although their overall plan cannot possibly succeed, they may cause immediate damage, as Satan, though he failed in his larger design, ruined Adam and Eve.

Pope's kind of evil is a small, grubby folly, too low for others to notice or waste time on, and so a danger that has been heretofore overlooked. It is a suffering, self-perverting, unhappy thing, as well as tempting and destructive. Like Dryden's and Swift's evil, it is impotent, weak, and without hope of survival: of the duces "scarce one is known to me by sight; and as for their writings, I have sought them (on this one occasion) in vain, in the closets and libraries of all my acquaintance" (5, 14). If it is weak, however, it is yet somehow indestructible:

> Who shames a Scribler? break one cobweb thro',
> He spins the slight, self-pleasing thread anew;
> Destroy his Fib, or Sophistry; in vain,
> The Creature's at his dirty work again;
> Thron'd in the Centre of his thin designs;
> Proud of a vast Extent of flimsy lines. (ll. 89–94; *4,* 102)

Here, in the *Epistle to Dr. Arbuthnot* (1735), the evil figure is as mixed and confused a thing as Sporus, who carries all the Satanic attributes associated with the Augustan agent of evil: he is attractive and nasty, tempting and impotent, "one vile Antithesis" (*4,* 119–20). The concessive sympathy, played down here, is much clearer in the portrait of Atticus, who, like Sporus, has perverted his own beauty, as Satan did his:

> Who but must laugh, if such a man there be?
> Who would not weep, if *Atticus* were he? (ll. 213–14; *4,* 111)

There are two versions of the villain in Pope's satire, however—the unsuccessful scribbler and the successful. The latter is the more dangerous, but the former's illusion is always capable, if taken seriously by any reader or critic, of becoming real. The poor and neglected scribbler is as dangerous, he says, as the scribbler with "his Lord, and whore." As with Vice, "Let *Greatness* own her, and she's mean no

more." In Pope's later satires the scribblers have been owned by
Greatness, and the first dialogue of the *Epilogue to the Satires* (1738)
ends with a vision (barely distanced by a subjunctive opening) of
Vice's triumphal procession:

> In golden Chains the willing World she draws,
> And hers the Gospel is, and hers the Laws:
> Mounts the Tribunal, lifts her scarlet head,
> And sees pale Virtue carted in her stead!
> Lo! at the Wheels of her Triumphal Car,
> Old *England*'s Genius, rough with many a Scar,
> Dragg'd in the Dust! his Arms hang idly round,
> His Flag inverted trails along the ground! (ll. 147–54; 4, 309)

The projected vision of the future that ended the earlier versions of
the *Dunciad* is made here and now in the closing lines of the 1743
Dunciad, in which all the lights of civilization go out one by one,
"And Universal Darkness buries All," including the satirist.

Whether in the satire of Dryden, Swift, or Pope, however, the
basic rhetorical strategy of Tory satire involved isolating individuals
and produced two general fictions. *Absalom and Achitophel* and *A
Tale of a Tub* followed *Don Quixote* in that they presupposed a
world that operates according to orderly principles, a Christian universe in which Satan and Achitophel, when they try to impose their
views, appear ridiculous and alone. It was important to show the
evil cutting itself off, and so many of the Augustan satires were
written from the point of view of the evil agent, either by ironically
regarding him as he would himself or by an outright imitation of his
speech. But although the evil agent isolated himself, the effect, noticeable to unsympathetic contemporaries, was that of the Tory satirist
isolating and even, in extreme cases (Curll, Dennis, Partridge),
maiming and destroying him.

The other form of Tory fiction, found in *Mac Flecknoe, The Dunciad,* and parts of *Gulliver's Travels,* presents an absurd universe in
which the assumptions of Quixote—or Achitophel or Satan—have
come true. Here it is the good man who is defeated and alone, a descendant of the alienated Juvenalian satirist. The isolated Satans and
Quixotes have taken over and are running society according to their
wildly individualistic ways; the good man is isolated in this chaos.

These then were the assumptions and the fictions with which Fielding openly linked his early works and which he employed at one time or another in his novels. However, he also must have been aware of the fiction of the Whig satirists, Addison and Steele. The obverse of the Tory fiction, their satire was written from the point of view of the normative *honnête homme* and his friends, with the evil agent peripheral and often absorbed, even without being reformed, into the good society. The *Spectator* (1711–12) presents a club, a social microcosm, an England in miniature, of which the reader is meant to think he is a part. The representative of Tory values, Sir Roger de Coverley, is neither excoriated nor revealed to be infamous, but only shown with his punch bowl and hounds, and the reader is left to conclude that the Tories, though good hosts and drinking companions, are incompetent, simpleminded old men who have lived beyond their time. Mr. Spectator *loves* Sir Roger, "that good old Man," and in spite of his follies, Sir Roger is accepted as part of the club, absorbed into the group, in effect forgiven because he is so harmless and lovable.[4] The club has room for Tories as well as a Whig (Sir Andrew Freeport), a Whiggish mediator (Mr. Spectator), and various other types who bear no direct relation to politics at all but carry their own distinctive interpretations of experience. This is a very different group from the Scriblerus Club, which contained only Tories who shared the same view of politics, literature, and life.

While the Spectator Club descends from Horace's circle of Maecenas, it also derives from the periodical convention of a variety of correspondents or experts holding forth on different subjects. The experts who answered questions in the *Athenian Mercury* became Defoe's Scandalous Club in the *Review* and Isaac Bickerstaff's reporters in the *Tatler*.[5] These remain points of view rather than characters; Steele has observers who submit articles on "gallantry, pleasure, and entertainment" from White's Chocolate-house, on poetry

---

4. So far as I know this interpretation is first recorded in John Aikin's "On the Humour of Addison and the Character of Sir Roger de Coverley," *Monthly Magazine*, 9 (1800), 1–2. C. S. Lewis has developed the idea persuasively in his essay, "Addison," in *Essays on the Eighteenth Century Presented to D. Nichol Smith* (Oxford, Clarendon Press, 1945), p. 2. My text for the *Spectator* is Donald F. Bond's (Oxford, Clarendon Press, 1965).

5. See Walter Graham, *The Beginnings of English Literary Periodicals* (New York, Oxford University Press, 1926), pp. 40–41.

from Will's Coffee-house, on learning from the Grecian, and on foreign and domestic news from St. James' Coffee-house. These are of course different points of view on different subjects, but applying different points of view to a single subject was also a popular device. All of these related, of course, to the various pseudosatires and journalistic writings of the time, such as Gildon's *The Post-Boy Robb'd of his Mail* (1692), whose subtitle explains its satiric method—"The Pacquet Broke Open. Consisting of Letters of Love and Gallantry, and all Miscellaneous Subjects: In which are Discover'd the Vertues, Vices, Follies, Humours and Intrigues of Mankind. With Remarks on Each Letter." A club of friends decides to expose the hypocrisies of men and have some amusement at the same time, and so they rob the postboys on their way to and from London, break open their packets, and read the letters. Each letter is followed by the comments of the various members of the club, whose names express their particular points of view—Mr. Temple, Mr. Church, Mr. Chappel, Mr. Grave, Mr. Summer, Mr. Winter, and so on. These comments bring out different aspects of the folly of each letter, but they are also present for the light they shed on different points of view.

The important element selected by the *Spectator* is the relative equality of the points of view. They are no longer simply right opposed to wrong but a spectrum either of values or, more often, of attitudes presented for their own intrinsic interest. As a fiction, the Spectator Club sanctioned satire that is less concerned with particular contemporary persons than with general comic types, that is more realistic and lifelike in the sense that its judgment is less rigorous, more tolerant, and more understanding. Much of the time the satiric emphasis is so slight that the *Spectator* seems to be engaged in a study of manners, comically juxtaposing different people with different origins, assumptions, and attitudes. In this mildly satiric setting, the *Spectator* projects many of the character types that populate the novel for the next hundred years—the hunting squire, the businesslike city merchant, the pedant, and the superannuated rake. They came together not to narrow by unfavorable contrast down to a single point of view but rather to portray a rich and varied society. The *Spectator* also established the discrete unit, the limited society—whether a club, a family, or a neighborhood—that would replace the unlimited wandering of the picaro as the milieu of the novel, and with this, the characteristically novelistic (at least eighteenth-century novelistic) atmosphere of comfort, deep roots, and security in friendships.

Thus in placing Fielding in relation to the Augustan satirists, we must keep in mind the assumptions and fictions of the Whigs as well as the Tories. Moreover, accompanying the Whig satire of the *Spectator* is the denial that it *is* satire. Addison and Steele stop frequently in both *Tatler* and *Spectator* to excoriate satire or at least satire written by Tories. Their attack on satire is in fact an attack on personal invective. Addison more than once equates satire and lampoon and calls it a violent weapon in the hands of a violent man (as opposed to a gentleman). While this view reflects the growth of a general reaction against satire, we must be careful to distinguish the actual satiric doctrine of Addison and Steele from the feeling generated by Addison's papers on satire and his casual references to it. Steele explicitly distinguishes in *Tatler* No. 242 (of Oct. 26, 1710, which became one of the central documents of satiric theory for the period) between what he calls "true Satyr" and "false": true satire is good-natured and general; false is malicious and personal. Recalling the great satirists of the past, Horace and Juvenal, he asserts

> that good Nature was an essential Quality in a Satyrist. . . . Good Nature produces a Disdain of all Baseness, Vice, and Folly, which prompts them to express themselves with Smartness against the Errors of Men, without Bitterness towards their Persons.

But he concludes that satire as it was being practiced in his day (i.e. by Tories) was "aimed at particular Persons" and informed by personal malice. The same definition of satire remains in the 1750s when Samuel Johnson defines it in his *Dictionary:* "Proper *Satire* is distinguished, by the generality of the reflections, from a lampoon which is aimed against a particular person; but," he adds, "they are too frequently confounded." (By "proper" he means the same as Steele's "true.")

None of the Tory satirists would have disagreed in theory with this definition of satire. As the development of Gulliver's character in Houyhnhnmland shows, they at least claimed to agree with Steele that "In all Terms of Reproof, when the Sentence appears to arise from Personal Hatred or Passion, it is not then made the Cause of

Mankind, but a Misunderstanding between Two Persons." They would not, however, have agreed with the corollary that the satirist must be good-natured or ridicule only the general follies of mankind. Swift claimed to write the most generalized kind of satire, whereas Pope, in the two versions of his letter to Arbuthnot on the subject, argues for attack on the particular malefactor. But these were only different ways of saying the same thing: the generic vice or vicious man was the object of satire, but satire cannot operate unless it approaches the general through those "living examples, which inforce best."[6]

To Steele then true satire is presumably a generic creation such as Sir Roger de Coverley or Will Honeycomb. But Addison, in his *Spectator* papers on the subject, does not explore true satire and, by his emphasis on the false, strongly suggests that he thinks there is no other kind (e.g. *Spectator*, Nos. 23, 35, 355, 451). His statements can hardly be called a theory, and if pinned down he probably would have agreed with Steele. However, for a variety of reasons, many of the post-Addisonian writers on satire choose to apply his strictures to all satire, no longer accepting the distinction between true and false satire: a satire *was* an ill-natured attack on a particular enemy of the satirist.

Behind Addison and Steele's attacks on satire was a basic belief, shared by an increasing number of their contemporaries, in the greater value of "such Passages as represent humane Nature in its proper Dignity" than of passages that "depreciate humane Nature, and consider it under its worst Appearances" (*Tatler*, No. 108). Addison's strictures on lampoon tend to give the impression that satire as a malicious attack on individuals is being challenged by a more generous comedy, which laughs at (or even with) general types. In this sense, Sir Roger de Coverley is an example of the transition from satire to comedy, from a more to a less rigorous mode, and an anticipation of certain major characters of Fielding and Sterne. Sir Roger is of course a humor-character and his follies are humors. In *Spectator* No. 101 Sir Roger is conceded to be "a great Humourist in all the parts of his Life," and in No. 106 he is again "something of a Humourist," "his Virtues, as well as Imperfections, are as it were

6. See Swift's letter to Pope, Sept. 29, 1725, and the letter from Pope to Caryll, Sept. 27, 1732, in *The Correspondence of Alexander Pope*, ed. George Sherburn (Oxford, Clarendon Press, 1956), 2, 325; 3, 316.

tinged by a certain Extravagance, which makes them particularly *his,* and distinguishes them from those of other Men." By this time, as Stuart Tave remarks, "Sir Roger's humors cannot be changed, and one does not want them corrected; for not only are they his natural manner and color, peculiar to him as an individual and delightful for their own sake, but also they cannot be touched without destroying his virtues."[7] The authors are evidently very fond of "the good old Knight," "the good old Man," not in spite of but because of his peculiarities. In No. 107 he is "A Man of Honour and Generosity," and in No. 116 (by Eustace Budgell) even his hunting dogs are too Sir Rogerish to kill a hare. He becomes Addison's "favourite," and his purity—which began with his failure to make contact with the real world—becomes so overpowering that rather than risk a stain on his character Addison (according to tradition) kills him.[8] In No. 517 all weep for "our good old Friend," and in No. 544 he is remembered as "that honest plain Man." Here easy to see and early in the century is a character who begins as a humor-character in the old sense,[9] representing politically objectionable principles, and who soon becomes the author's "favourite," loved rather than ridiculed for his follies.

The old meaning of "humor," used by Ben Jonson and his imitators and still in general critical use, was an aberration from the norm, an obsession which usurped all the person's other vital impulses. To Samuel Butler a humor

is but a Crookedness of the Mind, a disproportioned Swelling of the Brain, that draws the Nourishment from the other Parts, to

7. Tave, *The Amiable Humorist,* p. 105. Addison appears to distinguish humors of this sort from what he calls "pedants" in *Spectator,* No. 105: "Everyone that does not know how to think out of his profession, and particular way of life." The one carries overtones of freedom and expansiveness, the other of imprisonment.

8. See Eustace Budgell, *The Bee: or, Universal Weekly Pamphlet,* No. 1 (February 1733), p. 27; and John Campbell, "Addison," in the *Biographia Britannica* (1747). For the view that Addison was harder on Sir Roger than Steele was, see Emile Legouis, "Les deux Sir Roger de Coverleys: celui de Steele et celui d'Addison," *Revue germanique,* 2 (1906), 453–71.

9. Or "humorist," as he was called in the seventeenth century. To the Elizabethans "humorist" meant "satirist," the man who exposes the humors; in the eighteenth century, with characters like Sir Roger, "humorist" came to mean a person with endearing peculiarities (see Tave, p. 92).

stuff an ugly and deformed Crup-Shoulder. If it have the Luck
to meet with many of its own Temper, instead of being ridiculous, it becomes a Church, and from Jest grows to Earnest.[10]

Of course to the men attacked by Butler, Dryden, and Swift as fanat-
ics and madmen the excesses for which they were blamed seemed
good not bad things; and their views were in the ascendant. Criti-
cally, the distinction between humor as a good or an evil hinged on
whether it was natural or affected. To the extent that humor was
affected, Jonson and other satirists aimed their ridicule at it; theo-
retically the satirist could satirize only that for which a person is
himself responsible. "A satire," as Addison put it, "should expose
nothing but what is corrigible, and make a due Discrimination between those who are, and those who are not, the proper Objects of
it" (*Spectator,* No. 209). In practice, however, humor-characters were
of both types and uniformly ridiculed, although, of course, the character of the laughter differed markedly between that addressed to a
Volpone or Tartuffe and that addressed to an Arnolphe or Alceste.
By the end of the seventeenth century Congreve was making the
distinction that allowed for a character like Sir Roger. If man is born
with his humor and cannot change it any more than his face, he can
hardly be blamed for having it, but he may, being found diverting,
be admired for it. Congreve defines humor as "A singular and un-
avoidable manner of doing or saying any thing, Peculiar and Natural
to one Man only, by which his Speech and Actions are distinguish'd
from those of other men."[11] If the humor is peculiar to only one
man, it cannot be matter for satire, which supposes all men to be
much alike; if no one else has this humor, there is no point to the
satirist's exposing it.

The definitions of humor were predictably along party lines. The
Whigs, the low-church adherents, saw much oddity as amusing or
even admirable for its own sake—a heritage of the Revolutionary
settlement and a manifestation of English liberty. As Sir William
Temple put it:

10. "Humorist," *Characters,* ed. A. R. Waller (Cambridge, Cambridge University
Press, 1908), p. 139.
11. J. E. Spingarn, *Critical Essays of the Seventeenth Century* (Bloomington, Indi-
ana University Press, 1957), *3,* 248.

Plenty begets Wantonness and Pride: Wantonness is apt to invent, and Pride scorns to imitate. Liberty begets Stomach or
Heart, and Stomach will not be Constrained. Thus we come to
have more Originals, and more than appear what they are; we
have more Humour, because every Man follows his own, and
takes a Pleasure, perhaps a Pride, to shew it.

Congreve attributed English superiority over other nations in the
creation of humorous characters to "the greater Freedom, Privilege,
and Liberty which the Common People of *England* enjoy. Any Man
that has a Humour is under no restraint or fear of giving it Vent."[12]
The Tories, on the other hand, attacked these very qualities as uncon-
trolled and chaotic license. The dichotomy is the same one that made
the merchant an object of ridicule or attack by the aristocratic Tory
satirists and an object of defense by the Whig comic writers like
Steele: the same people are described, but their traits are ridiculed by
one and shown to be lovable by the other. In short, the developing
theory of humors as admirable eccentricities fulfills Swift's prophecy
in *A Tale of a Tub* that the moderns would soon be bragging about
their humpbacks and extravagant posteriors.

The meaning of humor, however, is only one aspect of the idea of
comedy itself. The history of the criticism of comedy is largely a
matter of whether *utile* or *dulce* is the more important consideration.
As long as audience-oriented theories of criticism held sway—which
lasted until the great Romantic revolution that began in the eighteenth century—art was judged in terms of its end and effects. The
Renaissance critics interpreted Horace's *utile et dulce* to mean that
pleasure contributed to the primary end of teaching, and so whenever comic forms were considered, even if the actual effect was purely
comic (as was often the case), the work tended to be analyzed as a
study in ridicule and therefore satire. The critical view that equated
comedy and ridicule persisted into the eighteenth century. Hobbes'
theory of laughter as "sudden glory" or pleasure aroused by another's
discomfort was only a cynical expression of what all theoreticians
felt. Even Jeremy Collier in his *Short View of the Immorality and
Profaneness of the English Stage* (1698) attacked the egoism of
Hobbes' theory but expressed the more conventional view that "The

exposing of knavery, and making *Lewdness* ridiculous is . . . occasion for Laughter; And this with submission, I take to be the End of *Comedy*." To John Dennis " 'tis the Business of the Copies [which comedy makes of the foolish and vicious] to expose, and satyrize, and ridicule those foolish and those vicious Originals"; elsewhere he notes that "without the *Ridiculum* Comedy cannot subsist, for the design of Comedy is to amend the follies of Mankind, by exposing them." As late as 1762 the author of *The Art of Poetry* was writing that "the design of Comedy is to make vice and folly appear ridiculous, and to recommend virtue."[13]

Nevertheless, beginning with Dryden, who tends to put *utile* and *dulce* in the order in which Horace himself placed them, making pleasure the final aim, we can detect the beginning of a transition in critical theory from comedy as a means to a moral end to an end in itself, sheer pleasure. Moreover, Hobbes' theory, with its bluntly degrading portrait of man (his laughter being part of his degradation), together with the suspicion that the court wits of the Restoration were using ridicule as a weapon against virtue rather than vice caused many respectable Englishmen to reconsider the whole matter. The danger of this otherwise beneficial weapon and of the pessimistic assumption about the nature of man became obvious to theorists long before they could find a theory to explain their feeling.

One solution was proposed by the third Earl of Shaftesbury in his *Letter Concerning Enthusiasm* (1708) and his *Essay on the Freedom of Wit and Humour* (1709). Shaftesbury simply vindicated ridicule by offering an alternative premise about the nature of man. Laughter is not, he argued, a sign of the laugher's felt superiority but an aspect of man's natural goodness and freedom by which he tests the world about him and exposes the encrustation of evil or (we might add, suggesting one part of his lineage) romance upon the real and good. Ridicule fits neatly into a Christian-Platonic ontology in which evil is not real, an illusion that can be separated from the real by a breath of laughter. Dryden, Swift, and Pope would have taken a less monis-

13. Collier, *Short View*, Chap. 4; Dennis, *The Stage Defended* (1726) and *Large Account of the Taste in Poetry* (1702), in *Critical Works*, ed. Hooker, 2, 313; *1*, 284, and *Art of Poetry*, Chap. 21. René Rapin's view in his twenty-fifth reflection (1674), widely accepted throughout the eighteenth century, was that the end of comedy "est de montrer sur le Théâtre les défauts des particuliers, pour guérir les défauts du Public, & de corriger le Peuple par la crainte d'être moqué. Ainsi le ridicule est ce qu'il y a de plus essenciel à la Comédie" (*Oeuvres* [Paris, 1725], 2, 196–97).

tic solution, arguing that evil is indeed real but utterly dependent, merely a perversion of the real (the good) in the sense that Satan is a perversion of the angel Lucifer. But Shaftesbury's theory of ridicule as a test of truth put into words, in an extreme formulation, a view expressed in the satire of the Christian-oriented Augustans.

Shaftesbury, in spite of his intentions, hurt satire in three ways. First, his doctrine acquired an unsavory reputation based on the false impression that he meant to apply ridicule to such truths as religion. In the hands of the impious, ridicule could in fact elicit laughter at the expense of true religion; this was the same danger Collier detected in the comedy of the Restoration dramatists. Swift's unlucky experiment in *A Tale of a Tub* helped to damage his reputation because, whatever his aims or results (like Shaftesbury he wished to attack the perversions of religion, not religion itself), it was thought too dangerous to juxtapose in any relationship ridicule and religion.[14] Shaftesbury's doctrine probed too far and touched a sore spot that reflected the growing feeling that the comic and the serious were irreparably separate.[15]

Second, Shaftesbury's basic assumption about the nature of man was very different from that of Swift and Pope, and the inferences he drew from it inevitably created a different satire. If, as he believed, man is essentially good, then evil is indeed an excrescence that can be blown away; it lies not in man himself but in externals to him, his environment, institutions, education, and customs. Shaftesbury's ridicule was a revolutionary unshackling, an opening of doors and windows, which in theory at least (had the Whigs not so soon become entrenched) would have been a truly Whiggish satire; it would have preserved the eccentric and individual and swept away the af-

14. Swift's own mentor, Sir William Temple, had used the example of *Don Quixote*'s ridicule leading to the ruin of the Spanish empire, and Leibniz, citing Temple, argued that ridicule even applied to superstition could only produce impiety. See Temple, "Of Ancient and Modern Learning," in Spingarn, *Critical Essays, 3,* 71–72 (also Steele, *Tatler,* No. 219); *Die Philosophischen Schriften von Gottfried Wilhelm Leibniz,* ed. C. J. Gerhardt (Berlin, 1875–90), *3,* 381.

15. Followers included Francis Hutcheson (*Thoughts on Laughter,* originally published in *Hibernicus' Letters,* 1725–27) and Anthony Collins (*Discourse Concerning Ridicule and Irony,* 1729). Opponents were more common, for example, Giles Jacob, who writes: "What has corrupted our modern Poesy is that Ridicule . . . as if nothing pleas'd but what provokes our Laughter. This Custom of Raillery and Ridiculing is very pernicious, not only to all Poetry, but indeed to all Virtue" ("Introductory Essay," *Historical Account of the English Poets,* 1720). See A. O. Aldridge, "Shaftesbury and the Test of Truth," *PMLA, 40* (1945), 129–56.

fected and insincere, making the same distinction that preoccupied Fielding a little later.

Third, the seriousness of the object of satire, under the circumstances, was considerably diminished. Allan Ramsay, elaborating on Shaftesbury's doctrine in 1753, declared that it was not good to ridicule the evil—"a man who even laughs at folly or vice, which are certainly the objects of pity or detestation, to sound and liberal minds, gives us as bad a sample of his morals as of his understanding." The real object of ridicule was "false opinions"; ridicule "operates by raising up fictitious characters to act in familiar occurences in life, upon principles false and chimerical, and by representing the obvious consequences of such a proceeding, convincing the reader of the falshood and absurdity of such principles and opinions."[16] Fielding had by this time embodied the doctrine in his preface to *Joseph Andrews* (1742), and the object of such ridicule was vanity and affectation or, in short, manners.

The change of climate revealed in Shaftesbury's philosophy can find a parallel in the softening of church doctrine through the influence of the latitudinarian divines—first, in the image of a benevolent, gentlemanly God and, second, in the belief in man's essential sinlessness and the loss of hell.[17] Pope mentions the preacher "Who never mentions Hell to ears polite," and Edward Young refers to the fashionable fiction of "A lady's soul in everlasting pain."[18] If man is essentially good, his worst actions are follies rather than vices—not follies in the old Horatian sense of that which pains oneself but in the Shaftesburyian sense of something transient and illusory, a mask or a misunderstanding, which does not affect the real self. A mid-century adaptor of Juvenal explains in his preface that he has "softened the harshness of vice, and made it, as more generally now-a-days experienced, the meer offspring of thoughtless folly."[19]

A second reaction to Hobbes accepted his explanation of laughter

---

16. "On Ridicule," later published in *The Investigator* (1762), pp. 69, 43–44 n.

17. Andrew M. Wilkinson says of the latter: "This assumption is by far the most important single factor in the decline of Satire, since it obviates the necessity for it" ("The Decline of English Verse Satire in the Middle Years of the Eighteenth Century," *Review of English Studies*, N.S. *3* [1952], 225).

18. Pope, "Epistle to Burlington," l. 150; Young, *Love of Fame*, Satire VI, in Chalmers, *Works of the English Poets* (London, 1810), *18*, 398.

19. Edward Burnaby Greene, *The Satires of Juvenal Paraphrastically Imitated and Adapted to the Times* (London, 1763), p. xvi.

as a partial truth but attempted to discredit ridicule and isolate a more amiable kind of laughter. Experience taught that all laughter is not a grimace or a showing of one's teeth, and that it is not aroused only by the ridiculous. This second, more benevolent laughter had of course always been present—one could and did point to Falstaff and Don Quixote—but it had never been explained or given prominence over ridicule, in part because it had appeared, as long as the more pessimistic view of man held sway, to be predominantly *dulce* without *utile*. Ultimately Lord Kames (in 1762) distinguished between laughter aroused by the ridiculous and that aroused by the incongruous, between the ridiculous and the risible (or the ludicrous, as it was later called).[20]

But before this philosophical distinction was hit upon, writers like Addison and Steele were turning to a "good-natured" satire, as opposed to the "ill-natured" satire of the Tories, and from a scornful to a rehabilitating laughter. In *Spectator* No. 249, Addison accepted Hobbes' explanation of laughter but tried to help matters by distinguishing between a specific feeling of superiority, which produces ridicule, and a more general one, which can be better called joy, and which produces laughter. Laughter brings "Reliefs," and it "breaks the Gloom which is apt to depress the Mind, and damp our Spirits with transient unexpected gleams of Joy." On the other hand, ridicule, "the Qualification of little ungenerous Tempers," becomes a synonym for satire with the same distinction we have already noticed between true and false—either "employed to laugh Men out of Vice and Folly" (as it used to) or (as in the present) "made use of to laugh Men out of Virtue and good Sense, by attacking every thing that is Solemn and Serious, Decent and Praise-worthy in Human Life" (in which category Addison would probably have included Shaftesbury as well as Swift). Here Addison has distinguished between comedy as release and satire as ridicule. He does not, however, go into comedy's subject matter or its moral, as opposed to psychological, usefulness.

There were two directions in which Addison's line of thought could proceed—toward sentimental comedy and toward what we

20. The important documents are Hutcheson's *A Collection of Letters and Essays on Several Subjects, Lately Publish'd in the Dublin Journal* (1729), *1*, 77–107; Alexander Gerard's *Essay on Taste* (1759); Lord Kames' *Elements of Criticism* (1762); and James Beattie's *Essay on Laughter and Ludicrous Composition* (1776).

\

think of today as pure comedy, laughter without moral judgment, *dulce* without *utile*. Steele picks up the first of these possibilities in *The Conscious Lovers* (1723); he explains in his preface that "anything that has its foundation in happiness and success, must be allowed to be the subject of comedy," and that the best comedy introduces "a joy too exquisite for laughter, that can have no spring but in delight." He presents virtuous characters for the audience to emulate rather than, in the manner of Restoration comedy (i.e. satire), examples of vice and folly to be shunned; these good people in certain situations, he says, will elicit sympathetic laughter. The problem had always been how to laud the virtuous in comedy when virtue was supposedly not a subject for comedy: the solution had been a cessation of comedy when virtue was in the foreground, and this continued to be distressingly close to the fact in Steele's comedies. Put into practice, his theory sounded the death knell of laughter (Cibber had to have him insert some farcical scenes in *The Conscious Lovers* in order to elicit laughter from the audience). At best, a comfortable, smiling comedy resulted, perhaps more realistic for the absence of laughter, and in time it contributed to the tolerant tone of the novel.

The humorous, as opposed to the virtuous, character, however, was obviously the answer; with the new interpretation of humors, harmless follies could be considered virtues of a sort. The upshot of all this was the shift from instruction to entertainment, from the didactic, either panegyric or denigration, to the incongruous, humorous, sympathetic, and pleasureful. In short, judgment disappears completely or is qualified out of existence, and instead of the virtuous or the vicious, the comic subject becomes merely the incongruous, the interesting or odd. As John Hughes put it in *The Lay-Monk*, No. 9, as early as 1713: it is "the Follies, the Singularities, and Humours; in a word, it is the Human Heart in all its odd Variety, pleasantly represented, that makes up the elegant Entertainment of Comedy."[21] In practice then the delineating of good and evil, the operation of judgment, moved out of the realm of laughter, while the laughable tended to become a pure experience, innocent of moral or meaning.

The antithetical theories of comedy and satire we have outlined

21. Cited from *The Lay-Monastery* (2d ed., 1714).

continued to flourish side-by-side after the middle years of the century, causing a fearful confusion in the statements of intention among novelists. "Satire" and "comedy" can mean almost anything unless carefully pinned down to their context, and then the resulting definition may be at odds with the practice it attempts to describe in the novel itself. Sorel's *Francion* in an English translation (1727) was called "The Comical History of Francion; Satirically Exposing Folly and Vice in Variety of Humours and Adventures." If satire offered a moral sanction to comedy, comedy also protected satire under its broad name and pleasant connotations.

Pope expressed the most prevalent feeling of the first half of the century when he argued that comedy encompassed both kinds of laughter without being prejudiced against either; he wrote to Cromwell, ending a long discussion of laughter: "To conclude, those that are my friends I *laugh with,* and those that are not I *laugh at.*"[22] The second is as necessary as the first to the construction of the novel.

Fielding remained ostensibly in the camp of Swift and Pope, asserting that comedy should not be morally neutral or an end in itself. In the *Champion* for January 3, 1739/40, he wrote that "when wit hath been used, like that of Addison or Steele, to propagate virtue and morality; when, like that of Swift, to expose vice and folly; it is then only, that these become commendable, and truly worthy of our praise and admiration." Like Addison and Steele, he attempted the first, but he was a consummate master of the second, and I shall contend that he came to the conclusion that only through some form of ridicule, however modified, could he portray the virtuous and moral.

Looking back from 1752, he wrote in the *Covent-Garden Journal* that he esteemed his chief models, Lucian, Cervantes, and Swift, "not indeed for that Wit and Humor alone which they all so eminently possess, but because they all endeavoured, with the utmost Force of their Wit and Humor, to expose and extirpate those Follies and Vices which chiefly prevailed in their several Countries."[23] His justification for satire is the old one (cf. Horace's *Satire* I.4) that the satirist's

---

22. *Correspondence, 1,* 112.

23. *Covent-Garden Journal,* No. 10, Feb. 4, 1752; ed. G. E. Jensen (New Haven, Yale University Press, 1915), *1,* 194. He trusts Rabelais and Aristophanes less, suspecting that their design was "to ridicule all Sobriety, Modesty, Decency, Virtue and Religion, out of the World."

design is the same as that of the Spartans, who "exposed drunken Men, to the View of their Children. Examples may perhaps have more Advantage over Precepts, in teaching us to avoid what is odious, than in impelling us to pursue what is amiable."

Fielding used the terms "comedy" and "humor" in the conservative sense accepted by the Tory satirists. His perennial opponent, Colley Cibber, was the man who, complacently parading his follies in his *Apology* (1740), asked, "But why make my Follies publick? Why not? I have pass'd my Time very pleasantly with them, and I don't recollect that they have ever been hurtful to any other Man living."[24] It was precisely Cibber's making a model of his follies in the manner of Swift's hacks, spiders, and moderns that drew Fielding's attack in *Joseph Andrews*.

In the *Covent-Garden Journal*, Nos. 55 and 56, Fielding acknowledges the new Whiggish meaning of humor as an amiable, individualizing foible, but argues for the old one, "a violent Impulse of the Mind, determining it to some one peculiar Point, by which a Man becomes ridiculously distinguished from all other Men." The best and worthiest men are liable to ridicule if all their qualities are drained into one characteristic, even if it is the pursuit of virtue. His explanation for the abundance of humorous types in England is very different from the Congrevian view that it arises "from the pure and perfect State of Liberty which we enjoy in a degree greatly superior to every foreign Nation." Fielding attributes it instead to the fact that in England the young of both sexes are given no education and that merchants rise to the ranks of the gentry "without having had any Education at all." Humor, in short, is "an Exemption from all Restraint of municipal Laws, but likewise from all Restraint of those Rules of Behaviour which are expressed in the general Term of good Breeding." By good breeding is meant the tendency to behave "with the utmost Civility and Respect" ("Behave unto all Men, as you would they should behave unto you"), which is of course "the very bane of the Ridiculous, that is to say, of all humourous Characters." Control, balance, and harmony are the contraries of humor.[25]

We shall not, however, find Fielding unaffected by the concepts he is here criticizing. The fortuitous alignment of Whig and Tory that

24. *Apology*, p. 2.
25. *Covent-Garden Journal*, Nos. 55 and 56, July 18 and 25, 1752; ed. Jensen, 2, 59–69.

joined the young Fielding with Pope and Swift against Walpole concealed the fact that in the generation separating them a new set of assumptions had arisen. While Swift was a devout high-church Anglican, and Pope was a Roman Catholic, both restrictive and authoritarian, Fielding was drawn to the beliefs of the Latitudinarian divines, which had appalled Swift and drawn his fire, and to the doctrines of Shaftesbury. It was Shaftesbury, in fact, who showed Fielding how to reformulate the satire of Swift and Pope.

He could adopt without any difficulty Shaftesbury's doctrine of ridicule as a test of truth, which was not very different from the views in the conventional satirists' apologies. Pope would have agreed that ridicule in the satirist's hands is a way to blow away the false and pernicious, which is insubstantial, without harming the good, which is real. Ridicule, writes Fielding, paraphrasing Shaftesbury from memory, "is one of those principal lights or natural mediums by which things are to be viewed, in order to a thorough recognition: for that truth, it is supposed, may bear all lights."[26] Thus Joseph Andrews is a Shaftesburyian when he says, "I defy the wisest man in the world to turn a truly good action into ridicule" (Bk. III, Chap. 6). In the preface to *Joseph Andrews* Fielding found this doctrine particularly useful in explaining satire as exposing evils that masquerade as goods and falsehoods as truths, for he recognized that Shaftesbury's ridicule was intended essentially as a test of false gravity or solemnity rather than of truth. As Shaftesbury's ontology suggests, imposture is a natural object of ridicule: "*gravity* is of the very essence of imposture," he writes. "It does not only make us mistake other things, but is apt perpetually almost to mistake itself."[27] The only way to distinguish true gravity from false, therefore, is to test it with ridicule. Indeed, the idea of testing itself became very important for Fielding.

The Villain of Fielding's Satire

There is no question that Fielding's emphasis in his early works falls on the deviant character. Most of these works are specifically

26. *Comment on Lord Bolingbroke's Essay*, in *Works*, ed. Henley, *16*, 317. He paraphrases Shaftesbury's *Essay on the Freedom of Wit and Humour* (Pt. I, Sec. 1; *Characteristics*, ed. J. M. Robertson [London, 1900], *1*, 44).

27. *Characteristics*, *1*, 10. Cf. Fielding's *Essay on the Knowledge of the Characters of Men*, ed. Henley, *14*, 285.

satires, but even his Congrevian comedies return in spirit to those satires in dramatic form, *Volpone, Tartuffe, The Country Wife,* and *The Plain Dealer,* rather than to the comical-romantic tradition of *Love's Last Shift, The Way of the World,* and *The Beaux's Stratagem.* Fielding's main characters are his "blocking characters," the Fainalls and Marwoods, the Volpones, Tartuffes, and Horners, not the Mirabells and Archers; and the main intrigue is of the knave's (as opposed to the hero's) contriving. As early as *The Temple Beau* (1730) the hero's intrigue shares the spotlight with the activities of the humor-characters, who emerge as the most memorable part of the play; and in *Rape upon Rape, or The Coffee-House Politician* (1730) the plot is subordinated to the portraits of Politic and Justice Squeezum, men whose obsessions have closed out the rest of life. The intrigue itself merely revolves around the central situation of Squeezum's corrupt use of power as a justice.

In the most ambitious of Fielding's comedies, *The Modern Husband* (1732), the Moderns' plot (she sells her favors; he blackmails her lovers) and its defeat make up the main action, not the pathetic but successful struggles of the Bellamants. The fulcrum of the action is simply the Moderns' moneymaking scheme, which exposes not only their greed and unscrupulousness, but also that of all the various parties who take advantage of their scheme. The situation is a satiric symbol of a society that permits such an undertaking and a touchstone for the members of that society, from the lecherous Lord Richly to the good but rash Mr. Bellamant and the virtuous Mrs. Bellamant.

If we remove the strikingly simple yet suggestive central situation or character of the comedies and present it alone, without the interference of intrigue plots and with two or three other analogical situations following, we have the typical Fielding farce. The symbol of folly is presented by itself, without even the pretense of comic trappings. The same emphasis appears in the picaresque novels whose conception, if not execution, can be assigned to the years before *Joseph Andrews.* The characteristic of *Jonathan Wild* that distinguishes it from the Spanish picaresque is the use of the main character as a symbol. Wild himself is the center of the novel; he is not a device for getting at the people he meets or a rogue whose tricks are recounted for their own sake (they are hardly that clever). His tricks are used only to prove his "greatness." Moreover, Wild does not serve masters; he is the master. He is more closely related to the Marlovian hero, possibly through such intermediaries as Don Tomaso, than to Laza-rillo de Tormes, and he is of course a narrative cousin of Tartuffe and Horner. The difference stems from his purpose. The continental pic-aro is usually an observer or mirror, a standard (however smudged) by which we judge what he encounters; Wild is the symbol of evil. As literary parody he derives from the criminal biographies which were simply about the rogue just hanged and all those exemplary bi-ographies that reached a climax for Fielding in Cibber's *Apology*.

Similarly, the longest part of *A Journey from This World to the Next* (which appeared in the 1743 *Miscellanies* with *Jonathan Wild*) is focused on Julian the Apostate, the evil man who passes through dozens of metamorphoses, each presenting another facet of evil. The survey is carried out by Julian's passing from body to body, trying to live a decent life so that he can get to heaven. This makes a very ele-mental picaresque tale in which the hungry soul instead of changing masters changes bodies, each with its own vices—a shifty slave, a mi-ser, a spendthrift, a flattering courtier, a fop, and various kinds of hypocrite such as the pretender to gravity, wisdom, and folly.

Julian the Apostate assuming the bodies of misers and courtiers gives us in its simplest dramatization the emphatic outward move-ment from a known fool or knave to other analogous but less obvious and more respectable fools or knaves. This effect, evident in all of Fielding's early satire, is a particular application of the Augustan use of analogy as a mode of thought. Like Swift and Pope, Fielding "felt the need of symbols that would allow him to comment at once on lit-erature and life."[28] In *Tom Thumb or the Tragedy of Tragedies* he uses the structure and diction to satirize heroic tragedies, the notes and scholarly apparatus to satirize pedantry, the size of Tom Thumb to satirize the pretensions of tragic heroes and "great men" in gen-eral, and the idea of the "great man" to satirize Walpole. He persist-ently throws his action onto another level by analogy—from the inci-dental simile, "The study of bookselling is as difficult as the law: and there are as many tricks in the one as the other" (*Author's Farce*, II.5; 8, 222), to the parallel action, the Apshinken family suggesting George II and Queen Caroline, with Robin the footman recalling their prime minister (*Welsh* [or *Grub-street*] *Opera*).

28. "Fielding's Early Aesthetic and Technique," *Studies in Philology*, 40 (1945), 547. This essay and several of the others referred to are reprinted in *Fielding: A Col-lection of Critical Essays*, ed. R. Paulson (New York, Prentice-Hall, 1962).

All of Fielding's lawyer, clergyman, courtier, and politician analogues may be thought of as part of the heroic level in a mock-heroic
satire. Fielding's particular effect, however, must be carefully defined.
In *The Dunciad,* for example, Pope parodies Virgil's *Aeneid* in order
to suggest an ideal against which the present-day Trojans who have
sunk to dunces can be measured. He uses the heroic or parody level
as a classical and religious ideal and thus suggests how different Theobald and the dunces are from Aeneas and the Trojans. Fielding, in
his *Dunciad* plays, conveys the heroic level in a style similar to that of
Pope's *Dunciad,* but he places both the high and the low in the present. His purpose is to suggest the correspondence, not the divergence,
between the heroic (or, for him, "great") world and the squalid
world of contemporary London. While Pope puts the unheroic contemporary world in the ideal context of Virgilian epic, Fielding puts
it in the unideal context of its own literary forms, heroic tragedy and
pantomime farce. The simple allegorical correspondence between
Queen Ignorance and ignorance is modified by an analogy between
this queen and the posturing queens of "heroic tragedy" on the stage.
In fact, Fielding's allegories in general, whenever they draw attention
to themselves, appear as parodies of high-flown writing. Pope's analogy between Theobald and Aeneas diminishes the modern in the
light of the ideal (the *Aeneid* itself is never satirized); Fielding's
analogy cuts in both directions, laying open the pretensions of Ignorance *and* her analogue, of the modern *and* his modern literature.
When he abandons the heroic postures of bad plays, Fielding continues the same effect in the rogue's posturing as a lawyer or a prime
minister.

John Gay's *Beggar's Opera* was Fielding's most important source
for the use of the heroic level as a parallel instead of a contrast to his
subject.[29] The diction and mock-heroic similes put into the mouths of
Gay's robbers and whores do not allude to an ideal but rather show
a correspondence between the activities of robbers and the heroic (or
upper-class) activities their words evoke. The Beggar who acts as
chorus makes the analogy between high and low explicit at the end
of the performance:

29. Although it seems likely that Gay introduced the young Fielding to this device
and to the particular low-high relationship, the motif was used in many of the Jonathan Wild pamphlets written before *The Beggar's Opera* appeared (see W. R. Irwin,
The Making of "Jonathan Wild": A Study in the Literary Method of Henry Fielding
[New York, Columbia University Press, 1941], p. 189).

Through the whole piece you may observe such a similitude of manners in high and low Life, that it is difficult to determine whether (in the fashionable vices) the fine gentlemen imitate the gentlemen of the road, or the gentlemen of the road the fine gentlemen.——Had the Play remain'd, as I at first intended [i.e. with the robbers hanged and transported], it would have carried a most excellent moral. 'Twould have shown that the lower sort of people have their vices in a degree as well as the rich: And that they are punish'd for them.[30]

Gay's robbers, pimps, and whores sound and act like the much-admired heroes of Italian opera and speak in similes that relate their actions to those of lawyers, merchants, courtiers, and politicians. The inference is that opera heroes and politicians, underneath their rhetoric and respectability, have the same cutthroat values as Macheath and Peachum, the highwayman and the fence, but only the latter "are punish'd for them." Besides the upward thrust of the low-high analogy, there is an equally deadly thrust outward from the actors on the stage, whatever their roles, to the merchants and gentlemen in the audience. The implication of the Beggar's substitution of a happy ending for the hanging of Macheath is that the latter would have made all the Macheaths in the audience too uncomfortable.

Gay's low-high analogy is an ingenious satiric device, but of paramount importance to Fielding is the attempt to embody the mock-heroic relationship in a variety of character types, turning it into an inappropriate diction that reveals a character's upward aspiration—his desire to emulate the more respectable citizen and/or his hypocrisy—his middle-class desire to avoid calling a spade a spade. Each group in *The Beggar's Opera* has its own mock-heroic equivalent, its own diction, and its own set of glancing similes. The Peachums and Lockits—the fences and jailers—talk like merchants. For example, when Lockit puts Macheath in leg-irons, he is a merchant trying to sell apparel to a gentleman.

Do but examine them, sir,—never was better work. How genteelly they are made! They will fit as easy as a glove, and the nic-

30. III.16; *The Poetical Works of John Gay,* ed. G. C. Faber (London, Oxford University Press, 1926), p. 531. Subsequent quotations are from this text.

est man in England might not be ashamed to wear them. (*He puts on the chains.*) If I had the best gentleman in the land in my custody, I could not equip him more handsomely. (I.7)

Both are very much aware of class distinctions. Macheath talks like a gentleman, with occasional lines from Shakespeare thrown in, and his diction is supported by the mock-heroic similes of the other characters. As Mrs. Peachum says of him, "Sure there is not a finer gentleman upon the road than the captain!" (I.4), adding that if Polly marries him she will be "as ill used, and as much neglected, as if thou hadst married a lord" (I.8).

The highwaymen's whores talk in the manner of ladies of fashion. "Pray, madam, were you ever in keeping?" asks Dolly Trull. "I hope, madam," replies Suky Tawdry, "I han't been so long upon the town but I have met with some good fortune as well as my neighbors." "Pardon me, madam, I meant no harm by the question; 'Twas only in the way of conversation," says Trull (II.5). In the same way, Polly Peachum and Lucy Lockit are essentially imitators of the heroines of romance or tragedy (Macheath has seduced Polly by giving her romances to read):

Lucy. [*speaking of Macheath*] Perfidious wretch!
Polly. Barbarous husband!
Lucy. Hadst thou been hanged five months ago, I had been happy. . . . Flesh and blood can't bear my usage.
Polly. Shall I not claim my own? Justice bids me speak. (II.13)

While, as Mrs. Peachum notes, Polly "loves to imitate the fine ladies" (I.4), her version of gentility is out of heroic plays and Italian operas and represents another variation in the play of parody styles.

The Beggar's Opera shows what can happen when mock-heroic irony is applied with some consistency to a character: the final effect is not so much to direct the satire to the thieves' betters as to dramatize social classes on the move upward and thus produce a comedy of manners. We observe the highwayman who sees himself as an aristocrat, flaunting his gentility and generosity, and the thief-takers and jailers who see themselves as merchants, with ledgers always at hand and talk of respectability and duty on their lips. The middle-class values of the Peachums and Lockits, based entirely on the profit motive, are contrasted with the disinterested love of Polly and Lucy. Lucy, for example, tells her father: "One can't help love; one can't cure it. 'Tis not in my power to obey you, and hate him [Macheath]" (II.11). The highwaymen also offer a contrast to the ledger-book success of the Peachums: they have to leave the counting room and risk their lives for their profits, and they are in general more loyal and more generous to each other (it comes as a shock to Macheath when he discovers that one of his gang has betrayed him). Even the whores, though also with traitresses in their number, "are always so taken up with stealing hearts, that [they] don't allow [themselves] time to steal any thing else" (II.4). There is a passion driving them that is totally lacking in the calculating world of the counting house.

These two elements, the opposition of economic motivation and love and Gay's particular use of the high-low analogy, will help to explain why, in the midst of satire bristling with efficiency, Fielding's attitude toward his image of evil seems curiously qualified.

Like Swift, Pope, and Gay, Fielding picked live models for his villains. One suspects, however, that he was more influenced by his models or prototypes than they; there seems to have been a split in his own mind between detestation for their effects or their motives and admiration for their vitality and success. The prototypes were Sir Robert Walpole, Colley Cibber, John Rich, and later, Samuel Richardson; perhaps the last is the most complex of all, since Fielding's parody of him became a kind of imitation, with his contempt for Richardson's ambiguous morality fighting against his admiration for the vital reality that Richardson created. However, Walpole fascinated Fielding the most, in the same way that Wharton fascinated and appalled Swift. What Fielding knew of Walpole—his power and endurance, his venality, his personal charm, and his notorious extramarital relations—provided the outlines of a symbol. But behind the symbol is also the Augustan convention of the small man trying to make over the world in his own image but ultimately doomed, by the nature of things, to defeat. Small, he tries to pass for large and is betrayed by the most commonplace reality.

Tom Thumb (1730) offers an early example. To begin with, for all his famous feats, Tom is after all only a few inches high, is incapable of having a woman (one of the cruxes of the play's action), and at the end is casually swallowed by a cow. The motif of the "great man" implicitly connects Thumb with Walpole: "The great Tom Thumb, / The little hero, giant-killing boy, / Preserver of my kingdom" (I.2; 9, 23). There is a sense of evil connected with his somehow inseminating Huncamunca, which is played upon until it reaches the height of absurdity in the parson's benediction: "Long may they live, and love, and propagate, / Till the whole land be peopled with Tom Thumbs." Then in a bathetic simile the parson develops *Dunciad* imagery:

> So when the Cheshire cheese a maggot breeds,
> Another and another still succeeds:
> By thousands and ten thousands they increase,
> Till one continued maggot fills the rotten cheese. (II.9; 9, 51)

Through a monstrous relationship with Thumb, the full-grown Huncamunca has become a breeder of mites, and the nation has been taken over by the busy, energetic, mindless little breed that Pope celebrates.

And yet, in the light of this hypothetical parturition, we tend to sympathize with someone so small and yet so mighty. Fielding expresses wonder (and this is part of his satire, as it is of Pope's) that something so diminutive could accomplish so much. There is no ideal opposed to him (except normal size), and the only sign of his wickedness is the preemptory slaying of the bailiff and his followers who tried to arrest Noodle (which was added in later versions of the play). On the one side is Thumb's obvious impotence (in terms of Huncamunca): "One fitter for your pocket than your bed! / Advised by me the worthless baby shun," says Grizzle, "Or you will ne'er be brought to bed of one" (II.5; 9, 42). On the other is Thumb's equally obvious reputation, which leads the giantess Glumdalca to cry: "Oh! stay, Tom Thumb, and you alone shall fill / That bed where twenty giants used to lie" (II.7; 9, 46–47). Then there are Thumb's own worries on the subject, "Yet at the thought of marriage I grow pale" (II.2; 9, 34), which suggest that he has simply fooled people, that his reputation is false. However, all of this can be answered by the fact that he did defeat giants, as he later defeats Grizzle's rebellion.

The gist of Fielding's satire is to oppose the "great man's" potency in political and economic spheres to his powerlessness in the more commonplace world of the barnyard animal who eats him. Justice Squeezum in *Rape upon Rape* is eminently successful in the world of his corrupt court jurisdiction, but when his wife appears or when he steps back into the domestic world, he suffers. Again, Jonathan Wild (another avatar of Walpole) is a character whose unluckiness in love strikingly contrasts with his success in business. His victory over Bagshot, from which he retires with three-quarters of the loot, is immediately followed by his amatory defeat at the hands of Laetitia Snap. He is not, like Thumb, afraid of women, but he is unable to cope with them (and is presumably unattractive to them); at any rate, as soon as he has beaten his retreat, the fop Tom Smirke emerges from hiding to enjoy Laetitia's favors. Wild's trouble with women extends to that other lady, Fortune, who causes him to lose "every farthing in his pocket," and a little later he is cheated of his loot by Moll Straddle.

Love stands as a norm of ordinary human activity; indeed, throughout Fielding's novels it signifies goodness. Wild's deficiencies are emphasized by his opposite, Heartfree (whose name tells us how he differs from Wild). Each has a "fides Achates"—Wild has Fireblood; Heartfree, Friendly—and each has a wife, Laetitia and Mrs. Heartfree. Fielding's contrast of the Wild-Heartfree groups can be seen in a single scene. At the end of Book IV, Chapter 10, Mrs. Heartfree, recounting her numerous stout defenses of her virtue, is interrupted by a clamor proceeding from Wild's discovery of Laetitia in the arms of Fireblood. The "great man" can be successful in killing giants and swindling fools and innocents, but his true frailty appears in ordinary human affairs. In Fielding's satires, there is always a Polly Peachum or Lucy Lockit opposed to the bourgeois-thinking villain; and in general Fielding develops Gay's contrast between the seemingly respectable merchant of crime and the highwayman. Fielding, however, more optimistic than Gay, goes so far as to make love the element lacking in the vallain, the element that either definitively sets him off from others or that eventually defeats him.

But there is a second source for the complexity of our reaction to Fielding's villains. Part of our sympathy can be attributed to the fact that Fielding is always presenting a surrogate or analogical image for

Walpole, and not Walpole (or the evil agent) himself. The pseudo-Walpole, however, is always implicitly related to the true Walpole not only as low to high but as unsuccessful to successful. The pervasive low-high analogy doubtless began for Fielding as a travesty device to discover "the sot, the gamester, or the rake" in "the cardinal, the friar, or the judge,"[31] but the effect in practice is not the Lucianic one of showing that the rake is the reality under the judge's wig; this would have involved the judge's alluding downward to the rake, as Lucian's gods do. Fielding, following Gay, gives the sots and gamesters the language of judges, which has the effect of saying that bad as these highwaymen and dishonest servants are they are not nearly so bad as their superiors, if for no better reason than that they do not get away with it. (Even Walpole, when he topples, becomes for Fielding a victim of other culprits just as bad—now the low half of the low-high analogy.)

He emphasizes the fragility of their lives, as when Gallono threatens Mother Punchbowl in *The Covent-Garden Tragedy*: "I'll give a crown / To some poor justice to commit thee thither / Where I will come and see thee flogged myself" (II.ii; *10*, 131). They are always in the shadow of the pillory, the prison, or the gallows, and their end is always contrasted to "the fate of greater persons."

> Great whores in coaches gang,
>> Smaller misses
>> For their kisses
> Are in Bridewell banged;
>> Whilst in vogue
>> Lives the great rogue,
> Small rogues are by dozens hanged.[32]

Even in the "happy ending" of *Jonathan Wild*, the hoodlum is, of course, hanged; but in this respect he is unlike his illustrious analogue, the prime minister. Most significantly, with the exception of Wild, we do not dislike these characters; our detestation is directed at the general (and vague) target of those "greater persons" beyond, while our immediate attention rests on the particular case. In fact, at

---

31. *Essay on the Knowledge of the Characters of Men*, ed. Henley, *14*, 283.
32. *Tumble-Down Dick* (1736), Air II (ed. Henley, *12*, 16).

times Fielding hints that the low are somehow good. When Mr. Spindle arrives at the Shavian hell of *Eurydice,* ready to recommend himself to the devil by the fact that he was hanged, Captain Weazel warns him: "No, hanged, no; then he will take you for a poor rogue, a sort of people he abominates so, that there are scarce any of them here. No, if you would recommend yourself to him, tell him you *deserved* to be hanged, and was too great for the law." As Fielding points out regarding punishment (*Champion,* Jan. 8, 1739/40), "It is not being hanged, but deserving to be hanged, that is infamous."[33] In these poor, rustic, underworld types Fielding shows us not pure evil itself but, in a way, the effects of evil. These people ape evil and so are, in that sense, victimized by it as much as is the good citizen.[34]

Now *Jonathan Wild* is a much more vigorously prosecuted case than *Tom Thumb,* but behind it is the same use of a surrogate, which is traced to Wild's remotest ancestors:

> O shame o' Justice! Wild is hang'd,
> For thatten he a pocket fanged,
> While safe old Hubert, and his gang,
> Doth pocket o' the nation fang. (Bk. I, Chap. 2; 2, 5)

In spite of the extreme stylization of the narrative, some human characteristics distinguish Wild from "greatness." His unattractiveness together with his unluckiness in love, his frequent failures (both professional and amatory), his breakdown when the warrant for Heartfree's execution arrives at Newgate, his overconfidence in Fireblood, his signs of cowardice in prison—all these, deviating from the straight line of satiric allegory, are small humanizing traits ("weaknesses"). An irony is created by the discrepancy between the narrator's ideal

33. *Works, 11,* 274; *Champion, 1,* 170.
34. For his particular emphasis on the unfortunate thief, Fielding may have recalled Steele's essay on greatness and the high-low analogy in *The Englishman,* No. 48 (Jan. 23, 1714), ed. Rae Blanchard (Oxford, Clarendon Press, 1955), pp. 191–95. Speaking of Alexander Smith's *The History of the Lives of the Most Noted Highwaymen:* "There is a satisfaction to Curiosity in knowing the Adventures of the meanest of Mankind; and all that I can say is, that I have more Respect for them than for greater Criminals, who are described with Praise by more eminent Writers." Steele takes his motto from Garth's *Dispensary* (ll. 9–10), which describes the place of punishment "Where little Villains must submit to Fate, / That great ones may enjoy the World in State."

Wild and the real Wild whom the reader sees. While the narrator persistently tries to maintain his greatness, we notice how in some ways he is just an ordinary person, reflecting the more monstrous (because more effective) crimes of his betters, and deluded and led on by the chimerical ideal of greatness—imitated from the behavior of his betters, whose language he mimics in mock-heroic style (to the count: "Sir, I am not insensible of my obligations to you, as well for the overvalue you have set on my small abilities, as for the kindness you express in offering to introduce me among my superiors" [Bk. I, Chap. 5; 2, 15]). He is most clearly the little man deceived by the ideal of greatness after Heartfree's death warrant has arrived: at one moment he cries, "I may yet prevent this catastrophe. It is not too late to discover the whole"; however, "greatness, instantly returning to his assistance, checked the base thought, as it first offered itself to his mind" (Bk. IV, Chap. 4; 2, 158). It is such "a weakness in Wild of which we are ourselves ashamed" or "these little sparks of which composed one of those weaknesses which we lamented in the opening of our history" that set him off from the ideal of the great who do not swerve from the path of crime or end on the gallows. The delusion (and our partial pity for Wild) is pointed up by the situation of the African king in the digression of Mrs. Heartfree's travels—there a man has to be almost mad with desire for greatness in order to take upon himself the burden, danger, and responsibility.

Fashion, in the sense of copying someone else's crimes, seems to be at the root of folly in Fielding's early satire. The power of fashion—of heroic tragedy, pantomimes, "honor," Walpole, greatness—is summed up in *Pasquin* when the mayor's wife, ready to set out for London, is asked by her daughter:

"But must I go into keeping, mamma?"
"Child, you must do what's in fashion."
"But I have heard that's a naughty thing."
"That can't be, if your betters do it; people are punished for doing naughty things; but people of quality are never punished; therefore they never do naughty things." (II.1; *11, 181*)

Or there is the courtier (Mr. Spindle) in *Eurydice* "who is so complaisant, that he sins only to comply with the mode; and goes to the devil, not out of any inclination, but because it is the fashion" (*11,* 275).[35]

These observations only corroborate Fielding's own statement in his preface to *Joseph Andrews:* "Great vices are the proper objects of our detestation, smaller faults, of our pity; but affectation appears to me the only true source of the Ridiculous."[36] His subject matter is properly these middling types rather than the great themselves, if there are such. He does not deny the possibility of their existence, but one suspects from their scarcity and abstractness that he never quite believed in the existence of such pure evil; when (in *Amelia*) he does present a more extreme evil, it has become a motiveless diabolism. If absolute evil seems to him unreal, the ordinary people he presents are eminently real; and by the contrast he tells his audience, in effect, that they need not divert themselves with considerations of the evil in diabolic natures when they have their own "flabby, pretending, weak-eyed devils" to contend with.

Fielding demonstrates the tendency of both the Scriblerians and, in their different way, the satirists of the Spectator Club toward humanizing the villain of satire, dealing in terms of character rather than idea, and dramatizing a middle area of evil rather than the melodramatic extreme. Fielding's effect, however, is closer to the benevolence of Addison and Steele than to the more sinister sense of evil that emerges from Swift's and Pope's satire. For example, the evil of fashion is a relatively innocent version of the interested imitation, in Swift's satires, of a philosophy that will vindicate one's own worst propensities or, at best, one's human weaknesses.

We can distinguish two different satiric villains in this period. One is concerned with changing other people or the world itself, the other with changing himself. The Swiftean, the true Satanic, villain is so proud of his own nature (whatever it may be) that, far from trying to conceal or alter it, he tries to change the external world to conform to it. If this is essentially a Juvenalian villain, then Fielding's is the Horatian outsider who tries to adjust to society—by lying about him-

35. A discussion of a similar effect in the contemporary prints of William Hogarth appears in my *Hogarth's Graphic Works* (2 vols. New Haven, Yale University Press, 1965), *1,* 26, 42–43. Cf. also Fielding's *True Patriot,* Nov. 5, 1745.

36. *Works,* ed. Henley, *1,* 23; see also *Champion,* Feb. 21, 1739.

self or by trying to change himself in order to conform. Fashion is a general trap for the weak, an easy way out by following the crowd. In this sense Fielding is criticizing society or social forms rather than individual wickedness. Behind his villain is a more optimistic view of human nature than Swift's. For Fielding the good man should be essentially himself, which is to some extent the folly and wickedness of the Swift villain (as it is the virtue of the Addisonian humor-character). The nature of evil is changing. To the Augustan a man is evil if he follows his own dictates even if they lead him against family, church, and state. To the new generation evil is becoming external restraint on an individual's natural bent for self-fulfillment.

The Satiric Structure

The main element in the action of Fielding's satiric plays is the middle, which becomes, in his most original creations, the farce. Farce, for Fielding, meant both a metaphor and a structure. One of his favorite analogies was between men and actors. He demonstrates in his parody farces how similar the wretched piece of play-writing is to the wretched piece of politics or religion. A bill in Parliament, the activities of great men, a village election with heroic speeches as well as bribery—all of these are symbolic farces, analogous in various ways to a puppet show or pantomime. Characters are always saying, "Why, what a farce is human life," or referring to "the grand pantomime played on the stage of life."[37] In life, as in Rich's productions, the audience sees only "the Sights of Serpents, Dragons and Armies, whereas indeed those Objects are no other than Pieces of stuff'd Cloth, painted Wood, and Hobby-Horses" run by "several Strings, wires, Clock-work &c." Newgate is "human nature with its mask off" and "the splendid palaces of the great are often no other than Newgate with the mask on." In the world Fielding explores "every Person . . . disguises his Mind, as much as Masque would his Countenance."[38]

Farce then is a general metaphor for contemporary life, and the

37. *The Modern Husband*, II.2; *Works*, ed. Henley, *10, 27*.
38. *Champion*, Apr. 22, 1740, in *Champion*, 2, 127; Preface to *The Miscellanies*, in *Works*, ed. Henley, *12, 243*; *Champion*, No. 120, Aug. 10, 1740, in *The Voyages of Mr. Job Vinegar*, ed. S. J. Sackett, Augustan Reprint Society, No. 67 (Los Angeles, William Andrews Clark Memorial Library, 1958), p. 25.

analogy between living and acting is a natural one in which to express a concern with either fashion or hypocrisy, the attempt to mask as what one is not. But the farce is also a formal structure for Fielding. By definition, and in the practice of Rich and his imitators, farce is comedy exploited for its own sake. Events are presented solely for their amusement value and have literally no meaning; actions do not necessarily follow from character, and reality is distorted to the point of sheer nonsense. This is the form Fielding parodies and ridicules as a symbol of a pervasive moral laxity, of life itself become meaningless. But, as some of the greatest dramatists have shown, farce is a two-sided instrument: it can be sheer nonsense, or its meaning can proceed through the higher logic of allegory or analogy. Fielding utilizes both possibilities; his plays-within-plays are at the same time farces and imitations of bad farces, so that he can call upon both ends of the farcical spectrum for his audience's reaction. In Rich's Covent Garden Theatre the action is unlifelike, illogical, and meaningless. But in Fielding's imitation, which on one level can be taken as similarly meaningless, the details are actually meaningful, and a higher (true) reality is implied.

Fielding explains the function of farce in the prologue to *The Lottery* (1731):

> Some follies scarce perceptible appear
> In that just glass which shows you as you are.
> But Farce still claims a magnifying right
> To raise the object larger to the sight,
> And shew her insect fools in stronger light. (*8, 267*)

Fielding's "authors" define the farces they write as having "several plots, some pretty deep, and some but shallow" or as "an Oglio of tidbits";[39] one author, Medley, suggests the form by his own name. Here is the basic imitative form of satire itself, which ridicules a chaos by dramatizing it. Being grotesque and comic, the satire can be interpreted as mere nonsense by the dull reader who likes this sort of literature, but it will be interpreted by the wise reader as a moral allegory. At the center of Fielding's early work is the farce that pretends to its dull audience that it is a poor play or a true account of Pamela's

---

39. *Pasquin*, I.1; *11, 341*; *Eurydice, 11, 277*.

behavior or, later, a Jacobite's newspaper, while its intelligent, morally aware readers, sensing the irony, see it as parody and moral commentary.

A peculiarity of Fielding's early satire is that he seldom allows the farcical situation or character at the center to stand alone; he surrounds it, cutting it off from immediate contact with the audience, by a romance plot, or, in his later plays, by the commentary of authors and critics.

The containing action of the earliest plays was the romance plot of Terentian comedy, and as Fielding's characteristic concerns emerged an ever wider discrepancy was revealed between the middle and the resolution of the end. The latter, in Fielding's hands, tends to echo the ending of *The Beggar's Opera,* where the Beggar, who is supposed to have written the play, gives up his poetically just ending for a happy one to satisfy the people both inside and outside the play—and by so doing further associates the two groups. The people inside the play are all about to be hanged or transported, and the people outside the play (seeing themselves on the stage) are eager for mercy.

One of the features of Fielding's satire from the very beginning is the mock recantation at the end. His earliest effort, a translation of Juvenal's sixth satire (on women), ends with a note gallantly explaining that "to the honour of the English ladies, the Latin is by no means applicable to them," and Wisemore takes back all he has said at the end of *Love in Several Masques:*

> And now ladies, I think myself bound to a solemn recantation of every slander I have thrown upon your sex: for I am convinced that our complaints against you flow generally (if not always) more from our want of merit than your want of justice. (8, 99)

The clearest example of the ironically happy ending (before *Jonathan Wild*) is *The Author's Farce,* where Luckless, the poet who has been fighting an uphill battle for recognition in a London of Bookweights and Marplays, turns out to be the heir to the throne of Bantom, with prospects of living happily ever after. Following from the parody of the heroic plays (e.g. Dryden's *Indian Queen*) in which such lucky discoveries are made, the ending only says to the audience: You like this sort of thing, so here it is. However, the very fact of the happy ending shows that the vice still exists. As in the third book of *The Dunciad,* the world of the farce has suddenly become real; it has extended from the play Luckless writes to the relatively realistic world of the frame action, which is now made over into a world of lost princes and hidden identities. And to point this up, as soon as Luckless succeeds to the throne of Bantom, he reverts to the very standards he has resisted and lampooned throughout most of the play. He takes Don Tragedio, Signor Opera, Marplay, and the rest along with him to entertain the Bantomites. Fielding shows under the disguise of a happy ending, with a comic feast to which even the bad characters are invited, that the forces of nonsense are indestructible.

In a more general way, throughout his career, Fielding draws upon the sort of happy ending Molière attached to *Tartuffe.* The situation is so bad, Molière says, that only a deus ex machina can remedy things; and the intervention of the king only tends to point up the impossibility of survival for normal virtue. Even at the end of *Tom Jones* and *Amelia,* we are left with the distinct feeling that *this one* got through by luck, but the corrupt world is unchanged. Often, in fact, it takes luck that seems almost supernatural to bring the hero through. Fielding's resolution does not necessarily change satire into comedy; it produces a particular muffling effect that seems to be Fielding's final comment on his subject.

In the farces that imitate heroic tragedy, ending in universal death and destruction, the conventions of the works parodied and the satire coincide in the defeat of the value principle and the encompassing and destroying of the sane by the insane. But this Juvenalian action is not allowed to stand alone either; it is surrounded and set off by a containing action of commentary. In a few of his plays Fielding hits upon a containing action that almost fits this framework of satiric exposition. For example, in *An Old Man Taught Wisdom* (1735), he presents a girl interviewing prospective husbands. The types pass in review—an apothecary, a dancing master, a singing master, and a lawyer; after their follies have been exposed, she marries the footman. Fielding makes her not a chastising or vituperative satirist, but an ironic commentator who leads her beaux on to reveal their particular follies. She knows all along what she wants, and her constant standard is Mr. Thomas the footman, against whom she judges these pretentious fools, and whom she brings in as her choice at the end.

Above all there is *Don Quixote in England* (1734), in which Quixote, like Fielding himself, sees the world as rich with analogy; thus he can point to each example as he sees it. Since Fielding concludes that the prevailing evil in England is play-acting, vanity, or hypocrisy, Don Quixote is the ideal person to be confronted with it: he sees through it and detects the true rogue underneath; more characteristically, he sees in the quack or the highwayman the prime minister, in the low the high. In this sense he is a prototype of Fielding's whole satiric approach. He sees the giant "at the head of his army, that howl like Turks in an engagement" (i.e. the mock-heroic attitude), and Sancho Panza sees "a country squire at the head of his pack of dogs." (Of course, when we see Badger at his most elemental, after getting drunk, he *is* much as Quixote sees him.) Thus we, along with Sancho, see the ordinary country squire, and Don Quixote sees his real significance—he is the leader of the country who abandons his responsibility for his pleasure, who at the head of an army would be the same as at the head of his pack of dogs. He too has something in him of the evil giant who hunts women "like hares." Don Quixote points out that if the squire were to be taken literally he would be seen as a "dog-boy" or a gamekeeper, not as a lord. The lawyer and doctor appear to be mere quacks and rogues, but Quixote sees them as "the prince of Sarmatia, and . . . of the Five Mountains," implying the similarity between the lowest and the highest, the merely annoying and the powerfully dangerous. When informed who they really are, he remarks: "Monstrous enchantment! what odd shapes this Merlin transforms the greatest people into!" (II.14; *11,* 481). The breaking up, the refracting of reality that takes place whenever Quixote appears is a version of the satiric experience; things are jumbled and a truer reality revealed.

The other side of the satire is the reaction of fools and knaves to Quixote himself. When a coachload of people debouch in the innyard, in spite of his efforts to prevent them, the problem offered them is Don Quixote, who thought their coach was a giant. Mr. Brief the counselor advises the landlady to see a justice of the peace to get the knight thrown out, and Dr. Drench the physician recommends physic. In fact, the whole play works on this general principle: what will be X's, Y's, and Z's reactions to Don Quixote? The politicians try to use him as an opposition candidate for parliament so that the other candidate will have to offer bribes; Squire Badger sees him as a rival for Dorothea; Sir Thomas Loveland sees him as "a philosophical pimp"; in short, each character interprets Don Quixote's motives in his own image. Presented with an apparently inexplicable action, each looks for a motive and in the process reveals himself.

Seeing him in their own image, the characters also become analogues of Quixote: they are juxtaposed and compared with him, and their madness contrasted with his. The lawyer sees him as a rogue, the doctor as a sick man. Badger is a sort of alter Quixote, riding his hounds toward the lady he is to court, being diverted at an inn, mistaking John (Fairlove's servant) for a lord because of his livery, mistaking Sancho for a country squire, in short, betraying all the classic Quixotic symptoms. Likewise Sir Thomas sees Badger through his madness for money as a good mate for his daughter (Quixote makes the analogy explicit, III.14; *11, 65*), when any normal person sees that Badger is a fool. Thus Fielding has taken the conventional situation of the father who wants his daughter to marry X while she wants to marry Y and, by placing Don Quixote in the midst of it, created a wholly satiric picture: madness becomes the common denominator of all actions. As Sir Thomas concludes, "I don't know whether this knight, by and by, may not prove us all to be more mad than himself" (III.16; *11, 70*). The action ends with the dehumoring of characters like Sir Thomas, not of Quixote himself, whose madness is normative.

Finally, with Don Quixote, the reactions of other characters do not stop with meditation; his bruises make him something of a victim, and a brief action becomes an aggressive one. Here Fielding traces the interplay between a commentator, a victim, and a series of aggressive characters, with the emphasis shifting from one element to the other; this will be essentially the structure of his novels.

In the more schematic relationships of the burlesque farces another tendency makes itself known. In *Pasquin* Fielding removes the satiric observer from the action upon which he comments. Pursuing his theatrical metaphor (in the *Champion,* May 10, 1740), he argues that if men and women are players, the satirist is the stage manager. He has the Moon explain that he is like the "Man behind the Scenes at your Play-Houses . . . who, tho' he may behold Objects in the truest, sees them at the same time in the most odious Light, and is not so agreeably deceived as those to whom the painted Side of the Canvas represents a beautiful Grove or a Palace."[40] Fielding secures this effect by creating two independent actions, one blatantly farcical and unreal, the other—though still stylized—representing the real world of moral and aesthetic judgment. Of course, one world can still, as in *The Author's Farce,* usurp the other.

This figure of the satiric observer is materialized in a commentator or series of commentators who, in the frame action, sit around and watch the farce being played. One is the author, another the critic, and another perhaps an aristocratic member of the audience or a beau. If there is no commentator, there are footnotes and glosses in the printed text (as in *Tom Thumb*). The device of the frame action comes from well-known sources—the commenting playwrights and critics from Molière's *Versailles Impromptu* (1663) and Buckingham's *Rehearsal* (1671); the footnotes from *The Dunciad*. (Pope's commentaries in *The Dunciad,* however, are an integral part of his fiction, adding to the images of his dunces; Fielding's usually assume the simpler role of interpreting but not modifying the dunces' characters.) These interpreters are not always normative; the truth may be arrived at obliquely through simple ironies, but they do in one way or another tell us how to take the play. In fact, to a large extent, they inform with meaning the farcical actions that are otherwise merely "farcical." But this structure also gives Fielding a device with which to catch the maximum number of people gathered around the central object, the farce, and in this respect it resembles the structure of *Don Quixote in England*. At the center is the play itself, as both object and touchstone, as both disjointed farce and a symbol for the "farce" of the times. Around this, illuminating it and themselves, are the critic Sourwit, the gentleman who makes up the fashionable audience, Lord Dapper, the playwright himself, and the actors.

One of the commentators is always the author of the play, and in the later plays he becomes increasingly prominent and normative, producing a somewhat simpler effect than the commentator-scapegoat Quixote. In *Pasquin* there is still a discrepancy between the play-

---

40. *Champion,* 2, 199. See also *Essay on the Knowledge of the Characters of Men,* in *Works,* ed. Henley, *14,* 283, and *Champion,* Apr. 22 and May 3, 1740.

wright as bad writer and as satiric commentator, between the heroic bombast of his play, which is itself ridiculed, and its subject, the defeat of Queen Common-Sense by Queen Ignorance. As the play proves, Fustian himself is one of the playwrights he is attacking in his own play. His explanation for the extraneous characters—"the business of the play, as I take it, is to divert, and therefore every character that diverts is necessary to the business of the play" (IV.1; *11,* 211)—is not essentially different from the function of the "singers, fiddler, tumblers, and rope-dancers" that make up the army of Queen Ignorance. Fielding's point is the irony of a playwright attacking a ridiculous kind of play in an equally ridiculous play. This confusion is eliminated in *The Historical Register* (1737), where the author Medley is given the awareness of Luckless in *The Author's Farce;* his play's purpose, he explains, is "to divert the town and bring full houses" (Medley as the hack playwright), while at the same time its "design is to ridicule the vicious and foolish customs of the age" (Medley as satirist—I.1; *11,* 242). His ode to the new year, with which he opens the play, is a conscious parody of Cibber's effusions as poet laureate and serves as a way to show how insipidly the year opens in England. "There, sir," he says, "there's the very quintessence and cream of all the odes I have seen for several years last past" (I.1; *11,* 244).

Indeed, the scene hardly exists without Medley's explanation. We have to be told by Medley that "this, sir, is the full account of the whole history of Europe, as far as we know it, comprised in one scene" in order to understand the pointless scene with which the play begins; it serves as a correlative to Medley's explanation of the briefness of his whole play considering that it is the record of a whole year (I.1; *11,* 246). At other times his function is to generalize. In the second scene, showing that ladies are now the arbiters of taste, Medley's comment is explicit: "if we go on to improve in luxury, effeminacy and debauchery, as we have done lately, the next age, for ought I know, may be more like the children of squeaking Italians than hardy Britons" (II.1; *11,* 249). Later, in the scene in the theater, Medley again explains so that no one will miss the point: there is "a strict resemblance between the states political and theatrical" and, when Apollo advises, "Let them hiss . . . as long as we get their money," he adds, to underline the identification with Walpole, "There, sir, is the sentiment of a great man" (II.1, III.1; *11, 257, 263*). The other commentators—the critics Sneerwell and Sourwit—do not express divergent points of view so much as contribute (sometimes ironically) to a single interpretation of an event. The event itself is never allowed ambiguity.

The same structure is found in the picaresque narratives, in which Julian the Apostate's journey is framed by commentary, Wild's actions are constantly admired and held up for emulation by an ironic narrator who is presented as an advocate of "greatness," and the whole is surrounded by Fielding's very explicit preface to *The Miscellanies*. Julian the Apostate has an almost authorial awareness in his memory. Like Le Sage's Gil Blas, he is looking back and judging his own actions, and so he speaks with irony or adds commentary. A typical Fielding spokesman now that he is completely purged and in heaven, he says of Zeno's court, "nothing could be more gay, i.e., debauched" or:

> Several poets, likewise, addressed verses to me [a general], in which they celebrated my military achievements; and what, perhaps, may seem strange to us at present, I received all this incense with most greedy vanity, without once reflecting, that as I did not deserve these compliments, they should rather put me in mind of my defects. (Bk. I, Chap. 12; *2, 264*)

There is, in fact, a veritable Chinese box of commentaries here— Fielding the author on the outside, the I of the narrative, Julian in heaven, Julian in each of his metamorphoses, and finally the other people involved in each metamorphosis. It is clear that Fielding's basic form is the presentation of a brief epitome in action, followed by a meditation on its meaning.

In all of his work, satiric and nonsatiric, Fielding is reluctant to leave the reader or viewer to see the connotations for himself; he consistently informs him that this *is* a farce and what its significance may be. An important difference between Swift's and Fielding's satire is that, while both use the obtuse speaker who damns his own cause without realizing it, Fielding uses the device much more sparingly and will not let him stand alone but surrounds him with Lucianic frames. In the periodicals a self-damning letter is usually followed by

Vinegar's or Drawcansir's commentary on it. Only once does Fielding leave his ironic persona to speak for himself without any frame; in the *Jacobite's Journal* (1747–48) John Trott-Plaid, a Jacobite, explains the mysteries of Papism and Jacobitism, and only the exaggeration lets the reader know that he does not express Fielding's own views. Still, the result was not altogether what Fielding wished. When he switches to a more conventional persona, he comments:

> I have observed that tho' Irony is capable of furnishing the most exquisite Ridicule, yet as there is no kind of Humour so liable to be mistaken, it is, of all others, the most dangerous to the writer. An infinite Number of Readers have not the least Taste or Relish for it, I believe I may say do not understand it; and all are apt to be tired, when it is carried to any Degree of Length.[41]

Fielding seems always to have been somewhat unsure of the device. Swift's use of the ironic persona leaves open the possibility that some Whig or Dissenter *did* write this pamphlet, that Whigs are really that mad; but Fielding bolsters his ironies with translations and commentaries. He explains in a preface what he is going to do in *Jonathan Wild,* and he even translates his ironies as he nears the end of his story: "completely great, or completely low," and "so great, *i.e.,* corrupted" (Bk. IV, Chaps. 4, 12; 2, 159, 188).

A certain fear of being misunderstood, a hint of the growing distrust of irony among Englishmen, only partly explains Fielding's use of commentators. After all, the commentators themselves are consistently ironic, although the simplicity and consistency of the relation between stated and implied prevents serious misunderstanding. More important, the directing hand of a commentator or "author" is present to impose order on the chaos which satire describes and to make perfectly certain the meaning of the action. We have already noticed the generalizing turn Fielding gave to Pope's *Dunciad*. Pope is more concerned with the closely-woven texture of his poetry than with a visualized fable, with a great chaotic mass of particulars than with broad, heavy outlines of action. He also conveys a much stronger sense of the sights, sounds, and smells of London—of the shocking particularity of the dunces' behavior—than does Fielding,

41. *Jacobite's Journal,* Mar. 26, 1748.

who holds more closely to the classical concept of decorum and does not allow the imitation to blur the clarity of his argument and his art.

Unlike Swift, Fielding shows less interest in his commentators as attitudes or points of view than simply as devices for establishing the objective meaning of an action. The clear reality of the external world is his arena, not reality as it looks, feels, or smells to the individual. He remains throughout his career more concerned with the problem of understanding, of fixing meaning, than with the problem of conveying the sense of felt reality—with the reader's, as opposed to his character's, understanding. It is significant that he thought of Swift himself as the ironist in *A Modest Proposal,* the Lucianic rhetorician who assumes various poses without losing his own identity.[42] While Swift merged the satirist and the satiric object in a single character whose perception was of prime interest, Fielding once again separates them, producing essentially the same commentator-scene relationship that characterized the satire of Lucian. His narrator, as we shall see in a later section, is at times related to the Lucianic questioner, and his form to the dialogue.

The Judicial Metaphor

One further inference to be drawn from Fielding's use of the object-commentator form deserves a section to itself. If one of Fielding's basic metaphors to which he returns in all his works is theatrical, another, less noticeable perhaps but equally important, is judicial. Implicit in some of the discussions of the farces, this metaphor becomes pervasive in the *Champion,* which was Fielding's first literary outlet after the Licensing Act (1737) deprived him of the stage and made him turn to the law as a profession.

Besides frequent references to judgment and punishment and the employment of legal terms, he introduces the earliest of a long series of mock courts, Hercules Vinegar's "Court of Judicature" (sometimes called a "Court of Censorial Enquiry"). This court, following the traditional claim of the satiric tribunal, is for those criminals not covered by the laws—"invaders and destroyers of our lives and fortunes, and of the persons and honour of our women, whom no laws in being can any way come at" (Dec. 22, 1739). Again Vinegar pre-

42. *Covent-Garden Journal,* No. 11; ed. Jensen, *1,* 201.

sides at a mock trial to determine such questions as which of the London fops should be chosen "Prince of the Coxcombs" (Apr. 8, 1740) or what is the nature of Colley Cibber's violation of the English language in his *Apology* (May 17, 1740).

The metaphor that makes the satirist and, later, the reader himself a magistrate, and every character or action a case for judgment, becomes a central one in *Tom Jones* and, in a somewhat different way, in *Amelia*. To begin with, it involves a modified definition of the satirist—a more legal, even social, interpretation with less sense of urgency; a transition from a prosecuting attorney to an impartial judge with a more or less even balance of alternatives before him. Besides the metaphor itself and one of the possible forms through which to convey it, Fielding also developed in his periodicals a persona that began to move in the direction of the detached, fair-minded judge who would later be equated with the artist-creator or historian in the characteristic figure of the Fielding narrator. It is no coincidence that one of Fielding's larger preoccupations in the *Champion* is with an ethos for his commentator. In his later plays, action is increasingly dependent on the commentator, and it is only a small step from the almost newspaper-like quality of *The Historical Register* to the real newspaper, the *Champion*.

Certainly one reason for Fielding's turning to journalism was that the periodical offered him a wide arena for the exploration of satiric forms. With every issue new and different forms could be employed. Fielding explores them dutifully but in much the manner of a classroom exercise, and he adds little of his own. He uses the conventional dream vision of the *Spectator,* the extended pursual of an analogy (e.g. between politicians and fishermen), the letter-to-the-editor, the imaginary voyage, the "character," and the lost-and-found column (lost: honor, opportunity, merit, etc.). Fielding's main concern, however, is with the supposed writer of the paper: this is the mask he adopted and maintained as the basic fiction of the periodical. Within the limitations of this persona, variety is achieved by introducing his friends or relatives, by plunging into his subconscious (his dreams), by publishing letters written by supposed readers, and the like. Another limiting factor for the periodical writer is his audience: its broadness and low level of intelligence gave Fielding a sample of the "common reader" that he would address in his novels. He had to be even clearer and less ambiguous, using fewer allusions, than in his plays.

Fielding starts with a persona he calls Hercules Vinegar, a heroic, chastising satirist (complemented by the "prudent Coolness" of his wife Joan):

> I have now determin'd to lay aside the Sword [he tells us], which, without Vanity, I may boast to have us'd with some Success, (though few Captains now living, can say the like) and take up the Pen in its Stead, with a Design to do as much Execution with the one, as I have already done with the other; or, in other Words, to tickle now, as I before bruised Man into good Manners. (Nov. 15, 1739)[43]

He is, in short, a "champion," and as such, he gives the pedigree of his magic club: the "very strange and almost incredible Quality belonging to it, of falling, of its own Accord, on every egregious Knave who comes in its Way." An equivalent of Juvenal's automatic indignation ("difficile est saturam non scribere"), it has gone after Cardinal Wolsey, Henry VIII, quack doctors, and beaux: "The Club is, in this Reign, reported to have beaten 100 Lawyers, 99 Courtiers, 73 Priests, 8 Physicians, and 13 Beaux, (whereof 12 died of the first blow) besides innumerable others." Gallantly, it has cudgeled no women, though "It hath indeed sometimes expressed very odd Motions at the Sight of particular Women" (Dec. 8, 1739).[44]

Vinegar has a family with a variety of interests and points of view, like the Bickerstaff family in the *Tatler* and the Spectator Club in the *Spectator*, but Fielding does surprisingly little with them. He finds it difficult to get involved in a very dramatic situation in the periodical, and so he usually lets Vinegar speak through the length of a paper or, more often, simply drops the crotchety character of Vinegar for a more normative persona. This figure, or point of view, represents the emergence of a public mask for Fielding, a *vir bonus* pose which apparently corresponds to the young lawyer and later to the Bow Street Magistrate and social reformer, the thoughtful husband and friend, and the conscientious citizen, as described by Wilbur Cross and

43. *Champion, I, I.*
44. Ibid., pp. 69–72.

James Work (mostly, it should be noted, in terms of the periodicals and pamphlets in which Fielding speaks out most clearly in this persona).[45]

This is the man who talks to us much of the time in the *Champion* —about subjects from the relation between fools and knaves to the defense of the clergy. He is a good man who tries to lead men into a decent mode of behavior, not the old Vinegar with his club; a descendant of the Horace of the *epistolae* rather than of the *sermones* (and no relation to Juvenal); and a lawyer or a judge first, a satirist second. He is not a moralistic figure, but a balanced, attractive one who explores the extremes of the strategies he uses in his fictional works—for example "roasting" people (Mar. 13) or "good nature" (Mar. 27). In one issue of the *Champion* he may present a sermon on virtue in which he is the moralist; in the next number he may introduce a letter in which an anti-mask treats the same subject satirically by expressing the opposing point of view. He shows sympathy for his fellowmen, as when a letter writer explains he is hypocrite, and Vinegar (as *vir bonus*) replies that a man who can write such a letter, so revealing and self-aware of his own character, has already taken the first step toward salvation. However modified this mask may have become by the time Fielding ended the *Champion,* it derives originally from his search for a satiric ethos.

In the periodicals Fielding begins to develop the most pervasive and important forms of his mature novels. The relation between the periodical essay and the Fielding chapter is obvious. The latter bears the form of the *Spectator* essay, beginning with a generalization or a moral aphorism, then presenting the scene itself, and ending with a pithy conclusion. But the *Champion* also heralds the larger structure, where the public mask guides the reader (often "you") through a maze of good and bad examples, defining a positive and detailed code of proper conduct very much in the manner of Horace. Bad examples are sprinkled along the way, but the end of the essay is to educate the reader in a decent mode of conduct, not to explore the nature of evil or to examine its universal infiltration. Evil has become

45. See Wilbur Cross, *History of Henry Fielding* (3 vols. New Haven, Yale University Press, 1918), and James A. Work, "Henry Fielding, Christian Censor," in *The Age of Johnson: Essays Presented to Chauncey Brewster Tinker* (New Haven, Yale University Press, 1949), pp. 139–48.

individual, what will affect oneself, not all mankind. In *An Essay on Conversation* "Fielding" has an intimate, discursive talk with a reader; in *An Essay on the Knowledge of the Characters of Men* he presents examples of hypocrisy for the reader to beware of; and in the novels a central example of "good nature" (or decency) is shown gradually learning wisdom in a corrupt world by means of contrary examples.

Fielding the "champion," the poet as the voice of society, is squarely in the Augustan tradition. But the *Champion* led him to jostle the role of satirist with that of moralist. To say that Fielding was a moralist means essentially that he proposed a coherent plan of life and conduct; to the extent that this figure held the center of the stage, he ceased to be a satirist. In all of his periodicals except the early issues of the *Jacobite's Journal,* the commentator has a larger part than the scene, the normative elements a larger part than the evil ones.

My own supposition is that Fielding began as a satirist in order to be in the proper tradition of writing, and that as he became more and more immersed in his undertaking he became increasingly interested in the moral imperatives which satire requires. Put another way, he began not for but against certain things, a typical satirist; as time passed he became knowledgeable of the positives to which panto-mimes and political corruption are opposed, and so his persona, and perhaps he himself, became increasingly the orthodox Christian which Pope used as his persona in his ethic epistles. Certainly the positives became more important as he grew older, partly due to his reformer's instinct, his career in the law, and his belief in man's posi-tive potential. He became more interested in the causes and motives —in the lure of fashion and emulation—than in the criminal act itself.

❀ *Chapter 3* ❀

FIELDING THE ANTI-ROMANTICIST

Fielding vs. Richardson

In the context of his earlier work it would appear that when Fielding came to write the first of his novels his intention was to correct the unhealthy tendencies of the Richardsonian novel in the same spirit in which he had earlier corrected the excesses of the pantomimes and operas. *Pamela* (1740), in one sense, represented the culmination of the forces of bad writing and fraudulent morality that Swift had attacked in *A Tale of a Tub* and Pope in *The Dunciad*. Like Swift, Fielding may have seen the new literary forms as dangerous because of their aggressive abandonment of classical models or any formal standards of excellence, their exaltation of the new and disordered, and their effect of raising the ego to an unprecedented prominence.[1]

Of course the same discrepancy resulted between intended meaning and the meaning communicated by the action itself which Fielding had explored in the hack writing that drew his attention before 1737. In fact, *Pamela* could stand at the end of our survey of mixed conventions in the emergent novel (Chap. 1). It was "the first novel," the final anti-romance, in that it produced an ultimate in formal realism through the immediacy, prolixity, and verisimilitude of the letter form, which expresses the inner workings of a mind and effectively immerses the reader in its simulacrum of the real world. But if *Pamela* was the prototype of the modern novel as defined by Ortega y Gasset and others, it was also a descendant of the romance and, in a sense, the prototype of the popular or romantic novel of the fleeing heroine, the interrupted seduction, and the happy marriage.[2] Al-

---

1. Cf. Swift's "Dedication to Prince Posterity" in *A Tale of a Tub* and Fielding's *Covent-Garden Journal*, No. 40, ed. Jensen, *1*, 362.

2. See Ian Watt, *The Rise of the Novel* (Berkeley and Los Angeles, University of California Press, 1956), and Leslie Fiedler, *Love and Death in the American Novel* (New York, Criterion Books, 1960).

though the novel's main concern seemed to be with the momentary and ephemeral, Richardson was very much concerned with eternal verities; he had a great moral to convey about virtue and vice, with his subtitle "Virtue Rewarded." This moral imposed certain conditions on the narrative that were not met by Richardson's account of the immediate workings of his heroine's mind. What led contemporaries to attack *Pamela* was, besides its immense and enviable success, the unstable compound Richardson created by mixing conventions of realism, romance, and morality play.

The romance convention probably caused the most trouble, requiring that the girl and the seducer be united at the end and thus preordaining the nature of virtue's reward. Since Richardson combined the figures of the lover and the ogre (we should also notice traces of fairy-tale romance, Cinderella, Beauty and the Beast, etc.), Mr. B. became such a monster that Pamela's ultimate acceptance of him seemed hypocritical self-advancement. Moreover, Richardson further tended to subvert his paragon by keeping her in a situation of pursuit and defense—the basic plot of romance—while at the same time granting her pious knowledge of Mr. B.'s nefarious intention and plentiful opportunity to leave his service. At his best Richardson used these contradictions to create a convincing picture of divided minds, both Pamela's and Mr. B.'s, struggling between conscious and unconscious drives—between Pamela's ideal of chastity and her love for Mr. B.; between his notion that a servant girl should be his for the asking and his growing love for Pamela as an ideal woman. At worst the jumbled conventions created the impression of double-dealing on the part of Pamela and her creator.

When *Pamela* came into Fielding's sights he seems to have sensed —certainly before his contemporaries—the peculiar danger of Richardson's hold over his readers. The effect of *Pamela*'s particularity, piled-up minutiae, repetitions, and prolixity was to draw the reader as close as possible to the heroine's immediate experience and mind, in fact to suck the reader in and immerse him in her experience. "Such a record," A. D. McKillop writes of Pamela's letters, "gives the reader a continuous and cumulative impression of living through the experience, and thus creates a new kind of sympathy with the character whose experiences are being shared."[3]

3. *The Early Masters of English Fiction* (Lawrence, University of Kansas Press, 1956), p. 57.

Immersion may lead to a sinister titillation in *Pamela's* erotic scenes, but more serious, it allows the reader to identify himself so much with the character that he tends to lose a sense of relationships, the wholeness of the moral design, and his moral perspective on the character. The reader becomes uncritical, a "friend" of the character, and having accepted Pamela's rationalizations as completely as he would his own, he emerges ready to modify his own conduct accordingly. The situation, as Fielding evidently saw it, was analogous to the blindness inflicted upon people by fashion and the conventions of "greatness" and "great men," all of which hindered not only the judgment of other people's actions but the decisions by which one takes one's own actions. Identification with a character was, of course, a prime ingredient of romance, the same danger that Cervantes perceived in *Amadis de Gaula*. But Fielding sensed that in this bourgeois story, laid in contemporary England with all the realism that particularity of description and immediacy of the letter form can give, immersion was much stronger than in a chivalric romance laid in the Middle Ages.

Samuel Johnson, writing in 1750 (*Rambler,* No. 4), also recognized this phenomenon at work, but his solution was more conservative— and perhaps more realistic—than Fielding's. He simply argued that the novelist, recognizing the power he wielded over his reader, must make his protagonist a virtuous man:

> if the power of example is so great as to take possession of the memory by a kind of violence, and produce effects almost without the intervention of the will, care ought to be taken, that, when the choice is unrestrained, the best examples only should be exhibited; and that which is likely to operate so strongly, should not be mischievous or uncertain in its effects.

In the right hands, Johnson thought, the novel could be a transcendent force for moral reform; the reader, sympathizing with the good man, would then go out and behave in the same way. But Fielding, seeing more danger than Johnson did in the example of Pamela, believed that with such an instrument in the hands of a bourgeois like Richardson, a man with enormous talent for "writing to the moment" but with a narrow, uncertain, even obtuse morality, the only answer was an alternative form that never for a moment left the reader in doubt about the author's intention as to who was good and who evil.

Seeing *Pamela* as a moral chaos in which the reader was invited to wallow self-indulgently, Fielding began his alternative, *Shamela,* by adding the objective commentator that *Pamela* lacked. Richardson, however good his intentions, could only appear as a sententious editor, a lone voice in an occasional note which was effectually outside the fiction and could be ignored. The reader had only Pamela and himself; almost everything was seen through Pamela's eyes, and she (Fielding believed) carried Richardson and the reader away with her.

Fielding's initial response was the Swiftean solution—letting the Pamelian speaker condemn herself. But even when he has made the dramatic irony unmistakable, if not coarse and obvious, and simplified the action, he surrounds Shamela's letters with commentary, offering viewpoints other than the heroine's which place her actions in clearer perspective. *Shamela* still uses the farce's approach to parody, surrounding the action with comment and not allowing it to stand by itself, and thus it remains halfway between the plays and *Joseph Andrews*. In the latter, however, Fielding replaces the directly imitated voices of the heroine and the commentators (Parsons Oliver and Tickletext) with one voice which controls and conveys the whole action.

While Medley was as close as Fielding came in the farces to a normative commentator, in *Joseph Andrews* the narrator is in temperament close to the persona of the periodicals—like him, an arbiter of morals and manners. He is, to begin with, a creator and/or historian, who sets before the reader an object that can be accepted as objectively true. The effect is evident if we compare the portraits of two ill-favored women:

[Mrs. Jewkes] is a broad, squat pursy, *fat thing,* quite ugly, if any thing human can be so called; about forty years old. She has a huge hand, and an arm as thick as my waist, I believe. Her nose is flat and crooked, and her brows grow down over her eyes; a dead spiteful, grey, goggling eye, to be sure she has. And her face is flat and broad; and as to colour, looks like as if it had been pickled a month in saltpetre.

[Mrs. Slipslop] was not at this time remarkably handsome, being very short, and rather too corpulent in body, and somewhat red, with the addition of pimples in the face. Her nose was likewise rather too large, and her eyes too little; nor did she resemble a cow so much in her breath as in two brown globes which she carried before her; one of her legs was also a little shorter than the other, which occasioned her to limp as she walked. This fair creature had long cast the eyes of affection on Joseph.[4]

While Richardson undoubtedly intended his portrait of Mrs. Jewkes to arouse our contempt if not ridicule, even drawing upon satiric conventions to do so, he put the description into the mouth of a character, Pamela, and thus made it subjective. When Pamela describes Jewkes, we see a portrait distorted by fear and apprehension. Almost at once, as if to make sure that there is no mistake, Richardson has Pamela add: "This is poor helpless spite in me:—But the picture is too near the truth notwithstanding." Her nightmare fantasies are collected in her portraits of Jewkes and Colbrand ("great staring eyes . . . a monstrous wide mouth; blubber lips; long yellow teeth, and a hideous grin"), and all the evil she is unwilling to see in her master is transferred to his underlings, as in another instance it is transferred to a bull (who turns out to be a harmless cow). But when Fielding describes Slipslop, we know that, however fantastic, in the context of his fiction she looked that way.

Second, Fielding's commentator is a manipulator. When an appalling event like the abduction of Fanny by the squire's men takes place, the narrator juggles scenes so that the reader does not lose sight of the overall structure of meaning in his concern for Fanny. Instead of closely following her fate in the Richardsonian manner, he switches to "a discourse between the poet and the player; of no other use in this history but to divert the reader" (Bk. III, Chap. 10; *1*, 293). The poet and player, sycophants of the squire who wants Fanny, and participants themselves in the abduction, casually discuss drama. This scene is followed by a dialogue between Joseph and Adams concerning Fanny, in which Joseph's anguish is counteracted by Adams' insistence on stoic acceptance. Only then is the reader returned to Fanny herself and her predicament. This diversion and the various

4. *Pamela* (London, Chapman and Hall, 1902), *1*, 141; *Joseph Andrews*, Bk. I, Chap. 6; *1*, 40.

parodic devices that follow set off the narrative and the characters from immediate contact with the reader and keep the reader aware of the author's controlling presence and his message. The juxtaposition also dramatizes the total unconcern of the poet and player about Fanny or any moral issue, as well as Fielding's favorite analogy between the shoddiness of art and morals, between the stage and life. The effect of the pause after the abduction is therefore essentially to allow contemplation. Beginning in *Joseph Andrews,* the important formal elements in Fielding's novels are the scene and the relationship between scene and commentary and between one scene and another.

In the third place, the commentator is an ironist. His ironic mask produces the impression necessary to Fielding's conception of the novel—the impression of neutrality and authority, as opposed to the disreputable, prejudiced, and limited vision of a Pamela. The ironic attitude implies a contrast between a limited and conventional view and a more generous, inclusive one. The effect is very different from Richardson's inclusiveness—gathering a great mass of minutiae and particulars within a narrow compass in order to submerge the reader. Irony holds the reader at some distance from the action; as Rebecca Parkin has noted, it "implies a sophisticated reader and a sophisticated poet, together with an awareness and acceptance, on the part of both, of their sophisticated status."[5] This is the old poet-audience relationship assumed and fostered by Dryden, Swift, and Pope. With them Fielding accepts the assumption that the air of artifice is compensated for by the sanity of the exposition, the clarity and, in that sense, realism of the picture—the impression that the author is aware of more than one aspect of his subject.

If Richardson's realism is one of plenitude, Fielding's is one of opposite and larger reference; if Richardson achieves verisimilitude by an oppressive intimacy, Fielding does the same by polarizing his views of people, his kinds of people, and their experiences and motives. The analogues he introduces in *Joseph Andrews* have the effect of suggesting both the complexity and the interrelations of life; ironic similes thus connect Slipslop and a tiger, Adams and Colley Cibber, Lady Booby and Cupid, Joseph and the biblical Joseph. The effect is exactly like that of Fielding's earlier satires, to extend the behavior of

5. *The Poetic Workmanship of Alexander Pope* (Minneapolis, University of Minnesota Press, 1955), p. 31.

a Lady Booby to the outside world of art, politics, religion, and the reader's own behavior. When Fielding wants to show how passion transforms sensible people, he compares it to Rich transforming (in his pantomimes) men into monkeys or wheelbarrows and to Cibber transforming the English language into something new and strange (Bk. I, Chap. 7). The implications involve not only the theatrical quality of Lady Booby's passion but the irrationality that is at the bottom of Rich's and Cibber's behavior.

The "reality" generated by Fielding's irony is a kind of control or discrimination, a depth of understanding—what Ian Watt has called "realism of assessment."[6] We might distinguish between reality as placement of something in a proper or true relationship to everything else in the world (Fielding's type), and reality as exposition of the authenticity of something (Richardson's). It follows that by reality Fielding means moral or factual truth apprehended by the reader, whereas he sees in Richardson a reality that means the true workings of a character's mind, without any concern for the truth or falseness of apprehension in relation to the external world.

Irony also serves Fielding as a controllable equivalent of Richardson's presentation of the workings of a mind. He puts mock-heroic speeches in his characters' mouths: Lady Booby cries, "Whither doth this violent passion hurry me! What meanness do we submit to from its impulse!" and reveals that she sees herself as a tragedy queen and her lust for Joseph as a grand passion.[7] But the narrator's ironies, in the manner of Dryden and the mock-heroic poets, also expose Lady Booby's mind. As soon as she is alone,

> the little god Cupid, fearing he had not yet done the lady's business, took a fresh arrow with the sharpest point out of his quiver, and shot it directly into her heart: in other and plainer language, the lady's passion got the better of her reason. (Bk. I, Chap. 7; *1,* 45)

This passage tells how Lady Booby would describe her feelings about Joseph (in terms of Cupid and hearts) and what actually happened

---

6. Watt, *Rise of the Novel,* p. 288.
7. Maynard Mack has pointed out this effect in his introduction to *Joseph Andrews* (New York, Rinehart, 1948), p. 6.

("passion got the better of her reason"); the passage not only sets her lust in perspective but also demonstrates her self-delusion, revealing an unhappy, misguided woman who rationalizes her petty affair into a great Didoesque love. Its effect in the larger context of Lady Booby's character is to suggest that her hypocrisy (calling her lust virtue) may be only a means to an end that is beyond her control.

Mrs. Slipslop "at last gave up Joseph and his cause, and with a triumph over her passion highly commendable" went off to get drunk. The author's ironic praise is obvious, but what it says in context is that she *felt* that she had triumphed and should be commended. Fielding's irony almost consistently, whether in speech or the author's comment, suggests the character's rationalization, just as Pamela's moral interpretations of her actions do (less self-consciously) in the novel he is criticizing. The mock-heroic of *Jonathan Wild* works in the same way, except that the self-delusion is mixed with aspiration to a false ideal, "greatness." Whether from the character's own lips or from those of the commentator, the irony tends to become an expression of the character's psychology.

Fielding does not call *Joseph Andrews* a satire; he infrequently refers to the word "satire" and holds firmly to the designation "comic epic in prose." Comedy, of course, still contained the idea of the satiric in the early eighteenth century and, by this time, had better connotations. But Fielding had other reasons as well for using the broader term.

To begin with, he specifically rules out certain kinds of satire he had used in the earlier part of his career as unsuited to the comic epic in prose. By the word "burlesque" he means, first, literary parody: he is not writing a parody of *Pamela* or of anything else, a strategy he had already handled in *Shamela*. His second meaning of "burlesque" is the more general one, "the exhibition of what is monstrous and unnatural"—a Shamela, a Pistol in *The Author's Farce,* or a Queen Ignorance in *Pasquin*. This meaning, the literary equivalent of caricature, applies to a particular kind of satire, travesty or mock-heroic, "appropriating the manners of the highest to the lowest, or *è converso*." Although *Joseph Andrews* betrays unmistakable elements of parody and high and low burlesque, they are, as Fielding claims, incidental and decorative rather than essential; they help to determine our attitude toward a character but do not ordinarily alter the character himself and certainly do not caricature him.

Fielding intends to set up not an exaggerated image of what he detests, in the manner of *The Dunciad* or his own *Shamela,* but rather an alternative of his own. This is, I think, the basic reason for his avoiding reference to satire. Throughout all three of his major novels he continues to refer to the importance of the new form he has created, but though he connects this form at various times with comedy, epic, and history, he never does with satire. His intention is not finally satiric. Although he may include the idea of satire, he means by "comedy" a more general imitation of reality or what he calls a "just imitation" of nature. Since satire remains an important part of his point of view, however, he wishes to dissociate himself from the particular kind of satire he had written a few years earlier in *Pasquin* and *The Historical Register* and more recently in *Shamela.* In one of the few occurrences of the word "satire," he gives us the *Spectator's* view that the preference of the general to the particular in subject "distinguishes the satirist from the libeller," and that in *Joseph Andrews* "we mean not to lash individuals, but all of the like sort" (Bk. III, Chap. 1; *1,* 216). This was a conventional definition, but Fielding would have to do some explaining to apply it to some of his earlier satires.

Fielding's analogy between his novel and the works of Hogarth makes his point clear. Hogarth's prints, which had become enormously popular after the publication of *A Harlot's Progress* in 1732, offered the best example of what Fielding himself wished to do: replace the fantasy of traditional, emblematic, and Augustan satire with a more restrained delineation, closer to experience, and reliant on "character" rather than "caricature," on the variety rather than the exaggeration of expression. Both, moreover, sought a more secure place in the classical hierarchy of genres than satire, the grotesque, or even the comic by itself could command (or, for that matter, than the rootless Richardsonian form could lay claim to). As Hogarth steered a course between the flatulent history painting of his time and the popular forms of satire and burlesque, Fielding sought to establish a genre between the romance he discerned in Richardson's *Pamela* and the grotesquerie of travesty.

The point that Fielding makes by bracketing *Joseph Andrews* between romance on one side and burlesque on the other is that he intends to write according to his own definition of realism. Both romance and burlesque are used by Fielding in this connection to show the different ways in which reality may be distorted—to glamorize and to vilify. He equates *Pamela* with the romances of Jack the Giant Killer and Guy of Warwick as he equates his own early work (though perhaps not so wholeheartedly) with burlesque and caricature. But his claim, like that of Defoe and Richardson, is to seek truth and reality; he says—and this is an important contribution of his preface—that the novel is a search for the real.

Fielding's idea of reality is, of course, quite different from Richardson's, and while he claims to be following a middle way, his realism is largely (like anti-romance realism) a contrary to Richardson's. Richardson sees life as a single-minded conflict between two people, one good, the other evil. He is interested only in the sensibility of one woman, alone in a closet with her daydreams and wish fantasies. His setting is usually indoors, in drawing rooms, hallways, and bedrooms —the "close, hot, day-dreamy" world Coleridge noted.[8] To what he considered the narrow world of *Pamela* Fielding opposes the wide world of epic with all classes and all manner of locales. His settings are out-of-doors, on roads, in inns, in coaches, on horseback, as well as in the places used by Richardson. Life is not a private relationship between a man and a woman but a journey on which one passes through all kinds of experiences and meets a great variety of people.

The analogy between epic and novel was a conventional one made by critics when attempting to justify the new fiction in terms of classical genres.[9] In his preface to *Joseph Andrews,* Fielding claims that to present true reality the novelist must correct his personal bias with reference to the larger view of tradition, developing the novel's affinities with the classical genres and in particular those genres associated with broad scope and objectivity of attitude. His preference for the *Odyssey* was natural, as he explains in the preface to the second edition of his sister Sarah's novel, *David Simple* (1744). The *Iliad* and *Odyssey* "differ principally in the action, which in the Iliad is entire and uniform; in the Odyssey, is rather a series of actions, all tending to produce one great end." He argues that "those who should

---

8. Samuel Coleridge, *The Complete Works,* ed. W. C. T. Shedd (New York, 1853), 4, 380.

9. See André Le Breton, *Le Roman au XVIIIeme siècle* (Paris, n.d.), and Dorothy Frances Dallas, *Le Roman Français de 1660 à 1680* (Paris, 1932), Chap. 1.

object want of unity of action here, may, if they please, or if they dare, fly back with their objection in the face even of the Odyssey itself." He also implies the distinction he feels between this form and satire. The comic epic in prose should not "set before us the odious instead of the amiable." By this he means that the central character should not be subject to attack on any serious grounds; he should be neither a villain like Milton's Satan nor a mock-hero like Shadwell or Cibber. Thus *Joseph Andrews* would be a comic epic; *Jonathan Wild* would not.

In *Joseph Andrews* Fielding inserts the action of the *Odyssey* or the *Aeneid* (the uprooting of a protagonist and his attempts to find his way home) in the middle of the seduction scene of the Richardsonian novel. As if to point out that one must break free from that small room and narrow relationship, he allows Joseph to escape and follows his flight. Each of the subsequent actions moves Joseph toward his final goal.

The action of *Joseph Andrews,* with its movement toward a positive goal and a happy ending, is clearly not satiric, but the picaresque novel, the contemporary equivalent of the *Odyssey*-type epic, naturally influenced Fielding's conception. By placing the emphasis on the various incarnations of Lady Booby that block or delay the hero's return, without sacrificing the generally epic intention, Fielding renders a greater part of the overall effect satiric. For his alternative to Richardson's novel he turned to the epic, but in practice he drew upon the conventions and techniques, the externalizing and expository forms with which he was most familiar in satire.

Anti-Romance

In *Shamela* Fielding parodied the formal conventions of the Richardsonian novel in the heroine's letters, in her circumstantial lists of wearing apparel and books, and in her furious scribbling "to the moment": "Odsbobs! I hear him just coming at the door. . . . Well, he is in bed between us, we both shamming a sleep; he steals his hand into my bosom."[10] Fielding's strategy is to travesty the Richardsonian style, dramatis personae, and, in an abbreviated form, plot, shifting it downward toward cruder and more extreme situations. *Shamela* is

10. Letter VI; *Joseph Andrews* and *Shamela,* ed. Martin C. Battestin (Boston, Riverside Editions, 1961), p. 313.

the simplest kind of anti-romance, the "true history" that travesties romance by revealing the real schemer beneath the pious phrases and coyness of Richardson's heroine. Thus Fielding reveals Mrs. Jervis to be a bawd, Parson Williams to be Pamela's lover, and "our old friend Nanny Jewkes" to be a rival for the love of Parson Williams. Mr. B. becomes the Booby he appeared to be in his bungling attempts to seduce Pamela, and Pamela becomes the designing slut that Mr. B. occasionally suspected her of being and that she appeared to be in such slips as when, with her pursuer close upon her, she recalls: "I found his hand in my bosom; and when my fright let me know it, I was ready to die; and I sighed and screamed, and fainted away. And still he had his arms about my neck."[11] Fielding simply gives us the *true* Pamela: "I thought once of making a little Fortune by my Person. I now intend to make a great one by my Vartue" (Letter 10; p. 325).

Shamela is conceived in the tradition of Jonathan Wild and Fielding's early villains, a central symbol of vice. But she is also, like some of them, a surrogate or apprentice, and in this sense *Shamela* is related to the *Don Quixote* kind of anti-romance. The hero acts according to a romantic ideal ("greatness") that is external and not entirely appropriate to him. Just as Quixote reads his romances, Shamela reads Whitefield and listens to Parson Williams' sermons advocating faith over works. Fielding's point is not only that these sermons are used as hypocritical masks but that they contain the code of hypocrisy that Shamela is teaching herself to follow. Worst of all, however, are her mother's letters, which continually exhort her to pursue her calculating end and capture Mr. Booby. Like Wild she is shown stretching to reach a mark held up to her by a hard taskmaster; her mother keeps urging her on and she, in her own way, always falls a little short.[12]

11. *Pamela*, I, 72.

12. The situation is perhaps even more reminiscent of *The Beggar's Opera* with the Peachum-Polly-Macheath relationship repeated in Mrs. Andrews-Shamela-Parson Williams. Gay offered Fielding a model for the interpretation of the middle-class mind that must have contributed to Fielding's interpretation of Pamela as Shamela. Mrs. Peachum sounds like Mother Andrews when she explains that "the first time a woman is frail, she should be somewhat nice, methinks, for then or never is the time to make her fortune. After that, she hath nothing to do but to guard herself from being found out, and she may do what she pleases" (II.8). Polly herself puts it this way: "A girl who cannot grant some things, and refuse what is most essential, will make but a poor hand of her beauty, and soon be thrown upon the common" (I.7).

Her trouble is that she cannot control her passion for Parson Williams, and in spite of her mother's warnings this leads to her downfall; Mr. Booby catches them in bed together and the whole scheme comes to nothing. The obverse of Wild's failure at personal relationships, Shamela's passion is her tragic flaw. Love as a lack, Fielding seems to say, helps to characterize the bad man and foretell the disintegration of his designs; but love as a positive force, even in so crude a form as Shamela's lust, must destroy hypocrisy and calculation, just as Shaftesbury's ridicule must destroy sham. It is not certain whether Shamela's love affair with Parson Williams is supposed to be more important as an act of hypocrisy or as a sign of her passion that obtrudes to destroy her hypocritical fabrication. What should appear to be vice punished may be interpreted as Shamela's one sincere action discovered. The Shamelian context admittedly warrants a less positive construction; but whatever the emphasis in *Shamela,* the love-profit contrast is central to *Joseph Andrews.*

Here Fielding creates an action that is roughly parallel to *Pamela*'s but at a remove. The death of Sir Thomas Booby, like the death of Mr. B.'s mother, sets the plot going, but Lady Booby is not simply a parody of Mr. B. She is a distinct person, a relative of Booby's, just as Joseph is (or rather appears to be) a relative of Pamela's, and the two sets of characters, Fielding's and Richardson's, carry on their own stories in *Joseph Andrews.* They are connected only by the reader's memory, Joseph's two letters to his sister, and the eventual meeting at Booby Hall. By that time Mr. Booby has married Pamela and Lady Booby has begun her last concentrated effort to corrupt Joseph. The Mr. Booby-Pamela action is not travestied, except perhaps in Pamela's insistent snobbery that is a sequel to her marriage.

As we have seen, Fielding conceives *Joseph Andrews* less as a parody, like *Shamela,* than as an alternative.[13] He starts with Colley Cibber's *Apology* and Richardson's *Pamela,* just as Cervantes started with the romances of chivalry; here, says Fielding, we are shown an "ideal" male and female, models for their respective sexes. But they, like those knights and ladies, are neither real people nor real ideals; *Joseph Andrews* will show what a true ideal is and what real people are like. This involves, first, an adjustment of values. Self-seeking

---

13. Cf. Martin C. Battestin, *The Moral Basis of Fielding's Art: A Study of "Joseph Andrews"* (Middletown, Conn., Wesleyan University Press, 1959), pp. 8–9.

that uses chastity as a means to an end (Pamela) and vanity that calls unchastity a virtue (Cibber) are offered their opposites, chastity and natural goodness (Joseph and Parson Adams). Second, it involves stripping off what appear to be virtues in most people and revealing the self-interest underneath. The latter, only half of the intention, corresponds to the travesty of *Shamela*.

In one of the many epic similes attached to Parson Adams, we are told that

> he did not more than Mr. Colley Cibber apprehend any such passions as malice and envy to exist in mankind; which was indeed less remarkable in a country parson, than in a gentleman who hath passed his life behind the scenes,—a place which hath been seldom thought the school of innocence, and where a very little observation would have convinced the great Apologist that those passions have a real existence in the human mind. (Bk. I, Chap. 3; *1, 30*)

Adams' inability to detect malice and envy is compared to Cibber's, and the audience notes the irony—that Adams is unable (from simplicity and goodness) to recognize malice when it appears, while Cibber (all too aware of it) is unwilling to admit that it *is* malice. The parallel continues to be enforced from time to time, as in the chapter heading, "A curious dialogue that passed between Mr. Abraham Adams and Mr. Peter Pounce, better worth reading than all the works of Colley Cibber and many others" (Bk. II, Chap. 13).

In much the same way, Lady Booby and Joseph are contrasted in a crucial scene with the further analogue of Potiphar's wife and the biblical Joseph.[14] Slipslop, whose pretended gentility and literacy recall Pamela's, is contrasted with Adams, whose shabbiness hides his true learning; a high churchman is contrasted with a low, a bad with a good. Whenever Fanny is in trouble at least two people come along, one to react selfishly and one (for either good or bad motives) to save her. When Adams asks a favor of two men, the first is rude, the second kindly.

14. Another sort of parallel may also be present. Battestin believes that Fielding uses a mock-heroic structure similar to Pope's, but with the *Bible* instead of the *Aeneid* as the second term. Abraham Adams and Joseph, he argues, should suggest to us overtones of the biblical Abraham and Joseph (see *The Moral Basis*, pp. 41, 48).

Thus the novel begins with a discussion of examples (Bk. I, Chap. 1) and a comparison of the examples of worldly wisdom, Pamela and Cibber, and the examples of simple goodness, Joseph and Adams. Once this comparison has been set up, Fielding takes the examples he has presupposed into the world of experience as Richardson and Cibber took theirs. By inference, Pamela and Cibber would have come through far differently. When Joseph maintains his virtue against Lady Booby's advances he is discharged; Pamela, for neither surrendering nor protecting hers, receives her master's hand in marriage. Adams is hardly an example for ambitious young Cibbers to follow: at forty he is still a curate; when he had the influence of his nephew at his disposal he did not know how to use it. We are told from time to time what a different sort would have done in the same circumstances: the men who have captured him and Fanny, thinking them robbers, are so busy arguing among themselves over the reward "that a dexterous nimble thief, had he been in Mr. Adams' situation, would have taken care to have given the justice no trouble that evening." Adams, however, makes no attempt to escape, trusting "rather to his innocence than his heels" (Bk. II, Chap. 10; *1, 165–66*).

True virtue is repeatedly rewarded by abuse, blows, or even imprisonment in place of the vicious. Joseph is beaten by robbers and left naked in a ditch and is then subjected to equally brutal treatment at the hands of several decent citizens who pass him in a coach. The progress of Joseph and Adams from London to Booby Hall is one long succession of such violent encounters: Adams is brained with a blood pudding, chased (as a substitute hare) by a pack of hounds, tormented with practical jokes, and dropped into a tub of water. The punishers, it is made abundantly clear, are the Cibbers and Pamelas.

Joseph Andrews is similar to *Shamela* in that it treats the "romances" of *Pamela* and Cibber's *Apology* not as the reading of an isolated Quixote, but as a pernicious ideal to which most people aspire. Fielding has ironically shown that the romance world is the real (in the sense of practical) world. The Quixote parallel, introduced on the title page, is enforced from time to time, as when Adams and his friends have difficulty getting away from an inn where they owe the reckoning: "they had more reason to have mistaken [this inn] for a castle than Don Quixote ever had any of those in which he sojourned, seeing they had met with such difficulty in escaping out of its walls" (Bk. II, Chap. 16; *1*, 196–97). The imaginary world of Quixote is quite real here: these innkeepers and clergymen *are* monsters.

In the romance world characters' virtues are miraculously synchronized with their surroundings, and so Pamela saves her virtue and wins a fortune. Joseph and Adams, put into a real world where Pamela's virtues are as inappropriate as Quixote's delusions about chivalry, are notably unsuccessful. The explanation, Fielding insists, is that Pamela's virtue is feigned for self-interest; this, he implies, accounts for the strange synchronization of her "virtue" and her world. Appear virtuous and act viciously: this is the Pamelian formula for success. Neither vice nor virtue can finally succeed, only pseudo-virtue.

The romance in the old Quixotic sense then is embodied in Joseph and Parson Adams. They have a true ideal that does not agree with the world around them, which behaves according to the code of the Cibbers and Pamelas. The romance values are chastity and charity, Christian virtues, all ironically exposed as inappropriate to eighteenth-century England. In short, Fielding has adopted the interpretation of *Don Quixote* that attacks the accepted morality and criticizes it by the standard of an absolute. His interpretation of Quixote always carries this emphasis, sensing that in this world Richardson and Cibber, the innkeepers and merchants, express the real and Quixote the romance.

One effect of making both sides of the reality-romance contrast forms that are imitated or codes of conduct is to suggest that the characters act not independently or by storybook conventions but in terms of divergent sets of manners.

The Alternative Hero: Quixote

Although Richardson presents an unromantic, bourgeois milieu, Fielding detects beneath the psychological and sociological realism the old outlines of the romance heroine, knight, and dragon. The heroine, taken at her own and her author's valuation, is much too good, and the villain much too bad; moreover, the subject is the pursual of the angelic by the diabolic (Mr. B. is frequently called Lucifer), the latter extending downward into the sexual and sadistic.

For Fielding, the middle area between the romance and the burlesque is the "ridiculous," still a satiric domain where no man is above censure. "Great vices," Fielding tells us, explaining his meaning, "are the proper objects of our detestation, smaller faults, of our pity; but affectation appears to me the only true source of the Ridiculous." This area excludes the noncomic experience—the absolutely good and absolutely evil. Within this middle area, however, are worse kinds of affectation: people who take pride in their real or supposed virtues, their folly being evident to others but unknown to themselves (vanity); and people who, practicing a vice, consciously pretend to virtue (hypocrisy).

Fielding's earlier villains in the farces and *Jonathan Wild* were, despite their vicious acts and employment of incidental hypocrisy, essentially of the first type. In these characters Fielding avoided the detestable by dealing with those who imitated without attaining it; they differed from the vain mainly in their conscious effort to be "great," but like the vain they were always falling short. Pamela's particular vice, however, leads Fielding in *Joseph Andrews* to deal with those who pursue selfish ends while affecting virtue. In one key scene he contrasts the robbers who waylaid Joseph with the respectable folk who came upon him in their stagecoach. The robbers simply robbed and beat Joseph, making no excuses for their villainy and taking the risk of hanging; they are contrasted with the fine gentlemen and ladies who are just as ruthless and brutal but in no danger of being called robbers and hanged. The admitted villain is followed by the woman who is appalled at the idea of being asked for a dram but later, when held up by a highwayman, is shown to carry a flask.

Beyond the comedy of hypocrisy is the plain wickedness of the robbers and the malignant, melodramatic evil of the rapist and murderer. The latter appear only occasionally—in the squire who pointlessly kills the little dog of Wilson's daughter, in the man who tries to rape Fanny, or in the squire who torments Adams and attempts to abduct Fanny. Though sometimes appearing as threats, these acts are ordinarily averted. Such true villains, Fielding adds in his preface, recalling the Satanic villain, "never produce the intended evil." The mistreatment of Joseph and Adams, for example, stops after it passes a certain degree of brutality, and the squire himself is ducked; knavery is present in life, incidental to follies, but is carefully placed in relation to the more universal area of the ridiculous. Furthermore, all of the typically satiric situations are resolved happily. Having drawn out the full effect of the satire, Fielding cancels it with a happy ending. One example is the nightmare situation in which Adams finds himself when he saves Fanny from a rapist and is then accused of robbery and attempted murder by the would-be rapist. He is brought before a justice and remanded to prison until the next assizes; having reached its satiric climax, after which only pathos could follow, the scene is suddenly interrupted, someone recognizes Adams, and all is saved, except that in the confusion the real culprit slips away. The ending does not cancel the effect of the scene (it preserves the good without altering the fact of the evil), but it does restrain satire from becoming melodrama.

A more difficult problem for Fielding was how to create a good character. I wish to approach his solution from two directions, both somewhat tentative but, I think, illuminating for the development of satiric conventions into novelistic ones. The first is through the surrogate villains of the early satires, and the second is through one particular form of this villain, Don Quixote.

Following Gay's example, Fielding had begun by dividing evil into the general and the particular. The general was abstract "greatness," pure drive for power; the particular was an ordinary imitator of the general, a Peachum or Lockit, a below-stairs type, and thus a comic reflection of the more serious, but only implied, upper plot. Only occasionally, as in *The Modern Husband,* was the plot played out on its higher level, and then it failed dismally, perhaps because it had to be taken too seriously. The hero of the early works was all love or feeling, contrasted to the fools who sacrificed their real selves to an imaginary and delusive ideal. Much of the sympathy the reader may have felt for the surrogate villains resulted from the fact that, in terms of the types of affectation listed in the preface to *Joseph Andrews,* vanity, not hypocrisy, was the predominant vice—a character merely follows fashion, aspires to be something he is not, without any intent to deceive (indeed, quite the opposite). Even the hypocrite Wild, who pretended to be Heartfree's friend while ruining him, was, in terms of the theatrical metaphor, wearing as his mask the "great man's" face.

The hero of Fielding's novel, as a reaction to Pamela the "paragon," has to be complex—in the sense that appearing bad or foolish, he is good or wise, and that he is also a mixture of these qualities. Thus if the bad character was complex in the early works (in the sense of being two things at once), in the later works the complexity is transferred to the good character. The bad character can be said to derive from the Wild who pretends to be Heartfree's best friend while betraying him; but the good derives from the Wild who is striving for an ideal of greatness but is betrayed by his own humanity.

Both hypocrisy and vanity appear on the spectrum of the "ridiculous" in *Joseph Andrews,* part of that middle area where there are neither paragons nor Satanic villains; the evil characters tend toward the hypocrisy end, and the good, aspirers to inappropriate ideals, tend toward the vanity end. At the outset, Joseph is ridiculous as an imitator of London fashion and, over a more extended period, an imitator of his sister Pamela's ideal of chastity, which is being imparted to him by her letters (cf. Shamela and her mother's letters). The abstraction of chastity is soon dropped, and Joseph's love for Fanny is substituted as his motive for remaining intact. By then Parson Adams, whose vanities are his conviction of his great knowledge of the world, his classical learning, his abilities as a schoolmaster, and his sermons, especially the one on "Vanity," has entered the story. In terms of fashion, Adams, though naturally a good, charitable man, is ridiculous because he conforms to certain doctrines of the Stoics and the Church Fathers, which, whether good or bad in themselves, are at odds with his own natural goodness.

In a very real sense, Fielding approaches Adams, his great comic creation, through ridicule. Arthur Murphy, analyzing the scene in which Adams assures a stranger that he is rich by showing his half-guinea, experienced "an Emotion of Laughter attended in this Instance with a Contempt for *Adams's* Want of Knowledge of the World."[15] We may not agree, but the point, of course, is that Adams' innocence is accompanied by claims that he *is* knowledgeable. In the scenes after Fanny and Joseph are joined, he is juxtaposed in scene after scene with Joseph, and in each case a judgment has to be made against Adams.

However, if Fielding approached Adams through ridicule, it is im-

15. *The Gray's-Inn Journal,* No. 96, Aug. 17, 1754.

portant to note the peculiar effect that renders the word inadequate. Fielding's hero, contrasted to Pamela as hypocrite, had to be a representative of feeling over form; contrasted to Pamela as paragon, he had to be a mixed or middling character. Fielding chose a hero who expressed the virtue of feeling so completely that he was somewhat ridiculous on that account; part of the point, of course, was that heroes, in order to escape being paragons, have to be slightly ridiculous. Don Quixote offered Fielding his prototype for the man who reacts to stimuli from his basic good nature, often in complete opposition to custom, convention, and even prudence.

The paradigm Cervantes introduced in *Don Quixote* is a remarkable satiric device which Fielding was quick to grasp and exploit, presumably as early as 1729, when he wrote the first version of *Don Quixote in England*. Quixote, as he saw, can offer a satire either on the visionary who wished to change the world, or on the innkeepers who will not be changed, or on both. Quixote is too impractical, too inward; the innkeepers are too practical, too much of the world; since both are excesses, they act as criticisms of each other.

English satirists recognized the usefulness of one or both of these aspects of Quixote as early as the Civil War, when Samuel Butler made a Quixote out of a hypocritical Puritan enthusiast. Fielding explored one aspect when he made his early villians Quixotic—obsessive characters like Politic, Justice Squeezum, Sir Avarice Pedant, Sir Simon Raffler, even Jonathan Wild, pursuing his chimera of "greatness" as Quixote pursued his chimera of chivalry. The second possibility which informs Fielding's novels is to see Quixote as representative of idealism and simplicity, of a dedication to unfashionable and inward ideals that makes him the opposite of all the conformists or pretenders to conventional and fashionable immorality. His idealism, by comparison, makes the crassness of the world stand out in strong satiric relief.

The Quixotic hero is opposed by the officiousness of innkeepers, the crude reality of windmills and sheep, and the cruelty of masters and the officers of the law. Though Cervantes at the time condemns Quixote, there remains something noble about his freeing the prisoners on their way to the galleys—something deeper and more real, as well as more generous, than the officialdom that sent them there. In short, Quixote's madness is socially and prudentially bad, but spiritually good. His motive is always the best, whatever his action. In fact if one were to look for an example of feeling at odds with form, or motive at odds with action (in the opposite sense from Pamela), he could not find a better one than Quixote.

The emphasis of disapproval in a Fielding hero falls more decidedly on the society through which he moves than on the impractical hero himself, but there is just enough of the visionary in him to make us wish for some of the Pamelian prudence that would keep him on his guard, ready for assaults with more than a crabstick or his fists. Adams is given the obsession of charity and Joseph the obsession of chastity. Joseph's is the more Quixotic in its origin, having been learned from his sister Pamela's letters, and also the more easily outgrown. By the time he is reunited with Fanny he has become the passionate lover—an equally Quixotic figure in this economically oriented society. Adams' basic obsession, seemingly natural but perhaps learned from the works of the Church Fathers, is a belief in the tenets of Apostolic Christianity, which, like Quixote's chivalry, no one else believes any more. Adams sees the world differently from most people, acts according to his vision, and sometimes tries to convert the people he meets. He argues the true nature of charity with Barnabas, Trulliber, and Pounce; he argues the necessity of truth-telling with the innkeeper; and he instructs Joseph in what he considers to be Christian submission to providence. Unlike the Swiftean version of Quixote, however, he never imposes physical coercion on those he tries to convert. There is no action and response, only response—from the wicked whom he meets.

As many critics have pointed out, Adams is the first great comic hero of the English novel. He is comic because of the constant jangling of the spiritual and physical in his makeup. He is wholly the parson, and yet he is hindered and jostled (dragged down in the Quixotic sense) by his ragged, unpriestly clothes, his physical grossness and athletic prowess, his bout with Parson Trulliber's pig, and so on. He is comic in the same sense as Dr. Johnson, the great lexicographer and moralist who, aroused in the middle of the night, is always willing to come down and frolic. Adams goes trotting ahead of the coach carrying the rest of his party: "Mrs. Slipslop desired the coachman to overtake him, which he attempted, but in vain; for the faster he drove, the faster ran the parson, often crying out, 'Aye, aye, catch me if you can' " (Bk. II, Chap. 7; *1*, 150). It is this Quixotic incongruity that makes him comic *and* sympathetic, a completely new combination and precisely what Fielding must have been seeking as the center of his comic epic in prose.

The Touchstone Structure

If the general effect of Fielding's comic epic in prose is indeed comic, the detail is drawn from the satiric forms and devices he knew so well. His particular use of scenic juxtaposition consists most often of a profession followed by an action in which the profession is exposed. To show that appearances or professions like Pamela's can be misleading, he fills his novel with situations in which a character speaks in high-flown terms, such as Lady Booby rationalizing her passion for Joseph, or in heroic terms, such as the gentleman discoursing "on courage, and the infamy of not being ready at all times to sacrifice our lives to our Country" (Bk. II, Chap. 9; *1*, 158). Shortly thereafter the character's words are belied by his actions: Lady Booby's self-control dissolves and her lecherously leering face appears, or the gentleman runs away at the first sound of a woman's cry of rape. A conventional pose gives way to reveal the real person through his action—whether it be a worse person or occasionally a better. A third element is often present, which makes satiric judgment obligatory—an Adams, a quiet sort who makes no professions, but who rescues the girl who is being attacked or translates the Latin correctly, and thus gives us a norm by which to judge the other performers. With the most important unit of exposition established, Fielding launches into the elaboration of the central part of the novel —the adventures of the road. Throughout this section punishment of the innocent acts as the central structural device, keeping the reader's attention focused on the Trullibers and Tow-wouses, whose unamiable qualities are exposed by contact with Joseph and Adams.

Around the central touchstone of Joseph or Adams flock a series of characters, each classified and judged by his response. While the continental picaresque often employs its protagonist as a touchstone, nowhere does one find the device used so schematically and extensively as in *Joseph Andrews*. The most famous instance takes place in the scene where Joseph, robbed and left naked in a ditch, is met by the coachload of respectable folk. Here is Joseph, the prototypical touchstone, suffering humanity stripped of everything, but instead of stimulating charity, he reveals various forms of selfishness in the passengers: prurient prudery in the lady; greed in the coachman who wants his fare; in the lawyer, fear that the passengers will be called to account if Joseph dies; and in the old gentleman, fear that the robbers may still be about but eagerness for an opportunity to show off his wit in front of the lady. In this satiric structure the ideal is indicated by the poorest, most un-Pamelian of the group, the postilion who lends Joseph his coat (and is later transported for robbing a hen roost). The whole scene, in typical Augustan fashion, carries overtones of the parable of the good Samaritan (*Luke* 10:25–37), preparing the reader for the long series of similar scenes that follows.

This fan-shaped structure can be discrete, as in the stagecoach episode, or it can spread over several chapters. Joseph continues as a touchstone when he is taken to the Tow-wouses' inn, and reactions follow in quick succession. (1) The doctor, learning that Joseph is not a gentleman, goes home to bed. When he does get to Joseph the next day he reveals his professional incompetence (or his desire to gain credit for healing a hopeless case) by claiming that Joseph is as good as dead. (2) Mr. Tow-wouse shows charity, wishing to send Joseph one of his own shirts. (3) Mrs. Tow-wouse, however, will not let him ("Common charity, a f——!"); she is concerned because if Joseph dies they will have to pay for his funeral. (4) The servant girl Betty, another un-Pamelian character, secures Joseph a shirt from one of her lovers. A normative character like the postilion, she is later caught in a compromising situation and punished by her "betters." (5) Mr. Barnabas, the clergyman, though informed that Joseph is dying, spends his time guzzling punch. Chapter Thirteen describes Barnabas' circuitous route to Joseph's room, his haste to be finished and back at the punch bowl ("For no one could squeeze oranges till he came"). The chapter ends with Mrs. Tow-wouse refusing Joseph the tea he desires, and Betty buying him some herself (it should be added, however, that Betty is much attracted physically to Joseph). When Joseph's situation has been thoroughly exploited, Fielding turns to the highwayman who has been taken prisoner (one of those who nearly killed Joseph). The prisoner—or rather his loot—calls forth the constable's dishonesty, the legal arguments of the surgeon and Barnabas, Mrs. Tow-wouse's blame of her husband, and Tow-wouse's fear that he might be held liable.

Each new inn, each new encounter, presents a new "stagecoach" and a new set of characters to be met, tested, and judged. When the story of Leonora jilting Horatio for the richer Bellarmine is told (and it too is made up of such situations), the listeners react automatically:

> "Poor woman!" says Mrs. Slipslop; "what a terrible quandary she must be in!" "Not at all," says Miss Grave-airs; "such sluts can never be confounded." "She must have then more than Corinthian assurance," said Mr. Adams; "ay, more than Lais herself." (Bk. II, Chap. 4; *1*, 130)

Every action is capable of revealing its observers—Slipslop's lust, Graveairs' prudery, Adams' moralizing, naïveté, and vanity in his classical learning. Some situations catch Adams and even Joseph, but the first purpose of such scenes is to contribute to the gauntlet run by the heroes on their way back to Booby Hall and to pit against these innocents the Cibbers and Pamelas. When Fanny appears before the justice, the whole gamut of reactions is run through:

> the justice employed himself in cracking jests on poor Fanny, in which he was seconded by all the company at table. One asked, "Whether she was to be indicted for a highwayman?" Another whispered in her ear, "If she had not provided herself a great belly, he was at her service." A third said, "He warranted she was a relation of Turpin." To which one of the company, a great wit, shaking his head, and then his sides, answered, "He believed she was nearer related to Turpis." (Bk. II, Chap. 11; *1*, 168)

With the good Samaritan echoes now building to unmistakable echoes of the trial and punishment of Christ (Adams and Fanny condemned; the real criminal released), Fielding presents the irresponsible justice, the lecher, the vicious-minded, and the great wit revealing themselves as they collect about the helpless innocents. The tricks played on Adams by the squire and his hangers-on, leading to the attempted rape of Fanny, are only the climax of these encounters.

In terms of the profession-performance form, which is central in a work concerned with hypocrisy, the touchstone becomes the second half, the exposing action, with the profession either assumed (these are often pious-seeming folk) or implicit in the pompous terms they use to cover up the brutality of their reactions. These satiric structures do not disappear in the beginning and end of the novel but are subordinated to the story of Lady Booby's passion for Joseph. Yet even here, when all that is necessary is for Lady Booby to corrupt a corruptible lawyer, the reader is treated to a small anatomy of the unethical lawyer in his speeches and plans for thwarting the Joseph-Fanny marriage. Nor is it sufficient for Mr. Booby to rescue Joseph from the court; the reader is also presented with lawyer Scout's deposition, which demonstrates the shiftiness, illiteracy, and legal jargon of the justice who wrote it. The most conventional of all satiric expository forms appears in the narrative of Mr. Wilson, who simply recites a list of the evils of London, ending with his withdrawal to an Eden (or Golden Age) in the country. But here the form has not been absorbed, and the purely satiric piling up of vice upon vice, crowding of incident upon incident, carries an imitative effect that is closer to Richardson than to Fielding.

The profession-performance and touchstone forms, on the other hand, support the initial and sustaining point of the novel about Pamelian appearance and reality. More than satire, these forms represent Fielding's image of the way life operates, and they demonstrate his continuing concern with the meaning of an action. In the *Champion* (Dec. 11, 1739), he argues that

> The only Ways by which we can come to any Knowledge of what passes in the Minds of others, are their Words and Actions; the latter of which, hath by the wiser Part of Mankind been chiefly depended on, as the surer and more infallible guide.[16]

Faces, he adds, are no more reliable than words. This discussion, which is used to introduce a hypocrite's letter-to-the-editor, is transformed into the theme of *Shamela*. Reminiscent of Pamela, Shamela tells us "That to go to church, and to pray, and to sing psalms, and to honour the clergy, and to repent, is true religion; and 'tis not doing good to one another." And in Parson Williams the maxim is "That

16. *Champion, 1,* 79.

'tis not what we do, but what we believe, that must save us."[17] In *Joseph Andrews,* where Josephs and Shamelas are placed in the same world, the central fact is that actions alone can be relied on as tests of men's character or inner being. In the *Essay on the Knowledge of the Characters of Men,* published in the *Miscellanies* of 1743, Fielding goes into more detail on the subject, which clearly interests him more and more. Here he argues in the typically satiric vein that "the actions of men seem to be the justest interpreters of their thoughts, and the truest standards by which we may judge them. By their fruits you shall know them." He then examines the various factors that obscure a proper judgment of actions: "when we take their own words against their actions" and "when we take the colour of a man's actions, not from their own visible tendency, but from his public character: when we believe what others say of him, in opposition to what we see him do" (*14,* 289–90). The first of these is the subject of *Joseph Andrews;* the second, anticipating a new phase of Fielding's career, becomes the subject of *Tom Jones,* where the reputations of Tom and Blifil render judgment difficult.

It is important to see that the touchstone structure is a logical development of the multiple commentators of Fielding's satiric farces. The normative aspect of these commentators led to the Fielding narrator: their apparently different points of view in the farces resolved into a single one that unambiguously explained the action they observed. In the *Champion* essays, where Fielding again began with a group of commentators, the Vinegar family tended to narrow into one person, the normative speaker, who subsequently became the narrator of *Joseph Andrews.* But the suggestion of multiple opinions and their reflection back on the commentators remained to some extent throughout the *Champion* and leads in *Joseph Andrews* to the multiple reactions to an action that is unambiguous (perhaps made so by the normative narrator) and by which the spectators are judged.

Already the device begins to imply the difficulty of judging an action, but as yet the difficulty lies in the observers, not in the action itself. The device may also, in the generally epistemological context of the anti-*Pamela,* suggest a range of attitudes rather than a group of different kinds of vice. Finally, as part of an anti-romance situation, it brings together a number of people from different professions and

17. *Shamela,* p. 319.

social classes and records their reactions to a social situation or crisis, something out of the ordinary routine that will reveal their true selves and (the crucial element) juxtapose the social appearance and the animal reality. In short, it suggests that revelation of character through an action is the point in question rather than the proof of a satiric theorem.

We cannot accept these forms as exactly what Fielding claims them to be or what they may appear to be. They are not in fact honest searches for truth or reality. Even if their extremely schematic anatomy-like structure did not argue against their objectivity, it would be clear that their purpose is a satiric one—to support Fielding's general premise about the relationship between his heroes and Cibberian and Pamelian society. As A. D. McKillop puts it, in Fielding's novels the discrepancy between appearance and reality "is not treated as an ultimate metaphysical problem, as in *Don Quixote*. Fielding is not trying to present or to pluck out the heart of a mystery; he is continuously corroborating a position which he has made clear from the first."[18] Nevertheless, Fielding's basic unit became a basic unit of the novel and, in his next novel, outgrew its satiric origin. The sense of a test and a judgment emerges, as does the leisurely pace, which as much as anything creates the mood of the novel as it developed in his hands.

The Debt to Pamela

Joseph Andrews is an anti-*Pamela,* but in more ways than one it verges on being a pro-*Pamela.* The most important element of *Pamela* and, later, *Clarissa* was the portrait of the individual defending her personal integrity, her very identity against threats from outside. Since Coleridge, however, readers reacting to Richardson's hot, stuffy sickroom tend to forget what a moral intention meant to Richardson, Pope, Bishop Slocock, and other conservative contemporaries who went on record in praise of *Pamela.* It meant, on the one hand, presenting an ideal of conduct, a Christian passing through trials and tribulations; on the other hand, it meant showing the evil threats to this virtue in their true colors. The most effective method for the latter was, of course, satire.

18. "Some Recent Views of Tom Jones," *College English, 21* (1959), 19.

Mrs. Jewkes and Colbrand, both epitomes of the malevolent guardian, are presented by conventional satiric portraits, emblematic and perhaps derived from the picaresque. They are domesticated in Richardson's novel because they are seen through Pamela's eyes and thus thoroughly assimilated to her psychologically convincing situation. She is satirizing a particular enemy, with only her own fear as motive and with no sense of exposing a general vice. Nevertheless, it is interesting that embedded in such a work should be fragments of the old satiric conventions.

More significant for Fielding is the touchstone form with which Richardson begins his novel—the treatment of a helpless servant girl at the hands of a wicked master, self-seeking servants, and the master's self-satisfied relatives and neighbors. A central character in a difficult situation is reacted to by a series of good and bad people. The vague outlines of this form occasionally emerge in a structure very much like that of *Joseph Andrews,* as in Parson Williams' letter recounting his failure to secure aid from the neighboring gentry. Lady Jones does not care to make an enemy of B.; Lady Darnford puts the responsibility on her husband, who sees nothing wrong with a young gentleman's seducing his waiting-maid ("He hurts *no family* by this"); Mr. Peters, the minister of the parish, sees ulterior motives in Williams' defense of Pamela, says it is "too common and fashionable a case to be withstood by a private clergyman or two," claims that any action on his part might turn B. against him, and, besides, " 'tis what all young gentlemen will do"; even Williams has some doubts, since "the gentleman is dying, whose living Mr. B. has promised me" (*1,* 168–70).

The novel, however, changes direction when B. arrives at his Lincolnshire estate: the touchstone structure and the anatomy are replaced by the simple battle of wills, a contest between B. and Pamela. The domain of satire, as Frye has pointed out, is the time *after* the forces of evil have defeated those of good; this precludes any active conflict between good and evil which is not one-sided. If Richardson had included letters from B. as well as from Pamela (as he did with their equivalents in *Clarissa*), his whole novel might have taken on the form of a battle of wills. The single point of view renders the larger part of the novel the pursuit of an innocent. Richardson is drawing in a vague way on Mrs. Manley's *chroniques scandaleuses* (even in the sense that he began with a true story); while his form is conventional, however, his conclusion and general effect are not.[19]

Once Pamela and B. are married, she again becomes a persecuted maiden and touchstone. This time she runs the gauntlet of the outraged reaction of Lady Davers, the foppish one of her nephew Jackey, and the jealous one of Lady Davers' maid. Pamela's confrontation of Lady Davers is less a conflict between strong-willed characters than the high point in the introduction of the new wife to a satiric portrait gallery of snobbish relatives. First she is the virtuous person tormented by these unfeeling, snobbish boors, and then she is the female satirist goaded into rebuke—the same figure who appeared occasionally in Lincolnshire. In his efforts to make the reader aware of Pamela's biting retorts, Richardson has Jackey point to her satiric strength whenever she completes a sally. Her remarks, however, are too direct, too prolix and realistic, too much a result of her situation to create a genuine feeling of satire.

Thus whenever the possibility of a dramatic conflict is past and the situation becomes relatively static, Richardson slips into popular conventions, which are sometimes satiric, although to him they were probably less specifically satiric than a way to the moral tone of denunciation through ridicule. The greatest force working against any possibility of sustained satire, as well as moral doctrine, is the character of Pamela. In the usual moral work the central character is not so central as she is, so closely felt, so absorbing as far as the reader is concerned. When she describes someone as vicious, he is only vicious through her eyes, to her way of thinking; when she explains one of her own actions, it is only from her point of view. This unreliability of the narrator, of course, notoriously destroys the intended direction of Richardson's structure, which is to contrast Pamela's angelic flight to the evil pursuit of Mr. B. and with the good and bad people who react to her during flight. But it does create, among other things, a new scene based on satiric conventions, in which one character sati-

19. This is not to deny anticipations and analogues in France that were strictly amorous. Prévost employs pursued heroines, and Mlle. de Theville is pursued by the wicked comte de Versac in Crébillon fils' *Egarements du Coeur et de l'Esprit* (1736); the heroine of Duclos' *Histoire de Mme. de Lux* (1741) is forced to give herself to a blackmailer and is also subsequently drugged and raped. While these carry *Pamela's* erotic theme, they do not carry the other un-French qualities that distinguish Richardson's novel—its echoes of satiric and picaresque forms.

rizes another without reference to anything outside their own private situation. This is a scene to which we shall return later.

Joseph Andrews is an alternative to Pamela, and yet Fielding places him in a situation roughly parallel to hers. Fielding has taken from Richardson the satiric situation of the innocent pursued and punished by the guilty and turned it into an obviously satiric principle of structure. It is even somewhat unfair of Fielding to contrast Joseph repulsing Lady Booby's advances and being discharged with the consequence of Pamela's less unequivocal repulses; after all, Pamela is threatened and put upon for a long time before she arrives at her happy ending. In a sense Fielding is merely showing that interim period, though extending the scope of Joseph's experience beyond sexual attack. Attacks on Joseph begin with his virtue but go on to more general and physical assaults and finally extend to Adams and even Fanny—to all the good, innocent people. The point is that this is how a virtuous Pamela would be treated in this real world, but it is also very close to the treatment accorded to the actual Pamela during the first and best-known part of Richardson's novel.

The influence is largely formal, since Fielding never dwells on Joseph's or Fanny's feelings; most of the time the reader is not allowed sympathy for the victim (as in *Pamela*) but indignation at the persecutor. Richardson is not a more important source for the persecuted hero than Cervantes; but from Richardson, the "enemy," Fielding was able to pick up an older strain of the picaresque, in which the low social status of the protagonist contributes to his troubles (not one of Quixote's problems) and in which the servant-master relationship plays some part.[20] Joseph, however, like Richardson's second

20. The idea of the servant girl probably came to Richardson from the large conduct book literature of his time, but consciously or not, he has connected his book with the basic servant-master relationship of the early picaresque novels, though characteristically narrowing his focus to only one episode. In the first third of *Pamela*, during the assaults on her virtue, he constantly refers to the proper relationship between Pamela and B. and B.'s perversion of it. "Well may I forget that I am your servant," Pamela tells B., "when you forget what belongs to a master"; she accuses him of "demeaning" himself "to be so free to a poor servant" (*1*, 18). "When a master of his honour's degree demeans himself to be so free as *that* to a poor servant as me, what is the next to be expected?" Pamela talks on and on, referring to "the distance between a master and a servant" (*1*, 33–34). Pamela of course derives less directly from the Spanish picara like Justina than from Defoe's heroes and heroines whose final goal, however disguised by moral platitudes, is simply survival.

heroine Clarissa, refuses to come to terms with his corrupt society and in this sense derives from the Quixote tradition.

Parson Adams is another of Fielding's original and brilliant contributions to this compromise form. By a weird logic Adams corresponds to Parson Williams, as Joseph and Fanny correspond to Pamela; Fielding gives his hero a clergyman, like Pamela's, to assist him to escape. Adams is as effective in preserving Joseph as Williams was in preserving Pamela (an irony Fielding had already explored in *Shamela*). By shifting the focus, on the one hand, to the pursuers and, on the other, to the figure of the comic clergyman-helper, Fielding has created a result not too far from Richardson's, yet comic and satiric. He has both the moral truth and the psychological truth Richardson attempted to join. Richardson's mistake may have been attempting both in the same figure, Pamela.

It is from *Pamela* (novel *and* character) that Fielding took his immediate inspiration. Looking at Richardson's novel he could see both strains of the potential novel; he could see the one he was interested in, the moral commentary, perverted and ruined, and so he set about correcting it, naturally following to some extent the basic situation of Richardson's novel. He changed the focus from the pursued to the pursuers, particularly in the middle part of his novel, but not so much as to deny the connection with Pamela or the alternative version he was presenting. But like Pamela, Adams and Joseph are positive, fully explored proposals for the good; they have to be, as alternatives to Pamelian virtue. Figures so fully developed were not common in satire prior to this. It is, in fact, in the development of these good characters that Fielding establishes *Joseph Andrews* as a transition between satire and the novel.

Joseph Andrews is the great watershed of Fielding's career. In all of his work the evil character appears either as the protagonist or as the persecutor of the protagonist: as the spider at the middle of a web dotted with trapped flies or as the cutthroat lying in wait along dark streets for the good man to pass. In *Jonathan Wild* both situations appear—Wild by himself and Heartfree and his wife being waylaid by Wild. In the satires that can best be called Augustan the evil agent is a larger-than-life symbol of man's perversity attempting to engross, amoeba-like, all that comes within reach. Certain mitigations accompany his portrait, but he remains bad and more or less in the center of the canvas. In *Joseph Andrews,* however, the evil agent receives much attention and even in the aggregate is still the subject of the satire, but he is no longer in the center, no longer dwelt on so lovingly, and is in fact less interesting than Parson Adams. His pride and swagger have been reduced to hypocrisy, and his exposure is that of a coward who affects bravery or a slut who affects gentility. So long as the character aspired to "greatness," a fashionable ideal, hypocrisy was secondary—one might use it as a way to achieve "greatness." But when Fielding turned from opera heroes and politicians to Pamela, who aspired not to "greatness" directly but disguised this quality by the term "virtue," he became concerned primarily with hypocrisy. Evil is no longer the adhering to a fashionable but wrong standard, but adhering to this standard while making loud protestations of a morally right standard; the character's motive has now become the subject of exposure.

With *Pamela* goodness became a problem for Fielding. The relative complexity of the evil man is transferred to the good man who is in the center of the narrative. It is altogether possible that *Pamela* may have made Fielding conclude that a hero could be as interesting as a villain. His moral essays, though assisting him, could not have shown him the way. His reaction against *Pamela* did show him that if the ordinary evil man is a mixed lot, so is the ordinary good man.

Chapter 4

FIELDING THE NOVELIST

The Lucianic Satirist

Fielding's growing interest in motive shows how far he has gone beyond the self-imposed limits of the satirist. As a satirist he is overwhelmingly interested in actions, and his aim is to distinguish the good from the evil—thus he places commentators around actions in his earlier works so that both can be readily understood. In *Joseph Andrews* he shows that by analyzing the action itself, one can see through the individual's professions. Pamela says she wants to escape from Mr. B., but if her reactions are examined by themselves it becomes obvious that she really does not. Even at the outset, action with Fielding is a way of dramatizing motive. But inevitably Fielding must also ask himself: what of those undeniably pious actions such as Pamela's resisting Mr. B.'s lecherous advances and fleeing at his approach? Here the action by itself cannot be interpreted, he would argue, without reference to Pamela's motives. How much is it her virtue of chastity and how much her mercenary desire to substitute the role of wife for the less profitable one of mistress?

Richardson is interested in Pamela's professions and actions; Fielding, in her motives. Richardson claims that her professions and actions tell us her motives; Fielding suspects a radical discrepancy. The satirist ordinarily makes much the same claim as does Richardson (he admits that motives are slippery and thus relies only on concrete examples of conduct), but he is never accused of hypocrisy because he keeps an external and firm control on his characters. By contrast, Fielding's concern with motives, which begins to be noticeable in *Joseph Andrews,* is distinctly un-Augustan; there is never a question of a discrepancy between an action and a motive in Swift's satire, only between words and motives or actions. But in the Good Samaritan scene of *Joseph Andrews* character is judged as much through motive as action: the lawyer would take Joseph into the coach, but for the wrong reason (he is afraid, being among the last people in Joseph's company, that he will be called to account for his death). Betty the chambermaid is kind to Joseph but her motive is at least partly sexual attraction. Again, landladies of inns refuse Joseph service because they think him a peasant, and other equally bad landladies lavish service on him thinking him a lord.

Charity, as it often appears in *Joseph Andrews,* is an objective action and so far does not depart from the criteria of the Augustan satirists. But the Latitudinarians and, with them, Fielding tended to divorce the inner motive from the outer expression, or character from conduct. While agreeing that objectively a good action must be judged by its good effect on other people, they claimed that the only real criterion was the motive from which the action sprang. As Archbishop Tillotson, the first Latitudinarian Archbishop of Canterbury, put it: if we are good "only to serve our temporal interest, though the actions we do be never so good, yet all the virtue and reward of them is lost, by the mean end and design which we aim at in the doing of them."[1] In the same way, though an action directed by a good motive goes astray, it is nevertheless a good action. The motive of love or charity—already encountered in the Heartfrees as foils to Jonathan Wild—makes it good. Parson Adams, although he stresses works ("What signifies knowing your duty, if you do not perform it?"), is often prevented from carrying them out, despite his good intentions. When he offers the Catholic priest money, he finds he has none to give, and when he tries to comfort Joseph over the loss of Fanny, he in fact increases Joseph's grief. Although objectified in Adams' attempt to help the priest, and to some extent censured in the treatment of Joseph, the inwardness toward which Fielding is pointing can become in certain instances very difficult to prove; moreover, it is not unrelated to the Quaker's inner light and the Puritan's conscience, both more concerned with private salvation than public welfare and both venerable targets of the Augustan satirists. Fielding's Latitudinarian heritage may be thought to run counter to his satiric intention much as Richardson's own sense of objective reality does to his moral aim.

1. Sermon CCX, "Of Doing All to the Glory of God," *Sermons on Several Subjects and Occasions* (London, 1757), *11*, 39.

Though *Pamela* derives from a Puritan and middle-class sensibility, it expresses a certainty in the rightness of form, convention, and tradition that is also Augustan (with the radical exception of the democratic overtones of the servant girl's marriage to her master, which is wholly middle class). As Bernard Kreissman has noticed, "Being blind to the 'inwardness' of virtue, Richardson could not conceive a virtuous character like Parson Adams, who was outwardly hot-tempered, eccentric, and loud."[2] Neither could Swift and Pope. While they attack the ridiculous behavior in which vanity manifests itself, Fielding attacks the invisible motives in apparently proper behavior. This amounts, finally, to an attack on the reality beneath the card-game of Augustan form, which Pope smiles at in "The Rape of the Lock" but accepts as part of the world of order that extends upward to marriage, the state, and the church.

It is perhaps ironic that with opposed intentions Fielding and Richardson have, in one respect, come up with the result intended by the other. Fielding, intending to show the importance of character over actual conduct, uses the Augustan's external techniques of irony and authorial omniscience; he has to explain motives objectively, make them as schematic and visible as physical actions. On the other hand, Richardson, concerned with the forms of virtue, conveys a powerful sense of his characters' inner being. It is equally significant that Fielding attacked Richardson less for breaking with the old, traditional forms (as Swift, following from his *Tale of a Tub,* would have done) than for espousing a morality that maintained the primacy of appearances and forms over subjective character. Fielding tries to connect his form with the past, and a classical Odysseus or Aeneas, a biblical Joseph or Abraham, often stands behind his characters as a yardstick of value. But the ancient who influenced him most was neither Horace nor Juvenal, but the cynical Lucian, who believed that man's mind is for seeing through frauds and lies imposed on us by our fathers and grandfathers, by judges and lawyers, philosophers and priests.[3]

2. *Pamela-Shamela* (Lincoln, University of Nebraska Press, 1960), p. 46.

3. Fielding has Billy Booth remark in *Amelia* that Swift excelled every writer except Lucian (Bk. VIII, Chap. 6); cf. *Covent-Garden Journal,* Feb. 4 and June 30, 1752. Fielding's Lucianic imitations are legion—a vision of Charon's boat (*Champion,* May 24, 1740) is based on Lucian's tenth, and *A Dialogue Between Alexander the Great and Diogenes* on his thirteenth *Dialogue of the Dead.* The *Interlude Between Jupiter,*

More than any of the other great classical satirists, Lucian is rhetorician first and moralist second, and his constant striving for surprise sometimes suggests that the effect is achieved for its own sake. He depends on the surprise of exposure, on making the apparently indefensible defensible, the apparently guilty innocent, the apparently noble ignoble. Perhaps partly for this reason, Lucian has no strong bias to a particular good as Juvenal does and no desire to map a subtle spiritual course for the reader as Horace does. His aim is double—to expose the real, however deep he must go under the illusions man weaves for himself; and to discomfit his reader, shake up his cherished values, and disrupt his orthodoxy. Lucian is the epitome of the satirist who writes at what he regards a time of extreme stodginess and reaction, when values have become standardized and rigid.

The typical Lucianic fiction has a markedly mobile protagonist asking questions: he travels over the earth, or up to Olympus to question the gods, or down to Hades to question the dead—always probing appearances, idealization, myth, and custom. He is very different from the Horatian observer, solidly within society looking out, or the Juvenalian, a last fragment of the true society that has been isolated or expelled. He is not even necessarily a good man since his value is only as disrupter of orthodoxy and questioner of long-held assumptions. In the *Dialogues of the Dead* Diogenes, whom Lucian elsewhere attacks as merely another false philosopher, acts as a disruptive agent whose questioning, probing, and railing serve a useful corrective function.

Lucianic satire works for Fielding in two areas—in the character of Tom and in the commentator's point of view. Tom, like Diogenes or Rabelais' Panurge, represents an excess that must at intervals be placed in relation to other values, and his satiric function is split between being a touchstone to test other characters and a corrective to expose their formalism. These two roles, passive and active, explain Tom insofar as he carries the traces of a rhetorical device. The second is clearly related to the Panurgic life-force. At a time when the Au-

---

Juno, Apollo and Mercury and *Tumble-Down Dick* owe a general debt to the *Dialogues of the Gods*. The *Journey from This World to the Next* derives from the *Dialogues of the Dead*, the *True History, Menippus*, and *The Cock;* the voyage of Mrs. Heartfree in *Jonathan Wild* derives in a general way from the *True History*. For an interesting account of Lucian's influence on Fielding, see H. K. Miller, *Essays on Fielding's Miscellanies* (Princeton, Princeton University Press, 1961), pp. 366–86.

gustan reaction against freedom and individualism had perhaps gone too far, Fielding places his emphasis on a counter-reaction in favor of breaking stereotypes and outworn categories, espousing the value of feeling as well as form, instinct as well as reason. Hypocrisy, for example, was a vice usually attacked from the security of a conservative, decorous society; the subject was the man who pretended to be part of society but was in fact an outsider. Fielding, however, uses Tom to attack the hypocrite from a position virtually outside society, from which, momentarily at least, both the virtues the hypocrite pretends to and his pretense appear less real and true than the natural feeling of a Tom Jones.

Shaftesbury's doctrine of ridicule as a test of truth probably served as the mediator between Lucian's cheerful cynicism and Fielding's adaptation of disruptive satire as one strain of *Tom Jones*. Running through the novel is the belief (though qualified by other, sometimes contrary, doubts) that man, like all creation, is basically good and can only be corrupted by externals—education, institutions, and customs. Thus, if the satirist can bring ridicule to play, these will be cleared away. In general, as was evident in the case of Fielding's early villains, fashion clogs the natural wellsprings of good nature in man; the false ideal of the "great man" withered the good nature in him and made him a one-sided humor-character. This semi-Pelagian view of man, which may have contributed something to the ambiguity of Fielding's early villains, is exactly the opposite of the Augustan satirist's view. Swift would say that men are all born with feeble intellect and moral sense, but the best of men realize their limitations and seek the guidance of church and tradition. Institutions are necessary to curb man's dangerous proclivities. Fielding, however, tends to suggest in *Tom Jones* that they may corrupt the good-natured man.

Forms for Fielding, however, are usually carefully defined as those things which are essentially illusory—opinions, habits, rumors, and the like. Besides giving Fielding a philosophical rationale for Lucianic satire, Shaftesbury gave him the groundwork for a spectrum of good and evil in which nothing is finally evil except various kinds of misunderstanding; in short, a metaphysical basis for a novel of manners in which social patterns of behavior could be contrasted with natural inclinations. In *Tom Jones,* moreover, the Shaftesburyian platonism extends to the very limits of Tom's world and accounts for such questionable events as the sudden dissipation of the threatened catastrophe followed by the happy ending. Tom, having lost Sophia, lying in the shadow of Tyburn, and believing that he has committed incest, seems to be doomed. But Fielding shows that this is all the world of appearances with which Tom has been clashing from the beginning: appearance can breed only appearance, and the reality was the bread Tom cast upon the waters in his acts of benevolence to Mrs. Miller and others. Tom has on his side such staunch friends as Mrs. Miller, while Blifil's plot depends on those qualities of form listed above—opinion, rumor, and such supporters as Dowling. Toward the end of *Tom Jones* letters begin to arrive at the right time, as do people, and Blifil's shoddy creation, which all along has been shaky and doomed, begins to come tumbling down, exactly according to Shaftesbury's prophecy, and exactly like Achitophel's at the end of Dryden's satire. All that separates this happy ending from the Augustan assumptions is that evil leaves no marks, no Adams, Eves, or Absaloms ruined along the way, and so it is less a perversion of the real than an excrescence on it.

But forms also include qualities, indeed institutions, that are less illusory and closer to the values defended by the Augustans; and Tom, being a corrective in the tradition of Lucian and Rabelais, does not always distinguish real from illusory forms when his feeling comes into play. His "good nature," the positive part of Fielding's doctrine, is the equivalent of the burst of energy that characterized the disruptive activity of Diogenes or Panurge and the wide-ranging alternative to the narrow morality of sexual chastity (the single choice between marriage and infamy) of Richardson's world. Again following the Latitudinarians and Shaftesbury, Fielding sometimes suggests that moral judgment is based less on intellection than on feeling, which is connected, of course, with the belief that man is basically good. "Good breeding" is the social quality in Fielding's system—doing to others that which you would like them to do to you. But at the bottom of "good breeding" is "good nature," that innate, almost inner-light quality. The criterion for one's actions is charity, or "good breeding," and the person with abundant "good nature" will always act from a charitable motive in a given situation. He will feel a veritable and "glorious lust of doing good."[4]

A modern in the armor of the ancients, Fielding seems to have

4. See *Of Good Nature,* in *Works,* ed. Henley, *12,* 258.

carried with him both the need of authority and confidence in intuition. Authority is transmuted in *Tom Jones* into the commonsense quality called prudence, which should be used to check even the best of passions—but which may be very unpleasant by itself.[5] Thus Tom, as a character, is shown to be "mixed" in a more radical sense than Joseph and Parson Adams. His exuberance sometimes ends in pain to others as well as himself and is an extension of the physically vigorous young man, not, as with Adams, a contradiction of the spiritual. Perhaps closer to Adams than to Joseph, Tom is persecuted by a wicked society but deserves his persecution just enough to benefit from it and so become a more balanced person at the end than he was at the beginning. Tom's Quixotic aberration is his "good nature," his "good breeding," which makes him go to the extreme of giving his body to young or old ladies out of a deep inner compulsion to generosity and love. And so while his good nature may be interpreted on one side as the proper corrective to Thwackum and Blifil, on the other it may be called momentary self-indulgence. Fielding, however, interprets it according to Quixote: Tom fastens his attention on one aspect of an object and makes it into the whole: just as the whirling blades of a windmill became the flailing arms of a giant for Quixote, so the white breasts of Mrs. Waters or the generosity of Lady Bellaston or the appearance of youth and availability in Molly lead Tom to break with both prudence and moral laws. He is as oblivious to appearances as Quixote: Fielding keeps emphasizing this, and the need for prudence, throughout the novel, until at the end we are told that Tom has reached a balance between feeling (his Quixotic madness) and form.

It is not, however, Tom Jones—the corrective or the mixed character—but Fielding's commentator-narrator who best demonstrates the use of Lucianic satire. He is the observer and questioner who probes past appearances, dropping the arras that conceals Square, and

---

5. Fielding follows Shaftesbury in referring to the impulses of feeling that end in action as "affections"; one is happiest when the social affections are most highly developed, but a balance between these and the private is necessary, and so the element of prudence enters in: one's outgoing nature is qualified by his ingoing, and vice versa. The result of imbalance is unhappiness, perhaps the suffering of conscience, which Tom feels from time to time. (See Shaftesbury's *Inquiry Concerning Moral Virtue*, Bk. 2, Pt. 1, Sec. 3, in *Characteristics, 1,* 334).

exploring the mixed quality of experience. The commentator's most potent tool is once again his irony, but now it is a more complex instrument used to question rather than affirm.

In *Joseph Andrews* the irony directed at the lecherous Lady Booby serves as both denigration and an indication of her own false picture of herself—a rhetorical and a psychological effect. But there is perhaps a third effect, which William Empson characterizes when he says that Fielding "seems to leave room for the ideas he laughs at."[6] In some sense Lady Booby really is, as she claims, heroically battling her passions, just as Quixote's illusions in some sense contain truth. While this is a very slight impression as concerns Lady Booby, it does explain something about our reaction to Parson Adams, who *is* both wise (as he thinks) and foolish. In *Tom Jones* Empson finds what he calls "double irony" to be a controlling principle.[7] This might be called "both/and" irony, because it gives some credence to both "the contrary" and "what one means," or to the praise and the blame. When Fielding says that Black George, who has just stolen Tom's money, really does love Tom, he is saying a number of different things—that Black George has persuaded himself by rationalization that he loves Tom, but also that there is a sense in which Black George really does love him, even if at the moment he loves money more. While single irony implies the author's grasp of all circumstances and eventualities, with the proper subordination of the false to the true, double irony suggests a greater tolerance, a delicate poise, or mere uncertainty. The effect is close to the unsubordinated *copia* of Richardsonian realism and suggests an attempt to achieve "realism of presentation" as well as "realism of assessment."

Our study of *Joseph Andrews* has shown that Fielding was not impervious to the success of kinds of realism other than his own. In *Tom Jones* the Richardsonian signs can be recognized at once—more facts, more information about everything, more extenuating circumstances recorded, and more different motives and attitudes to choose from, all creating a general plenitude. The irony helps to generate this impression; instead of a single statement (such as the one about Lady Booby's passion) Fielding gives two or more possibilities, some very plausible. Here are Mrs. Wilkins' reasons for obeying Squire

6. *Some Versions of Pastoral* (New York, New Directions, n.d.), p. 197.
7. "Tom Jones," *Kenyon Review*, 20 (1958), 217–49.

Allworthy: "Such was [1] the discernment of Mrs. Wilkins, and such [2] the respect she bore her master, [3] under whom she enjoyed a most excellent place, that her scruples gave way to his peremptory commands" (Bk. I, Chap. 3; *3*, 26). Or we are told why Tom avoids a fight with Blifil: "for besides that [1] Tommy Jones was an inoffensive lad amidst all his roguery, and [2] really loved Blifil, [3] Mr. Thwackum being always the second of the latter, would have been sufficient to deter him" (Bk. III, Chap. 4; *3*, 118). Substantiating the apparent multiplicity of motives is the author's pose of ignorance: "I know not for what reason" Jenny jumps up when Mrs. Partridge enters the room where she and Partridge are studying Latin. Wherever we turn we encounter the word "perhaps" or phrases such as "a matter not so easy to be acounted for," "we will not determine," or "I shall leave the reader to determine" (Bk. I, Chaps. 10, 11; *3*, 51, 55). All this is the counterpart of the doubt, confusion, and lack of subordination that characterizes the nonironic Richardsonian realism.

It is easy enough to take "Black George really loved Tom" as an ambiguity, but in the cases where Fielding lists multiple possibilities and says, "Take them all," one detects the pose of the Socratic ironist. In the examples concerning Mrs. Wilkins and Tom above, (1) and (2) are commendable motives, but (3) is prudential and has the effect of exposing the other two as rationalizations. All of the author's alternatives simply point to the ironic recognition that Mrs. Wilkins obeys out of fear for her position and that Tom is shy of the birch. Again, the author's ignorance is surely a mock-ignorance when he meditates on the motive of Allworthy's friend in recommending Thwackum as a tutor: "doubtless" because of Thwackum's qualifications of learning and religion, "though indeed" the friend was M.P. for a borough controlled by Thwackum's family.

The author is revealing a discrepancy between words (or rationalizations) and deeds that is not unlike the exposure of Square behind Molly Seagrim's arras. He asks the reader to pass judgment on Mrs. Wilkins, Tom, and the friend of Allworthy. But the very recording of multiple motives and qualifying clauses invites the reader to embrace them in his assessment; and acceptance of the invitation is made easy in many instances by the fact that the truth, or a missing portion of truth, is not revealed until hundreds of pages later. The basic unit in *Joseph Andrews* is the word contradicted by action or by the revelation of motive, and this same contradiction takes place in *Tom Jones,* eventually. But the latter, unlike *Joseph Andrews,* deals in suspense and surprise, with facts and actions long unknown to the reader; thus the emphasis falls not on the contradiction but on the speaker's speculations of the moment—which, though solidified later, nevertheless give to the novel an air of complexity and doubt which is not swept away by the denouement. When we see Bridget Allworthy showing generosity and kindness to little Tommy Jones (deviating from the pattern of the Wilkins-like harpy we believe her to be), we feel that here is a real person, not a type. And when we eventually discover the "truth" this impression is not wiped out. Her prudence, like Wilkins', is made to appear no longer a ruling passion but only one aspect of a multifaceted personality.

Irony is transformed by Fielding from a satiric strategy to a technique for suggesting the complexity of reality and the mitigating forces that make the "mixed" character in whom he is most interested, without succumbing to what he considered the chaos that accompanied Richardson's method, without abrogating judgment.[8] Fielding's constant aim is to keep the reader from actually participating in the action, but have him merge himself in the author as a judge who can sympathize with the characters but never lose perspective on their actions. The psychological purpose of his irony is always subordinate to the analytic.

The Meaning of an Action

The basic structural unit of *Tom Jones* is once again the action or situation surrounded by reactions. Tom is a touchstone and throughout the novel characters are judged "as they meet this test."[9] Since socially accepted opinion is against bastards, reactions to him tend to

8. Fielding's irony is also used for simpler purposes in *Tom Jones.* It serves as a euphemism when he says "but something or other happened before the next morning [after the fight over Jenny] which a little abated the fury of Mrs. Partridge" (Bk. II, Chap. 3; *3,* 73). It is also a way of saying that the motive is obvious: why so-and-so did this "must be left to the judgment of the sagacious reader," Fielding says when the answer is quite evident, "for we never choose to assign motives to the actions of men, when there is any possibility of our being mistaken" (Bk. V, Chap. 10; *3,* 259). Yet even in these cases, Fielding has drawn attention to the problematic nature of motives.

9. McKillop, *Early Masters of English Fiction,* p. 212.

be violent and acceptance of him indicates true humanity; as a touch-stone he promptly sets up the dichotomy of form and feeling. The first part of the novel concerning Tom's youth is constructed on a series of actions taken by Tom: he refuses to give away his poaching accomplice; he sells his horse and Bible; and he tries to save Sophia's little bird Tommy. Each is followed (and in some cases preceded) by commentary, abstract and concrete, delivered by Thwackum and Square, with assists from Blifil and sometimes Allworthy. The commentary characterizes the commentator, as it did in *Joseph Andrews*. Even after Tom is on the road the form persists, though less obtrusively. The Quaker, for example, shows a spectrum of reactions to Tom: first he is friendly; then he decides Tom is mad; and finally, learning who he really is, he becomes indignant; and his reactions are compared with the innkeeper's (Bk. VII, Chap. 10).

In *Joseph Andrews,* however, the action—whether Joseph's or Leonora the Jilt's—stood as the norm, good or bad, by which we judge reactions to it. In *Tom Jones* Tom's actions themselves are questionable, as are *all* the actions taken by characters in this novel, and the reader's attention is divided between action and commentary. Indeed, it is through these scenes that Fielding brings about the effect of Tom's greater importance and centrality to his novel than Joseph's or Adams' to his. Fielding has progressed from a villain-centered to a hero-centered plot, and from a hero-centered plot in which motive is exposed in the evil characters who swarm about the hero to a plot that is hero-oriented, with motive being sought in the hero himself. In each episode Tom is himself defined by his deeds, and the people around him (protectors and schoolmasters) are specifically judges of his actions rather than persecutors—though physical persecution often follows judgment. Their judgments tell us something about Tom's actions as well as revealing their own characters.

Almost all of the characters assume at one time or another the role either of commentator or of the person commented upon. The search for the meaning of actions, and in particular of motive in relation to action, is one of the central concerns of the novel. At one extreme Fielding presents the expansion of action by gossip and slander into fantastic rumors; at the other extreme is the author's own search for true motives behind actions. The reprehensible behavior of Thwackum and Square, their reactions to Tom, are no longer the novel's theme. The question at the center of the novel is why Tom behaved as he did at Upton, and this is anticipated by other questions such as why he had sexual relations with Molly Seagrim or why Black George stole his £500.

The action itself was simple in *Joseph Andrews,* persistently dramatizing the discrepancy between the apparent and the real, the Pamelian profession and performance. The result was essentially exposure of motive through action. Words were ambiguous, but hardly ever actions, which were considered the equivalent of motives. In *Shamela* Mr. Booby at last catches Shamela and Parson Williams in bed together, and in *Joseph Andrews* Lady Booby's fine words are followed by gross actions and the gentleman's talk about courage is followed by his terror at hearing Fanny's cries of rape. But in *Tom Jones,* though there are examples of this structure (Square in Molly's bedroom is the most famous), and all false appearances are eventually resolved in revealing action, throughout most of the book Fielding seems no longer willing to rely on externals. Actions are present mostly to highlight his more subtle and analytic treatment of their wellsprings, and they are seldom allowed to stand and speak for themselves. Even the simple exposure of Square and Molly is not allowed to pass without some mitigating discussion of motives.

Every action is analyzed as to motive and judged by neighbors or chance acquaintances or enemies, whose own motives, of course, appear in their interpretations. When Allworthy is first introduced, the reader is told he "had not the least doubt" of meeting his late wife in heaven—"sentiments for which his sense was arraigned by one part of his neighbors, his religion by a second, and his sincerity by a third" (Bk. I, Chap. 2; *3, 21*). These are three of the kinds of people one must encounter and by whom one's actions are so partially judged. The discovery of Tom in Allworthy's bed is followed by a recounting of the motives assigned to Allworthy by his neighbors—that Allworthy must be the father; that he was cruel in his magisterial treatment of Jenny; and that he probably spirited her away and murdered her—and finally the author's summary of the effect of this talk—that it does no harm to Allworthy and makes the rumormongers happy.

At the outset Fielding's emphasis is deliberately balanced between the good man who must tread warily in the world to avoid such malicious misinterpretation of his decent actions, and the evil-minded neighbors who are made happy by the misinterpretation. The rumors do Allworthy no harm because he carefully and prudently maintains a proper public image of himself; thus the rumors about Tom's parentage are mere speculation, amusing for the neighbors in part because of their unreality. But the rumors about Allworthy serve to anticipate Tom's situation. There *are* imprudent people about whom such speculation can be accepted as fact and become harmful. The danger of such misinterpretation is shown soon after Allworthy has ceased to be grist to the mill. Partridge is attacked by his jealous wife and beaten; her women friends enter and believe that he has attacked her; and soon the whole county is ringing with stories of Partridge's cruelty. The story is magnified until Mrs. Partridge has a broken arm and Partridge—when the story of Jenny's maternity becomes known —has a proper motive and two bastards. But the imaginary scene which has usurped reality is not so fantastic as its consequences, which can only be described as nightmarish. As in a nightmare each consequence is worse than the last, moving in the direction of complete fulfillment or destruction—in this sense, of the Partridge family. Justice goes all awry as the good Allworthy accepts the fantastic story as true; Partridge is found guilty of both beating his wife and fathering Tom; his annuity is withdrawn (a backfiring of the plan on Mrs. Partridge); he loses his school; and finally Mrs. Partridge dies of smallpox and he leaves the neighborhood. Mrs. Partridge's interpretation of the fight has been accepted, thus making the fantasy effective and ruining herself and her husband. In this case an action is misinterpreted, and the misinterpretation is acted upon and grows to monstrous proportions, the circles of its influence reaching out to other people.

As a satiric convention this situation is related to the nightmare injustice that Fielding employs in such scenes as the apprehension of Adams for the crime he had just prevented. In *Tom Jones,* however, the emphasis is not so much on the satiric image of the innocent persecuted as on the perverse or merely mistaken interpretation of actions. Partridge's disaster can be taken as a gloss on Fielding's remark in his "Essay on the Knowledge of the Characters of Men" that actions are rendered difficult to interpret "when we take the colour of a man's actions, not from their own visible tendency, but from his public character: when we believe what others say of him, in opposition to what we see him do." The general drift of *Tom Jones* follows this view, taking little Tommy, the bastard left in Allworthy's bed, and the various fantasies that follow from Bridget Allworthy's original act and developing them into the myth of the wicked Tom and the good Blifil, which leads to Allworthy's misunderstanding of Tom's motive for laughing during his serious illness and consequently to a disaster similar to Partridge's. Thus we are frequently shown the "malicious tongues" that whisper about any behavior that is not immediately understood—"the public voice, which seldom reaches to a brother or a husband, though it rings in the ears of all the neighbourhood" (Bk. III, Chap. 7; *3, 130*). The Virgilian Rumor herself makes an appearance amid the confusion of the Pretender's invasion, and Sophia becomes Jenny Cameron, Prince Charles Edward's supposed mistress (Bk. VIII, Chap. 9; *4, 102*).

The characters within the novel are paralleled by the kinds of reader Fielding presupposes outside the novel looking in—the "sneerer" and the "grave reader," the "virtuous reader," "readers of the lowest class," and the "upper graduates in criticism." These readers, like the characters in the book, are considered a more or less prejudiced jury or audience at a play—those two metaphorical equivalents that run through all of Fielding's fiction. The judicial metaphor is the more intense and widespread in *Tom Jones*. Fielding is constantly referring to "judges" and "jurisdiction" and to different kinds of justice: Tom's "mercy" or Blifils (or Thwackum's) "justice," a "court of conscience" or a "court of justice." When Black George is trying to decide whether to take the money Sophia has sent Tom as well as the £500 he has already stolen, his dilemma is described in terms of a courtroom scene with his conscience "a good lawyer" on one side, Avarice ready to "urge" the other, and Fear stepping in to decide the case (Bk. VI, Chap. 13; *3, 327–28*).

But to bring his point out most forcefully Fielding turns to his theatrical metaphor (Bk. VII, Chap. 1; *3, 331* ff.). He points out that in the past the resemblance between life and the theater has been "taken from the stage only"; now he turns to "the audience of this great drama," "the behaviour of her spectators" as well as "that of her actors." The focus is still on Black George's action, and Fielding sketches in the various reactions of the upper gallery, the pit, and the boxes to his deed, each censuring Black George in its characteristic way. The "sagacious reader," to whom Fielding addresses himself, is invariably left as the final judge, the author himself having withdrawn: "we never choose to assign motives to the actions of men, when there is any possibility of our being mistaken" (Bk. V, Chap. 10; *3, 259*). One result of the reader's search for meaning is the introduction of suspense. Fielding makes him *want* to know motive: why did someone put the baby in Allworthy's bed? why did Jenny act suspiciously? Questions of motive become questions of meaning: what does Bridget's kindness to young Tommy mean? *Tom Jones* has in a sense the fascination of a whodunit.

While actions are made difficult by the prejudices of observers, they are, Fielding makes abundantly clear, ambiguous in themselves. To get at the meaning Fielding explains the motives behind the action, and then the causes and influences that affected it, and incidentally its consequences. The motives and causes behind the actions of Black George and Tom are as mixed as the various interpretations of them by others. Fielding gives three motives for Tom's helping Black George and his family—his simple friendship for George; his sense of guilt for George's loss of his job (this is rendered more complex by the fact that George should have admitted his guilt to save Tom a thrashing); and his physical attraction to Molly.

Approaching an important action Fielding marshals all the contributing factors available. Leading up to Tom's betrayal of Sophia with Molly in the grove (Bk. V, Chap. 10), he dwells upon (1) the setting, "so sweetly accommodated to love." It is "the latter end of June . . . a most delicious grove . . . the gentle breezes fanning the leaves, together with the sweet trilling of a murmuring stream, and the melodious notes of nightingales." (2) Tom's thoughts of Sophia, memories of their last meeting, in which they realized that they loved each other, and knowledge "that fortune . . . sets a distance" between them (*3, 256*). (3) Relief at the recovery of Allworthy after despairing of his life. (4) Drunkenness caused by his celebration of Allworthy's recovery. As Fielding insists, "the reader will be . . . pleased to recollect in his favor that he was not at this time perfect master of that wonderful power of reason which so well enables grave and wise men to subdue their unruly passions" (*3, 258*). Tom, hardly in control of himself to begin with, walks through erotically stimulating scenery thinking of Sophia, whom he can never marry, and sees

Molly, who makes advances to him ("Jones probably thought one woman better than none"). The situation is exactly analogous to the one in *Joseph Andrews* where the chambermaid Betty, having been disappointed in her passion for Joseph, is approached by Mr. Towwouse, whom she would have repulsed under any other circumstances, and she succumbs.

The consequence of Tom's sin, besides pangs of conscience, is expulsion from Paradise Hall. But the connection between the action and the punishment is extremely tenuous, depending on Tom's discovery by Blifil and Thwackum and ultimately on Allworthy's belief that Tom has insulted him.

Searching for a basis for judging an action, Fielding is driven back to the parts that he can be more certain of; and this only leads to further uncertainty. Words are completely unreliable, as Square for one shows. So Fielding moves back to the action itself: but Blifil's freeing of Sophia's bird Tommy might be considered objectively a good deed; as Blifil explained, it freed a poor imprisoned animal. But its consequences were bad: Sophia unhappy, Tom nearly drowned, the bird devoured; and Blifil's motive, to hurt Sophia and destroy something named Tommy, was also bad. Consequences, however, are not reliable either: Allworthy dismisses Tom for a fancied slight, not for his real crime, and Sophia (Fielding insists on the point by giving us authorial comment as well as Sophia's own words) repudiates Tom not because of his affair with Mrs. Waters but because Partridge has manufactured a story about Tom's using her name insultingly in a tavern. As Fielding learns how misleading not only words but even actions and consequences can be, he finds it increasingly difficult to judge actions except in terms of motives. He rejects the satirist's simple but commonsensical acceptance of effect as the chief criterion of virtue in favor of the belief that an action can be neither good nor evil in itself, but only as its motive is charitable or self-seeking.

Through the ironic complexity of *Tom Jones* Fielding also says that motive too is so difficult to assign that only much later, by surprise, by accident, can we see behavior as good or evil. Mrs. Honour's decision to help Sophia escape from her father and aunt is finally accidental (Bk. VII, Chap. 8; *3*, 362 ff.). She thinks of (1) all the advantages to be gained by revealing Sophia's plot to Mrs. Western,

(2) all the advantages in a journey to London, (3) her love for her mistress, but (4) "the length of time which must intervene before Sophia would be able to fulfill her promises." And finally it is (5) her chance quarrel with Mrs. Western's maid that decides her. Her action is good, her motive mixed but ultimately frivolous; it is only later when she goes completely over to Lady Bellaston that her earlier action can be used as an aid in judging Sophia's ironically named maid.

The action is made even more problematic by the fact that the reader as well as the character never knows all that he needs to know in a given situation. We and Tom know nothing about the possibility of incest at Upton until long afterward. Fielding has consciously separated the action from its motives and causes, even from its consequences. In *Tom Jones* he is still writing about conduct, action, and scenes to be judged, but now they are so overly complex that we must conclude that not so much Tom as the whole episodic structure is being judged. Fielding is saying that actions cannot be isolated and correctly interpreted by anyone—even the author himself—because of their very nature. After summarizing the reactions of pit, gallery, and so forth to the performance of Black George, he adds that

> we, who are admitted behind the scenes of this great theatre of Nature (and no author ought to write anything besides dictionaries and spelling-books who hath not this privilege), can censure the action, without conceiving any absolute detestation of the person whom perhaps Nature may not have designed to act an ill part in all her dramas. (Bk. VII, Chap. 1; *3*, 334)

At this point the analyzed action has been placed in perspective; the particular case of conduct is not enough because, as he adds, "the passions, like the managers of a playhouse, often force men upon parts without consulting their judgment, and sometimes without any regard to their talents" (*3*, 335). Fielding has pushed his search behind motive itself, suggesting that the action, even if understood, is not basis for a definitive judgment of a man. One must look to the general span of his life. Near the beginning of the book, though admitting that it is an ideal, he argues that character is more important than action (or conduct): "it is a more useful capacity to be able to

foretell the actions of men, in any circumstance, from their characters, than to judge of their characters from their actions" (Bk. III,
Chap. 1; *3*, 106–07). The double irony, in this sense, supports the general meaning of the novel. In both betrayals of Sophia, Tom has succumbed to natural instinct, not in the least condoned by Fielding; he
has betrayed Sophia but he obviously still loves her, just as Black
George in some sense still loves Tom.[10]

Fielding shows three ways of suggesting the complexity of character. The first, a factitious complexity, describes hypocrisy or delusion in a character, juxtaposing what he appears to be or thinks he is
with what he really is. The second gives the character two or more
impulses, actions, or professions that are contradictory, suggesting that
he is "mixed"; or else he commits a good action and then a bad. The
third relates the character's action to multiple causes or motives, in
effect destroying the integrity of the action and making it only a focal
point for a character study which is a continuum between past, present, and future.

In *Tom Jones* Fielding has reached a conclusion that is essentially
alien to the classical, and so to the satiric, tradition—that judgment is
only possible when made of a whole being and not of an individual
action. Harold Rosenberg, employing the same metaphor as Fielding,
has called this "the failure of the individual to conform in every respect to his role."[11] In coming to this conclusion, Fielding has moved
appreciably closer to Richardson, who tirelessly demonstrated that
experience is both continuous and cumulative. Truth, or understand-

10. The description of mixed character in Bk. X, Chap. 1, is paralleled by a discussion of false critics in Bk. XI, Chap. 1. The latter deals with slanderers of books, the
criterion for which is the same as for the slanderers of people—those who misinterpret
Tom's actions because they accept a false character of him. The false critic passes judgment "upon works he hath not himself read." He may "without assigning any particular fault, condemn the whole in general defamatory terms," or, finding "some
faults justly assigned in the work" (though "not in the most essential parts, or if they
are compensated by greater beauties"), he yet condemns the whole book. He is like
those slanderers who condemn Tom or Black George for one or two mistakes, or those
authors who do not believe in mixed characters. The novel Fielding is writing and
Tom Jones himself become parallel phenomena at this point; the aesthetic and moral
are one: "Cruel indeed would it be if such a work as this history, which hath employed some thousands of hours in the composing, should be liable to be condemned,
because some particular chapter, or perhaps chapters, may be obnoxious to very just
and sensible objection."

11. Rosenberg, "Character Change and the Drama," in *The Tradition of the New*
(New York, Horizon Press, 1959), p. 138. See above, Chap. 1.

ing, is a gradual unfolding via the establishment of place and time, contact with a character's immediate environment, and a number of significant experiences. Truth is not given but gradually found out; it is not simply an immutable yardstick like Aeneas or Augustus, but a long series of experiences and approximations. It is also cumulative, carrying ideas from past to present, and so there is the need to establish the past, the causes and motives. Thus every moment, however fleeting, has its own place in this structure and its own importance. While it complicates the basis for a judgment, it contributes to the gradual establishment of being in a character.

Fielding has attempted to explore the shadowy Richardsonian realm, but he sets out with very different equipment. He has simply moved his tools of assessment into the world of *Clarissa,* pointing out what Richardson never did, that the problem is in fact the opposition between being and actions, justice and law. His progression toward *Tom Jones* can be said to be from law and a study of actions (satire) to justice and an interest in being (novel), brought about perhaps by his intimate contact with the law and his awareness in practice of the discrepancy between law and justice.

Satire and History

In *Tom Jones* Fielding is even more emphatic about the special quality of his form than in *Joseph Andrews:* he calls himself "the founder of a new province of writing" (Bk. II, Chap. 1; *3,* 66) and his work "this kind of writing, of which we have set ourselves at the head" (Bk. V, Chap. 1; *3,* 205); he now calls his writing "this heroic, historical, prosaic poem" (Bk. IV, Chap. 1; *3,* 143) and "this historic kind of writing" (Bk. IX, Chap. 1; *4,* 154). The emphasis shifts from epic to history as the defining genre.[12] Indeed Fielding's changing employment of satire as we have traced it corresponds in certain particulars to the role of satire in history writing in Fielding's lifetime.

The Augustan historiographers, following the precedent of classical models, tended to confuse or blur the distinction between the

---

12. For Fielding's library, which included Bayles' *Dictionary,* see Robert M. Wallace, "Fielding's Knowledge of History and Biography," *Studies in Philology, 44* (1947), 89–107.

function of the historian and that of the satirist.[13] The historian must be a judge, "shewing the Rod to Tyrants, and advertising them of the Punishment [History] prepares. . . . Their future Fame keeps them more in awe than their Conscience." Thus in a history "Judgment follows the Narration of things." The historian's claim, in fact, was very much like the satirist's:

> He is Judge, and Judgment reaches the Bad as well as the Good: His Function is a publick Witness, and 'tis the part of a Witness to conceal nothing. And in fine, 'Tis the publick Interest, that great Men and Princes to whom the *Laws* are but *Cobwebs*, should have some Bridle to stop them. And to a People that take *Religion* for a *Fantasm*, and *Hell* for a *Bugbear Eternal Infamy* is prepared for them in History.[14]

A much subtler statement of this view appeared in Swift's opening of his *History of the Four Last Years of Queen Ann's Reign* (publ. 1758):

> Although in an Age like ours I can expect very few impartial Readers; yet I shall strictly follow Truth, or what reasonably appeared to me to be such, after the most impartial Inquiries I could make, and the best Opportunityes of being informed by those who were the principal Actors or Advisers. Neither shall I mingle Panegyrick or Satire with an History intended to inform Posterity, as well as to instruct those of the present Age,

13. See Herbert Davis, "The Augustan Conception of History," in *Reason and the Imagination: Studies in the History of Ideas, 1600–1800*, ed. J. A. Mazzeo (New York, Columbia University Press; London, Routledge and Kegan Paul, 1962), pp. 213–29, esp. pp. 218–29. I am also indebted in the following discussion to Ernst Cassirer, *The Philosophy of the Enlightenment*, trans. Fritz C. A. Koeln and James P. Pettegrove (Princeton, Princeton University Press, 1951).

14. Pierre Le Moine, *Of the Art of Both Writing and Judging History* (Paris, 1690; trans. London, 1695), pp. 32, 110, 117; cited, Davis, p. 218. Cf. Swift's explanation of his role in *The Examiner* (*The Prose Writings of Jonathan Swift*, ed. Herbert Davis [Oxford, Blackwell, 1939], *3*, 141). See also *Spectator*, Nos. 136, 170, 420, 483; E. C. Mossner, *The Forgotten Hume* (New York, Columbia University Press, 1943), p. 6; Bertrand Russell, *History of Western Philosophy* (New York, Simon and Schuster, 1945), p. 660; and Bonamy Dobrée, *English Literature in the Early Eighteenth Century* (Oxford, Clarendon Press, 1959), p. 378.

who may be Ignorant or Misled: Since Facts truly related are the best Applauses, or most lasting Reproaches.[15]

The last clause, of course, gives him away. Here then are the views that Fielding presumably included in his meaning of the word "history" as it became more prominent in each succeeding novel—the search for truth, but truth as "what reasonably appeared to me to be such"—and while it no longer mingles panegyric and satire with history, still "Facts truly related are the best Applauses, or most lasting Reproaches." In short, neither the function of judgment nor the exemplary use of historical personages has been lost.

But Fielding's novels suggest that he was also sensitive to the changing currents of historiography in his time. The new developments were French and evolved from Pierre Bayle's *Dictionary* (1690), a huge pile of unsubordinated facts with the dictionary entries often buried under footnotes and appendixes; however, the very formlessness was Bayle's answer to the over-formalized myths of earlier history, particularly ecclesiastical. For Fielding Bayle's test of myth by fact must have represented a historical counterpart to the Lucianic-Shaftesburyian doctrine of ridicule. In *The Jacobite's Journal,* Fielding's "Court of Criticism" convicts a Jacobite historian named Thomas Carte "of a very high Offence; no less than that of perverting the Intent of History, and applying it to the sordid and paltry use of a Party" (Feb. 20, 1748). Specifically, he is accused of passing on "one False, foolish, ridiculous, and absurd Story" about a man who was allegedly cured by the Pretender of the King's Evil. In the same way Fielding tests in his early satires the myth of the "Great Man" and in *Joseph Andrews* the myth of the noble heroine by the rule of fact.

But if the first phase of the new development in history writing involved the questioning of accepted history (as myth), the second demanded *l'histoire de l'esprit humain,* of manners, social institutions, and the forms of society. While, as Hugh Blair noted, Voltaire is the great name connected with this phase, Bayle, Fontenelle, and Fénelon had advocated such history before him. This history, Blair explains, deals with

laws, customs, commerce, religion, literature, and every other

15. *Prose Writings,* ed. Davis, 7, 1–2.

thing that tends to show the spirit and genius of nations. It is now understood to be the business of an able Historian to exhibit manners, as well as facts and events; and assuredly, whatever displays the state and life of mankind, in different periods, and illustrates the progress of the human mind, is more useful and interesting than the details of sieges and battles.[16]

In one sense, this development was a continuation of Bayle's campaign to test and perhaps destroy old assumptions and historical lies. Voltaire's attack on heroes, the same as Fielding's, was supported by reference to facts and to factual accounts of customs. Voltaire also advocated the study of manners as a corrective to the mere accumulation of facts—exactly Fielding's view in opposition to such writers as Richardson: facts alone only confuse; they must be ordered so that the reader can reach a detached judgment.[17] As to the study of manners, "I declare here, once for all," says Fielding in the introduction to the third book of *Joseph Andrews,* "I describe not men, but manners; not an individual, but a species" (*1,* 215).

The historical shift from political to cultural history, from battles to the conditions of society, family life, and the like, parallels the general change we have followed in Fielding from satire to the novel, from the novel as satire to the novel as a study of manners, and from a concern with the public realm to a concern with the social and the private. In *Tom Jones* satire remains in only one important sense (I do not include incidental satire)—as a critical tool for exploring, discovering, and judging. It is clearly a means to an end that is not satiric but, in the general eighteenth-century sense, historical.

David Hume sums up the view of history as a critical, analytic, and, in one sense, satiric undertaking. In his essay "On the Study of History" (1741), he maintains the moral function of history, which allows us to see the human race "from the beginning of time, pass, as it were, in review before us; appearing in their true colours, without any of those disguises which, during their life-time, so much perplexed the judgment of the beholders."[18] The aim of discovering

16. Lecture XXXVI in *Lectures on Rhetoric* (publ. 1783).

17. See *The Works of M. de Voltaire,* trans. T. Francklin, Tobias Smollett, and others (London, 1779), *6,* 168.

18. *Essays Moral, Political, and Literary,* eds. T. H. Green and T. H. Grose (London, Longmans, Green, and Co., new impression, 1912), *2,* 389–90.

truth specifically by penetrating the disguise of human action is essentially the view Fielding states in the preface to *Joseph Andrews* when he takes affectation as his subject matter. Hume further distinguishes the historian from the poets, who, "as they address themselves entirely to the passions, they often become the advocates for vice," and the philosophers, who sometimes "go so far as to deny the reality of all moral distinctions." Historians, on the other hand, "have been, almost without exception, the true friends of virtue, and have always represented it in its proper colours," by which he means placing "the objects in their true point of view," neither too close nor too far from the viewer (p. 391). Fielding's banishment of the romancer and the burlesque writer serves the same function of seeking a proper point of view for his novel. Fielding shares the historian's dramatic irony—the contrast between the actors' view of their conduct (or someone else's conduct) and the fuller view permitted by the detachment and larger perspective of the historian.[19] Detachment and larger perspective are covered by Fielding's term "history" as he uses it in *Tom Jones;* and in the preface to *A Voyage to Lisbon* (publ. 1755), in a passage that could be an echo of Hume, he argues that the ancient poets, Homer and Hesiod, "affected" if they did not "pervert and confuse the records of antiquity":

> and, for my part, I must confess I should have honoured and loved Homer more had he written a true history of his own times in humble prose, than those noble poems that have so justly collected the praise of all ages; for though I read these with more admiration and astonishment, I still read Herodotus, Thucydides, and Xenophon, with more amusement and more satisfaction.[20]

Genius, Fielding explains in *Tom Jones* (Bk. IX, Chap. 1; *4,* 157), consists of "those powers of the mind, which are capable of penetrat-

19. Gibbon is an example of the historian who wrote with both epic and satiric as well as historical conventions in mind; see E. M. W. Tillyard, *The English Epic and Its Background* (London, Chatto and Windus, 1954), pp. 510–27, and Harold L. Bond, *The Literary Art of Edward Gibbon* (Oxford, Clarendon Press, 1960).

20. *Works,* ed. Henley, *16,* 182. Hume also extended Locke's metaphor of the mind as an audience chamber to the one Fielding habitually used: "The mind is a kind of theatre, where several perceptions successively make their appearance" (*Treatise on Human Nature,* I, *4,* vi).

ing into all things within our reach and knowledge, and of distinguishing their essential differences." These powers are invention and judgment, the former being not, as generally believed,

> a creative faculty, which would indeed prove most romance writers to have the highest pretensions to it; whereas by invention is really meant no more (and so the word signifies) than discovery, or finding out; or to explain it at large, a quick and sagacious penetration into the true essence of all the objects of our contemplation.

In his *Treatise of Human Nature* (1739-40) Hume expresses a skepticism about the quick and sagacious "penetration" referred to above that is very similar to the position Fielding eventually arrives at in *Tom Jones:*

> If any *action* be either virtuous or vicious, 'tis only as a sign of some quality or character. It must depend upon durable principles of mind, which extend over the whole conduct, and enter into the personal character. . . .
> Actions are, indeed, better indications of a character than words, or even wishes and sentiments; but 'tis only so far as they are such indications, that they are attended with love or hatred, praise or blame (III, iii, 1).

Hume is out to destroy the Hobbesian theory that self-interest is the single motive behind all behavior—also accomplished by Fielding's irony—and indeed argues against any simple, neat, monistic explanation of behavior, showing that a variety of motives bear upon any action (III, iii, 3).

Further, Hume implies that moral good or evil is almost wholly subjective, although he stops short of complete subjectivism by arguing that there is a great deal of agreement in men's judgments. In the same way Fielding shows a variety of different reactions to or judgments of an action but makes it clear which simply reflect the observer's self-interest and which are disinterested, until in *Tom Jones* he shows an almost Hume-like sense of the real difficulty of judging action by reactions, when even the good man, Squire Allworthy, can be blinded by Tom's reputation or perhaps even by self-interest. The answer, as Fielding shows, is to back away and see man in all his complexity. As Hume put it, by "correcting the appearance of reflexion, arrive at a more constant and establish'd judgment concerning them" (III, iii, 3).

We have observed a movement in Fielding's fiction, paralleling the developing theories of history, away from castigation and rigorous judgment and away from the circumscribed symbolic action. This movement can be, and usually has been, attributed to Fielding's Latitudinarian-Shaftesburyian tolerance, or it can be attributed to his intention of showing his readers how difficult it really is to make a judgment. Tolerance of course is a comic attitude, summed up in the *komos* or feast of reconciliation, and may be the final effect of a work like *Tom Jones*. But Fielding must have arrived at this characteristic effect through the parallel phenomenon of Lucianic and Shaftesburyian satire, beginning with the attack on forms and the intention to shatter stereotypes, Pamelian and otherwise. This kind of satire, which uses the multifarious complexity of experience to ridicule the over-formalized reaction, is the one branch of satire that is more or less parallel to the aim of the novel, particularly if channeled toward a question like character or action.

I have tried to show how the Fielding novel derives from the original aim of anti-romance—to destroy romance—as well as from the Latitudinarian influence. From the humanist revolutionaries, Erasmus and Rabelais, Fielding draws his "subversion of forms,"[21] his overturned endings, his mixed characters, his corrective to the Richardsonian morality and point of view, his search beyond words and even actions to motives, and ultimately his conclusion that judgment can be based only on a whole character. This represents another important shift, seen in moving from *Joseph Andrews* to *Tom Jones,* from the habit (still evident in Richardson's *Clarissa*) of seeing things in terms of analogical or symbolic relationships to the scientific pose that sees them in terms of cause and effect relationships. Causality was stressed in *Joseph Andrews,* but only in the detail of the novel, in the explanations of why each rider in the coach repudiated Joseph. In *Tom Jones,* however, everything is tied together tightly by causation, and Fielding always wants to know what the causes of a given "accident" were.

21. Price, *To the Palace of Wisdom,* pp. 292–304.

The phenomenon Fielding represents is not unique, and it can be traced in history or biography, from proving an already established point (a simple moral exemplum) to shaking up values, exposing the fact beneath the lies of theologians and courtiers, and always leaving something of a question: what really did happen? what did it mean? what was X really like?

The Public and Private Worlds of Amelia

Fielding starts off in *Amelia* with the same problem that informed *Tom Jones*. The first chapter talks about the relation between fortune and causality, implying that people use the idea of fortune to conceal their own responsibility:

> as histories of this kind, therefore, may properly be called models of Human Life, so, by observing minutely the several incidents which tend to the catastrophe or completion of the whole, and the minute causes whence those incidents are produced, we shall best be instructed in this most useful of all arts, which I call the Art of Life. (6, 14)

But in his dedication to Ralph Allen Fielding also says that he is going "to expose some of the most glaring evils, as well public as private, which at present infect the country" (6, 12); that the satire will be general, not personal. The careful search for causality applies on one level, but the novel is also much concerned with those "most glaring evils," which are represented as effects rather than causes. Yet, as Fielding adds, the evils are "as well public as private."

In the prison scenes with which the novel opens the reader is shown why the various prisoners are there: Robinson, for instance, attributes his incarceration to fortune, but he is there for having cheated at cards. A series of typical profession-performance structures conveys an anatomy of the prison. There is the girl with "great innocence in her countenance" who damns Booth's eyes and discharges "a volley of words, every one of which was too indecent to be repeated" (6, 27); there is the innocent-looking girl who is held as a dangerous criminal on the word of her father-in-law; and there is the Methodist, whose words and deeds do correspond: he says that crimes have no effect on the saved and proceeds to pick Booth's pocket (Bk. I, Chap. 4). These incidents, which are experienced by

Booth as he tours the prison, prepare the reader for the entrance of Miss Matthews (Chap. 6), who is clearly not what she appears to be. She looks innocent but has just attempted to kill an ex-lover. This crime was one of passion, not calculation. "Indeed sir," she says, "one subornation of perjury would sit heavier on my conscience than twenty such murders as I am guilty of" (Bk. I, Chap. 10; 6, 64). And yet the reader follows her as she carefully exploits Booth's doctrine of passions as man's only motivation, playing upon his weaknesses until eventually she seduces him.

The climax of the first third of the novel is once again a betrayal—Amelia's, by Booth and Miss Matthews. Everything leading up to it has, in a sense, been presented to explain Booth's action. As in *Tom Jones,* Fielding adds:

> Let the reader set before his eyes a fine young woman, in a manner, a first love, conferring obligations and using every art to soften, to allure, to win, and to inflame; let him consider the time and place; let him remember that Mr. Booth was a young fellow in the highest vigor of life; and, lastly, let him add one single circumstance, that the parties were alone together; and then, if he will not acquit the defendant, he must be convicted, for I have nothing more to say in his defence. (Bk. IV, Chap. 1; 6, 175)

When Fielding precedes this recital with an obvious reference to Booth's own self-justification, that "Fortune seemed to have used her utmost endeavors to ensnare poor Booth's constancy" (6, 175), he is condemning Booth's rationalization but not quite condemning his action. As with Betty the chambermaid and with Tom, Booth falls from a combination of circumstances, some internal and some external, including his persistent thoughts of Amelia combined with her inaccessibility. At any rate, the reader is not allowed to forget that this is a casual affair and that Booth really loves Amelia.

Miss Matthews' conduct is also explicable in terms of causality: her recent disappointment in the man she loved; the meeting with Booth, who was her first and perhaps continuing love; the talk about love and Amelia, her retelling of her own story, and the details of love that she elicits from Booth to inflame him; finally, her relief at hearing that she is not a murderess, that her lover is going to recover (as Tom learns that Allworthy will recover). All of these do their work on her as well.

I have devoted this much space to the matter of Booth and Miss Matthews to show that Fielding emphasizes the relationship between character and conduct at least as much in *Amelia* as in *Tom Jones*. But one notices that he is dealing here with two kinds of experience, more widely separated than they were in *Tom Jones*. Miss Matthews is introduced as the climax of a series of profession-performance contrasts, but her own case is much too complex to fit into this shorthand form. Since we are not led to conclude that Robinson and the rest are also, if we could know them, similarly complex, we tend to accept both the caricatures and the character study as true but unrelated facts, one concerning a general public theme, the other a private. The two areas again come into conjunction as Booth and Miss Matthews tell their stories.

These narratives keep the same action-commentator form with which we are now well acquainted, and they are filled with satiro-melodramatic villains like Miss Harris and Hebbers. In each case the listener acts as commentator and corrects the reader's possible misapprehensions about the speaker and his story. Booth smiles at Miss Matthews' excesses, Miss Matthews gives the woman's view on Booth's errors of interpretation, and occasionally Fielding himself intervenes. The tone of Miss Matthews' narrative tends to make the reader take it (as she offers it) on the same level as Judge Thrasher's court and the prison, as another attack on vice, in this case on the seducer Hebbers. The melodramatic style corresponds to Hebbers' actions as the sentimental does to Amelia's. But, as the commentary of the listener and her own unconscious slips demonstrate, Miss Matthews is in fact not satirizing but producing bitter personal reminiscence, and her story is a scheme for seducing Booth. The reader is left with the impression that Fielding wants her story to do two things—present a lesson and depict Miss Matthews. Because these are so far apart, one very general, the other very particular, the reader is never sure to what extent she represents moral truth and to what extent psychological.

Much more than in any of Fielding's earlier works two kinds of writing exist side by side, the satiric incidents of Justice Thrasher and the prison and the stories of Miss Matthews and Booth, merging at

times as in the story of Hebbers. The treatment of setting and minor
characters is satiric in a way that goes back to the farces, while the
main characters are treated as private lives and searched for motive
and character, as in *Tom Jones*. Some of the later episodes, especially
concerning Mrs. Bennet (whose narrative is less a parody and therefore more convincing than Miss Matthews'), show a distinct advance
in subtlety and penetration.[22] Public evil becomes much easier to see
—from Thrasher to the Noble Lord—and private character is even
more difficult to judge. The old pre-*Tom Jones* system of judging by
a single action (conduct) applies to the public characters, while the
private characters are judged by the general sweep of their lives. For
the satirically regarded characters Fielding shifts away from motives;
indeed, the conventionality or lack of motive is part of his characterization of evil in *Amelia*. In *Joseph Andrews* the squire who "roasts"
Adams indicates a momentary plunge into a kind of motiveless evil
nowhere else present in that novel; when Blifil's lust for Sophia turns
(with the knowledge of how she loaths him) to the sheer desire to
make her suffer, he too is approaching the malevolent. In *Amelia,*
however, there is the sinister Noble Lord (rendered more sinister by
the generic designation), whose villainy is the same as Sempronius'
in Addison's *Cato:*

> I long to clasp that haughty maid,
> And bend her stubborn virtue to my passion;
> When I have gone thus far, I'd cast her off. (III, 7)

Captain Trent, Mrs. Ellison, and even Miss Matthews (once we lose
sight of her in the flesh) carry out their evil deeds for pure malice,
with selfish motives as only secondary inducements. The emphasis in
their actions and in Justice Thrasher's court is no longer on motive
or self-deceit or hypocrisy, but on effect—the injustice manifested in
imprisoning Booth and other "poor wretches" and freeing the
wicked. While the reader could, in *Joseph Andrews,* react with
laughter to Parson Trulliber or Mrs. Tow-wouse, here, where the
effects of actions are emphasized, he reacts with indignation.[23]

22. See John S. Collidge, "Fielding and the 'Conservation of Character,'" *Modern
Philology,* 57 (1960), 245–59.
23. Fielding shows his concern in two *Covent-Garden Journal* papers on the "mob"
(Nos. 47 and 49).

On the public level *Amelia* bears much the same relation to Fielding's earlier work as "The Epilogue to the Satires" and *The Dunciad*'s fourth book do to Pope's, *Gulliver*'s fourth voyage does to Swift's, and the *Tailpiece* and other late prints do to Hogarth's. In Fielding's case, however, physical suffering, rather than the collapse of order, carries the chief emphasis. Life has become essentially the gauntlet Fielding describes himself running in *A Voyage to Lisbon* as he is carried helpless on a stretcher past jeering sailors. Booth is the poor man with nothing to recommend him but his own meager qualities and his wife. He is a Joseph Andrews or Parson Adams, but his treatment is no longer a joke. As Captain Trent tells him: "if you have no other pretensions than your merit, I can assure you you would fail, if it was possible you could have ten times more merit than you have" (Bk. X, Chap. 7; 7, 224). But Booth has a beautiful wife, and all that he and she need to do to succeed in "the way of the world" is to dispose of her virtue when it is called for. The Booths, however, have chosen to be virtuous, and so Booth passes through a corrupt aristocracy seeking advancement on his own terms, being refused, and, for good measure, being imprisoned and impoverished in order to make Amelia more accessible; meanwhile Amelia passes through a series of threats to her fidelity and virtue.

In *Amelia* Fielding has returned to the Juvenalian world in which the evil men are entrenched and the good man is isolated—here in his ineptitude (the private plot) as well as his weakness (public). Centered in London, and recalling in many respects Juvenal's "Rome" (*Satire* III), *Amelia* presents the situation of Umbricius, the last upholder of Roman values in an un-Roman Rome where money now controls preferment, justice, and of course chastity and honor. It begins with a version of the story Umbricius tells of the innocent man who stands up to hoodlums, is beaten up, and subsequently committed to jail for assault (ll. 281–300) and ends with Booth and Amelia retiring, like Umbricius, to a house in the country. Booth is a neat modernization of the Juvenalian "client": raised as a gentleman, he may not become a tradesman, cannot make a living as a farmer or as a half-pay lieutenant, and thus is trapped in a social situation in which he is utterly dependent on the men in power (Juvenal's patrons). On all sides are the fools who have compromised themselves, men such as Trent, who has sold the favors of his own wife and suggests to Booth that he do the same. Money, lust, and sheer restless vice are the motive forces of this world—from Sister Betty's greed to Colonel James' passion and the Noble Lord's sinister destructiveness. The Trents and the Booths can either pander to Noble Lords or starve and suffer for their virtue.

Evil in the Juvenalian world is pervasive. *Amelia* makes monotonously regular all the isolated evils of the earlier books: whenever a good sergeant appears there is bound to be a fifteen-year-old colonel to countermand his wise order; if a man does a good deed, he will certainly be thrown into prison by the police. Every person to whom one turns is prepared to betray him, and whenever he leaves home a sister is bound to forge a will and take the family fortune herself. Friends are potential corruptors of his wife, philosophers are sharpers, and religious pretenders are pickpockets. When Booth, thinking of James, says, "how false are all universal satires against mankind" (Bk. III, Chap. 7; *6,* 138), Fielding is clearly engaging in dramatic irony. And Amelia probably speaks for Fielding more than he admits when she exclaims, "Indeed, my dear sir, I begin to grow entirely sick of [the world] . . . for sure all mankind almost are villains in their hearts" (Bk. IX, Chap. 5; *7,* 144–45). In spite of Dr. Harrison's orthodox rejoinder to Amelia's pessimism, her statement gives the tone of the novel.

The good are relentlessly persecuted and appear to be in a dwindling minority. But the few good people have become *very* good: as Booth says of that paragon Sergeant Atkinson ("the tears bursting from his eyes"), "I scarce ever heard of so much goodness" (Bk. V, Chap. 4; *6,* 244). The acts of young Atkinson are unambiguously good: while Tom Jones was caught poaching and would not implicate his confederate, Atkinson is caught restoring baby birds to their nest and accepts punishment for attempting to steal them rather than implicate the boy who did steal them (Bk. V, Chap. 3; *6,* 238).

If one aspect of *Amelia* is based on Juvenalian conventions, another catches the tone of *An Enquiry into the Causes of the Late Increase of Robbers.* Chapter 4 of Book I is an anatomy of a prison, but it is more exposé than satire. Even Fielding's usual contrasts of appearance and reality, such as the innocent-looking girl who damns Booth's eyes, are simply reported. The footnote that explains the technicality by which perjurers may escape punishment under English law is symptomatic, as is the chapter which, "though it contains no great matter of amusement . . . may at least serve to inform posterity concerning the present state of physic" (6, 232). The whole has the weary tone of the magistrate who has seen much injustice and suffering and must tell somebody about it. Fielding the public man has emerged and is saying: Now, at once, we must change certain laws.

Thus, on the one hand, there is the public plot which displays the evils of contemporary society on as many fronts as possible. On the other is the private plot, concerned with the individual Booth, his betrayal of Amelia, his personal flaws, and his eventual reformation; it shows a Christian individual overcoming adversity not by changing circumstances but by rising above them and coming to terms with himself. The public and private themes fail to mesh; indeed, they seem to conflict. In the end Booth's victory in the private realm (his conversion to true Christian beliefs) has little to do with the public theme or with his extraction from the myriad difficulties into which he has been thrown.

The happy ending is quite different from *Tom Jones'*, where the weakness of Blifil's schemes are evident from the first and the denouement is carefully prepared. The end of *Amelia* is miraculous: Robinson thinks he is dying and confesses at exactly the right time and place so that the one person who can understand and utilize his confession is present. Colonel James' decision to give up his pursuit of Amelia is almost as miraculous (in its way, the private solution is also remarkable: Booth's conversion from skepticism via the sermons of Barrow is reminiscent of the effect of Pamela's journal on Mr. B.). This is the world of *The Author's Farce* and the court of Bantom, not of *Tom Jones*, for the ending is in fact far from happy on the public level; the happy ending is only in terms of Amelia and Booth. George Sherburn writes, "Obviously, if the fears of political and social degeneracy were not to be justified, what was really needed was the conversion, not of Booth, but of some noble lord, who acting from pure desire to secure an able officer for the guards would get the long-coveted commission for Booth."[24] The society remains as corrupt at the end as at the beginning.

The case of Colonel James is rendered particularly interesting by

24. "Fielding's *Amelia:* An Interpretation," *Journal of English Literary History, 3* (1936), 14.

the ending. More than anyone else James effectively bridges the two areas and the two plots. He begins as an example of character opposed to conduct, who does good deeds for Booth but then, under certain circumstances, tries to ruin him and seduce his wife. The evil act reveals the motive that informed the good act and thus renders it less good. Yet at the end James goes unpunished, like Tom at the end of *Tom Jones*. As part of the public action, his being accepted is ironic, a parody *komos* as the Booths and Jameses eat dinner together; the point is pessimistic and Juvenalian. But as part of the private action, it suggests that James too is enough of a mixed case that his few bad acts (the reasons for which have been made clear) do not outweigh his acts of friendship, that though a weak, passion-driven man (and his friendship is only one of those passions), he has always in some sense, like Black George, loved the man he attempted to betray.

The two plots are most effective as a statement of the discontinuity between public and private areas of experience, or of the importance of a personal, as opposed to a social, solution. But there are none of Fielding's usual indications that this is *Amelia*'s overt aim. On the contrary, his performance in *Amelia* accentuates the success of his transformation of satire into a tool of analysis in *Tom Jones* and raises the problem that was Smollett's central concern—how the unmodified conventions of Juvenalian satire can be introduced in conjunction with this relatively subtle instrument. The characteristic effect of *Amelia* can, I think, be explained as a mixing of novelistic and Juvenalian conventions.

SMOLLETT:

THE SATIRIST AS A CHARACTER TYPE

In Smollett's novels satire itself is the main aim. The peculiarities that set off his novels from those of his contemporaries—his brutality and tastelessness (which is the obverse of his gusto), his formlessness, the unpleasantness of his protagonists, his personal attacks on contemporaries, and his leaning toward the exotic (homosexuality, mild madness, and Gothicism)—can all be explained if not justified in terms of satiric aim.[1] Satire may cohabit with sentimentality or melodrama in Smollett's novels, but even these are, I believe, directed by the satiric aim. Everything Smollett wrote demonstrates his concern with satire. He wrote formal verse satires in his youth and a formal prose satire in his maturity; he discusses *Roderick Random* and *Ferdinand Count Fathom* as satires in their prefaces; and the word appears with monotonous regularity in all his works—in his authorial commentary and in the speeches of his characters.

Smollett published his first novel, *Roderick Random,* in 1748, six years after Fielding's first response to the Richardsonian novel and a year before his second. Although *Random* superficially echoes details and situations from *Joseph Andrews,* Fielding tells almost nothing about the sort of work Smollett attempts. Smollett's own definition of the novel, in the preface to *Ferdinand Count Fathom,* is so conventional it suggests a lack of interest in the subject:

1. See, e.g., Wilbur Cross, *The Development of the English Novel* (1899; 1920 ed.), pp. 63–69, and Sir Walter Scott, "Prefatory Memoir," *The Novels of Tobias Smollett, M.D.,* in Ballantyne's Novelist's Library (London, Edinburgh, 1821), 2, xxxiv. Much that follows is based on my essay, "Satire in the Early Novels of Smollett," *Journal of English and Germanic Philology,* 59 (1960), 381–402.

A novel is a large diffused picture, comprehending the characters of life, disposed in different groups, and exhibited in various attitudes, for the purposes of an uniform plan, and general occurrence, to which every individual figure is subservient. But this plan cannot be executed with probability, or success, without a principal personage to attract the attention, unite the incidents, unwind the clue of the labyrinth, and at last close the scene, by virtue of his own importance. $(8, 3)^2$

In the preface to *Roderick Random*—which he described in a letter as "a satire upon mankind"[3]—he expresses accurately his theory of the relationship of satire to the novel:

Of all kinds of satire, there is none so entertaining and universally improving, as that which is introduced, as it were, occasionally, in the course of an interesting story, which brings every incident home to life; and, by representing familiar scenes in an uncommon and amusing point of view, invests them with all the graces of novelty, while nature is appealed to in every particular. (*1*, xxix)

Satire, Smollett says, is best and most effective when disguised as novelistic fiction; the realism of the story (as Dr. Johnson insisted) makes the moral lesson more convincing than in surroundings of fantasy. But satire also gives a special flavor to the novel, lifting its scenes out of the dullness of factual reporting. Thus satire is improved in the novel form, and the novel form is enlivened by satire.

Smollett, however, is presupposing a novel to begin with—the conventional picaresque narrative mentioned above. If Fielding tries to create a new genre with satire as one of his components, Smollett unashamedly attempts to write satire in the most conventional form of his time. His early novels show an interesting progression in the technique of a satirist who could (or would) no longer write in the forms of Pope and Swift. They reveal the problems the novel form,

2. My text (unless otherwise indicated) is *The Works of Tobias Smollett*, ed. G. H. Maynadier (12 vols. New York, Sully & Kleinteich, 1903).
3. Letter to Alexander Carlyle, December 1747, in "New Smollett Letters," *Times Literary Supplement*, July 24, 1943.

as transmitted by Defoe and Richardson as well as Cervantes and Le Sage, offered a writer who wished to write satire.

The Hero as Satirist: Roderick Random

For his model, Smollett tells us in the preface to *Roderick Random*, he has turned specifically to the picaresque of *Don Quixote* and *Gil Blas*. In some ways, as Robert Alter has recently shown, he is the closest writer in English to the original picaresque tradition of *Lazarillo de Tormes*.[4] He is careful, however, to distinguish between his own particular use of the picaresque and that of his models. Perhaps the most telling fact about Smollett is the self-consciousness, even pedantry, of his approach as a satirist. He rationalizes certain picaresque conventions in terms of their satiric usefulness and abandons others because they detract from the satiric design.

He explains the convention of the inexperienced orphan-outcast hero as providing an object so alone and exploitable as to bring out the best and worst in the people encountered along the road. The hero's "low estate," he points out, provides a milieu in which "the humours and passions are undisguised by affectations, ceremony, or education" (*1*, xxxiii). In this isolated system men are at their most elemental and are easiest to analyze. So far Smollett is explaining the practice of the Spanish novelists, emphasizing the types encountered rather than the protagonist. But a Lazarillo de Tormes or a Gil Blas acts as both a touchstone and a mirror: he is an ingénu who does not recognize the evil that surrounds him as he travels the road. Lazaro praises the vicious blind beggar who taught him how to steal and cheat, while the reader sees reflected the vicious world in which stealing and cheating are the only ways of survival. Gil Blas, recognizing vice, does not castigate Dr. Sangrado's amazing cure-all, phlebotomy and warm water, but becomes the doctor's assistant and administers it himself. Irony is, of course, an essential ingredient of this form, since the protagonist blithely involves himself in the object of the satire.

This kind of satire does not seem to have been congenial to Smollett. The first of the picaresque conventions he alters is the degree of perception allowed the protagonist. Roderick has first been "allowed

4. *Rogue's Progress*, pp. 58–79.

... the advantages of birth and education" and then disinherited and cast out, dropped into the "low estate" of the picaro with the superior education and understanding of a gentleman. At the end, again unlike the picaro, he resumes his high estate.[5] This superior status not only allows Roderick a detachment from his surroundings unheard of in the picaresque, but it destroys one of the most important characteristics of the picaresque, the service of masters. Being a gentleman, Roderick himself has a servant,[6] and he can engage only in certain employments. He is an apothecary's assistant (like Gil Blas) and a doctor on board a ship, but when he becomes a common footman it is only in order to disguise himself. Usually his servant Strap earns the money for both of them. Roderick is only vaguely concerned with the problem of survival or security; rather, he seeks adventure for its own sake,[7] a circumstance which allows Smollett a larger range for his satire than was available to his models.

The service of masters is accordingly replaced by a characteristic noticeably absent in most picaros—pride.[8] The "mortification of my pride," as Roderick calls it, produces a violent, unyielding reaction more common in a Spanish grandee than in a prudent Gil Blas who is able to overlook his pride in a tight spot. "After giving way for a few minutes to the dictates of my rage," Roderick writes again and again, or "My indignation was too high to admit one thought of fear."[9] He is thus braver, as well as wiser, than Gil Blas; the streak of cowardice (or suppleness) in picaros is shifted, along with the responsibility of earning money, to Roderick's servant Strap.

The second change Smollett makes is a corollary to the first; he ex-

---

5. In this respect, as in others (see below, pp. 189–90), Smollett follows the tendency of English picaros to draw upon Don Quixote. Tom Jones, however—to take another English example—is never aware of his high estate and so operates from a very different point of view than Roderick or Peregrine Pickle.

6. Smollett believed that Fielding had stolen Partridge from his Strap. Certainly Smollett preceded Fielding in the use of a protagonist who has his own servant, but in this respect both are following Cervantes, and both Partridge and Strap show their debt to Sancho. Gil Blas still follows the usual servant-master relationship of the continental picaresque. In spite of his rise in the world and his eventual maintenance of servants, he remains in the relationship of a servant to a master, however exalted the master.

7. As Eugène Joliat puts it, "Il aime l'action pour elle-même" (*Smollett et la France* [Paris, 1935], p. 42).

8. See ibid., p. 41.

9. *Works*, ed. Maynadier, Chaps. 7, 6, 41; *1*, 52, 44; *2*, 187.

plains that he has done without the "disgraces" Le Sage attached to his hero. A disgrace tends to "excite mirth" at the protagonist's expense and "prevents that generous indignation which ought to animate the reader against the sordid and vicious disposition of the world" (*1*, xxxii). This change means, for one thing, that when chamber pots are discharged they fall on Strap, not Roderick. But it also means that Roderick is ordinarily outside the object of satiric attack. Sir Walter Scott observed that Smollett lacks "the grave irony of Swift and Cervantes," as well as of Fielding, and this tells us much about the tone of *Roderick Random*.[10] Roderick is not a cunning Lazaro or Gil Blas or a mad Don Quixote; he is not himself part of the foolishness and knavery at which the satire aims. When he does finally become implicated, as in his search for a rich wife, Smollett seems to be making less a comment on him than on his surroundings, which have now reached such a nadir of degeneracy that all one can do is try to live by those standards. But still unwilling to blacken his hero, Smollett has Strap make clear that Roderick is not really an exploiter of women but only a man who will make the young lady happy whose wealth will make him happy.

Only occasionally, and in pathetic (never ridiculous) circumstances, does Roderick become a satiric touchstone. The most Fielding-like episode in the novel is Roderick's being tossed up on the English coast, penniless, wounded, and exhausted (like Joseph Andrews after his encounter with robbers). He is "bandied from door to door through a whole village, nobody having humanity enough to administer the least relief" to him, until "an old woman, who was suspected of witchcraft by the neighborhood" (cf. the postilion or Betty the chambermaid), takes him in (Chap. 28; 2, 162). This is not to say that Roderick escapes persecution. A more typical example is his account of his schooldays:

> I was often inhumanly scourged for crimes I did not commit; because, having the character of a vagabond in the village, every piece of mischief, whose author lay unknown, was charged upon me. I have been found guilty of robbing orchards I never entered, of killing cats I never hurted, of stealing gingerbread I never touched, and of abusing old women I never saw. Nay, a

10. Scott, "Prefatory Memoir," 2, xxxvii.

stammering carpenter had eloquence enough to persuade my master that I fired a pistol, loaded with small shot, into his window; though my landlady and the whole family bore witness that I was a-bed fast asleep at the time when this outrage was committed. I was once flogged for having narrowly escaped drowning, by the sinking of a ferry-boat in which I was passenger; another time for having recovered of a bruise occasioned by a horse and cart running over me; a third time for being bit by a baker's dog. In short, whether I was guilty or unfortunate, the correction and sympathy of this arbitrary pedagogue were the same. (Chap. 2; *1, 11*)

The density of the passage, the piling up of persecution upon persecution, as well as the disorder of the world itself, points to a more Juvenalian than picaresque convention. But the important distinction between this and similar passages of punishment in picaresque novels lies in what follows.[11] The picaro accepts such treatment or adjusts to it; Roderick's reaction is that of the Juvenalian satirist:

Far from being subdued by this infernal usage, my indignation triumphed over that slavish awe which had hitherto enforced my obedience; and the more my years and knowledge increased, the more I perceived the injustice and barbarity of his behaviour. (pp. 11–12)

And at length Roderick materializes his moral insight (as well as his desire for personal revenge) in a physical chastisement of the schoolmaster. Roderick functions in the same way when Captain O'Donnell ambushes him: "I received a blow on my head from an unseen hand, that stretched me senseless on the ground; and was left for dead, with three stabs of a sword in my body." But his reaction is immediate. He begins to seek "some method of revenge against Squire O'Donnell" and fixes "upon a scheme of revenge"; after car-

11. Robert Alter, in a recent critique of my thesis concerning the Smollettian hero as Juvenalian satirist, has pointed out this passage to show the large proportion of violence that is (in picaresque style) meted out to Roderick. I suggest that he has overlooked the significant fact that in almost every case the persecution of Roderick is followed by Roderick's violent, unpicaresque reaction. (See *Rogue's Progress,* pp. 63–64 ff.)

rying it out he takes pleasure in having "every day an opportunity of seeing my revenge protracted on the body of my adversary by the ulcers of which I had been the cause" (Chap. 20; *1*, 198, 200–03).

The world's treatment of Roderick is brutal enough, but Smollett uses it to isolate him as a moral agent and elicit satiric responses. The climax of Roderick's persecution and isolation comes on Captain Oakum's ship—in the complete autocracy of a ship at war in the middle of an ocean. Roderick is "loaded with irons, and stapled to the deck, on pretence that he was a spy"; "lying in this helpless situation, amidst the terrors of a sea-fight; expecting every moment to be cut asunder, or dashed in pieces by the enemy's shot," he is spattered with the brains of an officer whose head is carried off by a cannonball and covered with a drummer's entrails;

> I could contain myself no longer, but began to bellow with all the strength of my lungs . . . I vented my rage in oaths and execrations, till my spirits being quite exhausted, I remained quiet and insensible of the load that oppressed me. (Chap. 29; *2*, 81, 83–84)

The final symbol of his isolation is the "curious trial" in which he finds that he cannot even prove that the Greek in which he has kept his diary is Greek and not a subversive cypher. Like Umbricius, the last Roman remaining in Rome, Roderick is the last man who knows what the truth is—and so has no way of proving it. It is hard to imagine a clearer example of Juvenalian convention transferred into prose fiction.

Roderick is therefore not a fool (to some knavish master) or a passive touchstone but a satiric observer who recognizes, reacts, and rebukes. When he is turned out by the Potions, he represents Mrs. Potion "in the most ridiculous lights my satirical talents could invent" (he is constantly talking about his "satire" or "satirical talents"), and when he has exposed Squire Gawky's cowardice in a duel, he is not content until he has published an account of it (even selling a gold-laced hat to pay for the publication). Sometimes, confronted with folly, he rigs situations to expose fools like Captain Weasel, whose courage he puts to the test by pretending a highwayman is attacking his coach. When he is jilted by the snobbish Me-

linda, he warns other men by exposing her true colors with the help
of a barber disguised as a marquis. Even when, upon occasion, Roderick acts the fool and must be satirized, he does so himself. When he
returns to London with Strap's money and sets out to find a rich
wife, he says, "I was guilty of a thousand ridiculous coquetries," and
derides the "absurd behaviour" and "fooleries" in which he is engaged; he is looking back from the time of his writing on another
Roderick Random, from whom he has detached himself.[12]

Smollett's changes in the old picaresque conventions reveal a conscious movement toward an approximation of Roman formal verse
satire, particularly as practiced by the Elizabethan imitators of Juvenal and Persius. To this synthesis can be attributed the peculiarity
of Smollett's protagonist.[13] Besides the overflowing of rage, the characteristics of Roderick's satiric temperament that stand out from the
innumerable incidents in which they figure are the motive of revenge
and the physical nature of the punishment he metes out. It is remarkable that every time something is done to Roderick, his first reaction
is that he must revenge himself ("revenge" is one of the most frequently repeated words in the novel).[14] To expose his cruel schoolmaster, for example, young Roderick, with the help of his uncle
Bowling, rigs a trap and has him captured, stripped, and flogged. To
the jealous gigolo Captain O'Donnell, who has had Roderick am-
bushed and stabbed, he sends an invitation to an assignation with an
apothecary's wife (luring him by his vice); the lecherous captain of
course shows up, and Roderick and his friends "rushed upon him all

12. *Works*, ed. Maynadier, Chaps. 7, 12, 50, 45; *1*, 54, 110; *3*, 34–35; *2*, 234–35.
The device of looking back from the moment of composition upon one's earlier blun-
ders—thus being one's own ironist—is probably derived from *Gil Blas*, where it is
used with a much greater consistency and so with a more Fielding-like effect.

13. See Scott, "Prefatory Memoir," *2*, xxxiv. Commenting on Smollett's expressed
desire to keep Roderick an ideal, Joliat has said: "Son héros Roderick . . . n'a absolu-
ment rien de recommandable. Il est curieux que ce soit précisément ce personnage, que
Smollett [in his preface] avait voulu nous rendre sympathique, qui nous plaît le moins
dans son premier roman" (*Smollett et la France*, p. 36).

14. Lazarillo de Tormes does revenge himself once on the blind beggar, but only
incidental to his escape and on the spur of the moment. Revenge is a luxury to the
picaro. The revenge motif appears briefly but is not developed in the English criminal
biography, *Don Tomaso*, ed. Petersen (1680), pp. 200–01, 204–05. Brutal vengeance
is of course found in some early Spanish and Italian prose fiction, but without the
satiric emphasis; see the tale of a scholar's revenge in Boccaccio's *Decameron* (eighth
day, novella 7) and the flaying of Afranio in the *Jugement d'Amour* (cited by Reynier,
Le Roman réaliste au XVIIe siècle, p. 83).

at once, secured his sword, stripped off his clothes even to the skin, which [they] scourged with nettles till he was blistered from head to foot" (Chap. 20; *1*, 202).[15]

Why then, if Smollett desires to keep Roderick sympathetic (as he claims in his preface), does he give him these characteristics? The frequently expressed view that the brutality and unsympathetic nature of Smollett's protagonists can be explained by a correspondence between the author and his heroes cannot be accepted as more than a partial truth. Roderick undoubtedly draws upon the convention of punishment traced in picaresque literature. Smollett the physician doubtless found it convenient to employ the correspondence between physical and moral: a good whipping will strip off moral disguise; a blow on the head helps a fool to see his way; a chamber pot over the head reduces the victim's pride in his human reason. Roderick's schoolmaster, for example, is treated as he had treated his pupils, laid over a bench "and his bare posteriors heartily flogged with his own birch" (Chap. 5; *1, 31*). But while the moral-physical equation pervades all of Smollett's novels, a major difference remains in *Roderick Random*: Smollett has made the picaro the punisher rather than the punished; while this occasionally happens in the picaresque, the protagonist is either as bad as the person he punishes or, like Don Quixote, completely ineffectual. Roderick is good and effectual. Moreover, Roderick and Smollett point in another direction by using the vocabulary of the formal verse satirist.

Roderick's revenges are appropriate satiric punishments that usually involve one of the conventional weapons of the satirist. "Ile send abroad a Satir [satyr] with a scourge," writes the Jacobean satirist George Wither, "That to their shame for this abuse shall strip them, / And being naked in their vices, whip them."[16] Roderick clearly owes a great deal to the humorless, malcontent satirist of the Elizabethans who metaphorically beats, bastinadoes, bleeds, and purges his enemies; whose satire is always "Begot long since of Trueth and holy

---

15. Smollett later (*Peregrine Pickle*, in *Works*, ed. Maynadier, 6, 273) refers the term "practical satire" to this sort of thing. While, as Putney pointed out ("The Plan of Peregrine Pickle," *PMLA, 60* [1945], 1058), "this practical satire" is in the tradition of the rough-and-tumble scenes of *Don Quixote* and *Joseph Andrews,* there is the important difference that Roderick is the castigator, not one of the confused participants.

16. *Abuses Stript and Whipt* (1613), Sig. T7.

Rage," as Joseph Hall puts it; and who is usually the injured and betrayed. But like Roderick, and unlike the classical Juvenalian, the satyr-satirist is specifically motivated by either revenge or envy, although his satire is not less true for that:

> Enuie waits on my backe, Truth on my side:
> Enuie will be my Page, and Truth my Guide.[17]

If we look ahead a moment to *Peregrine Pickle,* we are told that Peregrine, having been gulled by lords and ministers,

> lived, therefore, incessantly exposed to all the pangs of envy and disquiet. When I say envy, I do not mean sordid passion, in consequence of which a man repines at his neighbour's success, howsoever deserved; but that self-tormenting indignation which is inspired by the prosperity of folly, ignorance, and vice. (Chap. 96; 7, 141)

One critic sees this as Smollett's tendency "to undervalue the merits of more successful men";[18] but what it is, in fact, is an exact statement of the satyr-satirist's view of the relation between envy, truth, and satire. What the malcontent satirist sacrifices in disinterestedness and personal intrepidity he gains in the extra force that his personal concern gives to his invective.

These characteristics, derived from the old erroneous derivation of "satire" from "satyr," were available to Smollett in the works of the Elizabethans and Jacobeans, in the works of Oldham (whose motive for satirizing the Jesuits is said to be revenge), and in the popular broadsides and ballads of his own time. Swift's promise of a revenge on Lord Allen which included dissection and display (in his *Epistle to Lord Carteret*) was certainly known to Smollett. He was probably aware of all of these sources, but like the Elizabethan satirist, he saw Juvenal as his master. Among his earliest published works was a pair of Juvenalian satires, "Advice" and "Reproof," which imitate the conventional self-defense of the satirist. Structur-

---

17. *Virgidemiae,* in *The Collected Poems of Joseph Hall,* ed. A. Davenport (Liverpool, Liverpool University Press, 1949), pp. 47, 11.
18. Putney, "Peregrine Pickle," p. 1058 n.

ally the "Reproof" follows Horace's first satire of the second book, but its tone is closer to the "Difficile est saturam non scribere" of Juvenal's first satire.[19] In this poem Smollett speaks through the conventional figure of the satirist who cannot restrain his anger; he explains that looking around him he sees "What vices flourish still, unprun'd by [him]" and cannot help applying his "scourge" and "the vigour of [his] chast'ning hand" to the offenders.[20]

This metaphor of scourging is made concrete in scenes in *Roderick Random* and runs through the metaphorical language of the novel in Roderick's references to "the lash of my resentment" (Chap. 6; *1, 39*). Most of Roderick's peculiarities are explicable if we assume that Smollett has simply, in his academic manner, transferred the figure of the satyr-satirist from "Advice" and "Reproof" to his novel. His motive was probably double—to find an expression for his own particular view of satire and, by the satirist's conventionality, to shift his emphasis further onto the vice satirized. The result, far from being simply a projection of Smollett himself, is an extremely conventional figure.[21]

But if Smollett's particular version of the Juvenalian conventions came to him filtered through the Elizabethan satirists, his general notion that these had a place in the novel followed from one strain of the picaresque. Le Sage's *Diable boiteux* (1707) tells where Smollett got his "large diffused picture, comprehending the characters of life." In the run-of-the-mill narrative satires of the seventeenth and eighteenth centuries, the Picaresque relationship between two people dwindled to the relationship between an eye and an object. A decided shift of emphasis took place from the master-servant relation to the master or (since the master as such tended to disappear) the character, object, scene, or place observed. As a relatively uninvolved observer, the picaro could assume any tone from urbane Horatian to savage, sarcastic Juvenalian, from ingénu to *vir bonus* and heroic de-

---

19. The two epigraphs, from Juvenal's second and thirteenth satires, bespeak a more than nodding acquaintance with Juvenal. Peregrine Pickle also "produced an imitation of Juvenal, and lashed some conspicuous characters, with equal truth, spirit, and severity" (Chap. 93; *7,* 104).

20. *The Works of Tobias Smollett,* ed. George Saintsbury (12 vols. Westminster and New York, 1899–1900), *12,* 18.

21. Even Smollett's thrashing of Peter Gordon can be regarded as merely an extension of satiric conventions in the same way that Pope's administering a purge to Curll was. By 1753, when he beat Gordon, the ethos had long been established.

fender of the faith. For variety a traveler, an animal, or even an inanimate object like a coin passing from pocket to pocket could present a series of more or less vivid satirically perceived scenes. The satirist's skill went undivided into the tableaux that were framed. Recognizing the convenience and flexibility of the picaresque form, satirists tended to overemphasize its satiric lines, turning it into a close approximation of formal verse satire. When the observer was thematically appropriate, as when a coin holds together a series of scenes portraying greed, the result was very close to a satire of Horace or Juvenal or, more likely, one of their Elizabethan imitators.

Le Sage's *Diable boiteux* was a typical and influential example of the picaresque transformed into an imitation of a formal satire. Asmodée, the spirit of passion (when not disguised as Cupid, he is an ugly and crippled dwarf), is the string upon which the scenes and incidents are hung. He guides the neutral narrator through Madrid, showing him the sights, appropriately illustrating various kinds of passion—for gold, for one's youthful appearance and desirableness, and so on. He offers his biting commentary on all that he shows. As Asmodée takes the narrator to visit prisons, madhouses, and cemeteries, Le Sage explores the possibilities of punishment, madness, and death as satiric structures in the Lucianic manner.

Similarly, as the reader follows Roderick Random's travels, he is given the gamut of satire on schools, country life, travel, low-life in London, service in the navy, village life, war in Germany, high-life in London and Bath, and prison life in the Marshalsea. Smollett's unifying theme, as he phrases it in the preface, is "the selfishness, envy, malice, and base indifference of mankind" (*1, xxxii*)—surely general enough to cover almost anything he might decide to introduce in his novel. All of the characters Roderick encounters either exhibit a self-centeredness that extends from indifference to willingness to exploit others or, like Roderick's uncle Bowling, his servant Strap, and his love Narcissa, exhibit just the opposite, acting as proper norms of behavior. Very simply, Smollett presents a long series of bad examples, vaguely linked to a single broad sin, to be judged against a scattering of good examples. Even his digressions are merely explorations of some further aspect of the central vice. Thus a prison in a Smollett novel is not so much a plot-link as a place in which as many representative satiric types as possible can be brought together. Particularly in *Peregrine Pickle, Ferdinand Count Fathom,* and *Sir Launcelot Greaves* the prison becomes a "microcosm" (the word appears in all three novels) of the real world, with its own laws and justice, vices and virtues, and, for that matter, plot. Smollett offers a Cook's Tour of English jails: Roderick is thrown into the Marshalsea, Peregrine into the Fleet, Fathom into the King's Bench, Greaves into Justice Gobble's jail (though the prison device here is fulfilled by the King's Bench Prison he tours and the madhouse in which he is confined near the end of the book), and Humphry Clinker spends some time in Clerkenwell Prison. Prison becomes a metaphor for society, and criminals are exaggerated tendencies of "honest" men;[22] the other Smollett trademarks, the coach-ride, the inn, and the "college," serve the same purpose.

On a smaller scale, the satiric portraits of grotesques like Lavement or the usurer, whose "whole figure was a just emblem of winter, famine, and avarice," become frames for satiric commentaries on their equivalents in the great world (Chap. 11; *1,* 95). The apothecary Lavement (whose name was the French euphemism of the time for enema) is described as a combination of snake, fawning simian, and dog and sounds very much like one of Nashe's emblematic portraits in *The Unfortunate Traveller;* he is never seen so vividly again, nor does he ever do anything to justify so striking a description. Such microcosms and set-pieces are too discrete to merge completely with the surrounding material of the novel, and they illustrate rather than advance the novel's theme.

Fielding's picaresque, with the mediation of Augustan ideals of unity and economy, gives the impression of being single-minded, a straight line in which intensity of gaze makes up for variety. Every detail or encounter contributes to the development of an argument concerning the relationship between greatness and goodness or form and feeling; the narrator's gravely ironic stance makes the reader aware at every step of an author standing between him and the material, preventing any irrelevant information from reaching him. Smol-

---

22. The only time that Fielding approaches such a structure is in the early chapters of *Amelia,* and he may have been consciously or unconsciously falling in line with the same conventions used by Smollett. *Le Diable boiteux* offers the best parallel to Smollett's transformation of scenes into satiric microcosms.

lett's picaresque goes to the other extreme; where the movement of Fielding's satire is centripetal, Smollett's is centrifugal, away from the hero and toward a general exploration. Moreover, the central "I" who is seeing, being acted upon, and reacting produces a heightened reality that goes far beyond the portraits of a Slipslop or Mrs. Towwouse. He appears to be in the very middle of the chaotic action, describing what it feels like, while Fielding's normative and controlling narrator is on the periphery. Roderick is in this respect more closely related to the letter-writing Pamela than to Joseph Andrews. As with Pamela's frightened description of the monstrous Jewkes and Colbrand, everything Roderick sees appears to be distorted by his point of view, and to the extent that the reader accepts these monsters, he becomes immersed in Roderick's experience. With Smollett's lack of detachment—his first-person speaker, whose nightmare observations can be taken partly as a reflection of his indignation—comes a much greater sense of immediacy, or sensuous contact, almost totally lacking in Fielding's novels and much closer to the effect of the Richardsonian novel.

In either kind of novel, however, realistic assumptions relate that clash with unmodified satiric conventions. Smollett's miscalculation in *Roderick Random* is dropping a poetic convention—or perhaps, better, an incompletely transformed one—into the realistic world of the post-Richardsonian novel. As Scott pointed out, a scene like the flogging of the schoolmaster seems wanton and cruel in its context;[23] to see it in a true perspective it is necessary to remember the conventions of formal verse satire and imagine the scene in a discursive rather than a dramatic frame. The railing of a persona becomes something quite different when it is materialized in a concrete act of revenge. Roderick's attributes (pride, vengefulness, envy)—quite acceptable in formal verse satire where an author is always evident behind the convention and the strings of his manipulation—become character traits that have to be accounted for in the novel, whose conventions of realistic presentation and a search into motives Smollett has slipped into.

Smollett does not judge Roderick as a character immersed in an action but as an observer and satirist separate from that action. The reader, however, will not allow the observer and the observed an ex-

23. "Prefatory Memoir," p. xxxiv.

istence as separate as Smollett requires. His natural tendency to read *Roderick Random* as a story of the observer is increased by the piquant complexity of Roderick's character, and therefore much of the observed appears to be excessive and irrelevant, and much of the observer appears to remain unexplained. Roderick's thoughts are usually "engrossed," as he says, "by the knavery of the world, to which I must be daily exposed; and the contemplation of my finances, which began seriously to diminish" (Chap. 11; *1, 90*). The reader is constantly presented with this mixture of the general and the personal but with no indication that Smollett intends two conflicting areas of experience. Moreover, if there is a definite impression of disunity (a better word perhaps than formlessness) about his novel, it can be attributed at least partly to the mixture of the two conflicting forms, satire and novel, an anticipation of Fielding's difficulties in *Amelia*, here taking the form of a split between the themes of the observer and the observed.

In retrospect, we can see the importance of Roderick as a character for one strain of the novel. Satire's signal contributon to the novel is the militant search for reality under deceptive appearances. Smollett —like Fielding, Goldsmith, or almost any novelist writing after 1740 —demonstrates the need to see beneath worldly contrivances and so fills his novels with imagery of disguise, but he stands apart from them in his emphasis. While Fielding, for example, is concerned with the wiles of vanity or hypocrisy (with the satiric object, so to speak, as masquerader), Smollett is groping toward a concern with the problem of knowledge. As essentially a writer of travesty, he focuses on the unadorned evil that is exposed rather than on its modes of deception; on the process of getting at it rather than the question of the degree of guilt; and on the effect the evil has on the satirist's rather than on the villain's state of mind.

Any development shown in Roderick is almost entirely in terms of his reactions and follows two lines—that of learning to recognize snares or hidden wickedness, and that of learning to control his reactions. His education brings him satiric knowledge, beginning with his persecution at school, which opens his eyes to injustice and barbarity under the disguise of authority; the squalor he suffers in Potion's house once his uncle Bowling's money is no longer forthcoming has the same effect: "my misfortunes had taught me how little the caresses of the world, during a man's prosperity, are to be valued by him" (Chap. 7; *1*, 54–55). Roderick's early encounters with evil, leading up to his arrival in London, involve self-interest under disguises and are presented in a series of small Fielding-like satires of words contrasted with deeds. Roderick's cousins feign sorrow as their grandfather dies but reveal real anger when they hear his will read; the innkeeper tries to look like a schoolmaster but reveals his true soul in his outrageous bill; Captain Weasel, who sounds and acts like a giant when he is invisible inside the coach, turns out to be tiny and cowardly when he emerges; even the nobleman, who tries to look brave by pursuing the highwayman Rifle, is reining in his horse so that he cannot possibly overtake him.[24] The conventionality of these incidents is somewhat mitigated, however, by the fact that Roderick learns from them to see better and, concomitantly, begins to expose follies to the sight of others. Perception or observation means for Roderick stripping away an appearance, or even rigging a situation that will make the person expose himself in his true colors, and finally punishing the culprit, a method which traditionally served in the picaresque as a way of observing the *real* man. Roderick is simply what he appears to be—what in *Humphry Clinker* Smollett will call an "original"; and his efforts are aimed toward setting things right, making other people be what they are.

The Fielding protagonist is always either a touchstone or an object that must be judged and corrected. In Smollett's fiction the protagonist begins as an observer, the role that Fielding keeps to his narrator outside the action, and never entirely loses this role or the resulting theme.

Satire as Theme: Peregrine Pickle

In his next novel, *Peregrine Pickle* (1751), Smollett shows that he has come to realize the problem inherent in his mixing of conventions, and, starting with much the same protagonist as *Roderick Ran-*

24. In a few places Smollett even slips into repetitions. For example, the business of the cowardly Captain Wessel and the false alarm of a highwayman that Roderick sounds in order to expose him is repeated in volume three: there is a captain in both cases, a coachride, a lady to be impressed, and highwaymen (though in the latter case they are real and not a part of Roderick's plan). See *Works*, ed. Maynadier, Chaps. 12, 54; *1*, 110; *3*, 83. These repetitions appear to have no function.

dom, he seeks to follow his singular characteristics through to their logical consequences. The result is, in one sense, less a satire than a novel about satire. Second, feeling that he must control this protagonist, Smollett has changed from a first-person to a third-person narrative, a mode to which he holds until his final novel. There is, accordingly, a court of appeal above and beyond Peregrine Pickle, the satirist within the novel.

While Roderick is a satirist to the extent that he pays back the enemies who have gulled him, Peregrine goes much further: he rigs practical jokes on people who have not even harmed him in order to reveal their foolishness or knavery.[25] Like Roderick he has a "satirical disposition," but in this novel such phrases are tied more closely to the plot. Before he is one year old his satiric bent is revealed: he pretends to be in pain so that when everyone comes running in answer to his cries he can "lie sprawling and laughing in their faces, as if he ridiculed the impertinence of their concern" (Chap. 11; *4,* 89). What establishes his pranks as satires is their aim to punish the victim's particular folly. The pranks Peregrine and Hatchway play on Commodore Trunnion are directed at his hatred of his kinsmen, his hatred of attorneys, and his belief in goblins (foibles enumerated by the innkeeper when we first meet Trunnion). But to a greater extent than in *Roderick Random* our attention is drawn to the punishment. When Peregrine punishes Trunnion for his pose of "Hannibal Tough" by stepping on his gouty toe, pain, not vice or folly, is revealed; and when Peregrine, having been gently caned, falls to the floor as if dead, Trunnion's anguish only serves to reveal a gentle heart. The potion Perry satirically substitutes for Mrs. Trunnion's spirits only serves to nearly kill the good woman. The effect of such emphases is to make Peregrine a most unlovable hero.

Our attention is also drawn from the vice to Peregrine's ingenuity as he sets up satiric scenes. When he learns that the painter Pallet is angry with his companion the Doctor, Perry

> resolved to *encourage* these sentiments of disgust, and occasionally *foment* the division to a downright quarrel, which he foresaw would *produce some diversion,* and perhaps *expose* the poet's

25. The revenge motif is not, however, lost; whenever he is gulled Peregrine's first thought is of revenge.

[i.e. the Doctor's] character in such a light as would effectually *punish* him for his arrogance and barbarity. (Chap. 48; 5, 119; italics mine)

Throughout the novel the reader is told that he "seized all opportunities of observing new characters," and the vocabulary associated with him is rich with "punish," "expose," "ridicule," "seek diversion," and "satirize." By telling Pallet, who is in prison for masquerading as a woman, that he is to be made *in fact* a woman ("reduced to the neuter gender"), he not only enjoys the ridiculous Pallet hopping about his cell in terror, but also produces a satire on the gullible, stupid, and terror-stircken painter and on castrato sopranos, wives, the English, and so on.

Smollett shows Peregrine's satiric inclination as, first, a sign of a superiority which leads him to set himself up as an impersonal nemesis. In the second stage, forced to defend himself against the enmity of his brother Gam and the curate Sackbut, Peregrine justifies his punishments of the unfortunate Sackbut on the moral grounds of the satirist punishing vice. Then, when brought into contact with the sophistication of high society and the continent, his satiric bent becomes a ruthless pride that preys upon the fools and simple souls around him for his amusement or worse.

On Peregrine's grand tour his satiric pranks are juxtaposed with the darker studies of his attacks on the virtue of Mrs. Hornbeck and Amanda, as his satire becomes an increasingly personal weapon. He seduces Mrs. Hornbeck, he believes, in order to punish her husband for keeping her locked up; then, the second time he makes off with her and Hornbeck comes after him for revenge, this solipsistic satirist debates whether to punish the cuckold:

but when he considered that Hornbeck was not the aggressor, and made that unhappy husband's case his own, he could not help acquitting his intention of revenge, though, in his opinion, it ought to have been executed *in a more honourable manner;* and *therefore* he determined to chastise him for his want of spirit. (Chap. 60; 5, 219; italics mine)

And so he captures and ducks poor Hornbeck. His satire, no longer disinterested, has become a rationale for vice and profligacy. He horsewhips Pallet, whose bungling schemes unintentionally kept him from indulging his lust on an innocent girl, and then tells Pallet "he had richly deserved the punishment he had undergone, for his madness, folly and impertinence" (Chap. 57; 5, 190). In this light Peregrine's attempt on the virtue of his beloved Emilia appears as merely another example of the relationship he has set up between himself and the objects of his satiric contemplation. The remainder of the novel, then, is spent curing him of his folly.[26]

The connection between solipsistic satire and the exploitation of other people is shown in the first half of *Peregrine Pickle*—the same theme as in *Roderick Random* but presented more originally and forcefully; in the second half, with the death of Old Trunnion, Cadwallader Crabtree makes his appearance, pointing up the totally nihilistic side of such satire. the negation to which unrelieved misanthropy must lead. Crabtree, who perhaps derives to some extent from that morose practical joker La Rancune in the *Roman comique,* is both an exploration of some of the possibilities in the role of satirist and an ingenious solution to the ideal functioning of a fictional satirist. He has knocked about the world for a long lifetime, attacking every evil he saw and landing in galleys and prisons, including those of the Spanish Inquisition. He has finally hit upon the perfect medium for his savage indignation: he pretends to be deaf as a stone, "an expedient," he explains, "by which I not only avoid all disputes and their consequences, but also become master of a thousand little secrets, which are every day whispered in my presence, without any suspicion of their being overheard" (Chap. 72; 6, 17). We can almost feel the author's sigh of admiration as he writes of a satirist who can ferret out evil and castigate it to its face without endangering his own person or curbing his own satisfaction.

While Crabtree is an ideal satirist, he is also a satirist who has divested himself of his human nature in his monomaniacal pursuit. He makes his first appearance just a few pages before Peregrine's attack on Emilia, more or less setting the stage with his memory of the spiders he studied while a prisoner in the Bastille:

Although I presided with absolute power over this long-legged community, and distributed rewards and punishments to each,

---

26. Peregrine's moral development, which I only sketch briefly here, has been well traced by Putney ("Peregrine Pickle").

according to his deserts, I grew impatient of my situation; and my natural disposition one day prevailing, like a fire which had long been smothered, I wreaked the fury of my indignation upon my innocent subjects, and in a twinkling destroyed the whole race. (Chap. 72; 6, 13).

He has fulfilled, in his cell in the Bastille, the satirist's dream of "absolute power" over his community, where he can "distribute rewards and punishments"; but he is dissatisfied with this too—he must rail to live—and so he destroys his kingdom. When he turns the light of his satire on Peregrine, the protagonist is made to see that Crabtree's misanthropic satire is "not so much incensed against the follies and vices of mankind, as delighted with the distress of his fellow-creatures," and that "detaching yourself from the bounds of society, and . . . moving in a superior sphere of your own" simply leaves you alone and unprotected (Chaps. 90, 91; 7, 79–80, 90). Through Crabtree Peregrine learns that too great a detachment is an absence of love; he must be able to love his fellowmen—thus subordinating himself—before he can gain Emilia.

In Peregrine, who progresses from a satirist making fun of foolish people to a monster exploiting simple people, Smollett has recognized and utilized the essential self-centeredness of the Juvenalian satirist. The satirist has become a protagonist, and the form of the anatomy has been subordinated to a more complex plot in which he registers a moral development—as opposed to the merely perceptual development of Roderick Random.

Why then is *Peregrine Pickle* still as a whole (and in spite of brilliant parts) an unsatisfactory performance? One pertinent answer is that every time Peregrine punishes a person, however unjust his motive, his satiric analysis of that person is true: Hornbeck *is* a Pynchwife and Pallet *is* a meddling fool; whatever one may think of Peregrine as a man (and Smollett is of course making this distinction), he is telling the truth as a satirist. As the Juvenalian satirist explains: "Enuie waits on my backe, Truth on my side." A second answer is also implicit in the ambiguous characterization of Crabtree —first, in Smollett's admiration for Crabtree as an ideal satirist, and, second, in his concern with the moral implications of Crabtree's satire. The situation, which is similar to Swift's in the fourth voyage of

Gulliver's Travels, is caused by mixing novelistic character and satiric device, where the character has to carry at once a private and public meaning.

Throughout the novel, the episodes that illustrate Peregrine's character and those that reveal the sins of society fail to coalesce. On the one hand, there is a conventional satiric structure—a satirist using various devices to reveal the corruptions around him. The reader moves, as he did in *Roderick Random,* through satires of school, university, grand tour, dueling, high society, and the rest; and Crabtree and Peregrine demonstrate other devices such as the old one of the parade of fools in their fortune-telling masquerade. On the other hand, there is the story of Peregrine's pride and detachment from humanity, and the incidents above, which stand on their own as satiric scenes, also become illustrations of Peregrine's misanthropy and coldness. The curious result is a satire which at the same time examines the nature of satire, one in which the reader never can be sure whether a particular satiric episode is to be accepted as true or as a reflection on the satirist himself. It is questionable, finally, whether the themes of Peregrine's satire and of his moral decline ever come together. For example, the episodic nature of the novel destroys any real sense of Peregrine's atonement for his behavior to Emilia. He says he regrets it, and then nearly a volume follows (other flirtations, the "Memoirs of a Lady of Quality," and some satiric pranks) before he encounters Emilia again. There is no indication that he has thought of her in the interval, and so the point is lost that this attempted seduction was an important event for which he has to atone.

One might argue that it was a mistake for Smollett to move further away from the static satiric structure he apparently desired. As Rufus Putney has observed, Smollett can build a sound, consistent structure, but not one that grows to the dramatic climaxes expected in a novel;[27] after the performance of *Peregrine Pickle* one can conclude that Smollett's forte is not the narrative of character development but satiric contemplation—the slow walk around an object, through which its various facets are exposed—a process which is essentially static and expository. He can produce brilliant portraits and tableaux, even prolonged scenes of action, but they do not lead anywhere. The satirist (Juvenal is again a good example) creates powerful individ-

27. Ibid., p. 1063.

ual scenes or situations, but his climax is always arrived at by juxta-posing these scenes and is cumulative rather than culminative.

Smollett's problem is how to find some sort of satisfactory balance between the satirist and his satire, between the observer and the ob-served, so that the vice he is anatomizing will be the center of focus. In *Roderick Random* the Juvenalian satirist, whose idiosyncrasies are not explained, excites too much interest in himself and draws the reader away from the object of attack. In *Peregrine Pickle* Smollett carries out the implications of these idiosyncrasies, and the story is *about* the observer. But, perhaps because Smollett wants to have his cake and eat it too, the observed maintains a disturbing—and distract-ing—existence of its own. The result is a plot and a satiric anatomy running side-by-side and almost equal in emphasis. The importance of *Peregrine Pickle* in Smollett's development is its discovery of the satiric theme; Smollett's problem has led him to search into the na-ture of the satirist and his function, into the difference between the satirist and the ordinary human being.

The Search for a Satirist

After *Peregrine Pickle* each of Smollett's novels is to some extent a search for a satirist, an exploration into the function and meaning of the satirist, just as each contains a solution of some kind to the problem of a satiric form. Roderick, Peregrine, and Crabtree offer three solutions to the problem of the satirist and his function: begin-ning his career with a mechanical adaptation, Smollett ends with a rather searching inquiry into the nature of satire in relation to the individual who practices it. Peregrine and Crabtree are useful sati-rists (in the sense that their attacks are "true"), but before they can be useful human beings as well, they have to be cured of their mis-anthropy. The distinction between man and satirist, private and pub-lic roles, runs through the rest of Smollett's fiction, receiving its defin-itive treatment in his last novel, *Humphry Clinker*.

This distinction arose, one suspects, as part of Smollett's attempt to square his Juvenalian satirist first with the current doctrine (Steele, *Tatler*, No. 242) that satire, and so the satirist, must be good-natured, and second with the picaresque form. His solution is related to the Jonsonian one, the theory of humoring and dehumoring. Both Ben

Jonson and Smollett recognized that satirizing is not the normal state of man and has to be explained. Smollett requires Peregrine to be cured of his pride and misanthropy, as Jonson did his malcontent satirists, when there is no longer any need for the envy and dissatisfaction that brought them into being. The return of his money, the timely inheritance of his estate, the love of Emilia, and revenge on his old enemies free Peregrine from the need for misanthropy; under Emilia's loving smile even Crabtree has become cheerful as the book ends.

There are also suggestions of dehumoring in the case of Roderick. All the important characters along the way gravitate back to the hero at the end; the evils have been repaid—Captain Oakum is dead and the loathsome Mackshane is in prison; the good have been rewarded —Morgan with a rich wife, Bowling with success, Roderick with father, wife, and fortune. There is no further need for revenge: "The impetuous transports of my passion are now settled and mellowed into endearing fondness and tranquility of love" (Chap. 69; 3, 260). It is clear that the satiric function is a sort of mask, assumed when the hero is dispossessed and discarded when his estate is returned to him, for both Roderick and Peregrine have streaks of good nature in them, invariably of a sentimental or benevolent kind; opposed to Roderick's passionate rages are his "sympathy and compassion" for the unfortunate and his "tender passion" for the good, and Peregrine's generosity, compassion, good nature, and "natural benevolence" are insisted on from time to time. By making misanthropy a mask for a tender heart Smollett suggests the idea that one is not simply a satirist but a man who is for a time forced into the role by intolerable circumstance.

This seems to be a general idea behind the character of Ferdinand Fathom, who is the malcontent satirist carried to its furthest implication. In his preface to *Ferdinand Count Fathom* (1753), Smollett says that Fathom is himself the evil that is being exposed; but running just below the novel's surface is a recognition of (or an unwillingness to pass up) the connection between the satirist and the criminal: both exploit and punish the folly of mankind. Take for example the seduction of Celinda. "Perhaps such a brutal design might not have entered his imagination," the reader is told, if Fathom had not noticed "certain peculiarities":

> Besides a total want of experience, that left her open and un-
> guarded against the attacks of the other sex, she discovered a
> remarkable spirit of credulity and superstitious fear . . . so deli-
> cate was the texture of her nerves, that one day, while Fathom
> entertained the company with a favourite air, she actually
> swooned with pleasure. (Chap. 34; 8, 274–75)

With aeolian harps and old wives' tales Fathom seduces Celinda; in
sections like this it is problematic whether the satire is more on
Fathom's viciousness or on Celinda's folly. In his commentary on the
episode, Smollett shifts his authorial emphasis from the victim's gullibility to Fathom's evil.[28] But one wonders whether by pointing out
that Celinda thereafter "grew every day more sensual and degenerate," ending in a life on the streets, Smollett is not presenting both the
evil example of Fathom and the punishment Celinda deserves for her
romantic illusions.

Fathom is to some extent that traditional figure of the English
picaresque, the criminal who unwittingly serves to reveal the folly of
his dupes as well as his own knavery. An example is his cheating of
Don Diego de Zelos, who reveals in his discourse to Fathom a great
fund of pride, vanity, and intolerance, as well as a tempting overconfidence in his own judgment. As if enough functions had not
been heaped upon him, Fathom is also one of the dupes, more often
than not gulled by the party he intended to gull.[29] Finally, he has
maintained all along an "ingredient in his constitution" which,
though not exactly a tincture of goodness, will ultimately "counteract
his consummate craft, defeat the villainy of his intention"; thus, like
Smollett's other satiric figures, he is permitted to return to a normal
life at the end—this time by repentance (Chap. 43; 9, 37).[30]

28. For other examples of the author's overemphasis of evil in his hero's actions, see
Works, ed. Maynadier, Chaps. 42, 49; 9, 32, 107–08.

29. The possibilities of the criminal as satiric observer were glimpsed near the beginning of *Roderick Random,* where the highwayman Rifle recounts his latest robbery:
"I likewise found ten Portugal pieces in the shoes of a Quaker, whom the spirit moved
to revile me with great bitterness and devotion" (Chap. 8; *1,* 65). The source of this
episode, incidentally, is probably the robbery in *Joseph Andrews* in which the highwayman reveals the prudish lady's secret penchant for alcohol (Bk. I, Chap. 12). Smollett
explored the possibilities of the confidence man as satirist in *Peregrine Pickle* in the
fortune-telling hoax set up by Peregrine and Crabtree and in the figure of Peregrine
himself.

30. This sentimental use of the tincture of goodness, ending in regeneration, should
be contrasted with Fielding's use of Wild's "weaknesses."

In Smollett's next novel, *Sir Launcelot Greaves* (1760–61), he uses the favorite solution of the Elizabethan dramatists who wanted to give their heroes license to rail—madness. Madness as a mask is very different from madness as a commentary on the protagonist. The essential difference between Sir Launcelot and Don Quixote, his prototype, is that Quixote goes out to attack imaginary wrongs while the real world of less spectacular but more dangerous wrongs lies all about him; Sir Launcelot attacks real wrongs which in his (and Smollett's) world cannot be cured in any way other than by the intervention of a madman. Sir Launcelot contrasts himself with Quixote: "I see and distinguish objects as they are discerned and described by other men. . . . I quarrel with none but the foes of virtue and decorum" (Chap. 2; *10, 19*). "It was his opinion," we are told, "that chivalry was an useful institution while confined to its original purposes of protecting the innocent, assisting the friendless, and bringing the guilty to condign punishment" (Chap. 18; *10, 245–46*). Smollett here proves the integrity of his satirist without concealing the fact of his madness—having his "truth" as well as his rage. Sir Launcelot is forced to revert to an older, nobler code by the sorrow he feels at losing his beloved Aurelia and the outrage he feels at her guardian's conduct; all combine to unhinge his mind and turn him into a foe of all injustice.

Unlike Quixote, he is not allowed to be mocked, however eccentric his appearance and actions; for that there is his Sancho Panza, Crabshaw (as there was Strap in *Roderick Random*). When Sir Launcelot finds himself among the unregenerate, he simply lays about him with his lance and disperses them. Confronting Justice Gobble, he is able to cow the ex-tailor and his wife by producing his name and rank. Like Peregrine and Crabtree, he fancies himself a higher justice. When all the prisoners flock around him "in accusation of Justice Gobble," he is reminded of the "more awful occasion, when the cries of the widow and the orphan, the injured and oppressed, would be uttered at the tribunal of an unerring Judge against the villainous and insolent authors of their calamity" (Chap. 11; *10, 140*).[31] In short, he thinks of himself as God's right hand, and with madness as

31. In this respect he is related to the Quixote who claims he "was born, by Heaven's will, in this our age of iron, to revive what is known as the Golden Age" (Cervantes, *Don Quixote*, trans. Putnam, *1*, 146). Cf. Samuel Butler's observation, "A Satyr is a Kinde of Knight Errant," etc. (*Characters*, ed. A. R. Waller [Cambridge, Cambridge University Press, 1908], p. 469).

a mask Smollett can accept him as such without having to postulate a set of psychological traits like Peregrine's to explain him. At the end, when order has been restored and Aurelia is safe, Greaves returns to his normal pursuits. Having put off his armor, he appears at his wedding in "a white coat and blue satin vest" (Chap. "The Last"; *10, 339*).

From the radical metaphor of this novel it appears that satire to Smollett is a vocation or a quest, and for eighteenth-century Englishmen like Greaves it must be a throwback of some sort to an earlier, simpler, or more sensible world. It is not an entirely admirable occupation, and even Greaves learns that recourse to law is the only answer. And so the pattern established in *Peregrine Pickle* is followed in the subsequent novels, although the satirists themselves represent different areas of exploration and experiment. They have in common a dislocation of some sort—whether a criminal mind like Fathom's or a sort of madness like Greaves', and they use these infirmities (Fathom unconsciously, Greaves consciously) to reveal the hidden corruption around them; finally, in one way or another, they are returned to a normal equilibrium when the satiric role is no longer required. One can distinguish between Smollett's treatment of the cause of the humor and his treatment of the humor itself. He early sensed what causes would be acceptable (loss of estate, loss of Aurelia), but two sorts of humor were available to him, an internal and an external one. It could be internal like rage, which is peculiarly individual and needs explaining; or it could be external like madness or sickness, which is beyond the individual's control and responsibility. The latter, which most clearly delimits the areas of the observer and the observed, as well as private and public experience, will be the method of Smollett's final works.

The Sick Satirist

Smollett returns in his last work to the connection between satire and abnormality established in *Sir Launcelot Greaves,* exploring its possibilities, both technical and moral. The satiric observers of his *Travels Through France and Italy* (1766) and *History and Adventures of an Atom* (1769) act as a bridge between the demented Greaves and the physically ill Matthew Bramble of *Humphry Clinker* (1771).

In the *Travels,* Smollett sees his journey in terms of the conventions of Juvenalian satire. His departure is the prototypical exile of the Juvenalian idealist, and this "Smollett" coincidentally has all the characteristics of the figure: he rails, threatens to cane rogues, and smells out evil beneath the fairest disguises. He is driven to travel the road of moral censure like the Juvenalian, first, by personal defeat (he is "traduced by malice, persecuted by faction, abandoned by false patrons, and overwhelmed by the sense of a domestic calamity"); second, by the general situation in England ("a scene of illiberal dispute, and incredible infatuation, where a few worthless incendiaries had, by dint of perfidious calumnies and atrocious abuse, kindled up a flame which threatened all the horrors of civil dissension"); and, third—the original touch that sets him off from the conventional Juvenalian—by the poorness of his health (he hopes "the mildness of the climate" in southern France will "prove favorable to the weak state of [his] lungs").[32] Although all of these motives for travel have their foundation in biographical fact, I suspect that Smollett sensed the connection between his own illness and his travels and Sir Launcelot Greaves' madness and his quest. The sick Smollett looking for health becomes the satirist seeking a place in which he can morally survive, and the sickness itself gradually develops into a satiric metaphor of man's condition.

Smollett's frail health and his background as a physician make up a central fact of his point of view. The chicanery and selfishness of the people who meet the friendless traveler are translated into the physical effect they have on him. The roguery of a ship's captain is dramatized by the effect on a delicate man of being put into a rough sea in an open boat and then having to walk a mile to an inn; the roguery of an innkeeper, by the effect of poor diet or of having to sit up in a cold kitchen until a bed is emptied in the morning. It is always the physical that Smollett attacks—inns, sanitation, even the white sand used on the paths of Versailles which hurts his eyes by the

32. *Travels* (London, 1766), *1,* 1–2. Smollett's complaints do, of course, like the journey itself, have a basis in facts: his work for the Bute ministry involved him in attacks and counterattacks, and his only child Elizabeth died in April 1763. When he reaches the general situation of England, however, he may be indulging in the pathetic fallacy. In spite of what he says about England as he sets out, his homeland remains a standard by which he judges the other countries he visits; every unsatisfactory place is "inconvenient, unpleasant, and unhealthy," and when he returns to England at the end he praises it as "the land of liberty, cleanliness, and convenience" (*1,* 33; *2,* 254).

reflection of the sun. The physical sensation in his bones or lungs tells him to look for a moral corruption in his surroundings; garbage in the streets connects with indecency in behavior and finally with a perverted morality.

The *Travels* is thus as much a guidebook to conduct as to the sights of France and Italy. It is related less significantly to travel books than to the imaginary visits made by Orientals to Paris and London, as in the *Lettres persanes* of Montesquieu and Goldsmith's *Citizen of the World*. Smollett's work shares with these a satiric intention and the convenience of the epistolary form, which is easily adaptable to the cumulative catalogue of formal verse satire. As Smollett must have recognized in writing the *Travels,* the letter form offered as striking an opportunity to the satirist as to the Richardsonian writer-to-the-moment. The letter lends itself not only to emotional crises but also to other moments of great intensity, from which indignation as well as sentiment may issue. As the Duchess of Newcastle wrote in her preface to *CCXI Sociable Letters* (1664), "The truth is they are rather scenes than letters, for I have endeavored under cover of letters to express the humors of mankind and the actions of man's life." Thus as a satire the *Travels* has an advantage over Smollett's satiric explorations in his novels: there is no need for either plot or character development, the emphasis being neatly balanced between the sight seen and the commentary. But the *Travels* is also a true memoir and so lacks the emphasis, the coherence, and the point, as well as the complexity, of Smollett's fictions.

The moral-physical parallel that underlies the satiric use of sickness in the *Travels* becomes the structural principle of Smollett's political satire, *The History and Adventures of an Atom.* The device of an object that passes from person to person making satiric observations on what it witnesses was probably taken from Charles Johnstone's *Chrysal* (1760, 1765), in which the object is a coin and the episodes are held together by the theme of man's lust for and dependence on gold.[33] Smollett follows Johnstone in combining the idea of the coin that passes from pocket to pocket (as in *Tatler* No.

---

33. The tradition in which both *Chrysal* and the *Adventures of an Atom* are written probably owes more to the French descendants of the *chronique scandaleuse,* Crébillon fils' *Sopha* (1740) and Diderot's *Bijoux indiscrets* (1748), than to the English specimens of Addison and Fielding.

249) with the idea of metamorphosis (as in *Spectator* No. 343 and Fielding's *Journey from This World to the Next*). Johnstone makes Chrysal not only a guinea but, at the same time, the *spirit* of gold, which can enter into the possessor's mind. Smollett's satirist is the indestructible atom whose travels from organ to organ, from body to body (via digestion, dysentery, and disease), give a moral history of the Newcastle, Pitt, and Bute ministries. Thus his point of view is, like Chrysal's, internal as well as external.

Smollett allegorizes the humiliating relations between George II and his prime ministers by a daily kick in the posteriors. In his earliest writings, the verse satires "Advice" and "Reproof," he uses such physical equivalents as sexual perversion as metaphors for corruption in political and social morality. So too in the early novels moral instruction is accompanied by practical jokes and beatings, and a character's villainy is suggested by his twisted shape. The terror that is expressed in Newcastle by defecation appears in Commodore Trunnion in similarly physical terms—the knocking of his knees, the bristling of his hair, and the shattering of his teeth. The difference between the allegory of Newcastle's fear and the objectification of Trunnion's is mainly in the degree of extravagance.

In the *Adventures of an Atom,* however, the moral-physical parallel is not only more obtrusive (and consistent) but more explicitly involved with sickness. One senses behind the atom a medical intelligence asking exactly what is wrong with Newcastle and Pitt, what makes them act the way they do? Like a dissector the atom examines the inside as well as the outside of bodies to discover the secret source of evil: inside Mura-clami (the Earl of Mansfield) it finds a "brain so full and compact, that there was not room for another particle of matter. But instead of a heart, he had a membranous sac, or hollow viscus, cold and callous, the habitation of sneaking caution, servile flattery, griping avarice, creeping malice, and treacherous deceit" (p. 309). The mixing of anatomical and moral terms (with the latter enlivened by adjectives of movement) creates a vivid picture of destructive and parasitic evil. But the result is quite different from that of the *Travels* and of less use in Smollett's search for an effective satirist. Here the satirist has access to the bodies of others and investigates them as vehicles of moral squalor; in the *Travels* the satirist's own body is the one under scrutiny. Smollett's use of disease in the

Adventures of an Atom is still conventional. The disease is an image of Mansfield's evil or, as seems likely from the passage above, the cause of his evil. The atom is looking for "the motives by which the lawyer's [Mansfield's] conduct was influenced."[34] It describes the organs in terms which suggest a disease preying on Mansfield; and if Mansfield is diseased, one might argue, he bears less responsibility for his villainy. Even taken merely as an equivalent of his abstract evil, disease must be regarded as reductive decoration; there is no *necessary* connection between sickness, perversion, and erratic behavior and the Pitt Ministry (except perhaps in Newcastle's physical peculiarities).

Smollett's original touch in the *Travels* is to attach the physical disorder not to the evil but to the good man. Sickness is a reflection of the evil and filth that affect an ordinary decent man, rather than a descriptive image of the evil itself. The evil person is not sick, Smollett says, but sick-making. As always, Smollett is finally more interested in the evil as it is reflected in the consciousness of an observer than as it exists in itself. He has advanced from portrayals of villainy that is punished by a hero to villainy that is reflected in the punishment of the hero. But when he turns to this second use of punishment, he qualifies it by making it sickness. People do not, as in *Joseph Andrews,* merely meet "Smollett" and abuse or cheat him; he does not need to have violent contact with people—merely by observing them he suffers the punishment of illness. Moreover, medical and anatomical imagery is not merely decorative when it is involved with a central character who is sick, and the result is a fiction of more compelling belief. On a naturalistic level it is credible that a sick man should be sensitive to his surroundings, and it is the matter of belief, or credibility, that holds the *Travels* within the area of the memoir, as it holds *Humphry Clinker* within the area of the novel.

In *The Expedition of Humphry Clinker* Smollett takes the idea of the valetudinarian traveler from his *Travels* and uses it to explain Matthew Bramble as a satiric observer and to relate him to the satiric objects that surround him. Bramble's reactions to his environment are more immediate, startling, and emotional than "Smollett's." In the *Travels* poor accommodations endanger "Smollett's" frail health; in

34. *The History and Adventures of an Atom,* in *Works,* ed. Saintsbury, *12,* 252.

Humphry Clinker Bramble has only to be in the presence of the morally corrupt for his body to react involuntarily: "his eyes began to glisten, his face grew pale, and his teeth chattered" (Apr. 24; *11*, 45);[35] this is followed by railing and sometimes by physical chastisement. Bramble's sickness is Smollett's most effective equivalent to Juvenal's "Difficile est saturam non scribere," the claim that merely confronted by vice he reacts much as Pavlov's dogs salivated at the ringing of a bell. In a crowded ballroom of Bath, when things got too bad, his "nerves were overpowered, and [he] dropped senseless upon the floor" (May 8; *11*, 98). In short, as he says at one point, "my spirits and my health affect each other reciprocally—that is to say, everything that discomposes my mind, produces a correspondent disorder in my body" (June 14; *11*, 234); his travels record a search for health which is a search for moral standards in a chaotic world. As Jery notes, "He is as tender as a man without a skin, who cannot bear the slightest touch without flinching" (Apr. 30; *11*, 73). Bramble is a man without defenses upon whom the least deviation from normal acts as upon a thermometer. In certain areas, the cities and spas of England, he is sick; the Scottish air brings improvement. Upon leaving Scotland Jery writes, "I never saw my uncle in such health and spirits as he now enjoys" (Sept. 21; *12*, 129). And, as the sick man who knows sickness at first hand, Bramble recognizes false cures and sickness in others who do not recognize the symptoms; when he is well, he knows that others must be too.

The analogy between moral and physical sickness does not end with the invalid Bramble. The chief images he applies to the conditions he sees are drawn from the vocabulary with which he is most familiar. Bath, "which nature and providence seem to have intended as a resource from distemper and disquiet," has now become "the very centre of racket and dissipation" (Apr. 23; *11*, 49). London is "a dropsical head, [which] will in time leave the body and extremities without nourishment and support" (May 29; *11*, 131). Under London's glittering exterior the sick Bramble can detect "steams of endless putrefaction"; its people have "languid sallow looks, that distinguish [them] from those ruddy swains that lead a country life" (June 8; *11*, 181). Beginning with disease, he extends his imagery to

---

35. Cf. Commodore Trunnion, whose "eye glistened like that of a rattlesnake" when his indignation rose (*Pickle*, Chap. 2).

imbalance, disorder, and collapse of other kinds. Starting with the unhealthy fumes of the waters at Bath, he goes on to see the new constructions as "the wreck of streets and squares disjointed by an earthquake," the houses "built so slight, with the soft crumbling stone found in this neighbourhood," that you can push a foot through the walls (Apr. 23; *11,* 53). Bodies, houses, cities, and the whole nation are organisms that are sick or conducive to sickness.

Bramble's diatribes take the form of letters written, appropriately, to his doctor (his first words are "The pills are good for nothing"). I have said that the epistolary form in the *Travels* accommodates the catalog form, the static scene, and the cumulative effect of the formal satire Smollett liked to write. Bramble's search for health is similarly compartmentalized. Each of his letters, reporting his condition to Dr. Lewis, is a self-contained satire, and together they produce a powerful cumulative effect. The most impressive of these units are the two tirades on Bath (one on its luxury, the other on its sanitation) and, more fully developed, the two great tirades on London (again, one on its luxury, the other on its unhealthfulness). The latter, reminiscent of Johnson's "London" (or Juvenal's third satire), gives an idyllic picture of the naturalness of Bramble's home in Wales, followed by a nightmarish, kaleidoscopic vision of London's perversion of nature: bread is turned into "a deleterious paste" in order to make it whiter, veal is bleached, greens are colored, soil is produced artificially, and the poultry is more quickly fattened "by the infamous practice of sewing up the gut" (June 8; *11,* 182, 183). Both London and Bath are described in terms of a terrible proliferation, with millions of shabby, crumbling, but new houses spreading in all directions, choking and stifling, crowding and crushing out value and even life itself; and paralleling the houses are the great aimless crowds of people. Bramble's descriptions of these cities, piling detail upon frightful detail, are reminiscent of the satires of Juvenal, Swift, and Pope, in which a chaos is described as moving ever outward to engulf all that remains of value and order.

But the general pattern of a formal satire presupposes not only an apocalyptic vision of the multiplicity and complete ruin to come, but also a glimpse of unity in the traditional ideas that are being defeated; this can be a picture of a golden age in the past, as in Juvenal's sixth satire, or simply a reference to the poet's own past, as in Pope's

"Epistle to Arbuthnot." Smollett presents the two visions as contemporary in time, and spatially the vision of ruin in England precedes the vision of the golden age in Scotland—a more hopeful progression than is usual in satire. Scotland is still, however, the past in the sense that, because of its backwardness, its feudalism and traditionalism, it is not strictly contemporary with England; its people live (as do Bramble and Sir Launcelot Greaves) according to the standards of an older, simpler time. Bramble's search for health causes the novel to fall into the traditional two-part structure of formal verse satire. The thesis-antithesis contrast is apparent both on the level of the individual letters (as in the opposition of good Wales and vicious London in the satire on London) and on the more general level of the novel's action, in the journey from unhealthy England to healthy, invigorating Scotland.

But with the pattern of a satire apparent, and the bitter denunciations of London and Bath, one might ask why the overall effect of the novel is not so disturbing as that of *The Dunciad* or *Gulliver's Travels*. One answer is that Smollett softens the force of his satire by delivering his criticisms of society through a mouthpiece whose habit of criticism he attributes to disease. A second answer is that Smollett, in various ways, subordinates Bramble to the larger plan of his novel. We shall take up others later.

It is clear that Smollett was conscious of the implications of Bramble's position. He balances the accuracy—or the truth—of Bramble's satire against the sickness of the man. Bramble's niece Lydia, for one, substantiates the truth of his observations. To her Bath appears to be "a new world. All is gaiety, good-humour, and diversion." Nevertheless the noise, heat, smells, and conversation give her "the head-ache and vertigo the first day" (Apr. 26; *11*, 57, 58). Even Tabitha Bramble's dog Chowder gets sick in these surroundings. So much for Bramble's accuracy; the sickness of the man—as opposed to the satirist—is closely bound up with the figure of Humphry Clinker. Humphry too is a reformer, though of an altogether different sort from Bramble: his proposal for stopping "profane swearing . . . so horrid and shocking, that it made my hair stand on end" is to "Make them first sensible that you have nothing in view but their good, then they will listen with patience, and easily be convinced of the sin and folly of a practice that affords neither profit nor pleasure" (June 2;

II, 151, 152). However inadequate this is as persuasion, it offers a revealing contrast to Bramble's misanthropic railing, particularly when one notices that it takes Humphry to budge Bramble into action on the notorious Chowder, and that it is Humphry who more than once rescues Bramble from drowning. Near the end, when the coach overturns a second time (the first time occasions the introduction of Humphry), Humphry hauls Bramble out of the river onto the bank nearest Dennison's property; this leads, with Dennison's arrival and the use of Bramble's former name "Loyd," to Humphry's being revealed as his son. With the baptism in the river Bramble loses his misanthropy and takes upon himself the responsibility for his past actions by acknowledging Humphry as his son. Humphry, in fact, offers a commentary on satirists of Bramble's type. His enthusiasm and visionary quality are necessary to get Bramble successfully through his travels, and the reader may recall, by contrast, the more usual role of the servant in holding down to earth the fancies of his master. Smollett has reversed the Quixote-Sancho Panza roles, giving the master the skepticism and the servant the enthusiasm, in order to emphasize the incompleteness of the sceptical character.

Bramble's sickness betrays a certain weakness in his position: however much his satire reveals about his surroundings and other people, it is really only a concern for his own comfort; the people he rails at are keeping him from being well. Thus, finding a simpler, more congenial countryside relieves only the symptoms of his disease. Ultimately he must find the cure in himself by turning from railing at others to recognizing the disorder within himself. His railing (we finally see) is a luxury roughly analogous to the one he secured from Humphry's mother, passing on (as he does from Bath to London) without accepting any responsibility for his pleasure.

Observation as Theme

Second, Bramble is only one of five letter writers (though he is the most important one). Their points of view qualify his own and contribute significantly to the novel's overall form and theme.

In *Peregrine Pickle* Smollett introduced at least one other satirist— Cadwallader Crabtree—as a contrast to Peregrine. In *Sir Launcelot Greaves* he again included other satirists along the way for comparison. Most reprehensible is the political lampooner, the misanthropic

Ferret, who looked "as if his sense of smelling had been perpetually offended by some unsavoury odour; and he looked as if he wanted to shrink within himself from the impertinence of society" (Chap. 1; *10, 2*). A Hobbesian, he believes that all men and laws are corrupt, but instead of seeking to correct them he tries to exploit their corruption to his own ends. After a speech reviling quacks he shows that he himself is one by selling an "Elixir of Long Life" to the crowd. Throughout the novel he questions the whole idea of the knight-errant and his efficacy. At the very beginning, at the Black Lion, he argues that a knight-errant is ridiculous, mad, and no more than a vagrant, and he stands face to face with Greaves—the satirist as cynic vs. the satirist as corrector of wrongs, the two figures who were one in Peregrine. At the end of the novel Sir Launcelot provides an apartment for Ferret at Greavesbury Hall (which Ferret leaves, however, disgusted with seeing his fellow creatures too happy).

Dick Distich, another satirist, is confined to a madhouse; he "reviled as ignorant dunces several persons who had writ with reputation, and were generally allowed to have genius." Confining Greaves in an asylum with an insane satirist has the same effect as putting him in Greavesbury Hall with Ferret. Then there is the secondary Quixote, Captain Crowe, who is closer to Quixote than Sir Launcelot because he is older, madder, and more often defeated. He attacks coaches containing beautiful maidens he fancies are in distress and (like Quixote) is beaten down by the realities of their servants. But, since he is a Smollettian satirist, however wrong or mad he may be, his satiric instinct is correct. It turns out that the lady *is* in distress, for she is Sir Launcelot's beloved Aurelia who is held captive by her evil guardian Antony Darnel.

Greaves himself, the crusading satirist, an ideal by which the passive or foolish satirists are tested, is only one aspect of a larger theme. The novel, Smollett's most thoughtful if not most successful to this time, is about the individual's relation to society, with its crux the question of justice in reality vs. justice in law. At the beginning justice and law are separate entities. Civil laws do not accord with real justice, and even natural law appears to be unjust in Greaves' loss of Aurelia. The most potent contrast is between the people in prison or the madhouse and the people who put them there. Distich explains of the madhouse "That it contained fathers kidnapped by their children, wives confined by their husbands, gentlemen of fortunes sequestered by their relations, and innocent persons immured by the malice of their adversaries" (Chap. 23; *10, 310*).

The satirist and the knight-errant are the traditional punishers of crime unreached by the law, and Greaves is both. Smollett uses Greaves to show that the situation is so bad that a madman is necessary to demonstrate exactly how bad. But while Greaves is an improvement and does set some things right, he is lawless. On the one hand there is the idealist Greaves, and on the other the exploiter of the law, Justice Gobble; in the middle is the honest lawyer Tom Clarke—at first another Quixote with his legal terminology, but ultimately sensible. He acts as a restraining influence on Greaves, interposing when the knight lifts a bench to dash open the cell door and "assuring him he would suggest a plan that would avenge himself amply on the Justice Gobble, without any breach of the peace" (Chap. 10; *10, 138*). Near the end Greaves, locked in the madhouse, comes to the realization that knight-errantry is futile against the legal chicanery that put him there and returns to his senses; he is released by Clarke's careful legal work. Once free, Greaves uses legal means to extricate Aurelia; to get Sycamore and Dandle he "practiced a much more easy, certain, and effectual method of revenge [than the satirist's], by instituting a process against them" (Chap. "The Last"; *10, 332*). Sad as it may be, Smollett says, legal restitution is the only true kind. Satire then has become part of a larger theme concerning the law, and the good and bad satirists become examples along a spectrum of judges running from the unjust Gobble to the good justice who frees Aurelia.

In *Humphry Clinker,* within the frame of an extremely conventional plot concerning the reunion of lovers and the reunion of a father and son, Smollett presents letters from five observer-correspondents visiting a series of cities—Bristol Hot Well, Bath, London, Edinburgh—which are the occasions for their meditations. He takes the device of the multiple letter writers from Christopher Anstey's verse satire, *The New Bath Guide,* published in 1766.[36] As in his earlier adaptations, however, Smollett's own intention is made clear

36. The *Travels* is a series of letters written by one man, while *Humphry Clinker* is a series of letters written by five different people. As a satiric device, however, the difference is more apparent than real. The singleness of a series of letters from one correspondent is dissipated in the *Travels* by addressing the letters to different audiences—to a woman for a satiric description of French fashions, to a man for a discussion of French politics, and so on.

by a look at the radical changes he makes in Anstey's form. Anstey employs a series of rather bland poetic epistles written by the members of a family sojourning in Bath; the chief letter writer is Sim B-n-r-d, a young man bothered with the wind, but there are also letters (hardly distinguishable from his) by his sister, their "Cousin Jenny," and their maid Tabby Runt. Perhaps the most obvious difference between the two books, in terms of what we have already seen of Smollett's satiric method, is that Sim quickly becomes a part of Bath and is absorbed into the satiric object. Smollett's commentators in *Humphry Clinker* are in varying degrees outside the object and remain critical. The second difference between the two books is that Smollett has grouped his letters around central incidents and locations. The characters move from Bristol Hot Well to Bath to London to Harrogate to York, and they give their separate comments about each city. This form is an improvement on the picaresque novel as a vehicle for Smollett's satire because the emphasis is of necessity shifted from the protagonist as actor to the object satirized and his opinion of it. Third, in terms of his interest in the nature and function of the satirist, Smollett's use of the collection of letters brings a number of different points of view (in varying degrees satiric) to bear on each situation; unlike Anstey, Smollett does not let slip the opportunity for utilizing grotesquely various temperaments in his letter writers. Their different views of an object act as spotlights on the various aspects of the evil. This is also a more economical solution to the problem of the satiric anatomy than presenting a long series of adventures that reveal the object's different aspects, as Smollett had done earlier in *Roderick Random*.

In contrast to the Juvenalian spirit of Bramble, there is the Horatian satire of his nephew Jery Melford (the Sim B-n-r-d of *Humphry Clinker*).[37] After describing his uncle's violent reaction to a situation

37. It is interesting that the figure in *The New Bath Guide* who may possibly have suggested to Smollett the role Bramble plays is the object of Sim's amused scrutiny. Sim and his companions dance in his room, disturbing "Lord Ringbone, who lay in the parlour below, / On account of the gout he had got in his toe." They hear him beginning "to curse and swear," sounding very much like Bramble. In *Humphry Clinker* the same situation is seen from the point of view of Jery Melford, whom Bramble sends up to quiet the dancers (as Ringbone sends his French valet); and it is Bramble who, a few pages later, rails. In short, Ringbone may have suggested to Smollett the possibility of his own favorite kind of satiric persona in this situation, the possibility of using the valetudinarian of the *Travels*, as well as the need for keeping this figure one of a group of observers.

Jery adds, "But this chaos is to me a source of infinite amusement. . . . These follies, that move my uncle's spleen excite my laughter" (Apr. 30; *11*, 73).[38] While his uncle scourges, Jery lets folly speak for itself and condemn itself. But with his objectivity he lacks his uncle's moral purpose and the personal involvement occasioned by his ill health; thus such an object of satiric contemplation as Lieutenant Lismahago he finds merely "a high-flavoured dish. . . . It was our fortune to feed upon him the best part of three days" (July 13; *12*, 18). As Bramble expresses the seriousness of his concern in his choice of a correspondent, so Jery characteristically corresponds with an Oxford chum who merely wishes to be entertained.

The other letter writers have considerably less to say. Lydia Melford is the naïve, impressionable young girl whose instincts (physical reactions) tell her that Bath is appalling, but whose sense of fashion makes her adjust to it. Winifred Jenkins, representing the servant's point of view, is all eager acceptance, to the extent that appearances dupe her fearfully. Tabitha Bramble, on the other hand, reflects her environment as much as a stone wall; her only concern as a letter writer is back at Brambleton-hall in her belongings, the price of flannel, and the affairs of her servants (she corresponds with her housekeeper). When she happens to mention Bath or Hot Well it is only as it affects Brambleton-hall. As a character (as opposed to a letter writer) Tabby's railing (reminiscent of her brother's) is directed toward getting a husband. In short, she rejects all the world but the narrow demesne of her current prospect (who again has reference only to her concerns back at Brambleton-hall).

Tabby's total rejection is one end of the spectrum, the other end of which is Win Jenkin's total acceptance of Bath and London. Between these extremes are the various degrees of acceptance and rejection of Jery and Bramble. Also along this spectrum are the points of view registered by the characters whom Bramble and Jery meet in their travels. Many of them have satiric inclinations—some bad, like Bul-

---

38. Jery's connection with a Fielding commentator like Medley is suggested by his frequent use of the stage metaphor. After Humphry's appearance in court, Jery writes that "the farce is finished, and another piece of a graver cast [is] brought upon the stage" (June 23); after describing Lishmahago at some length (in two letters), he remarks, "I suppose you are glad he is gone off the stage for the present" (July 18; *12*, 45). At the end he calls the journey a comedy on which the curtain has at last fallen (Nov. 8; *12*, 259).

ford, who exposes his guests' weaknesses with practical jokes; and some good, like S----t (Smollett himself), whom Jery meets in London. S----t simply invites the fools and knaves to dinner, observes their follies, and privately draws their attention to them; he suggests a resignation that is perhaps closest to the feelings of Smollett the author—at least those Smollett wishes associated with himself.[39] The most important of these satirists-within-the-action is Lismahago, the Scot who has lost a scalp to the American Indians, has his wisdom entirely from the experience of bloody deeds in the wilderness, and takes pains to qualify every apparent truth. Refusing to make a choice between England and Scotland, he acts as a corrective to Bramble, the seeker of health and comfort, and broadens the sick man's perspective during the crucial Scottish tour. But looking at the scenes between Bramble and Lismahago (reported by Jery) one has to conclude not that Lismahago is simply seeing a truth Bramble does not see, but that he is a disputatious malcontent, as Jery says. Lismahago, like Bramble, tells the truth or an important part of it, but for the wrong reasons: they are both incomplete men, only less so than others like Holder and Bulford or even Paunceford. Both have to be cured at the end of the book; once Lismahago is married and has the security he seeks, "His temper, which had been soured and shrivelled by disappointment and chagrin, is now swelled out and smoothed like a raisin in plum-porridge" (Nov. 8; *12, 260*).

The relation of points of view and satiric objects thus creates a reciprocal theme—the moral significance of the scene and the moral significance of the observer. Because the focus is usually on the scene rather than on the characters, the questions the reader tends to ask about the characters are in relation to the scene he observes; for example, what is X's reaction and what does it reveal about him qua observer? One character's point of view acts as a commentary on another's. Jery's Horatian attitude shows up an inadequacy in Bramble's Juvenalian; Bulford with his practical jokes and Jack Holder, who manufactures satiric situations for his own amusement, point up Jery's shortcomings; Tabby's self-centered railing is the most damaging commentary on her brother's.

---

39. Smollett is following the practice of Pope, Swift, Prior, and other eighteenth-century satirists by inserting a self-portrait (a "good-humoured and civilized" man Jery calls him), which represents a norm of behavior from which the deviations of the other characters can be measured.

The characters analyze not only the situations, but each other. Jery follows his uncle's every reaction with disapproval or admiration, and Bramble anatomizes all of the characters: Jery is "a pert jackanapes, full of college-petulance and self-conceit, proud as a German count, and as hot and hasty as a Welsh mountaineer"; Lydia "has got a languishing eye, and reads romances"; and sister Tabby, "that fantastical animal," is "the devil incarnate come to torment me for my sins" (Apr. 17; *11*, 15). Even when one character is contemplated in action by another, both maintain their roles of observers: ensnared by the romantic Wilson, Lydia (according to Bramble) is "a simple girl utterly unacquainted with the characters of mankind" (Apr. 17; *11*, 18); the nature of her reaction is the main thing in question.

Smollett has presented in *Humphry Clinker* a dramatic essay on the values of various kinds of satire, much as Ben Jonson did with Asper, Macilente, and Carlo Buffone, the objective satirist, the envious malcontent, and the mere buffoonish railer in *Every Man Out of His Humour*. But Smollett has also included many characters whose reactions fall outside the satiric range. The satiric attitude toward the world is simply the most critical; it is one end of the spectrum I have postulated; the other end is total acceptance or, worse, affected acceptance.

As in Roderick Random's satirizing, Bramble's diatribes are closely related to a theme concerning ways of looking at the world. "Sophistication" is the word he applies to all he hates in England: it is "a vile world of fraud and sophistication," to which he opposes "the genuine friendship of a sensible man" (like Dr. Lewis, Apr. 23; *11*, 55) or the time "about thirty years ago" when Bath was a healthy, simple spa, and the most crowded parts of London were "open fields, producing hay and corn" (Apr. 23, May 29; *11*, 49, 130). Sophistication for Bramble involves the change from a genuine, true form to something that may appear good but is really false, useless, and harmful. He attacks the fantastic shapes that are replacing the ordinary, functional houses of Bath; the idea that ordure can, if called perfume, be pleasant to smell; that Harrogate water owes "its reputation in a great measure to its being so strikingly offensive" (June 26; *11*, 247); that sickness requires so many doctors and so many elaborate (and actually unhealthful) cures. The theme extends beyond Bramble's and Jery's commentary. Because the indefatigable Wilson disguised himself in the first place he is not accepted as a suitor for Lydia. He is doing what he thinks is expected of a lover, according to the sophistication of London and Bath: part of this is disguise; part is the idea of elopement and the flowery letter that starts, "Miss Willis has pronounced my doom," and continues, "tossed in a sea of doubts and fears" (Mar. 31; *11*, 20). If Wilson had simply gone up to Bramble and announced his true name and intentions he would have had Lydia at once, and there would have been no novel (just as there would have been no novel if Bramble had given his true name to Humphry's mother).

The antithesis of British sophistication is the underdeveloped Scottish land and the old-fashioned Scottish customs; and so Bramble finds the immediate antidote to England in Scotland. But it is also the naked Humphry, without clothes or parents; Lismahago, scalped and exposed in his nakedness by Bulford; and, of course, Bramble himself, who is "a man without a skin."[40] Thus far Smollett is developing a conventional satiric contrast between false and true, affected and sincere, artificial and natural, apparent and real.[41] His originality lies in his noticing that, if the opposite of sophistication is the bare forked animal Bramble, it is also his act of stripping off the illusions of others. The sophisticate and the satirist are thesis and antithesis.

There is still some question, however, as to the exact value attached to the satiric attitude within *Humphry Clinker*. The word "original," which is applied both to satirists like Bramble and to some of the fools he observes, gives an idea of Smollett's intention. Applied to Bramble and the people he admires, "original" has the meaning of having existed from the first or of being "a thing (or person) in relation to something else which is a copy" (*OED*). This meaning connects "original" with that other key word "sophistication," a change from the genuine to something that appears good but is false.[42] Since the evil anatomized in *Humphry Clinker* is the conforming to a false standard and form, being what one is not, an orig-

<hr/>

40. For a fuller discussion of nakedness, and a slightly different interpretation of it, see M. A. Goldberg, *Smollett and the Scottish School* (Albuquerque, University of New Mexico Press, 1959), pp. 171–75.

41. Sophistication is also attacked in Smollett's *Travels*: women's paint and dress; vanity that makes a soldier wear fashionably long hair in spite of the inconvenience to fighting; the "absurd luxury" of having fifty scullions to cool an army meal; the empty and pernicious forms of dueling; false honor and gallantry.

42. See Jery's remark to his correspondent Watkins that "I was much pleased with meeting the original of a character, which you and I have often laughed at in description" (Apr. 18; *11*, 28); also, "perusing mankind in the original" (Oct. 14; *12*, 239).

inal is at least a more valuable person than the sophisticates of Bath and London. Bramble admires S——t as an original because he "had resolution enough to live in his own way in the midst of foreigners; for, neither in dress, diet, customs, or conversation, did he deviate one tittle from the manner in which he had been brought up" (July 4; *12, 5*). In this sense an original is true to himself, and Bramble, Humphry, and Lismahago are all originals. Gradually, however, it becomes apparent that whatever its meaning in a particular context, "original" in general refers to an eccentric or an oddity, and whatever the emphasis intended, it does not designate an ideal.[43] This is clear enough from the inclusion of Tabitha Bramble or Micklewhimmen or Newcastle within its ranks. Those to whom the word is not applied are, significantly, very bad or very good; noticeably missing are the affected and sophisticated, such as the Pauncefords, the Burdocks, and the Oxmingtons, as well as the unmistakably good people like Moore, Captain Brown, Dennison, the Admiral, and S——t.

Primitivism is not the ideal of *Humphry Clinker.* Bramble's misanthropy is as extreme a state as sophistication. Humphry is "innocent as the babe unborn," "a great original" (May 24, June 8; *11, 128, 162*), but that this is not altogether an ideal situation becomes obvious when we see that it has left Humphry open to the influence of Whitefield's sermons and to exploitation by the Tabitha Brambles and Lady Griskins of this world. Similarly, Lismahago, however free of illusions, has to compromise and find a wealthy wife and security for his old age. Even Scotland itself, which is "original" in the old sense and which has usually been taken as Smollett's ideal in *Humphry Clinker,* does not receive unstinted praise from either Bramble or Lismahago. Bramble tells the story of the stones that mar the fields in Scotland: the peasants leave them and grow their scanty crops; the philosopher has them removed, whereupon his crops decrease; when he returns the stones to his fields the crops again grow. The point

---

43. The *OED* cites *Humphry Clinker* for the sense of "original" as "oddity," perhaps because in at least two cases "original" appears in close proximity to "oddity" (June 8, 10; *11,* 186, 188). There also appears to be a distinction between kinds of "original" in Smollett's novel: Bramble speaks of "Those originals [the authors who praise themselves and damn others, who] are not fit for conversation" (June 2; *11,* 161), and on the next page Humphry "turns out a great original." The difference between good and bad originals is again implicit in Bramble's comment, "if you pick up a diverting original by accident, it may be dangerous to amuse yourself with his oddities. He is generally a tartar at bottom" (June 8; *11,* 186).

seems to be that things should be left as they are. When the philosopher offers his rational explanation for the effectiveness of the rocks
—that they restrain the perspiration of the earth and act as protectors
from the winds or reflectors of the sun—Bramble adds:

> But surely this excessive perspiration might be more effectually
> checked by different kinds of manure. . . . As for the warmth, it
> would be much more equally obtained by enclosures; one half of
> the ground which is now covered would be retrieved; the culti-
> vation would require less labour; and the ploughs, harrows, and
> horses would not suffer half the damage which they now sustain.
> (Aug. 28; *12,* 103)

This procedure of showing the virtue of originality, which now
comes to mean primitivism, and then qualifying his admiration is
employed by Bramble throughout the Scottish sections. The virtue
and limitation of primitivism is shown in Bramble's discussion of
the clans. He admires the patriarchal system, the solidarity of the
family, and the loyalty to a clan chief on purely family grounds
which cannot be destroyed by passing laws that free the family from
legal ties, but he regrets the clans' lack of property and independence.
Jery, a few pages earlier, while admiring the same qualities ("the
simplicity of ancient times") and even claiming he had never slept so
well as on the rush-strewn floor of the Campbells' great hall, laughs
at the useless and unpleasant traditions of the bagpiper (Campbell,
the clan chief, stuffs his ears with cotton) and the carousing funeral.
Bramble's praise of Scottish naturalness is balanced by his praise of
the progress of cities like Lieth and Glasgow.

If we notice that the travelers, having visited the bracing air of
Scotland and being improved in health by the contrast, return to
England and there encounter examples of the true ideal, we will see
that, instead of employing the thesis-antithesis mode of formal verse
satire, Smollett goes one step further and, presenting two extremes,
ascertains the golden mean.[44] In *Humphry Clinker* he offers a pro-

---

44. Smollett uses the dialectical structure elsewhere in details, but *Greaves* is his
only novel that anticipates *Humphry Clinker* in its general structure. The failure of
law and Greaves' lawless corrective are both shown to be excesses that must be resolved
in the proper administration of law.

gression from sophistication in Bath and London to an opposite primitivism in Scotland and finally to a compromise in northern England. The ideal estate, Dennison's, was put in order by Englishmen who withdrew from the city to a traditional home and "restored" it, and the chaos of Baynard's estate is being repaired by the same Englishmen. Running parallel to the progression of the journey are three kinds of people: the good, hospitable, wise people, scattered along the way (for contrast) but concentrated in the scenes at the end; the "originals," eccentric but better than the third group; and finally the affected, the poor hosts, the ungrateful, and those who affect originality. Members of the second group can, by losing their eccentricity, become members of the first, the most obvious example being Bramble with the recovery of his health.

Bramble's Juvenalian satire falls with Bramble into the second group (as does Jery's Horatian). Satire is one reaction to a sophisticated, corrupt world, and a useful one, but not sufficient in itself. It is needed as a jolt back to reality, as an extreme like Scotland. When this extreme has been seen, however, it must be qualified into a useful, livable reality like the Bramble or Lismahago at the end of the novel. Thus, in his last novel, Smollett has placed the satiric temperament in a world of various other attitudes and temperaments.

The Satirist as Point of View

Smollett's development shows a number of important facts about satire's situation in the second half of the eighteenth century. He becomes increasingly concerned with the character of the satirist, until in his last novel the evil object has become simply the reflection of a point of view—a symptom of sickness or isolation or a sense of fun. Satire tends to change from a form with a persuasive end to a subject, an attitude which Smollett regards with mixed feelings. In Peregrine Pickle and Ferdinand Fathom the satirist has become a villain, and although Greaves and Bramble are by no means villains, their condition as satirists is far from ideal and has to be remedied.

Unlike Fielding however, Smollett does not stand alone among his contemporaries. He is only one of a large number of writers who, attempting to fit satire into the novel, focused on the simple form of a satiric eye vs. a satiric object. As a weather vane he can be usefully placed in the context of two of his contemporaries, one lesser and one greater, Sarah Fielding and Richardson.

Mrs. Fielding's *Adventures of David Simple* appeared in 1744, between the publication of *Joseph Andrews* and *Clarissa*. *David Simple* is about friendship—the ideal relationship between two people, a private relationship—and so satire is seen as devisive, negative, and cruel. David, the observer who witnesses all the satiric scenes of evil, is anything but a satirist. Only at moments of shock, despair, and personal disappointment does he temporarily become a satirist; when his marriage proposal is rejected, he "walked about, and raved like a Madman; repeated all the Satires he could remember on Women." When he recovered, however, "instead of resolving to be her Enemy, he could not help wishing her well."[45]

David's faith in human love is shaken by his brother's treachery; he broods until he becomes "in this Point only as mad as *Quixote* himself could be with Knight Errantry" and sets out on a quest for "a real Friend" (*1*, 36). Whenever he encounters another example of the evil he has grown accustomed to find, he sadly moves on, continuing his Diogenes-like search. He even adopts disguises that allow him a better vantage for observation. Sarah Fielding, belonging to the Richardson as well as the Fielding camp, is more concerned than her brother with the effect of these incidents upon an observer's sensibility. To convey the detail of her indictment to David as well as to the reader, she introduces various expository figures who are themselves satirists. They also serve, significantly, as some of the false friends David meets on his journey.

Characters like Orgueil and Spatter, whose names suggest their function, strip away pretensions and false appearances of the people they know better than David; having accomplished their mission they are then discredited as poor friends. Mr. Orgueil takes David about town—for example, to a dinner or the theater—and the next morning he anatomizes all of the people who seemed so impressive to David the night before, until he is "quite exhausted with giving so many various Characters" (*1*, 118). We are told that he goes to the play "on purpose to make Observations on the Humours of Mankind; for, as all the Criticks commonly go from Taverns, Nature breaks out, and shews herself, without the Disguise which People put

45. *David Simple* [2d ed., 1744], *1*, 61.

on in their cooler Hours" (*1*, 119). This is, of course, what David has set out to discover (and even he breaks out railing at the wickedness of the audience come to hoot at success greater than their own); but Sarah Fielding attaches the unpleasant dissecting to characters she can discredit, while reserving for David the role of gentle, good-natured observer, whose sensitive soul is hurt by what he sees and is set to musing on man's fate. The satirist is moved to the side as one character type among many. What is wrong with Orgueil is not specifically his satire, but the motive behind it. He is like Smollett's Jery Melford: "for his part, the Follies and Vices of Mankind were his Amusements, and gave him such ridiculous Ideas, as were a continual Fund of Entertainment to him" (*1*, 125). Like Peregrine Pickle, "he has made *a God* of himself," although his rational god occasionally does do good "because it is suitable to the *Dignity of his Nature*" (*1*, 129).

Fastidious David leaves Orgueil as soon as he learns about his bad side and goes to live with Spatter, whose favorite word is "fools"—"a Monosyllable he always chose to pronounce before he went to Bed, insomuch that it was thought by some who knew him, he could not sleep without it" (*1*, 170). At length, "with the utmost Horror for his Principles" (*1*, 177), David leaves Spatter. But if Orgueil's motive discredited his satire, Spatter's, when it is discovered, places him somewhat higher on the moral ladder according to Addison and Steele. David notices that, though he "seemed to take such Delight in *abusing* People . . . no one was more willing to oblige any Person, who stood in need of his Assistance"; when he learns from Varnish that Spatter's "Ill-nature dwells no-where but in his Tongue; and the very People whom he so industriously endeavours to abuse, he would do any thing in his power to serve," he realizes that Spatter's real motive is "his *Love of Mankind*, which made him have such a Hatred and Detestation of their Vices, as caused him to be eager in reproaching them" (*1*, 148, 179). After learning Spatter's true character, he is glad to know that he was not "so black as . . . he began to suspect him," but also that "all the Characters of Men he had had from him were not so bad as he had represented them." (As with Bramble, this is one of the advantages of the partially discredited satirist). He is still determined to leave Spatter, however, "for nothing was more unpleasant to him than continual Invectives" (*1*, 181–82). And so he turns from Spatter to his opposite, Varnish.

Other satirists appear—for example, Cynthia, a sympathetic satirist, who is a Cinderella-type, observing high society from below-stairs and satirizing in self-defense. Most of the time, however, the satirist proves to be an ill-natured gossip, betrayed by his motive. If, as Steele said, the true satirist must write out of good nature, then a solution is to give one character good nature, let him utter meditation and vaguely liturgical complaint, and embody the ridicule and invective in other characters without good nature (Spatter being the hint of a compromise solution).

Richardson anticipates Smollett in regarding satire as one attitude on a spectrum of social and antisocial attitudes and by distinguishing between different kinds of satiric attitudes. It is significant that *Humphry Clinker,* like Richardson's novels, is epistolary, and that this is the direction in which Smollett's experiments naturally led him. In *Clarissa* too, letters bring different points of view to bear on the same experience, and one or more are overtly satiric.

When Pamela, with sufficient provocation, becomes a railing satirist in her descriptions of Mrs. Jewkes, Colbrand, and others, Richardson's intention is to suggest the fear they engendered in her *and* their actual loathsomeness. Like so many of the satiro-novelists, he wants it both ways and betrays himself by slipping into the use of conventional portraits (which would probably not have come to Pamela's mind). But while in *Pamela* he is clearly as interested in his heroine's interpretation of events as in the events themselves, he has only her point of view and so has to offer variations in her style. In *Clarissa,* however, he presents a story that is as much about the commentators as about the action they comment on; different letter writers illuminate the same events, and so the characters have to be distinguished not only as to histories, social classes, and actions, but as to points of view, attitudes, and prose styles. Richardson only completely succeeds, I believe, with Clarissa herself, whom he understands best; even the occasional pietism of her style is appropriate to a reader of edifying books.[46] But there also have to be points of view for the others, and both Anna's and Lovelace's are at times satiric—mocking, ironic, critical of events and actions.

46. William J. Farrell has shown that Clarissa writes in the pathetic vocabulary of "she-tragedy" and that Lovelace alternates between the style of courtly love letters and the plain style ("The Style and the Action in *Clarissa," Studies in English Literature,* 3 [1963], 365–75).

Anna Howe's satiric attitude is needed to cut beneath Clarissa's protestations, her familial piety, and her whole emotionally complicated situation in order to give distance and suggest certain hidden truths, such as Clarissa's attraction to Lovelace. It contributes to a realism of assessment lacking in *Pamela*. Also, Anna's constant ridicule of poor Mr. Hickman creates an attitude and a relationship in contrast to Clarissa's (while Clarissa regards Lovelace as Satanic, Anna calls Hickman "the lowest of Satan's servants").[47] Hickman, according to Anna, "is a sort of fiddling, busy, yet . . . *unbusy* man: has a great deal to do, and seems to me to dispatch nothing. Irresolute and changeable in every thing, but in teasing me with his nonsense" (2, 13–14). If this is somewhat abstract, later in the same letter she extends Hickman, as well as Solmes and Lovelace, into caricatures by "supposing them boys at school." Hickman, she supposes, "a great overgrown, lank-haired, chubby boy, who would be hunched and punched by every body; and go home with his finger in his eye, and tell his mother" (he has been trying to court Anna through *her* mother). Or take the "ugly likeness" of Solmes she sends to Clarissa, which fastens on his laugh:

> for his first three years, at least, I imagine, must have been one continual fit of crying; and his muscles have never yet been able to recover a risible tone. His very smile . . . is so little natural to his features, that it appears to him as hideous as the *grin* of a man in malice.

After he laughs, she is relieved to see "his features recovering their natural gloominess; though they did this but slowly, as if the muscles which contributed to his distortions, had turned upon rusty springs" (1, 178–79). As these examples show, Anna's "satire" concentrates on the individual—Hickman, Solmes, the Harlowe siblings, Lovelace, even Clarissa—not on the general fault.

Replying to one of Anna's letters, Clarissa writes a little essay out of Steele's *Tatler* on good and bad satire. Your satire, she writes to Anna,

> is intended to instruct; and though it bites, it pleases at the same time: no fear of a wound's wrankling or festering by so delicate

47. *Clarissa*, 2, 15.

a point as you carry; not envenomed by *personality,* not intended to expose, or ridicule, or exasperate. The most admired of our moderns know nothing of this art: Why? Because it must be founded in good nature, and directed by a right heart. The *man,* not the *fault,* is generally the subject of *their* satire: and were it to be *just,* how should it be *useful* . . . when every gash (for their weapon is a broad sword, not a lancet) lets in the air of public ridicule, and exasperates where it should heal? (2, 158–59)

While one may doubt whether Anna's satire is always "true," it is easy to see that it is used here to set off Lovelace's false satire. His venomous attacks on Clarissa's family, Clarissa, the faltering Belford, his various confederates in crime, and even Virtue itself, derive not from good nature but from selfish motives. His pose is a cross between Rochester's libertine spokesman in "A Satyr Against Mankind" and the self-exposing speaker of Oldham's "Satyr Against Virtue." Like the latter, Lovelace's satire has only his own personal aim, while Anna's is constructed on a firm moral basis of love and friendship.

Lovelace is much more than a satirist, but when Richardson gives him the pose and vocabulary of the rake, he also gives him—as his due—the rake's cynical satiric wit; thus he becomes the dangerous satirist who undermines society, who attacks particular people rather than general evils. The connection between false satire and the rake goes back, of course, to the moralists' distrust of Restoration comedy with its satirizing seducers, its Dorimants and Horners. By the mid-eighteenth century satire was coming to designate a convenient equivalent for a proud, aristocratic, cynical, inhuman, deceiving character type.

Lovelace is invariably exposed by his motive. Satire in him comes to represent a contempt for people—the aristocrat judging people and finding them wanting—that reaches ultimately to his "test" of Clarissa, which, like Peregrine's of Emilia, is a claim that he can expose her to be like others; that if he can seduce her he will reveal the true Eve beneath all the appearance and profession of virtue:

By my soul, Belford, I believe, that nine women in ten, who fall, fall either *from their own vanity* or *levity,* or for want of *circumspection* and *proper reserves.* (4, 310)

yet, sweet dears, half the female world is ready to run away with
a rake, *because* he is a rake; and for no *other* reason; nay, every
other reason *against* their choice of such a one. (5, 62)

Richardson's idea of the satirist extended to the clever Swift, who
played about with irony, fiction, and reality in his "projects"; with
many other contemporaries, he regarded works like *An Argument
Against Abolishing Christianity* as essentially Swift the satirist talking. For example, in Lovelace's project for new marriages every Val-
entine's Day (when the birds change mates), Richardson constructs
hypothetical happy consequences remarkably similar to Swift's in
the *Argument* or the *Modest Proposal:*

> such a change would be a means of annihilating, absolutely an-
> nihilating, four or five very atrocious and capital sins.—*Rapes,*
> vulgarly so called; adultery, and fornication; nor would *polyg-
> amy* be panted after. Frequently would it prevent *murders* and
> *duelling;* hardly any such thing as *jealousy* (the cause of shock-
> ing violences) would be heard of: and hypocrisy between man
> and wife be banished the bosoms of each. Nor, probably, would
> the reproach of *barrenness* rest, as now it too often does, where it
> is least deserved.—Nor would there possibly be such a person as
> a barren woman. (6, 54)

As in Swift's mock projects, the speaker, while exposing himself,
throws shafts of light on a number of subjects, from dueling to the
impotent husband who blames his wife for their childlessness.

If Anna's flippant, lighthearted satire, whose aim is to keep Clarissa
on an even keel, is at one end of the spectrum of attitudes in *Clarissa,*
and Lovelace's self-centered satire, motivated by his lust or desire for
revenge, is at the other, somewhere between falls the later letters of
his friend Belford. Belford begins as a rake but is converted by his
meeting with Clarissa; he warns Lovelace to stop, much as Anna
warns Clarissa earlier, though without Anna's satire. But after Clarissa's rape, and much more after her death, Belford turns, out of the
deepest sort of indignation, to railing. The most striking of such
scenes is the death of the bawd Mrs. Sinclair, who helped to bring
about Clarissa's ruin. In order to emphasize the contrast between this

and Clarissa's death scene, Richardson uses (and acknowledges in a footnote) Swift's imagery from his dressing room poems to characterize the corruption of Mrs. Sinclair and her whores:

> the paint lying in streaky seams not half blowzed off, discovering coarse wrinkled skins: the hair of some of them of divers colours, obliged to the black-lead comb where black was affected; the artificial jet, however, yielding space to the natural brindle: that of others plastered with oil and powder; the oil predominating: but every one's hanging about her ears and neck in broken curls, or ragged ends. . . . If thou *hadst* [seen them], I believe thou wouldst hate a profligate woman, as one of Swift's yahoos, or Virgil's obscene harpies, squirting their ordure upon the Trojan trenches; since the persons of such in their retirements are as filthy as their minds.—Hate them as much as I do; and as much as I admire, and next to adore, a truly virtuous and elegant woman [i.e. Clarissa]. (9, 64–65)

In short, once he discovers Clarissa, Belford becomes a Gulliver in Houyhnhnmland; the implication is, as in Smollett, that sufficient provocation—when good is being trampled underfoot—will produce satire that is valuable, if only as a corrective.

Like some of Lovelace's letters, which are intended to characterize the libertine, this letter goes beyond the needs of characterization and tends to stand by itself, a shocking image of sexual depravity. It approximates Smollett's satire in *Humphry Clinker* in which the reader is given the effect of the vice on an observer, who has been sensitized by certain circumstances. In both cases, the observer as well as the observed is part of the theme. Whether or not both or neither can be traced back to Gulliver's reaction to the yahoos, the effect is nevertheless analogous.

What has been said about *Clarissa* can also be said in part about *Sir Charles Grandison* (1754), but Richardson's last novel will be introduced more appropriately in a later section.[48] We can conclude that nonsatiric, even antisatiric writers have begun to use satire as an attitude which they contrast with more benevolent ones such as friendship, sentiment, and love. The good satirist and the bad are

48. See below, pp. 279–83.

taken as two ways of looking at experience, and this produces certain distinctive character types in the novels of Smollett and, to some extent, in those of Richardson and later Burney and Austen. The chief character type who emerges is the satirist-satirized, who runs through a whole gamut of mutations in Smollett's novels, from the equivocal satirist to the villainous satirist to the sick satirist. If in one manifestation satire is now an attitude, in another it is simply a character uttering ridicule or invective at another, whether indirectly as in Anna's letters or directly as in the exchanges between Clarissa and Betty Barnes.

The Satirist as a Comic Type

As the character of Matthew Bramble shows, another role was available to the satirist-satirized figure in eighteenth-century fiction. Anna is something of a "humourist," whose satiric thrusts at Hickman are qualified by her secret liking of him. Bramble's fierce denunciations clash with his secret benevolence, his rough exterior with his heart of gold, and his hatred of the general with his love of the particular. He is frequently discovered helping destitute widows on the sly, and his ecstasies over the good are as striking if less frequent than his spasms in the presence of the bad. In a metaphorical sense his sickness and health correspond to the public railing and private benevolence, but the result is as comically incongruous as Parson Adams with his spirituality embodied in a vigorous body wielding a crabstick and racing coaches. The contradiction of satiric commentary and motive can, in short, be comic as well as tragic.

The satyr-satirist on whom Sarah Fielding, Richardson, and Smollett patterned their critical commentators was a satirist whose public exposures and denunciations were explained by envy and the desire for revenge, in other words, by a sense of evil in himself. One of Smollett's accomplishments in *Sir Launcelot Greaves* was to substitute for the disreputable motive of envy the reputable one of benevolence. It was Greaves' passion for justice and reform that drove him to his *furor satiricus*. But in *David Simple* Sarah Fielding had already sketched in a character who railed at public evils while doing private acts of benevolence. In *The Citizen of the World* (1760–62), Oliver Goldsmith had introduced Mr. Drybone, the Man in Black, a misanthrope with a difference. While the traditional misanthrope (e.g. Fielding's Man of the Hill) is a sensitive, good man who is disillusioned by his experience in society and turns into a railing satirist, the Man in Black, having gone through his disillusionment and become a railing satirist, retains his original benevolence. His misanthropy is a consciously assumed mask which allows the sentimentalist to face the hostile world. As Lien Chi Altangi, his receptive student, notices,

> though his conversation be replete with the most sordid and selfish maxims, his heart is dilated with the most unbounded love. I have known him to profess himself a man hater, while his cheek was glowing with compassion; and while his looks were softened with pity, I have heard him use the language of the most unbounded ill nature.[49]

Lien Chi, more sensible than David Simple, recognizes both sides of the Man in Black and accepts him as a valuable friend.

Drybone probably influenced the conception of Matthew Bramble, but their effects are essentially different. The point of Drybone's assumption of misanthropy is his hypocrisy; moreover, Goldsmith uses misanthropy to mean cynical worldliness as much as satirical railing. Drybone allows Goldsmith to make the satire and the sentiment coincident, not consecutive as in most misanthropes; unlike Bramble, however, Drybone is never really a misanthrope. Bramble may be, in some sense, only posing as one. "He affects misanthropy," Jery says in his letter of April 24, "in order to conceal the sensibility of a heart, which is tender, even to a degree of weakness"; but Smollett stresses his satire rather than his cynicism, and his sickness leads the reader to think that his misanthropy, even if a protective reaction, is involuntary. Finally, both figures demonstrate Steele's dictum about satire's origin in good nature, but Drybone makes satire a conscious pose of an unsatiric personality, while Bramble makes it *difficile . . . non scribere.*

Thomas R. Preston, in an excellent study of the benevolent misanthrope, argues that this type "gains in satiric power" over the old

---

49. *Collected Works of Oliver Goldsmith,* ed. Arthur Friedman (Oxford, Clarendon Press, 1965), 2, 109.

satyr-satirist, and he points to "the ironic tension between speculative misanthropy and actual good deeds" and the fact that the "new satiric persona calls into question the whole theory of benevolence in human nature, since the new misanthrope is really a man of feeling forced into the position of a satirist to protect himself from imposition and to castigate a society which ironically believes that men are naturally good."[50] This ought to be the case, and in a few novels may be,[51] but in general the effect of these amiable misanthropes is not one of intensification but of mitigation and qualification. First, because the satirist opposes general satire to particular benevolence, his satire is so generalized that it lacks bite. Second, much of the time his satire functions mainly to characterize the speaker, who is such a mixed and comical character that he and not what he says is attended to. In *The Citizen of the World,* Drybone is more often exploited for the incongruity in his position than as a keen social observer; in the same way Lien Chi Altangi, the Chinese observer, tends to become interesting as an incongruous mixture of wisdom and naïveté, and his observations become chiefly amusing for the incongruity between a foreigner's view and our own.

While writers like Goldsmith still use their satiric observers as devices to whose words the reader is meant to harken, they betray their allegiance to the amusing possibilities of a satirist as a character type in action with other character types (perhaps other satirists). The satirist then disappears into a character who evidently refuses to believe his own satire, who speaks worse than he thinks, and whose sharp tongue is denied by his good heart—in short, not a satirist at all but a comic type. Such figures have been completely absorbed when their satire can no longer be taken as a truth independent from their characters and situations, when it no longer refers to anything external to the plot.

50. Thomas R. Preston, "The Good-Natured Misanthrope: A Study in the Satire and Sentiment of the 18th Century," Unpublished Doctoral Dissertation (Rice University, 1962), p. 57; see also his article based on the dissertation: "Smollett and the Benevolent Misanthrope," *PMLA*, 79 (1964), 51–57.

51. Preston's list includes Samuel Sarcastic in Melmoth's *Shenstone-Green* (1779), Sir Howell Henneth in Bage's *Mount Henneth* (1781), Albany in Fanny Burney's *Cecilia* (1782), Wyman in Bage's *Barham Downs* (1784), Paul Lamounde in Bage's *James Wallace* (1788), Partington in Melmoth's *Family Secrets* (1797), and Lindsay in Bage's *Man as He Is* (1792).

Chapter 6

SATIRE AND SENTIMENTALITY

Chroniques Scandaleuses

In the course of the last chapter satire (the word and the thing) has gradually been debased until it merely signifies a man revenging himself upon an enemy; at least, this was the meaning it had for most of Smollett's contemporaries. It is time to look at the final disappearance of satire as a meaningful term in amusement, scandal, melodrama, and sentimentality and try to explain why these antithetic qualities jostle each other in Smollett's novels; why he accompanies his satiric scenes and characters with threads of unmitigated romance plot, ending with the missing father found, the estranged lovers united, the paternal estate reclaimed, and a reward for the worthy. To an extent, of course, these romance conventions are added only to make a beginning and end that will be acceptable to the mid-century reading public. Occasionally, as when they convey the humoring and dehumoring of the Quixotic satirist, they are assimilated to the satiric intention. Most often, however, sentimental stretches, brimming with tender feelings and tears, lie inert beside lively satiric scenes.

Something of the decline of satiric forms into an observer-object relation has already been seen. By the end of the seventeenth century the satirist had become in many instances a convenient persona for reporting current events in a satiric style; "satiric," no longer a synonym for "realistic," now indicated only a sharp, lively style. Ned Ward's observer in *The London Spy* (1698) is a Londoner showing the sights of the city to a visitor from the country; Tom Brown in *Amusements Serious and Comical* (1700) uses an American Indian. The result in both cases is not so much satiric as entertaining—the intention being to report an incident or a curious type for the reader's

"amusement" (to use Brown's word). These "realistic, satiric 'jour-
neys' about town,"[1] written in verse by Tom D'Urfey and in prose by
Ward and Brown, traced their satiric ancestry to Juvenal, in particular to his third satire ("Rome"). Individual conventions, like the
dense crowd of the Juvenalian scene, are well conveyed:

> *Make Way there,* says a Gouty-Leg'd Chairman, that is carrying
> a Punk of Quality to a Mornings Exercise: Or a *Bartholomew-*
> Baby Beau, newly Launch'd out of a Chocolate-House, with his
> Pockets as empty as his Brains. Make Room there, says another
> Fellow driving a Wheel-Barrow of Nuts, that spoil the Lungs of
> the City Prentices, and make them Wheeze over their Mis-
> tresses.[2]

The speaker is always pointing: "Look, yonder is . . ." or "Pray mind
that worshipful lump of clay, that inanimated figure who lolls in the
elbow-chair, and takes no matter of notice of what is said in the company" (p. 69). "Here sits a holy sister, full of spiritual pride in her
face, the word of God in her hands, the passion in her eye, and the
devil in her tail" (p. 89). In each case the exhortation is followed by
an account of the person, usually more informative than satiric.
Brown combines a factual, specific location—a dissenter church or
Westminster Hall—with real people, such as Dr. Woodward, Daniel
Burgess, or Dr. Offspring Blackall, and with conventional subjects,
such as women in church, virtuosos, gamblers, and quacks. In a general way he produces a social and moral anatomy of London, with
satire as one popular ingredient, and the effect is not unlike that of
Bramble's letters in *Humphry Clinker.* Although Brown's *Amusements* lacks arrangement or a connecting theme and is a much duller
performance than Smollett's, it uses satiric scenes in the same way—
as part of a medley that includes much else.

If in one direction the observer-object relation in satire leads toward straight reporting, in another it leads toward the melodramatic
and sentimental. A spirit, an animal, or inanimate object as observer

1. See Benjamin Boyce, *Tom Brown of Facetious Memory* (Cambridge, Harvard
University Press, 1939), p. 134.
2. *Amusements Serious and Comical and Other Works,* ed. A. L. Haywood (New
York, Dodd, Mead & Co., 1927), pp. 11–12.

has the advantage of being able to gain access to places no human could enter and thus detect the reality beneath otherwise inviolable appearances. In Guevara's *El Diablo cojuelo* (1641) a "genius," out of gratitude, lifts off all the roofs of Madrid at night to expose its real life to his benefactor. By 1707 Le Sage hints in *Le Diable boiteux,* his adaptation of *El Diablo cojuelo,* at a further significance of the supernatural observer: Chimney C says to Chimney D (in the second "Dialogue of the Two Chimneys"), "This is the advantage we chimneys enjoy; we are witnesses to a thousand sights that men would pay any price for seeing."[3] Charles Gildon, in his adaptation of Apuleius' *Metamorphoses* (1709), replaces the ass with "a fine *Bologna* Lap-Dog" which will be more readily "admitted to the Closets, Cabinets, and Bed-chambers of the Fair and the Great."[4] In *The Island Adjacent to Utopia* (1725) Mrs. Mary de la Riviere Manley has her observer Cupid, who eavesdrops on "the soul-torturing anguish of that unfortunate lady" and on worse, crow that he "was witness of her secret pangs, her agonizing complaints, heard of no ear but mine" (*1,* 211).

At its best the *chronique scandaleuse* represents another form of anti-romance, a conscious effort to attain to the real in reaction to romance. This is the purpose of the "genius" who removes the roofs of Madrid and, in one scene, shows people in the privacy of their bedrooms. The observer who can see through walls also reveals the sexual aspects of reality and, perhaps even more important, the emotional and psychological; men and especially women are shown "with their hair down."

Mrs. Manley makes a great pretense, if nothing else, of writing satire. In her dedication to the second volume of *The New Atalantis* (1709), she claims that it is "written like *Varronian* Satyrs, on *different Subjects, Tales, Stories,* and *Characters* of *Invention,* after the Manner of *Lucian,* who copy'd from *Varro.*" She cites Dryden's dictum in *The Original and Progress of Satire* (1693) that "What is most essential, and the very Soul of Satire, is scourging of Vice, and Exhortation to Virtue. . . . Tis an Action of Virtue to make Examples of vicious Men." Defending herself against the attack of the *Tatler* (No.

3. *The Novels of Le Sage and Charles Johnsone,* in Ballantyne's Novelist's Library (Edinburgh, 1822), *4,* 303.
4. *The New Metamorphosis* (London, 1724 ed.), preface.

92), she turns her dedication into a satiric apologia, invoking "the *Precedent* of our *Great Fore-fathers* in *Satire,* who not only flew against the *general* reigning *Vices,* but pointed at *individual* Persons," and she lists the great satirists who, she says, wrote *chroniques scandaleuses.*[5] I quote these self-justifications because, to many at this time, precedent was as good as performance, and I strongly suspect that this was true of Smollett. But we might also acknowledge that, rather than a thin gilding of didacticism over sensational eroticism, Mrs. Manley in fact uses eroticism as a come-on to lure neutral readers into her labyrinth of anti-Whiggery. And her propaganda was successful if one may judge by the action taken against her by the infuriated Whigs, by Swift's praise of her, and by the large public she reached and the large body of imitators she aroused.

Her form is an elaborate facsimile of formal verse satire. It is discursive rather than dramatic, a conventional frame for a gallery of portraits and scenes; it simply juxtaposes a satirist with a long line of satiric objects for him to observe and criticize. In *The New Atalantis* Astrea (Justice), a cross between Juvenal's Umbricius and a supernatural observer, decides to return from exile and revisit the earth; she meets her mother Virtue in tatters and learns that men have set up a mock Astrea. Her stroll through the capital city (Angela, or London) produces a series of shifting scenes of corruption punctuated by Juvenalian outbursts on this sad state of affairs. Almost at once, however, Mrs. Manley's focus narrows to love; the scenes exposed are invariably concerned with love affairs. Sexual passion is Mrs. Manley's satiric metaphor for the human situation, and her satiric method is *cherchez la femme:* at the bottom of all the great Whig policies lurk dark private passions. The war in Europe is merely the largest of these: like the other issues it is reduced by her pen to the lowest common denominator, much as her friend Swift had reduced all the huffing and puffing of the moderns to the little vapor searching for an exit from the body. Her paradigm for the Whigs is a boudoir, and going behind the scenes for the damning reality she follows the method of travesty, showing the rape of a nation to be no more noble than the rape of a maiden.

5. *Secret Memoirs and Manners of Several Persons of Quality of Both Sexes, from the New Atalantis, an Island in the Mediterranean, Written Originally in Italian* (2d ed. London, 1709), 2, Sig. A3, A4.

Mrs. Manley produces a new kind of satiric situation in which a wicked man betrays a woman. In the notorious Fortunatus episode a lustful, foolish woman (the Duchess L'Inconstant alias the Duchess of Cleveland) is exploited by an ambitious lover (Fortunatus-Marlborough) who, once he has used her, betrays her, drops her, and later refuses to help her in her need. The Duchess' end shows both the wages of her folly and the exploitations of a wicked man. The same relationship, with the same denouement, appears in the story of the Duke (the Duke of Portland) who falls in love with his young ward Charlot, seduces her, and later abandons her. "Thus was Charlot undone!" cries Mrs. Manley, "thus ruin'd by him that ought to have been her Protector!" (*1, 72*). And Charlot, like the Duchess, goes steadily downhill after her betrayal:

> The remainder of her life was one continu'd Scene of Horror, Sorrow, and Repentance. She dy'd a true Landmark, to warn all believing Virgins from shipwracking their Honour upon (that dangerous Coast of Rocks) the Vows and pretended Passion of Mankind. (*1, 83*)

The Duke's passion makes him forsake his duty fighting at the side of King Henriques (William III). As in the Fortunatus story, however, this episode, whatever its satiric or moral intent, emerges simply as a psychological study of an older man's passion for a young girl— how it warps his life, destroys his honor, and crushes his innocent victim.

The tone of complaint is Mrs. Manley's usual satiric voice. She starts with the description of despair and defeat, of onrushing chaos, of the exploitation and annihilation of goodness (all conventions of Juvenalian satire), and carries this beyond pessimism or even despair into sentimental lament. The *saeva indignatio* of Juvenal, softened and made melancholy, becomes: "But oh! how despicable her Garments! how neglected her flowing Hair! how languid her formerly animating Eyes! how pale, how withered, the Roses of her lovely Cheeks and Lips!" (*1, 2*). If at one extreme she slips into the imagery of the weeping, forlorn, dishonored woman who is her chief symbol of the evil of the Whigs, at the other she uses a vocabulary of biblical lamentation full of abstractions that extend to the characters, some of whom are personifications. Solitude and Sincerity cry out against "false Glory! glittering Pomp! swelling Ambition! noisy Wisdom! pretending Loves! boasted Knowledge! seeming Piety! affected Honesty!"

Mrs. Manley's experiment is not an isolated case. Her disciple Mrs. Eliza Haywood repeatedly uses the device of a love story to get across her "satire," setting her stories in the familiar Manley frame. Both begin with a satiric, or at least propagandistic, intention and develop a kind of scene that gets across its point through stories of pathos and degradation which rely more heavily on the reader's sympathy than his indignation. Moreover, the characters are supposed to be real people—Marlborough, Godolphin, and the rest—and so added to the reader's sympathy for the heroine is shock, surprise, and perhaps indignation at the discovery that a great public man has (and is motivated by) such a sordid private life. The three main elements then are a private microcosm to illuminate a public macrocosm, an emphasis on sexuality as the central evil that reflects all public evils, and the conveyance of this by melodramatic diction.

To see the important shift in (or away from) satiric method that is implicit in the Manley *chronique scandaleuse,* one needs to recall the use of relationships and scenes of epiphany by earlier satirists. For one thing, the relationships presented were always social ones—between a patron and his dependent (in Juvenal), between a master and his servant (in the picaresque), between a writer and society (in Dryden and the Augustans). When the marriage relation was used, as in Juvenal's sixth satire, it was marriage as a social institution, stressing the wife's duty to her husband and family, not to her lover. In the early eighteenth-century works that have been discussed, marriage remains in the background as a kind of ideal relationship against which the relationship between a lover and a loved one develops into that between a seducer and his victim. One inference to be drawn from this seducer-seduced relation is that Mrs. Manley and her followers, who find love the secret motive for every action, while taking sanction from Restoration satire, in fact reflect by their emphasis the rise of the Puritan ethic that finds the epitome of evil in sexual misbehavior.

The progenitor and most respectable source of the sentimental convention of the seduction was, in all likelihood, Nicholas Rowe's *The*

Fair Penitent (1703). One of Richardson's sources for *Clarissa,* it shows how tragedy, like satire, was sentimentalized in the eighteenth century. Rowe's "she-tragedy" (as explained in the prologue) is no longer tragedy concerned with "the fate of kings and empires" (with "the great") but "A melancholy tale of private woes." Accordingly the subject of tragedy is now "sorrows like your own," and the effect of "ambition" on "the great" is replaced by the effect of "imperious love" on the ordinary person (specifically on the female). Rowe has taken the "misfortunes and distress" that are "one of the main designs of tragedy" and shifted them downward until the tragic dramatist's announced aim is "to excite [the audience's] generous pity." The villain of tragedy is now the rake—become an almost Satanic villain—who ravishes and then flees at the mention of "the marriage chain." Lothario is a darker Dorimant, made to account for his actions. Satire likewise sinks from anger to melancholy and complaint, from judgment to pity, from public concerns to private, from political affairs to domestic.

Yet, typically, there were various ways in which the emphasis on seduction could be justified. To the classical minded Augustan, for example, a reference to such a violation was sure to be accompanied by a reference to Virginius, who slew his daughter "yet unspotted to prevent / The shame which she might know" (IV.i), or to Lucrece, who took her own life after being raped by Tarquin. These were invariably symbols of Republican Rome vs. tyranny, and the Augustan could associate a girl's chastity with the inviolability of the individual against tyranny as easily as the Puritan could. Although Whigs like Rowe cultivated such symbols, the Tories too connected themselves with this tradition, taking the defense of Chastity as a fierce Roman virtue "worthy of that spirit / that sweld in ancient Latian breasts when Rome / Was mistress of the world" (V.i).

If, in these works and in Richardson's vastly greater novels, evil narrows to a sexual assault, it should perhaps be regarded as part of the larger change of emphasis from evil that is a desire to fulfill one's own nature at the expense of all other people to evil that is a thwarting of the individual's self-fulfillment. The old Augustan emphasis remains in the figure of Lovelace, the individualist who, like Satan, would ruin Clarissa or all the world to achieve his own private end. But the fact that, as Richardson complained, contemporaries often preferred Lovelace to Clarissa (and later critics thought that Satan was the real hero of *Paradise Lost*) shows how ambiguous selfish individualism could be as an evil. This is the figure that Smollett explored in the novels of his middle period, and like Richardson he sees the blackest evil not in the overthrow of social structures but in a sexual assault on a virgin.

Satire and Melodrama

In *Roderick Random* Smollett connects evil with the effects of egotism—the impingement of one individual upon the liberty, security, or serenity of another. He associates this with the authority of captains and generals, the rich and politically powerful. But in *Peregrine Pickle,* by which time *Clarissa* had been published, his emphasis changes from the public types of dominance to the private and, increasingly, the sexual. He shows the desire for power over other people in satirists, wives, and seducers; the first part of the novel is about marriage, the second about extramarital relations, and in both the unit of analysis is the relationship between a man and a woman.

The first volume gives various examples of subjection and freedom in a comic context. Two men appear at the outset, one completely passive, already dominated by his sister, and the other free. Gamaliel Pickle merely exchanges one keeper for another when he marries; but Hawser Trunnion is captured and subdued, his eccentricity curbed, by a wife. What at first seems their folly soon turns out to be innocence. In the society of these women they are "quite out of their element"; they have no chance against the "discretion," prudence, and scheming of the single-minded Grizzle and the new Mrs. Pickle. Smollett contrasts a preternatural simplicity with a dedication to deceit and domination. With Grizzle in charge of the Trunnion ménage, "in less than two hours, the whole economy of the garrison was turned topsy-turvy" (Chap. 9; *4, 75*); "in less than three months he became a thorough-paced husband" (Chap. 10; *4, 79*). Throughout the story poor Trunnion is compared with captive animals; "like a reluctant bear, ... he is led to the stake amidst the shouts and cries of butchers and their dogs" (Chap. 5; *4, 42*).

The story of Pickle and Trunnion in the first volume is a parallel and preparation for the whole story of Peregrine, with special emphasis on his heredity. But a significant change takes place as Smollett's focus narrows from the contrasted Trunnion and Pickle households to the story of Peregrine himself. The various kinds of exploitation narrow to a preoccupation with a single kind, sexual violation, and the various innocences of Trunnion and Pickle become the single, and supposedly far more important, innocence of the helpless virgin. Although the attempt to rape Emilia is not the exclusive consequence of Peregrine's will to power, Smollett seems to regard it as his climactic and most heinous crime, which must be elaborately expiated. Peregrine approaches the rape via the beating of Pallet and the ducking of Hornbeak, via the seduction of one wife and the attempted seduction of another. The worst is his nearly successful rape of a virgin. Such scenes of more-or-less bungled seduction are a commonplace of *Gil Blas* and the continental picaresque, but here the tone of moral concern or indignation is much stronger; the reader feels that Peregrine is doing something evil as well as foolish, and not that this is simply the way of the world. The style reflects the situation:

> Instead of awful veneration, which her presence used to inspire, that chastity of sentiment, and delicacy of expression, he now gazed upon her with the eyes of a libertine, he glowed with the impatience of desire, talked in a strain that barely kept within the bounds of decency. (5, 284)

Although Peregrine's attempt to rape Emilia is motivated by his pride and (Smollett adds for good measure) his adherence to the false ideals of high society, the heightened feeling Smollett engenders around the act derives almost exclusively from the idea of Peregrine's forcibly deflowering the girl who loves him and (the irony of his self-delusion) whom he loves. One of Smollett's direct sources is Mrs. Davys' *Accomplish'd Rake* (1727), and the difference is instructive. He omits the large quotient of Sir John Galliard's obligations to the Friendly family and the elaborate consequences to them as well as to the raped Miss Friendly;[6] the horror of the unaccomplished rape in

---

6. Sir John Galliard, it will be remembered, attempted to lure Miss Friendly from a masquerade to a bagnio; failing, he later fed her drugged macaroons and succeeded in raping her in a country inn. Even the jargon Smollett uses is already present: Miss Friendly becomes "the innocent sacrifice" to lust, "his victim," the "poor innocent Miss Friendly" upon whom "the base, ungenerous" Sir John is going to work "his base design." The same authorial addresses are made to the rapist: "O Man! How strong the passions, how exorbitant the desires," etc. (McBurney, *Four Before Richardson*, pp. 292–93).

Peregrine Pickle is made to arise more exclusively from the sexual situation.

In *Ferdinand Count Fathom* the seduction/rape becomes Smollett's chief symbol of evil (the robbery is a less heinous analogue), and his approach to sexual evil is less equivocal, perhaps because he now has an almost completely unsympathetic hero. Fathom's schemes and attempts at sexual violation mark his progress toward an absolute in depravity. The five seductions (or attempted seductions) are a major unifying element in the novel and appear increasingly worse as the women attacked are progressively more innocent.

Teresa, the first victim, is merely an unscrupulous servant, no better than Fathom, who helps him cheat the Melvils. The second victim, Wilhelmina, is an unattractive girl who succumbs to gross flattery, and her stepmother, who receives the same treatment, is played off against her. Wilhelmina has such clearly designated weaknesses of character as "unenlightened pride" and (with her stepmother) a certain "appetite for pleasure" (Chap. 12; *8, 76*). The reader is told in passing that Fathom debauches the landlord's daughter in Antwerp and leaves her four months pregnant (Chap. 27; *8, 221*), but there are no details given. The next victim, Elenor, is a more complex and pathetic case. Fathom meets her on the stage to London and quickly convinces her that she has "captivated the heart of a man who could raise her to the rank and dignity of a countess." She is essentially "an innocent, unsuspecting country damsel, flushed with the warmth of youth, and an utter stranger to the ways of life" (Chap. 30; *8, 242*), and her fate is accordingly darker than Wilhelmina's. Celinda, as we have seen, is motivated by excessive sensibility, but her consequences are the most dismaying, a plunge from degradation to degradation. Significantly, Mlle. de Melvil and Monimia, who have none of these follies, do not follow the path to seduction. With them, as with Emilia, the seducer cannot succeed, and Smollett has settled into the world of melodrama in which villains are thwarted and heroines preserved.

Smollett informs this scene of sexual threat with the vocabulary of melodrama and its appurtenances of tears, religious overtones, and physical fear. The diction heightens three areas—the evil seducer, the pursued innocent, and the atmosphere that surrounds the act of evil. Peregrine is "the insidious lover" who works upon Emilia with "his hypocrisy" until "her heart should be so far entangled within his snares" that he can seduce her (Chap. 75; 6, 36). Fathom "marks" Elenor's "chastity for prey to his voluptuous passion" (Chap. 30; 8, 242). On the supposed death of Monimia, the narrator addresses Fathom thus: "Perfidious wretch! thy crimes turn out to be so atrocious, that I half repent me of having undertaken to record thy memoirs; yet such monsters ought to be exhibited to public view" (Chap. 49; 9, 108). This is still clearly the Juvenalian world in which Swift flays Lord Allen and puts his carcass on display, but the satiric grotesque is becoming monstrous, sublimely horrible. Juvenal's wives who poison their husbands and the sons who poison their fathers are only somewhat more grotesque and less melodramatic.

Another extension of the Juvenalian situation is the pitiful victim— the Umbricius who is driven out of Rome. When Fathom tells Monimia his lies about her beloved Renaldo, "her fatal conjecture" about Renaldo's love brings out "signs of extreme agitation"; "a flood of tears gushed from her enchanting eyes"; "she indulged her sorrow to excess" (Chap. 45; 9, 53). She "endeavoured to devour her griefs in silence; she in secret bemoaned her forlorn fate without ceasing; her tears flowed without intermission from night to morn, and from morn to night" (Chap. 46; 9, 59). And so "her cheeks grew wan, her bright eyes lost their splendour, the roses vanished from her lips, and her delicate limbs could hardly support their burden" (p. 60). As Fathom moves in for the kill, she resists his "detested embrace," and the resulting clash is almost "supernatural" (to use Smollett's word) : he "would have acted the part of young Tarquin, and violated by force that sacred shrine of honour, beauty, and unblemished truth" (Chap. 49; 9, 98). She, with sword in hand, is like the archangel Michael; her aspect "seemed to shine with something supernatural, and actually disordered his whole faculties" (p. 99)—and he, like Satan, retreats.

The virgin is only the extreme instance of innocence and pitiableness. The reaction of Monimia's beloved Renaldo to Fathom's plot is much the same: separated from Monimia his life becomes "a sacrifice to the most poignant distress"; "he beheld the mistress of his soul abandoned to the blackest scenes of poverty and want" (Chap. 44; 9, 43, 45); and he too "wept and raved by turns" (Chap. 46; 9, 65). As Smollett tells the reader in a chapter heading, "Renaldo's Distress

Deepens, and Fathom's Plot thickens" (Chap. 45). Much as Fielding does in *Jonathan Wild,* Smollett shows a thesis, Fathom, and an antithesis, Renaldo Melvil: the first volume is about Fathom, the second increasingly about Melvil—in particular about the reactions of the innocent as they are exploited by the evil Fathom, and so about their suffering. The focus on Melvil and his particular suffering at Fathom's hands shows how, by shifting to the victim, Smollett has changed from the comic or grotesque to a melodramatic evil, from the vigor of evil to the agonies of the persecuted innocent, and from indignation to compassion.

In such surroundings evil becomes palpable, an atmosphere, as in parts of *Macbeth.* The well-known interlude of Fathom's seeking refuge from a storm in a lonely house on the way to Paris introduces this atmosphere. The house in which guests are murdered for their money, the stormy night, the "dismal soughing of the trees," lightning and thunder and rain, and a murdered man still warm elicit from Fathom "unspeakable horror" and "transports of . . . dread" (Chap. 21; *8, 147*). Smollett's point in introducing this scene is presumably to warn Fathom (and the reader) of the depths to which he will sink—that murder for money is not far beyond murder for lust (which appears to be Monimia's fate). More important are the elements of the Gothic and the sublime which Smollett associates with the manifestation of evil—as he does later in the visit to Monimia's "grave" and in her "ghost" and "resurrection."

Smollett's introduction of such scenes and imagery is, in one sense, a matter of decorum. Critics increasingly warned satirists that evil and vice should not be ridiculed; ridicule was to be reserved for lighter follies. Moreover, ridicule remained a low form compared to the "finer perception" of the sense of sublimity which was supposedly beyond the satirist. One solution was Smollett's—to modulate from one tone to another or to show the close connections that existed between satire and Gothic horror and other aspects of the sublime.

Smollett's melodrama operates by the same externalizing of emotion and generalizing of diction that characterizes his satire. When terror comes to Commodore Trunnion, "a cold sweat bedewed his limbs, his knees knocked together, his hair bristled up, and the remains of his teeth were shattered to pieces in the convulsive vibrations of his jaws" (Chap. 7; *4, 55*). If Trunnion batters his teeth to pieces in comic terror, with Fathom "the whole surface of his body was covered with a cold sweat, and his nerves were relaxed with an universal palsy" (Chap. 21; *8,* 149). Rape and seduction are only the obverse of the satiric violence of broken heads and violent purges. Smollett's theory can be described either as the belief that satire and melodrama are complementary and can be mixed—that they are, after all, both heightenings of reality—or that such melodramatic episodes as the seduction scene are an extension and darkening of satire, much like the harsh railing style that the satirist assumes when the world becomes too incorrigible for any other approach.

There is satiric precedence for Smollett's linking satire with melodrama in parts of Juvenal's satires and in Elizabethan satire (especially in a work like Nashe's *Unfortunate Traveller*). But it is more probably from the novels of Mrs. Manley and Mrs. Haywood, which called themselves satires, that Smollett derived the plausible idea that scenes of raped innocence, sexual violence, and heavily emotional trappings could complement or intensify satire. The seduction of Celinda, for example, could have been written by Mrs. Manley; it leads to the familiar consequences, with the poor girl growing "every day more sensual and degenerate" and ending as a streetwalker. Her omniscient Cupid or Virtue or Justice may even have exerted some influence on Smollett's railing and—in *Fathom*—lamenting satirist and certainly on his omniscient atom in *Adventures of an Atom.*

Manley and Haywood, as well as Ward and Brown, offered another useful precedent to Smollett. If the satiric form can, under certain circumstances, absorb a series of melodramatic scenes, it can with equal ease be "intensified" into journalistic exposé. Again Juvenal offered an ultimate sanction in his lurid particularity, which could be interpreted as a *chronique scandaleuse* of Roman vice, but Mrs. Manley and the "secret histories" of the various "spies" were closer to hand. Smollett's narrative of Miss Williams' sad sexual experiences in *Roderick Random* is an early example of one aspect of the *chronique scandaleuse* (Melopoyne's story is another), but the most obvious is "The Memoirs of a Lady of Quality," which fills nearly a whole volume of *Peregrine Pickle* and deals with contemporary characters thinly disguised in a sentimental and sensational way, but with satiric touches. With Smollett, however, it is not altogether certain that his satire was not aiming toward some version of the actual, and that his long interval of composing histories and compendiums of knowledge was not in fact part of a straight line connecting *Roderick Random* and *Humphry Clinker*. Certainly one of the impressive accomplishments of the latter novel is its incorporation of journalistic elements.[7]

Looking back from *Humphry Clinker,* we can see that exposé, the travel book, and the melodramatic and sentimental scenes are not only areas of subject matter but projected attitudes toward experience. In one sense all of the different tones—satiric (Horatian and Juvenalian), melodramatic, sentimental, reportorial—are attitudes, reflections of sensibility that resolve themselves into the general points of view of the letter writers in *Humphry Clinker*. However, they pose the central question of whether Smollett's use of them is, in intention and effect, the broadening of a spectrum or a transformation downward from Horatian satire to good-natured banter, from Juvenalian satire to melancholy, melodrama, and sublimity, and from admiration for the good to sentimental rapture? In one sense Smollett is consciously attempting to extend the satiric tone from indignation to horror and sympathy and the satiric subject matter from fool and knave to villain, from dupe to innocent virgin, from social to private, and from fancy to fact. This is, I think, the crucial intention, but one cannot discount the desire to write a popular work, because almost all the forms Smollett employs are popular contemporary ones—the *chronique,* the romance of rape and redemption, the journey about town (or country), and many more. In each case he borrows a form that has satiric roots but has lost most of its satiric inspiration. His motive was partly to revivify the satiric impulse but very likely partly to write popular fiction.

Peregrine Pickle was published in February 1751 and Fielding's *Amelia* in December of the same year (the dedication is dated December 12). From what is known of Fielding's activities at the time, *Amelia* seems to have been written mainly in the course of that year. It is possible that Fielding read *Peregrine Pickle* upon publication, since the first edition contained scurrilous attacks on him and his friend Lyttelton; he alludes to the "Memoirs of a Lady of Quality" at

7. See Louis L. Martz, *The Later Career of Tobias Smollett* (New Haven, Yale University Press, 1942).

least twice in the course of *Amelia*. Whatever the relationship between these novels, Amelia, the epitome of goodness, represents a remarkable reversal of her author's values. As the central symbol of value she is presented as the object of seducers, and the evil under consideration becomes the violation of sexual fidelity. Indeed Amelia is another Clarissa, whose problem is treated within the marriage relation, and who is ultimately successful in maintaining her integrity: she represents the "virtue rewarded" ending that Fielding claims to have wished Richardson would accord Clarissa. Mrs. Bennet's exclamation after the "fatal consequence" of the Noble Lord's attack on her virtue, "happy had I been had this been the period of my life" (Bk. VII, Chap. 7; 7, 48), exactly echoes Pamela's "May I never survive, one moment, that fatal one in which I shall forfeit my innocence!" While Mrs. Bennet does not escape Fielding's irony, in this instance her own sad fate is a warning to Amelia.

This is not to say that Fielding has suddenly adopted the Puritan ethic. Sexual intemperance in both *Tom Jones* and *Amelia* is a serious offense only when it injures someone, when it betrays Sophia or Amelia. It is not vague and irrational as in the works of Smollett. Moreover, Booth, driven by passion and seduced by Miss Matthews, is clearly less culpable than Colonel James, who is driven by passion to destroy his friend and an innocent woman; even worse are the Ellisons and Trents, who betray for pay, or the Noble Lord, who betrays for his own amusement. Nevertheless, in *Tom Jones* the sexual is only one of many kinds of violation; in *Amelia* it is the central one, with Booth's various misfortunes merely leading toward or away from the potential seduction of Amelia.

Fielding apparently felt that this aspect of *Amelia,* among others, needed some justification. Not long after *Amelia*'s publication he wrote some pieces about his "favourite child" in his current periodical, the *Covent-Garden Journal*. One of these essays (although not mentioning *Amelia* by name) discusses the idea of evil,[8] those men "by whom [women] are deceived, corrupted, betrayed, and often brought *to Destruction, both Body and Soul.*" The crime as he outlines it is appropriately Satanic—evil hating and wishing to destroy the good. In *Amelia* Satan, the Seducer of Man, becomes more specifically the Noble Lord, the Seducer of Women. He has all the Sa-

8. *Covent-Garden Journal*, No. 20, Mar. 10, 1752; ed. Jensen, *1*, 253–58.

tanic trappings, whether satiric or Richardsonian. He is "the handsomest and genteelest person in the world" (Bk. VII, Chap. 6; 7, 43), a consummate actor, who carries out his seductions with masks; he corrupts his victims and then leaves them—corrupting is all that interests him. "What is this appetite," cries Mrs. Bennet, one of his victims, "which must have novelty and resistance for its provocatives, and which is delighted with us no longer than while we may be considered in the light of enemies?" (Bk. VII, Chap. 9; 7, 58). She has the last word on his crime:

> my doubt is whether the art or folly of it be the more conspicuous; for however delicate and refined the art must be allowed to have been, the folly, I think, must upon a fair examination appear no less astonishing: for to lay all considerations of cruelty and crime out of the case, what a foolish bargain doth the man make for himself who purchases so poor a pleasure at so high a price! (Bk. VII, Chap. 6; 7, 45)

By the last phrase she means both the enormous time and expense the Noble Lord went to in accomplishing his scheme and the price of his own soul. Fielding has once more put his villain in the Augustan context of Satan-Quixote.

As Fielding shows, the satirist could do one of two things. In his early work Fielding tried to establish some perspective on sexual evil, opposing the trivial evil of Pamela's situation to the real evil in ordinary social relationships. The other possibility was to accept the assumption of sexual evil; but since sexual evil was no laughing matter, the seduction would have to receive the overtones of Juvenalian indignation and melodramatic complaint.

Perhaps the most remarkable fact about both *Amelia* and the novels of Smollett, however, is their alternation of satiric and satiromelodramatic scenes with visions of the good which are idealized and sentimentalized. A scene in Fielding's best satiric manner will be followed by a depiction of goodness painted in sharply contrasted colors. While Fielding leaves the reader to react to the satiric exposure, in the sentimental scenes he lets his characters do the reacting: Booth "stopped, and a torrent of tears gushed from his eyes—such

tears as are apt to flow from a truly noble heart at the hearing of anything surprisingly great and glorious" (Bk. II, Chap. 1; 6, 67). Virtuous behavior is also as stylized as the grotesque wambling of satiric
characters: fearful for the safety of her son, Amelia "staggered toward him as fast as she could, all pale and breathless, and scarce able
to support her tottering limbs" (Bk. IV, Chap. 7; 6, 209).

Although Smollett spends considerably less time than Fielding on
the good characters, his villains tend to weep when confronted by the
goodness they are in the process of destroying. Peregrine, when he
attempts to ravish Emilia, finds "the tears gushing from his eyes"
(Chap. 76; 6, 46), which recalls his final attempt on Amanda, when
"the tears ran down his cheeks" (Chap. 58; 5, 204). Smollett, with his
curious protagonists, is able to bring satire and sentimentality together in a single figure. Roderick's satiric railing is a symptom of a
tendency to overreact to stimuli, which is also reflected in its opposite, pity, as when, finding Miss Williams in distress, he cries, "What
effect, then, must it have had on [my heart] that was naturally prone
to very tender passion?"[9] A sentimentality that is the obverse of an
extreme sensibility to evil or folly in its various disguises is best conveyed in Matthew Bramble, who, witnessing noble scenes like the
return of Captain Brown, "sobbed, and wept, and clapt his hands,
and hollowed" (Step. 21; 12, 132). His nephew Jery explains that
"His blood rises at every instance of insolence and cruelty. . . . On the
other hand, the recital of a generous, humane, or grateful action,
never fails to draw from him tears of approbation, which he is often
greatly distressed to conceal" (May 10; 11, 100). Satire and sentiment,
which appear rather unconvincingly side by side in Smollett's early
and middle novels and in *Amelia,* are successfully embodied in
Bramble as alternating reactions to experience.

If Smollett and Fielding demonstrate a willingness to see satire and
various forms of sentimentality as complementary aspects of experi-

9. It is true, as Albrecht Strauss has pointed out ("On Smollett's Language," in
Style in Prose Fiction, ed. Harold C. Martin [New York, Columbia University Press,
1959], pp. 33–34), that Smollet often undercuts a sentimental scene, as when, after
long separation, Roderick's old schoolmate Strap "leaped upon me in a transport of
joy, hung about my neck, kissed me from ear to ear, and blubbered like a great school-
boy who has been whipt" (Chap. 44). This is only true, however, when for some
reason comic characters are involved in a sentimental situation (e.g. the scene from
Fathom, analyzed by Strauss, where the comical Jew Joshua is present).

ence, it is not surprising to find a tradition of satire in the novel that carries this premise deep into the nineteenth century. Dickens is only the greatest example of the satiric logic we have examined carried to an extreme. The passage at the beginning of the fifth chapter of *Martin Chuzzlewit* (1843) sums up the distinctive quality of Dickens' satire (though not of course its most sterling qualities). The chapter begins with a brilliant satiric portrait of Pecksniff by describing his horse, in whom his enemies

> pretended to detect a fanciful resemblance to his master. Not in his outward person, for he was a rawboned, haggard horse, always on a much shorter allowance of corn than Mr. Pecksniff; but in his moral character, wherein, said they, he was full of promise, but of no performance. He was always, in a manner, going to go, and never going. When at his slowest rate of travelling, he would sometimes lift up his legs so high, and display such mighty action, that it was difficult to believe he was doing less than fourteen miles an hour; and he was for ever so perfectly satisfied with his own speed, and so little disconcerted by opportunities of comparing himself with the fastest trotters, that the illusion was the more difficult of resistance. He was a kind of animal who infused into the breasts of strangers a lively sense of hope, and possessed all those who knew him better with a grim despair.

This portrait, in which the high and the low are both realized, is immediately followed by a passage describing the horse's driver:

> Blessings on thy simple heart, Tom Pinch, how proudly dost thou button up that scanty coat, called by a sad misnomer, for these many years, a "great" one. . . . Who, as thou drivest off, a happy man, and noddest with a grateful lovingness to Pecksniff in his nightcap at his chamber-window, would not cry: "Heaven speed thee, Tom, and send that thou were going off for ever to some quiet home where thou mightest live at peace, and sorrow should not touch thee!"

The pairing of the satiric and grossly sentimental is a Dickens trademark. The evil is fantastic in its symbolic vividness, and so is the good. If one regards satire as a propagandistic device of persuasion which employs fantasy, irony, and other devices, he might well conclude that portraits of both the good and the evil were called for in an equally "satiric" or fantastic tone. In Dickens' novels the satiric symbol like Pecksniff is complemented, on the one hand, by the sentimental ideal he is grinding into the ground, Tom Pinch, and, on the other, by the murderous and melodramatic Jonas Chuzzlewit. The rape of the innocent girl, the exploitation of the child, and the murder of the rival all involve both a murderous exaggeration of a satiric vice (as Chuzzlewit is of Pecksniff) which is the center of the novel, and an innocent virgin or orphan who is persecuted, but brave and good.

The other extreme to which the satiric-sentimental dichotomy can lead is a Gothic novel like Mrs. Radcliffe's *Mysteries of Udolpho* (1794), where the emphasis is on the sentimental-melodramatic elements, which are alternated (or padded) with satiric portraits and scenes. M. Quesnel, Mme. Cheron, Count Morano, and others engage in situations in which manners are juxtaposed and criticized and the innocent heroine is isolated and persecuted. Once again the satiric and sentimental are related as different versions of a similar tone: the satiric scenes of tyranny with the Quesnels and Cherons work up to the "sublime" scenes at Montoni's Udolpho. Although these characters have their prototypes in Clarissa's family, they are observed satirically with Smollettian exaggeration; they are not real people with complex motivations but, in their own way, obsessed souls like Montoni.

The Sentimentalization of the Satirist

One way to understand the disappearance of satire as a major genre in the eighteenth century is to observe its transformation into (or absorption by) the sentimental novel. Such a merger sounds paradoxical, but, as *Peregrine Pickle* and *Amelia* show, satire has enough in common with the sentimental novel, as to both tone and form, to afford, when it softens, an easy accommodation. Both claim the moral aim of improving society, employ scenes of strong feeling and symbolic import, of horror and aggression, of evil and corruption, and tend toward the use of a catalog form for their essentially expository purpose. The main difference lies in the satirist's placing his emphasis on the activity of the evil and the sentimentalist's placing his on the benevolence of the good. But in the second half of the eighteenth century this is not always a clear distinction, for the sentimentalist increasingly dwells upon the suffering, mental as well as physical, of the good. Satire, of course, claims that a man is evil as a result of what he has done, not what he has caused others to suffer. As early as the first decade of the century, however, the sentimental works of Mrs. Manley and Mrs. Haywood played upon the prestige of satire as well as on the demands of a female audience. In *Joseph Andrews,* although the hero's suffering is never sentimentally dwelt upon, it contributes strongly to the reader's condemnation of the lawyers, prudes, and innkeepers who mistreat him. In Smollett's novels and in *Amelia* the suffering of the victim and the guilt of the aggressor are often balanced scene for scene. "Satire and sentiment," R. L. Brett writes, ". . . were both important features of this diverse age; superficially so dissimilar, they were allies in a common cause."[10] Both sought to produce a more intense reaction from the reader as well as an increased awareness of the finer shades of right and wrong, and satire, by its extensive vocabulary of expository and analytic forms, worked hand in hand with sentimentalism. The initial questions to be answered are how the satirist became a sentimentalist and how the sentimentalist became a satirist.

The satirist was influenced by the demands and conventions of satire whose logic could lead toward sentimentality. The Juvenalian conventions involving savage indignation, an isolated protagonist, and sensational scenes are the most obvious. But clearly a sentimental temperament is necessary for the transformation of satiric conventions into satiro-sentimental ones. The natural tendency of satirists to resolve their satire into the simple relationship between an observer and an object can, depending on the century, show a basic interest either in the object or in the observer. One side of Smollett was intensely interested in the scene portrayed or reported, while the observer was merely a convenience; but another side, often at odds with the first, sought new and original points of view and ways to justify the observer in terms of ethos and verisimilitude. This second side shows that Smollett was aware of the contemporary views that insisted on the satirist's good nature, but the ingenuity of his search and

10. Brett, *The Third Earl of Shaftesbury: A Study in Eighteenth-Century Literary Theory* (London, Hutchinson's University Library, 1951), p. 185.

the shifting emphases that accompanied it suggest that he was also interested in the character *as* observer. An interest in sensibility, in the emotions, may have helped to channel his work on the satirist's character toward a greater emphasis on the feelings of the observer (and thus often of the victim) than on the vigor of the evil itself.

The crudity of Smollett's medical detail cannot obscure the general family resemblance of Bramble's disease to fashionable melancholia and the vague illnesses which stimulate the tenderest emotions. Bramble's sickness, with its automatic concomitant of satire, relates him in a wry way to the Romantic image of the poet, whose sensitivity and suffering are greater than others', and whose reaction is to produce out of his suffering beauty and truth. Byron sums up the therapeutic or cathartic theory of poetry when he writes that "art comes over me in a kind of rage every now and then . . . and then, if I don't write to empty my mind, I go mad."[11] There is, of course, a connection between all Juvenalian satirists and the Romantic theory of poetic inspiration. The sentimental element in Bramble's misanthropy also helps to convey the impression that he is a thwarted poet. In relation to the whole body of Smollett's writing, he represents an almost Romantic reversal of the old correlation between the shape of one's body and of one's soul: in Bramble the sick or crippled exterior denotes a finer, more sensitive soul.

Fielding reflects only indirectly the growing emphasis on feeling over reason. Even Tom Jones' dependence on feeling as a guide is strongly qualified. The matter of judgment is Fielding's main concern, and he agrees with Hume on the difficulty of arriving at one. He does not finally use feeling as his criterion of right and wrong, although he does tend to approach the reality of the evil action through the consciousness (the motives) of both the agent and the observer; his final acceptance of justice or mercy over law shows that feeling, in his own case, has won over reason. Therefore he arrives at a position of more sympathetic acceptance than is usually possible for a satirist.

Smollett, on the other hand, is almost wholly unconcerned with motive or the mind of the evil agent. His satire is divided between his observer, in whom he does become psychologically interested, and

11. *The Works of Lord Byron, Letters and Journals,* ed. Rowland E. Prothero (London, 1898–1901), 5, 215 (Jan. 2, 1821).

an object, which always remains for him an emblem—the only development being from a real emblem in the external world to (in his last works) an emblem in the consciousness of the observer. The matter of the satirist's judgment, which in Fielding is a system of delicate checks, balances, and ultimately human sympathy, emerges in Smollett as pure feeling. It is hard to imagine a more irrational, intuitive satire than that of the angry, vengeful man, the madman, or the sick man. From Roderick Random to Matthew Bramble, Smollett followed the course of eighteenth-century sentimentalism in his satire. The Juvenalian satirist, in the most general terms, reacted more from feeling than from reason, and this was Smollett's starting point. Lothario's words to Lucilla in *The Fair Penitent* (I.1), "I see thou'st learned to rail," are appropriately answered, "I've learned to weep." Rage and tears are two sides of the same coin. Shaftesbury's view that awareness of right and wrong is conveyed by a "reflex sense," which makes one "incline to" or recoil from the perceived object, supported this aspect of the satirist. With the advent of Bramble, the satirist's reaction to vice became analogous to Harley's reaction to virtue in Mackenzie's *Man of Feeling*. Both are equally related to Madame de Staël's belief that virtue is a "spontaneous impulsion, a motive which passes into the blood, and which carries you along irresistibly like the most imperious passions."[12] Smollett is echoing in his own way, as Fielding did in his, Hume's conclusion that "morality is more properly felt than judged of."

Smollett, however, was no Latitudinarian. He replaced reason with feeling but still maintained the strict necessity of judgment and condemnation; feeling was his agency for judgment and moral castigation rather than, as Fielding would have it, an agency for sympathy. Fielding, although he gives Tom Jones something of a "reflex sense" of morality, stands back as author, distanced by his irony, and dramatizes the difficulty of judging. Two kinds of sentimentalism emerge: one leads to exaggeration, strong contrasts of good and evil, benevolence and censure; the other leads to a refinement of feeling, a more delicate judgment arrived at by reason and sentiment, by careful lists of causes and effects. The distinction is perhaps more significant for their followers than for Smollett and Fielding themselves. In *Amelia,*

---

12. *De la littérature: Discourse préliminaire,* cited by Louis I. Bredvold, *The Natural History of Sensibility* (Detroit, Wayne State University Press, 1962), p. 25.

Fielding ended by employing Smollettian sentimentalism, and Smollett ended in *Humphry Clinker* by qualifying his strict moral judgment.

Turning from the satirist to the protagonist, one notices that English writers from Fielding on tend to soften the picaresque, making the servant-master or punished-punisher relation of the Spaniards into a victim-persecutor relation. There is a progression from the persecuted picaro (Joseph or Adams) to the persecuted pair of lovers (Joseph and Fanny or Booth and Amelia) to the persecuted maiden (Monimia in *Ferdinand Count Fathom*). This progression is paralleled in Smollett's fiction by the satirist himself—Greaves, "Smollett," and Bramble, the good man in an evil society. As they descend from Roderick Random, they show their relation to a Juvenalian satirist-protagonist. The physical defeat of the satirist is counteracted by a spiritual victory, just as Clarissa's physical defeat followed by death amounts to a spiritual victory. As the emphasis shifts from the cruel vitality of the oppressor to the pitiable suffering of the oppressed—Monimia's terror or Bramble's seizures—satire loses its identity in sentimental fiction. The protagonist-observer shared by the sentimental novel and satire was a man or woman of feeling in a hostile society, often a virgin pursued by a seducer with no help from any side. Fielding approaches this figure from the direction of satire. He attacks *Pamela* by putting a man of feeling into a world of calculating Pamelas, but his satiric effect is not too different from Richardson's nonsatiric effect in parts of *Pamela*.

The sentimentalist like Richardson usually starts from a thesis about "virtue," the good man as a man of benevolent feeling or sensibility. "The example of a beneficent spirit, gracefully exerted," he writes, "will awaken in others a capacity to enjoy the true pleasure that arises from a benevolent action."[13] He begins as a moralist by advocating a positive ideal, while the satirist begins by attacking a false ideal. If the positive ideal is to escape abstraction, to have persuasive impact and practical feasibility, the exemplar of feeling has to be put in exemplary situations in contact with men of form and prudence (Cibbers and Pamelas). If the tale is to be at all realistic the man of feeling will come off second best in the clash: Joseph's encounter with the coachload of people shows essentially what happens.

13. *A Collection of Moral Sentiments* (London, 1754), p. 259.

The sentimentalist therefore finds himself in a Juvenalian situation. As Walter Allen puts it, the sentimental novel "may primarily have as its end a description of the impact of the world upon a young man 'obedient to every emotion of the moral sense,' but it is also, by implication, a statement of the case against the world, against society."[14] And so the sentimentalist often becomes, in spite of himself, a Juvenalian satirist, and at times it is hard to tell whether the good is being praised or the evil censured.

The situation was not, however, quite so accidental as it sounds. The sentimentalist was more of a rhetorician than he is usually given credit for being; very often he combined a belief in original sin with his literary image of human perfectibility, arguing that man will never improve if he does not think he is capable of radical improvement.[15] It was only toward the end of the century that the moral aim disappeared and emotion was sought for itself.[16] The man of feeling was therefore often as much a corrective as a self-sustaining ideal, and so, like Panurge and, in his own way, Tom Jones, he lent himself to the satiric contrast of vitality and excessive formalism. The effect, of course, was quite un-Panurgian, as Mackenzie shows when he says that Harley's grave evokes such virtue that "it will make you hate the world—No: there is such an air of gentleness around, that I can hate nothing; but, as to the world—I pity the men of it."[17] The intense contemplation of virtue intensifies the contrasting evil of the surrounding world, but the result is less condemnation than pity or melancholy.

The man of feeling was in fact an anti-Panurge, an anti-Tom Jones, in that he was passive and receptive, a person to whom things happened. In searching for a form and a fiction through which to present his encounters with the world, the sentimentalist adapted the picaresque journey, usually modifying it with a frame of pastoralism. The hero leaves idyllic surroundings which correspond to his own good nature, goes to the city, where he is put upon, and at the end retires to the country again. The beginning and end are as necessary

14. *The English Novel* (New York, Dutton, 1958), p. 89.
15. Preston, "The Good-Natured Misanthrope," pp. 5–12.
16. See Erik Erämetsä, "A Study of the Word 'Sentimental' and of Other Linguistic Characteristics of Eighteenth Century Sentimentalism in England," *Annales Academiae Scientiarum Fennicae,* Series B, 74 (Helsinki, 1951), 70.
17. *The Man of Feeling* (New York, W. W. Norton, 1958), p. 94.

as the golden age at the opening of Juvenal's sixth satire or the beginning and end of *Humphry Clinker* to set off the world of artifice in the middle. Like Smollett, the sentimentalist plays down the protagonist as actor and emphasizes his role as observer and reactor. Joseph Andrews is simply trying to get home and must pass through an obstacle course, but David Simple and Harley must set out to learn something, and their reactions are usually less stoic than Joseph's. Whether David is searching for a true friend or merely seeing the sights of London, he makes a survey or anatomy of a vicious society, covering all its aspects; and the author is as concerned with his reaction as with the stimulus. The catalog form is ideal for presenting the sentimental experience, which consists of a series of delicious or devastating emotional encounters.

In Henry Mackenzie's *Man of Feeling* (1771) Harley leaves his pastoral setting to visit London in order to acquire a lease to some land that is rightfully his, is cheated out of it, and returns to the country. The central part of the story offers a cross section of London, each scene presented in its grossness or horror and then reacted to by Harley. The scenes portray conventional satiric types—a philosophic but cheating beggar, a foppish footman who passes himself off as a gentleman, madmen in Bedlam (both satiric madmen and an Ophelia-like persecuted maiden), a misanthrope, some sharpers, and a poor prostitute. Harley's reaction is as expected. He does not robustly combat evil or even spend much time getting to know it; he savors it (after Edwards' sad story, he says, "let me imprint the virtue of the sufferings on my soul" [p. 66]), sympathizes with its victims, and when possible succors them. But as to the evil itself, like David Simple he flees it. Already in *Humphry Clinker,* we recall, Bramble only rails, while privately helping society's victims, and then withdraws rather than fight. The world Harley explores is much the same, equally full of mixed Juvenalian and sentimental conventions. It is a world in which the proud, newly rich merchants and sons of stewards are invading the ancient domain of his family, and its cast of characters includes the footman who grows rich by pimping and secures the lease sought by Harley. Everywhere material prosperity is attained at the expense of spiritual degradation.

Since Harley, as called for by the ethos of the man of feeling, is an observer and a patient rather than an actor, Mackenzie relies on all the time-honored satiric structures of exposition. The characters Harley meets expose themselves with their words or deeds, or a second character of more experience serves as a guide and strips off their appearances. Along his way Harley encounters a beggar who points out selfishness and gullibility but proves to be a cheat; a footman who passes for a gentleman but exposes himself with his own words (to the reader, though not to Harley), followed by a man at the ordinary who exposes him to Harley; and a Bedlam guide who analyzes the madmen's delusive notions and then calls equally delusive notions "the motives of the greatest part of mankind" and the world "a large madhouse," before proving to be one of the inmates himself. Like the beggar and the madman, all the commentators are exposed, though their words ring with truth. The bottle-companions who reveal a benevolent-looking old gentleman to Harley as a cardsharp follow this bit of insight with an obtuse attempt to argue him out of his appointment with Miss Atkins, the unhappy prostitute. They know some facts unavailable to Harley, but his natural feeling leads him to truths unavailable to them. There is also, of course, a railing misanthrope who has "the spirit of Diogenes" and applies "his talents to the vilifying of his species." But, as a friend tells Harley, the nature of truth "may be changed by the garb it wears; softened to the admonition of friendship, or soured into the severity of reproof: yet this severity may be useful to some tempers; it somewhat resembles a file, disagreeable in its operation, but hard metals may be the brighter for it" (p. 29). Many of the satirist's character types are used here as Sarah Fielding and Goldsmith used them—to serve as guides for the innocent protagonist and as other interesting points of view.

In a sense, the satirist and the sentimentalist found themselves in complementary dilemmas in the late eighteenth century. The sentimentalist needed an active hero, but unless the man of feeling became worldly himself, he remained forever passive, an ethereal ideal (Fielding's solution was to teach him prudence). The sentimentalist needed a man of feeling who could cope with and understand the world without sacrificing any of his naïve essential goodness. The satirist needed a satiric commentator who was good-natured and generalized in his commentary, but who at the same time uttered particularized satire. Thus both satiric and sentimental works had benevolent characters uttering general complaint and, nearby, unsatisfactory or comic types uttering particular satire. The common area was, as has been suggested, the melancholy satirist, whose reactions extended from (under dire provocation) generalized satire to sympathetic tears. The benevolent misanthrope, as Preston has argued, offered a compromise; but only in a few instances, like Paul Lamounde in Bage's *James Wallace* (1788), does he come close to being a central character. Though an interesting technical solution, he remains almost always a secondary character in a novel in which the conflict continues unabated in the major characters.

The Sentimentalization of the Satiric Object

The scene observed by the sentimental satirist is the last element shared by the two genres. These encounters are the center of both the satiric and the sentimental experience. The satirist has always said with Dryden, Swift, and Pope that a corrupt piece of writing implies a general loosening of moral fiber, that a specific action symbolizes a whole lifetime; and the sentimentalist clearly agrees. The sentimentalist's scene presents three kinds of action: the good act, the bad, and the questionable. By the time *Humphry Clinker* was written the satirist was turning into a visionary who could detect hidden evils apparent to no one else. In time Blake would recognize in a commonplace street cry the disintegration of society; and "A dog starved at his master's gate / Predicts the ruin of the state." The importance of the symbolic action in the sentimental novel led to the same intense reaction of the observer, analysis of the scene, and judgment found in satire, and accordingly to satire's tools of analysis. The observer's response might be flight or helpless tears, a softer version of the Juvenalian indignation, complaint, meditation, or even occasional railing. The sentimentalist, however, sees this as a trait shared by all men who are sensitive: "I'm persuaded, to a man who feels for others as well as for himself, every rainy night, disguise it as you will, must cast a damp upon your spirits."[18]

While the satirist argues that an evil act has a powerfully metonymic effect, he sees a single good act as relatively meaningless unless it is related to a lifetime of orderly behavior. The sentimentalist, how-

18. *A Sentimental Journey Through France and Italy,* ed. Wilbur Cross (New York, Liveright, 1926), p. 36.

ever, sees a man's true character in a momentary, perhaps careless act of charity. For example, when Yorick in Sterne's *Sentimental Journey* (1768) admits that he has no French passport, he makes himself both touchstone and observer:

> The master of the hotel retired three steps from me, as from an infected person, as I declared this————and poor La Fleur [his servant] advanced three steps toward me, and with that sort of movement which a good soul makes to succour a distress'd one ————the fellow won my heart by it; and from that single *trait,* I knew his character as perfectly, and could rely upon it as firmly, as if he had served me with fidelity for seven years.[19]

But while the good act is sometimes used to intensify the bad by contrast (as in *The Man of Feeling*), it is a purely sentimental convention and can be dismissed from our attention.

The bad act can be either sentimentally or qualifiedly bad. In the sentimental novel that descended from Richardson the evil is relatively uncompromised, except in the direction of melodrama or Gothic horror. The emotional authority of the man of feeling leaves no doubt as to the evil, and his assistants, the ironists and misanthropes who fill in the detail, do not much mitigate the severity of the condemnation; in fact, they tend to merge with the evil object. But while this is true in theory and in many actual scenes, there is a pervading sense of mitigation in most satiric and sentimental novels after Fielding showed how to use Don Quixote as a device for expressing qualified disapproval.

Quixote is, of course, present in the good characters—David Simple, Sir Launcelot Greaves, and even Harley. Following from Fielding's example, he was used to represent idealism and simplicity which, by comparison, made the crassness of the real world stand out in strong relief. Very little change of emphasis was needed to transform him from a satiric to a sentimental hero. But he still remained (and was sometimes used as) a symbol of the imagination gone out of control, trying to distort reality. Quixote's madness thus served to mitigate the severity of his attack. He could serve as a satirist satirized or as a man of feeling satirized, in either case a corrective but

19. Ibid., p. 103.

not an altogether trustworthy ideal to follow. After *Tristram Shandy* and *A Sentimental Journey,* the sentimental observer is believed but at the same time satirized for his excessive emotionalism, and the author's attitude toward the evil object changes accordingly. Closely related to the Quixotic ambiguity of attitude is the alternation of satire and sentiment, disapproval and acceptance, which characterizes the novels of Sterne and most subsequent sentimental novels. In Smollett, as later in Dickens, the alternation of satire and sympathy is aimed at different, alternative objects—the bad person and the good, the Pecksniff and the Tom Pinch. The result is undeniable satire side-by-side with undeniable sentimentality. A second possibility is to alternate satire and sympathy aimed at a single object and so produce an ambiguous or mixed attitude.

The mitigated or ambiguous act, when presented to the observer, can become the questionable act. While the sentimentalist approaches the Juvenalian satirist in the excess of his reaction, he also owes something to the analytic methods of the Horatian satirist like Fielding, who used satiric forms to get at the meaning of actions and reactions. Harley's approach to analysis is similarly delicate. The old situation of the man of apparent consequence who turns out to be a nobody elicits the following response from Harley:

[1] Harley began to despise him too, and to conceive some indignation at having sat with patience to hear such a fellow speak nonsense. But [2] he corrected himself by reflecting that he was perhaps as well entertained, and instructed too, by this same modest gauger, as he should have been by such a man as he had thought proper to personate. And [3] surely the fault may more properly be imputed to that rank where the futility is real than where it is feigned: to that rank whose opportunities for nobler accomplishments have only served to rear a fabric of folly which the untutored hand of affectation, even among the meanest of mankind, can imitate with success. (p. 19)

As Fielding set up courts with defense, prosecution, judge, and jury or theaters divided into pit, gallery, and orchestra, Mackenzie sets up opposing forces within Harley to decide some delicate question of conduct. Should one give a dishonest beggar a shilling?

Harley had drawn a shilling from his pocket; but Virtue bade him consider on whom he was going to bestow it. Virtue held back his arm; but a milder form, a younger sister of Virtue's, not so severe as Virtue, nor so serious as Pity, smiled upon him; his fingers losed their compression, nor did Virtue offer to catch the money as it fell. (p. 14)

The irony, though gentle, remains, but the final conclusion is in favor of generosity.

The emphasis, as Harley suggests, almost always falls on sympathy or acceptance—an effect which Dickens criticized in Thackeray. If Dickens descends as a satirist from Smollett, Thackeray is related to Sterne. Put into *Little Dorrit* as Henry Gowan, Thackeray's characteristic sentiment is "Clarence is a great ass, but he is one of the dearest and best fellows that ever lived!" Dickens, as narrator, replies:

It appeared, before the breakfast was over, that everybody whom this Gowan knew was either more or less of an ass, or more or less of a knave; but was, notwithstanding, the most lovable, the most engaging, the simplest, truest, kindest, dearest, best fellow that ever lived. (Chap. 17)

Dickens criticized Thackeray (as Fielding or Smollett no doubt would have Sterne) from the point of view of a moralist. This criticism may explain why, in spite of its claim to be a satire and its satiric structure, *Vanity Fair* does not read like a satire. Sterne and Thackeray, whatever their failings, did not share what Edmund Wilson has called Dickens' inability to "get the good and bad together in one character."[20]

Sterne: The Subversion of Satire

The oddness of Dr. Slop in the world of *Tristram Shandy* has often been noticed. He is the only caricature; his physical description, the muddy fall he takes before the reader first sees him, and his boorish behavior are all from the world of Smollett and the picaresque writ-

---

20. *The Wound and the Bow* (New York, Oxford University Press, 1941), p. 65.

ers. Slop makes one suddenly aware of how different this world is in which the attack is ambiguous, reproof is mixed with love, and evil has become good. But each of the other characters carries a Dr. Slop within him, as well as Slop's contrary.

Walter, Toby, Yorick, and the rest are, of course, humor-characters, for whom humor means an amusing and endearing oddity; they are the amiable humorists of whom Stuart Tave writes. In a general sense public assumptions have changed, the Tory being replaced by the Whig. Sterne is a writer who is still aware of the Tory assumptions, however. Immensely pleased to be told by the old Earl of Bathurst that he was the successor of Swift and Pope, he makes us see his characters and situations first as the old satiric ones and then as the new recipients of comic-sympathetic laughter. The thesis is as much a part of the effect as the antithesis, and the transition becomes for Sterne a basic theme.

Tristram Shandy is constructed like a satire rather than a novel and presents within the first volume all the elements of the Tory fiction as composed by Swift. The plot is, as with Swift, the book itself, and the form closely resembles Swift's epitome (in *A Tale of a Tub*) of the seventeenth-century literature that can be called wit-writing or writing-as-process and the hack-writing that derived from it. These forms of expression disdained all tradition, authority, or rules, and their only virtue was the reflection of the writer's own eccentric mind.[21] In both cases the object ridiculed is the same self-sufficiency of mind, except that by Sterne's time it had taken the form of the Richardsonian novel.

Sterne apparently saw the same difficulty as Fielding in *Pamela* and *Clarissa*—a discrepancy between the moral structure of the novel and the psychological reality portrayed. It is this discrepancy that Swift had brilliantly dramatized and exploited in the *Tale* and his other first-person satires, making the discrepancy convey a meaning of his own. His strategy was to put the story in a single first-person speaker who was allowed to follow the wanderings of his

---

21. *Tristram Shandy* was originally to have been a travel book like *Gulliver's Travels* (see James Work, Introduction, *Tristram Shandy* [New York, Odyssey Press, 1940], p. xlvi). Sterne acknowledges the *Tale of a Tub* as a model: "for what has this book done," he writes of *Tristram Shandy*, "more than the Legislation of Moses, or the Tale of a Tub, that it may not swim down the gutter of Time along with them?" (Work, p. 610). All quotations are taken from Work's text.

random thoughts rather than chronology or the careful juxtapositions manipulated by the Fielding narrator; he used realism as an appearance that concealed the satirist's imposed order, thus to a startling degree maintaining realism while, through the natural juxtaposition of ideas in a rambling discourse, conveying his own commentary on the apparent chaos presented. Sterne follows the same procedure, but with a story instead of a discourse (though he is often close to discourse) and with a more thoroughly realized speaker. Thus the same ironic or informative juxtapositions that in a Fielding novel always run the risk of appearing contrived are in *Tristram Shandy* perfectly explicable as the accidental association of ideas of a wandering mind.[22] Tristram explains the method in his madness (something Swift's consistency would not allow his speaker to do):

> I was just going, for example, to have given you the great outlines of my uncle *Toby's* most whimsical character;—when my aunt *Dinah* and the coachman came a-cross us, and led us a vagary some millions of miles into the very heart of the planetary system: Notwithstanding all this you perceive that the drawing of my uncle *Toby's* character went on gently all the time. . . .
>
> By this contrivance the machinery of my work is of a species by itself; two contrary motions are introduced into it, and reconciled, which were thought to be at variance with each other. In a word, my work is digressive, and it is progressive too,—and at the same time. (pp. 72–73)

In the first volume four subjects, or events, are covered that have no temporal or narrative connection whatever but are associated in Tristram's mind—Tristram's conception, Yorick's life and death, Walter's theories, and the character of Uncle Toby. Each, showing the wounding or maiming (even destroying) of a person, is closely connected thematically to the others. Thus as the *Tale of a Tub* pretends to be a piece of egregious hack-writing, so *Tristram Shandy* pretends to be the autobiography of Tristram; actually, being devoted largely to the period before and immediately after his birth, it is about his father and uncle and the relation of the free-wheeling mind to reality. It pretends to be a novel to end all novels, but it is actually a satire on novels and all examples of the unbridled mind.

22. Cf. Watt, *Rise of the Novel*, pp. 290–91.

Before qualifying this statement (as every generalization concerning *Tristram Shandy* has to be qualified), one should look at a specific example of the unbridled, traditionless mind in the narrator, Tristram. As Swift's Grub Street Hack or Richardson's Pamela repeatedly says, "I am now writing" (or "this very moment" or "this present month of August, 1697"), so Tristram speaks of a memorandum "which now lies upon the table" (p. 9) or refers to "this very day, in which I am now writing this book for the edification of the world [cf. the Hack's "for the universal benefit of mankind"],— which is March 9, 1759" (p. 44) or says "that observation is my own; —and was struck out by me [cf. "strike all Things out of themselves"] this very rainy day, *March* 26, 1759, and betwixt the hours of nine and ten in the morning" (p. 64). Most of all, there is Tristram's laborious attempt to establish the exact moment and circumstances of his own birth. Both Swift and Sterne are satirizing the importance of the present moment in the traditionless, unstable modern world. This moment is all the modern has to hold to because he has only himself; and so he makes it a rallying cry of defiance.

Like Swift, Sterne satirizes the author-reader relationship that such a notion implies. As the Grub Street Hack tells the reader exactly how he must read his book, even down to taking purges and living in a garret, so Tristram peremptorily orders his reader to "immediately turn back, that is, as soon as you get to the next full stop, and read the whole chapter over again" (p. 56) or "Lay down the book, and I will allow you half a day to give a probable guess at the grounds of this procedure" (p. 17). Tristram echoes the Hack's claim of "an absolute authority in right, as the freshest modern, which gives me a despotic power over all authors before me" in his refusal to follow any tradition, any authority. He at once dissociates his work from the precept of Horace (do not begin ab ovo), "for in writing that I have set about, I shall confine myself neither to his rules, nor to any man's rules that ever lived" (p. 8).

Sterne begins then with the Swiftean villain and his characteristic expression. He ignores the Fielding villain (unless Dr. Slop qualifies) who hides his natural impulses under masks that conform with the dictates of accepted social standards. His protagonist, like Swift's, tries to eliminate or deny discrepancy rather than conceal it and so attempts to shape reality to accord with his own image of what it should be. The hypocrite is a conformist; the world-changer, a non-conformist.

But although the Tristram who is narrator is a world-changer, the Tristram of the narrative is a passive and wholly innocent victim; if anyone could be more innocent than the young Joseph Andrews it is the newborn babe Tristram. The narrative is constructed around a series of satiric scenes of frustration, violence, and pain, either involving Tristram or contributing to one of his disasters—his begetting, Dr. Slop and the knots (and his excommunication of them), the crushing of Tristram's nose, the bungled christening, Phutatorius and the chestnut, the death of brother Bobby, the drastic circumcision, and so on. Approached from the direction of satire, the story Tristram tells is one great anatomy of the fools and knaves who affect him. His recollections are a long list of consequences to himself. Walter Shandy is more obviously than Tristram the Satanic villain who tries to reorder the world because of the effects of his work and his defeats at the hands of reality. Another kind of world-changer, he "was systematical, and, like all systematical reasoners, he would move both heaven and earth, and twist and torture everything in nature to support his hypothesis" (p. 53). "What is the character of a family to an hypothesis?" he asks (p. 69). This man, "a philosopher in grain,—speculative,—systematical" (p. 68), is of course a descendant of Swift's crazy and dangerous speculators in religion, learning, and science. The Grub Street Hack, in order to arrive at his particular interpretation of reality, intended "to lay open, by untwisting or unwinding, and either to draw up by exantlation, or display by incision." One after another, Walter's hypotheses, like the Hack's, are proved wrong when they come face to face with reality. In every case, however, defeat is accompanied by the consequence to young Tristram.

For the idea of the pedantic father, the lover of hypotheses who plans his child's birth, christening, and education all according to some fantastic theories derived from the ancients, Sterne drew in particular upon *The Memoirs of Martinus Scriblerus*. This product of the Scriblerus Club offered a prototype for Walter and even a general model for Sterne's plot. The emergence of Tristram as a participating character in Volume VII is not unlike young Martin's emergence toward the end of the Scriblerian fragment. In both cases the emphasis is clearly on the father up to this point. Indeed perhaps because the Scriblerian project petered out and thus less was written on Martin, Sterne was initially led to put his emphasis predominantly on Walter.

Cornelius Scriblerus begins to plan for his child before conception, believing that the state of the homunculus is crucially important. He follows the prescription of Galen, "confining himself and his wife for almost the whole first year to Goat's Milk and Honey"; he will have sexual intercourse with his wife only when the wind is right; and once Martin is conceived, he has a concert performed every day ("according to the custom of the Magi"). Long before it is time for Martin's birth he prepares "two Treatises of Education; the one he called, *A Daughter's Mirrour,* and the other *A Son's Monitor.*"[23] All of these theories are based on his love of the ancients—on precedent, custom, old books, everything except common sense and experience.

It is Cornelius' wife and young Martin who suffer for his theories. He causes his wife to undergo an abortion and is very pleased when he learns the aborted child was female. He nearly kills Martin when he attempts to christen him according to old custom. His idea is to have Martin christened on an ancient, rusty shield, but a conscientious maid polishes off the rust, and at the sight "Cornelius sunk back on a chair, the Guests stood astonished, the infant squal'd" (p. 106). He drops both shield and child to the floor, and his only concern is whether the former has been damaged.

Walter's theories parallel Cornelius', down to his theory of the homunculus, his once-a-month intercourse, and his *Tristrapoedia.* In the same way, it is Tristram and his mother who suffer as a result of Walter's pedantic interpretation of the marriage contract and his choice of a male midwife who wrote a book on the subject instead of an experienced midwife. Martin's christening is the single episode in the *Memoirs* that may have suggested to Sterne all the various disasters that befall Tristram and Walter's plans for him. Walter's own suffering, though hardly minimal, is, like Cornelius', directed at

23. *Memoirs of the Extraordinary Life, Works, and Discoveries of Martinus Scriblerus,* ed. Charles Kerby-Miller (New Haven, Yale University Press, 1950), pp. 96, 97. J. M. Stedmond has shown a number of more specific parallels between Scriblerus and Shandy ("Satire and Tristram Shandy," *Studies in English Literature, 1* [1961], 53–54).

his ruined theory rather than the ruined child. When news reaches him of the forceps accident or the false christening, he flings himself down on a bed or whatever is handy, but he never does the first natural thing—run up to see his wife or son. He worries about the body politic, which he describes in vivid concreteness, but not about the bodies of his wife and child.

Walter's overreliance on mind at the expense of body is the cause of his error. Like all the Satanic villains of the Augustans, he is in various senses impotent. There is a Shandy tradition of sexual failure, but it is essentially Walter's emotional impotence that prevents him from feeling any sexual passion. He begets children "out of principle" (p. 116), and his conception of Tristram, which I earlier compared to Achitophel's conception of his "lump of anarchy," has nothing to do with passion. His desire is to mold the unborn Tristram into an abstract pattern of his own formulation.

His first defeat is appropriately at the hands of his wife, who endangers Tristram's homunculus by asking about the clock at the wrong moment. But if, like Jonathan Wild and others, he is thwarted by the opposite sex, he is also drubbed by the world as a whole. Swift uses the hard realities of objects like forceps and sash weights to suggest the immutable order of the universe which a speculative mind like Walter's cannot alter to his own ends. Sterne follows this equation closely, creating all the typical scenes of reality collapsing theory, but he emphasizes the irrationality of the real world, not its order or even ideality. For example, after explaining how, as a result of his elaborate theories of naming, Walter hates the name Tristram, Tristram writes:

When this story is compared with the title-page,—Will not the gentle reader pity my father from his soul?—to see an orderly and well-disposed gentleman, who tho' singular,—yet inoffensive in his notions,—so played upon in them by cross purposes;—to look down upon the stage, and see him baffled and overthrown in all his little systems and wishes; to behold a train of events perpetually falling out against him, and in so critical and cruel a way, as if they had purposedly been plann'd and pointed against him, merely to insult his speculations.—In a word, to behold such a one, in his old age, ill-fitted for troubles, ten times in a day suffering sorrow;—ten times in a day calling the child of his prayers Tristram! . . . By his ashes! I swear it,—if ever malignant spirit took pleasure, or busied itself in traversing the purposes of mortal man,—it must have been here. (pp. 55-56)

By playing with the time sequence, Tristram shows Walter as old and worn, a tiny human on the great impersonal stage of the world, and suggests a lack of connection between men's minds and the objective world under any circumstances.

It is suggestive that the Swiftean villain Walter Shandy was chosen by *The London Magazine* of 1782 as one of its two favorite comic "humourists." He came to represent the Shandean philosopher or system-builder, whose soaring imagination was comically contrasted with its petty defeats at the hands of reality—a Quixote, in short. It is equally significant that the second of these favorite "humourists" was Matthew Bramble, the satirist transformed into a comic type.[24] The two types that are polarized in Bramble and Walter Shandy and continue in novels of the nineteenth century were neatly distinguished by Congreve:

a Character of a Splenetick and Peevish *Humour* should have a Satyrical Wit. A Jolly and Sanguine *Humour* should have a Facetious Wit. The Former should speak Positively; the Latter, Carelessly: For the former Observes and shews things as they are; the latter rather overlooks Nature, and speaks things as he would have them.[25]

Here is the basic attitude of the fictionalist toward satire near the end of the century. Satire is a necessary means to observe and show "things as they are," but it is an excess in itself and thus can appear in only one way in the novel—divided between the satirist and his satiric object, in a splenetic character who will keep the characters in line and a ridiculous character who is his foil.

A comic character is, however, by no means the end of Sterne's effect in *Tristram Shandy*. He accomplishes the undermining of

24. "Imaginary Dialogue Between Walter Shandy and Matthew Bramble," *London Magazine, 51* (1782), 322.
25. "Concerning Humour in Comedy," in Spingarn, *Critical Essays, 3,* 244.

Walter to a large extent by making Tristram, the writer-to-the-moment, a foil to Walter's straitjacketed mind. Both Tristram the child (as victim) and Tristram the man (as liberated mind) act as the reality with which Walter's theories come into constant conflict; they, along with Uncle Toby's nonsensical common sense, represent the real world. In a sense Sterne interprets *A Tale of a Tub* as many of Swift's contemporaries did, as simply advocating the chaos of experiential reality. He does with the image of chaos almost the reverse of what Swift did, restoring the positive value it had for Rabelais and Erasmus. The irregular and vital are even connected with Hogarth's "Line of Beauty," the natural curving line opposed to the geometrical symmetry of Palladian architecture and neoclassicism. Corporal Trim, when he begins to read the essay on conscience, is presented first in a hypothetical military posture, "dividing the weight of his body equally upon both legs;—his eye fix'd, as if on duty," and then in his actual stance, with his knee, for example, "bent, but that not violently,—but so as to fall within the limits of the line of beauty;—and I add, of the line of science too," for otherwise all orators "must fall upon their noses" (pp. 121–23).

This is not, however, the complete effect. In *The Memoirs of Scriblerus* the plot was split between Cornelius and Martin, father and son, who were made to represent the two extremes of eccentricity —the mad ancient and the equally mad modern. While Cornelius reduced everything to the narrowest interpretation of the ancients' precedents, Martin went out hither and yon to collect scientific specimens and seek a "modern" education. In Scriblerian satire the unbridled and too bridled mind are two extremes of the same evil, and Sterne retains this implication by suggesting that Walter and Tristram are equally mad. Finally, they tend to represent two kinds of experience, two ways of ordering that are opposed and left to comment *on each other* and are comic in juxtaposition.

Much the same applies to the rest of the dramatis personae of Augustan satire as they appear in *Tristram Shandy*. Yorick is the satirist who is isolated from "decent" society by his propensity for seeing and telling the truth and subsequently is driven to his grave. The other character, Uncle Toby, is both a commonsensical foil to Walter (an ingénu satirist) and in his own right a modern who tries to impose his version of reality (here the battle of Namur) on his contemporaries just as Walter tries to impose his theories; he is always explaining, explaining, and is never understood. Even Yorick, to his contemporaries, is a madman who cannot be understood. Thus, although Walter is shown to be completely isolated and alone, like the Grub Street Hack or the astrologer Partridge, so are his victim and the satirist and the whole cast. Moreover, the impotence of the Satanic villain, both as to his deeds and his sexual prowess, while evident enough in Walter, is famous in Toby and Tristram and, in a somewhat different sense, in Yorick. Walter's world-changing theories are defeated, but so in various ways are the plans of all the other characters. All of them are presented as not only contrasting but parallel cases. From the idea of the thwarted hypothesizer Sterne develops the suffering figure of Walter and the equally suffering figure of Tristram: they have become real people, not symbols. From the argument between Cornelius and his brother (or brother-in-law) Albertus comes the wonderful conversations between Walter and Toby. These also doubtless owe something to Quixote's talks with Sancho Panza. As usual in the eighteenth-century novel, Don Quixote is the extra ingredient added to the formula of the Scriblerus memoirs. Cornelius becomes Don Quixote and thus lovable; Albertus becomes Sancho. Sterne's curious wildness of tone, which makes the whole matter of satire somewhat questionable, comes from the Quixotic nature of the follies examined. As Quixote went out to save maidens in distress, so Toby relives the war of the Spanish Succession, Walter weaves his elaborate theories, and Tristram tries to write his life "to the moment." Both Walter and Toby go wrong by reading the books in their ancestral library—Walter, the works of the logicians and the philosophers, the makers of minute and elaborate hypotheses; Toby, the romances of war and adventure, *Guy of Warwick* and *The Seven Champions of Christendom.*

One is reminded of Sterne's earliest published work, *A Good Warm Watch-Coat, or The Political Romance* (1759), in which he presents a very Swiftean allegory, reminiscent of the story of the brothers and their coats in the *Tale,* with various letters and the like tacked on (at the end in this case) to set the allegory in perspective. His workmanship is skillful but conventional, with a touch of life here and there, but in the "key" that is appended to the "romance," he reveals his more characteristic manner. This second fiction has a

club that reads and discusses the allegory, more reminiscent of the old
Post Boy satire showing a club reading and commenting on the mail
than of the Spectator Club. While the allegory is a fair imitation of
Swift, the round-table discussion is pure Sterne. It abandons the conventional playing off of true and false views and instead introduces
the interplay of different and incompatible points of view that are
mutually personal and obtuse, much as Smollett does a decade later
in *Humphry Clinker*.

Swift's *Tale* attacked the impossibility of communication—the intellectual impotence that results from pride in one's own mental gy-
rations. When Sterne's second volume specifically extends the theme
of sexual impotence to a less elemental equivalent, communication,
one can see that the book has been, from the start, about this problem.
It is about hobbyhorses—Toby's, Walter's, and, by implication, Tristram's. In volume one hobbyhorses characterize the man; in volume
two the various hobbyhorses or streams of associations of ideas col-
lide. Toby's crosses Walter's, Dr. Slop's crosses these, and so on.

Toby's hobbyhorse, with which the volume begins, is the outcome
of an attempt to communicate; he has to make himself understood as
to exactly how and where he was wounded, and so he ends by building Namur in his bowling green. At the beginning of the volume, he
offers a close parallel to Tristram's hobbyhorse: both are searches into
the past to determine and communicate the exact nature and causes
of their woundings. Toby traces trajectories and plots exact coordi-
nates of his position at the crucial moment, and this leads him to
other woundings, other battles, and even whole wars. Tristram begins the same way and branches out to other "small heroes" who, like
himself, are crushed by the world—the LeFevers, Marias, Tobys,
Yoricks, and Walters. The account of Toby's fortifications (the
growth of his hobbyhorse) in volume two is a concrete illustration of
Tristram's own adjustment to life: in volume one Tristram indicates
the sort of buffets life has given him and suggests an analogue in
Toby; then in volume two he shows how Toby adjusts to his situation via a hobbyhorse. By the constant asides to the reader it becomes
obvious that Toby's solution tells why Tristram himself is writing.
The only way to survive in such a world is to have a hobbyhorse.

Speaking of Toby's futile attempts to convey his meaning, Tristram says, " 'Twas not by ideas,—by heaven! his life was put in jeopardy by words" (p. 87). It is, of course, words that cause the collision of hobbyhorses. Curtius and hornworks, which are seige equipment to Toby, are bed curtains and cuckold horns to the lecherous Dr. Slop. Words come to mean outer forms that conceal reality; they come to have an utterly false and arbitrary meaning that is beyond an individual's control. To dramatize this, Sterne introduces a series of conventional documents in the first two volumes—in volume one, the marriage contract and the opinion of the doctors of the Sorbonne; in volume two, the Sermon on Conscience. The first two are examples of attempts to rationalize and legalize, to write the letter of the law, on important subjects that will not allow it (a husband-wife relationship and the nature of a human being). "I was doom'd," says Tristram, "by marriage articles, to have my nose squeez'd as flat to my face, as if the destinies had actually spun me without one" (p. 41). The Sermon on Conscience comes as a further caveat against overreliance on external forms of control and also against conscience itself when it is self-deluded and sets up for king.

Against these ordered documents, Sterne places the shiftiness of the potential meanings of words. He turns again to Swift's *Tale,* where the Grub Street Hack's failure to order reality according to his own eccentric vision appears most strikingly in his failure to control the meaning of words. The tub to which he compares his writing becomes, in a slightly different context, the literal tub in which dissenters preached or in which syphilitics were sweated. Once tub has established the idea of a container, it moves to analogous shapes (the rotten nut, the sack posset), always with the modern's equation between any product of his brain and the modern himself (they are, Swift maintains, the same). These images reach a climax in the concrete figure of the Aeolist who makes his body a mere container of air (spirit), and the spider (in the *Battle of the Books*) whose body is a self-sufficient tub of dirt out of which he constructs his cobwebs.

Thus Tristram, who has been talking about his birth, refers to the joke Yorick makes on one of his pompous parishioners in terms of gestation: the effect of the joke grows in the victim (though forgotten by Yorick) until finally, when the opportunity shows itself, out comes a full-grown revenge. The result, Yorick's loss of preferment, leads to a general disillusionment with mankind that kills Yorick; he tells Eugenius as he is dying to look at his head, "so bruised and mis-shapen'd with the blows which ***** and *****, and some others have so unhandsomely given me in the dark" (p. 31). This image is picked up in volume two when Dr. Slop knocks at the Shandy door, which "crushed the head of as notable and curious a dissertation as ever was engendered in the womb of speculation;—it was some months before my father could get an opportunity to be safely deliver'd of it" (pp. 102–03); later one sees the result of Dr. Slop's forceps on Tristram's head.

Words never mean the same thing to one person as to another, to Walter as to Toby, or to Tristram as to the reader; each goes his separate way, contributing to the general meaning of the novel. In *Tristram Shandy* words are part of man's original dislocation. They are like Walter's theories, analogous to the clocks that are not wound, the hinges that do not get oiled, the sash weights that are not replaced, the fields that are never cultivated, and the coats of arms that are never repaired. Appropriately, words keep slipping into their sexual meanings, and verbal misunderstandings lead to the malfunctioning of objects which, in turn, leads to the literal or figurative emasculations of the characters. Sterne implies that the difficulty in communication is caused by the external forms of the words themselves or at least by man's inability or unwillingness to use them correctly. Tristram is accordingly compelled, in order to convey his meaning, to adopt the most unorthodox methods, which include introducing marbled pages, violating chronology, and introducing a dedication out of place. Even the "digressive . . . progressive" mode of his work is no longer a satiric strategy as much as a proper means of communicating a nonrational meaning. The puns on gestation and crushed heads, for example, suggest the analogy between Yorick and Tristram and (whether by Tristram or Sterne) connect all these battered people—the unborn Tristram, his father whose disillusionment is to come with Tristram, Toby already twenty years older than his wound, and Yorick who dies years later when Tristram is a grown man. The multi-meanings of words help to focus these four crucial incidents, scattered in time, on Tristram's birth.

On the level of the characters, Toby has to show the location of his wounding by maps and models and (for the Widow Wadman) in the flesh; Trim's stance as a "Line of Beauty" and later his dropping his hat to convey the death of Bobby are more important than spoken words with strict denotation. Walter is constantly flying into rages when Toby applies common sense to his theories or gets astride his own hobbyhorse, but by gesture or some other nonrational means, Toby does communicate his love to Walter. "My uncle Toby stole his hand unperceived behind his chair, to give my father's hand a squeeze—" (p. 586). When Toby, angry at Walter's ridicule of his hobbyhorse, puffs so hard on his pipe that Walter begins to cough, he at once leaps up in sympathy, despite his painful groin. Toby's actions, in turn, "cut my father thro' his reins, for the pain he had just been giving him" (p. 212). On the other hand, a strain of *Lillibullero* or a look from Toby can transform Walter (p. 115), and they communicate sensitively through "hems" (p. 274), short broken sentences, and dashes simulating silence. Even Dr. Slop can be communicated with by a "humph" (p. 129), and the Widow Wadman and Mrs. Shandy talk with their eyes. In volume three these modes of communication are illustrated in the stories of the Abbess of Andouillet and the ass and of Tristram and the ass in the doorway. Words do not suffice to move the ass; neither does food; but a good blow from behind does. The nonrational that rises above these is the reality Sterne is trying to represent, and so communication is achieved by gesture, irrational sounds, and often complete silence. At this point Sterne is consciously connecting Tristram with those Augustan fools who, like the Grub Street Hack, convey their meaning through eccentricities of form, italics, and whatnot. Walter and Toby are the enthusiasts who communicate through coughs and belches. Sterne has taken the step from Swift's world to Wordsworth's. As Toby and Walter cannot understand each others' words, so Wordsworth is unable to understand the words of the solitary reaper. But there is a higher kind of communication—by love or feeling—that takes place naturally between Toby and Walter when all else has failed. Addison, Pope, and Fielding continue Swift's attack on the senseless sounds of the Italian opera singer and the hack poet, but Sterne sees this pure sound as the final reality and truth.

Fielding demonstrates in his novels a movement in this direction. In *Tom Jones* the "gentle pressure" of the baby Tom's hand "seeming to implore his assistance" has more effect on Allworthy than "the eloquence of Mrs. Deborah" who wants to cast out the baby. But these examples of natural reactions opposed to formalized ones bear little relation to the extremities to which Sterne goes for his examples. He consciously takes up the old satiric object, lets one see that it is a satiric object, and then modifies it into a good. In his own terms he arrives at irrational communication not as an ideal but as a last feeble hope. It is not, after all, a very effective means of communicating: it does not prevent any of the physical catastrophes; it only signals the lowest common denominator—that we are all related in some sense. *Tristram Shandy* is not so much praise of the irrational modes of understanding (as Wordsworth's "Solitary Reaper" is) as an attack on the faulty rational ones and thus on the Swiftean assumption that there is an alternative to the enthusiast's exalted coughs and hems.

In the same way Sterne shows that the particular moment—"this very rainy day, *March* 26, 1759, and betwixt the hours of nine and ten in the morning"—is transient and insignificant, but he also suffuses it with irrational importance. His particular effect is, as I have said, the romantic irony of complicating the reader's reaction through satire followed by acceptance. It must also be concluded that, in relation to our general study of the novel, he has picked up one strand of the anti-romance tradition and written the ultimate expression of a-literature in the eighteenth century. He accomplishes this feat by subverting the conventions not only of Richardson but of Swift and Fielding as well.

Yorick: From Self-Revelation to Self-Analysis

In his second novel, *A Sentimental Journey Through France and Italy* (1768), Sterne deals again with slippery words, adding ambiguous actions and gestures. Almost everything has two meanings, from the horse called a bidet to the beggar who whispers to ladies in the streets of Paris: one meaning is innocent, the other carnal. But the betrayal of language is very different from in *Tristram Shandy*. There it was comic, with Widow Wadman taking the carnal and Toby the innocent meaning. In *A Sentimental Journey,* however, we are given a single character, Parson Yorick, who combines two characters' understanding. He regards himself as a spiritual man but whenever he does so he exposes the carnal beneath.

The error in his basic assumption that sentimental love is pure is made clear in both external and internal actions. The love-letter in French by Jaques Roque, which keeps saying "L'amour n'est *rien* sans sentiment," slips into indecent puns: "On dit aussi que Monsieur le Corporal [his rival] monte la garde Mercredi: alors ce sera mon tour. / *Chacun à son tour*."[26] In the next chapter Yorick, left in his chamber to meditate on his sentimental attachment to the lady he met in Calais, expresses himself in the following ambiguous terms:

> I walked up gravely to the window in my dusty black coat, and looking through the glass saw all the world in yellow, blue, and green, running at the ring of pleasure.———The old with broken lances, and in helmets which had lost their vizards—the young in armor bright which shone like gold, beplumed with each gay feather of the east———all———all———tilting at it like fascinated knights in tournaments of yore for fame and love ———(p. 79)

The "ring of pleasure" of the tilt field is an extremely unfortunate image for Yorick to have chosen to express the world preoccupied with sentimental love. The next paragraph continues with his self-urging to "seek———seek some winding alley, with a tourniquet at the end of it, where chariot never rolled or flambeau shot its rays." More often a comic self-deception is involved, as when he tells the Count de B**** that he "cannot bear the shock of the least indecent insinuation" but proceeds to use the most compromising images to describe his search into "the nakedness of [women's] hearts" (pp. 120-21). Actions betray him in the same way—not, as in Fielding, betraying his conscious but concealed motive, but revealing his subconscious. He can reach out in a gesture of Christian charity and catch "hold of the *Fille de Chambre's*———" (p. 169).

But if the effect begins as satiric, it changes as we approach the crucial chapters with the fille de chambre. Yorick, we discover, though unaware of the intrusion of his carnal self in his double entendres, is very much aware of the conflict in his nature between spiritual and carnal. Bevoriskius' digression on copulating sparrows in the middle of his grave and learned *Commentary upon the Generations from*

26. *A Sentimental Journey*, ed. Cross, p. 78.

Adam elicits the following Shandean self-portrait: "Ill-fated Yorick! that the gravest of thy brethren should be able to write that to the world, which stains thy face with crimson, to copy in even thy study" (p. 126).

Everything in Yorick's subconscious conspires toward his seduction of the fille de chambre, and as the two sink without conscious volition onto his bed double entendres fly thick and fast: "I'll just shew you," says the fille de chambre, "the little purse I have been making to-day to hold your crown" (p. 130). Their gestures relating to her purse, her shoe, and so on are equally suggestive, but now the tension between the two meanings has become conflict. The chapter called "The Temptation—Paris" is followed by the key chapter, "The Conquest" (again with a double meaning), in which Yorick explains in effect that being human he contains both spiritual and carnal forces within himself, but that what matters is his control of the latter in a physical test:

> If Nature has so wove her web of kindness that some threads of love and desire are entangled with the piece——must the whole web be rent in drawing them out? . . . whatever is my danger——whatever is my situation——let me feel the movements which rise out of it, and which belong to me as a man ——and if I govern them as a good one, I will trust the issue to thy justice! for thou hast made us, and not we ourselves. (p. 132)

He takes the fille de chambre by the hand, leads her out of the room, puts the key in his pocket, *"and then*——the victory being quite decisive," he kisses her and leads her to the gate.

At this point Yorick has become a Swiftean villain turned hero, a man who is aware of the dross in his spirituality and both willing and able to conquer its physical, conscious manifestation even if (as he admits) he cannot conquer all its subconscious rumblings. Swift never attacks the subconscious itself, only the subconscious as it is allowed to project its fantasies into actions. In Yorick it has become one element (perhaps the spice) in a delicate compound of character.

The true import of *A Sentimental Journey* depends on the fact that Yorick is both satiric object and observer. In *Tristram Shandy* he is the Fieldingesque satirist with an invincible dislike and opposition in his nature to gravity;—not to gravity as such; . . . but he was an enemy to the affectation of it, and declared open war against it, only as it appeared a cloak for ignorance, or for folly; and then, whenever it fell in his way, however sheltered and protected, he seldom gave it much quarter. (p. 26)

But he is also, we saw, the Juvenalian satirist who is maliciously misunderstood, and far from a mitre or even a deanery, he gets nowhere by preferment. In *A Sentimental Journey* Yorick is given himself for a satiric object, and becomes his own satirist. One Yorick approaches a monk, determined to give him no alms: "there was something, I fear, forbidding in my look: I have," adds the second Yorick, "his figure this moment before my eyes, and think there was that in it which deserved better" (p. 25).

Sterne takes the device (perhaps from *Gil Blas*) of the protagonist-narrator looking back on his own actions and satirizing them, and, as with Yorick as a self-exposing fool, he uses it to get at a state of mind which interests him—the clergyman's sentiments played off against his reason, his desires against his conscious spirituality. Yorick's self-concern, the problem of coming to understand and control the grosser aspects of himself, is a subtler and more subjective version of Fielding's analytic approach in *Tom Jones*. Satire is used for analysis, but it is now turned on the narrator by himself—dividing and viewing him from a new perspective. If the end of Swift's satiric monologues is self-exposure, Sterne's is self-analysis. He combines the self-incriminating speaker with the observer who delicately analyzes the significance of an external scene by making the observer analyze his own past actions. Satire thus joins with sentimentalism in the delicate balancing of one against the other, leading not only to mitigation and qualification of what starts as a satiric object, but also ultimately to subtle psychological distinctions—or refinements of sentiment—that can be established only through a modified satiric process.

❈ *Chapter 7* ❈

THE NOVEL OF MANNERS

This final chapter will seek some kind of synthesis of the various novelistic transformations and absorptions of satire by examining their most interesting product, the novel of manners. The scene of the novel of manners, for example, draws on both the satiric touchstone scene in which guilt is diffused and the satiro-sentimental scene of sexual threat and tears. Both the ironic observer of the Fielding novel and the Smollettian observer of delicate sensibility—one a controlling intelligence, the other a character—contribute to the heroine of the novel of manners. Those assistant satirists who surround the dumb man of feeling are as important as the spectra of different points of view in the Spectator Club and *Humphry Clinker*. The essential elements, however, are the controlling and analytic intelligence of the Fielding novel and the Richardsonian concern with consciousness; but the latter, before it could influence the novel of manners, had to pass through satiric intermediaries.

It is possible to trace a line from the anti-romance of Cervantes, Sorel, and Furetière through the novels of Fielding, Smollett, and Burney to the novel of manners written by Jane Austen. The anti-romance contributes the basic structure for a study of manners not concerned exclusively with conduct book problems (what to do when two equally stringent rules apply at once) or with a reportorial description of different manners (the various "spy" and travel narratives). The basic situation simply involves the juxtaposition of two sets of values or manners (ideal-real, aristocratic-bourgeois, natural-unnatural, free-confined, individualist-conformist) and a protagonist who touches both. The protagonist is between the two areas; not completely committed to either, he is insecure, an unknown quantity seeking to discover his true position in relation to them, or else he is solidly on the lower level but trying to pass himself off as the higher, or perhaps even trying to become the higher. The spectrum of possibility runs from the bastard or foundling who seeks self-identity to the fop who apes the externals of his betters.

The Richardsonian novel is a novel of manners in the sense that it is concerned with the relationship between the manners of the rising middle class and those of the declining aristocracy. If an analogy is possible between *Don Quixote* and *Pamela* or *Clarissa,* its usefulness lies in Richardson's employment of the romantically alluring image of the aristocratic rake to draw Pamela and Clarissa, with much talk of reforming him, to their respective fates. Richardson's aim is not criticism or analysis, however, but conflict, ending happily for Pamela, tragically for Clarissa. Neither heroine is presented primarily as aspiring to the aristocracy, but rather as pursued and persecuted by it. Clarissa in particular is ground to death between the wheels of the two classes. In both cases, Richardson expresses the feelings of the emergent bourgeoisie—a servant may marry her master, and a middle-class girl should be married, not raped, by an aristocrat (a view at variance with the Restoration comedy of manners); in short, the individual's integrity is paramount and depends on freedom of choice.

It was left for Fielding to turn from the dramatization of a conflict to an analysis of the relationship involved. Fielding, however, was not concerned with the relationship between the classes, but with the anti-romance subject of the relationship between the instincts of the individual and the code of manners that does not at every point fit them—either painfully distorting them or serving as a convenient mask for the hypocrite. Thus in *Joseph Andrews,* his anti-romance on *Pamela,* he opposes the real human behavior of Adams and Joseph to the middle-class manners of the Pamelas and Cibbers, which conceal or justify self-seeking. Quixotism is interpreted by Fielding as the ability to see through (or be unaffected by) the manners of one's society. In *Tom Jones* he uses the man motivated by natural feeling to criticize the conventions and customs of his society, including the aristocratic manners of the Bellastons and Fellamars. In a sense all of Fielding's work is constructed on the anti-romance situation; in his early works he shows the foppish imitators of fashion, which in this case is the false ideal of "greatness." But he treats Jones as Cervantes did Quixote, putting him and the Fellamars side by side, as feeling and form, and letting them comment on each other. To the extent that the virtues and vices of feeling and form are balanced—some virtue on both sides—*Tom Jones* becomes a novel of manners.

Fielding's novel also enormously broadens the scope of satiric irony in order to express a point of view that is judicious, understanding, and sympathetic and can encompass both form and feeling. However, it still leaves a broad gap between *Tom Jones* and *Pride and Prejudice*. One of the important breaks is the relationship between persuasion and dramatization, between reader and protagonist. Fielding's technical equipment permitted the reader's growing awareness, but it worked less well when he wished to dramatize the growing awareness of a character. In *Tom Jones* he attempted to make Tom's self-recognition correspond to the reader's. As early as Book VIII Tom speaks out to correct the Old Man of the Hill, whose experience, like Tom's, has been colored by betrayal but whose generalization is that all men are evil. Tom has discovered, somewhere along the line, about the same time as the reader, that this is an oversimplification. He shows this even more strikingly with the puppet-master who, unwilling to acknowledge man's mixed nature, presents only paragons to instruct his audience. Jones tells him that he should have included Punch: "so far from improving, I think, by leaving him out and his merry wife Joan, you have spoiled your puppet-show" (Bk. XII, Chap. 5). When the puppet-master's wife discovers her maid making love with the Merry Andrew on the stage, the truth of Tom's view becomes apparent, and the gypsy episode confirms Tom's and the reader's realization that mercy is better than strict justice, that evil is in many cases a spot that darkens a character but does not destroy it. Tom later appears to see Black George's failure (stealing the £500) as an objectification of his own at Upton and elsewhere, when he pleads for him: "you must suffer me to call it weakness rather than ingratitude; for I am convinced the poor fellow loves me" (Bk. XVIII, Chap. 11).

One wonders, however, if the knowledge of mixed character is connected with Tom's more important disasters. It shows understanding in his relations with Black George and Molly but has no effect when applied as self-knowledge to his own case; indeed one goes from his talk with the Old Man to his escapade with Mrs. Waters, after which his views about mixed character sound like special pleading. The knowledge administered helps the reader but not Tom. It is the reader who needs to know about the complexity of actions in order to understand Tom; Tom only needs to learn prudence and to know himself. Therefore in terms of the main action of the novel—the need to complement Tom's feeling with form—the enlightened party remains the reader, and the character seems unaware of his problem. Knowledge that all people are fallible is hardly a help toward self-knowledge or self-discipline. The truth, I suspect, is that Fielding is still primarily interested in Tom as a corrective and as an example of character vs. conduct; he is not really interested in Tom's perception —the sine qua non of the novel of manners.

An ingénu cannot serve as the protagonist of a novel of manners. Joseph Andrews' innocence (and to a lesser degree Tom's) forces the reader to focus on the evil glaringly exposed, not on the hero's problems that may have caused him to become entangled with knaves. Joseph is never embarrassed: to be embarrassed one must see as well as be seen. Tom's embarrassment (for example, when he learns that Sophia knows of his behavior at Upton) points in a direction that Fielding never fully explores. Among the satirists, Smollett is responsible for this strain. The novel of manners protagonist and many secondary characters descend from the satiric observer as a character, whose gradual transformation we have followed from a public figure (whose motives and concerns are external and moral) to a private one (whose concerns are strictly internal and personal). Roderick Random acted as a satirist of society out of both desire for revenge (private) and moral conviction (public); by the time one reaches Captain Mirvan in *Evelina* personal considerations are the sole motive. However, only when an author can balance an interest in what happened per se with how it appeared to X, Y, and Z, can a novel like *Pride and Prejudice* be produced.

Dr. Primrose: The Ironic Hero

One of the missing links, the step beyond Fielding in the exploitation of irony as a fictional device, is supplied by Oliver Goldsmith's *Vicar of Wakefield* (1766). This novel, so brilliant for at least half its length, is strangely underestimated, remaining a memory from childhood which, unlike *Gulliver* or *Crusoe,* cannot shake off the childish reading. There is perhaps no level the child has missed, and the pleasure of the adult is almost the same as that of the child. The *Vicar*'s great popularity and its influence on continental literature were due to Goldsmith's building his story on fairy-tale motifs and archetypal patterns that touched a sensitive chord in all readers and showed a way toward introducing romance into the realistic novel form. (Similar patterns in *Clarissa* were submerged under the close texture of observed experience—though they played their part in Richardson's popularity too.) As Smollett builds his novels around a structure of satiric exposition (with some romantic or sentimental plot elements), so Goldsmith builds his novel around the myths of the god who descends among humans as a traveler in search of hospitality, the ruler who passes among his people in disguise, and Jack and the Beanstalk. The most striking and central of the myths is the story of Job—his fortune lost, his house burnt down, both his daughters abducted, one (supposed) dead, his son about to be hanged, etc. The *Vicar* is a typical product of mixed genres, with many theatrical elements thrown in at the end.

In part, however, it is a close eighteenth-century precursor of *Pride and Prejudice,* and it still shows the scaffolding that has been shed or more thoroughly disguised by Austen. To begin, we must go back to a slightly earlier work. The first *Chinese Letters* were published early in 1760; they were reworked as much as possible and published as *The Citizen of the World* in May 1762. Goldsmith wrote the *Vicar* at this time or shortly after, although it was not published until 1766. In other words, Dr. Primrose follows chronologically hard on Lien Chi Altangi. Goldsmith's Chinese observer carries the associations of a country very unlike the Persia of Montesquieu's *Lettres persanes,* with its seraglio, passion, and adventure; China recalls wisdom, tradition, conservatism, and the like. Unlike the noble savage (Voltaire's Huron), Lien Chi Altangi brings something more with him than simplicity; his comments are often sharpened by irony, particularly as he becomes accustomed to the new country and can analyze both it and China with some detachment, juxtaposing their different manners. But this is not to suggest that he is only an ironic observer. Often he sees the truth through a child's eyes or through the haze of conflicting conventions, and often at the beginning and occasionally at the end his divergent point of view exposes him to satire. In a memorable scene he is charmed by a young lady he meets on the street, from whom he generalizes about the kindness of English ladies; he never suspects that she is a prostitute until she fails to return the watch she has volunteered to have repaired for him. His true criticisms of the fantastic fashions of London women are followed by his adverse comments on their white teeth and unconstricted feet. He is, after all, Goldsmith points out, from a country with as many foolish customs of its own. The effect in general is of two sets of manners —some good, some bad—juxtaposed, rather than one set (bad) criticized by the other (good).

There is nothing new about this figure. The satirist tries to invent a central figure who can convey as much varied satire as possible. When Goldsmith came to write the *Vicar,* however, he must have begun with two ideas—to present a Parson Adams character and to have a Fieldingesque commentator as his supposed "author." The *Vicar,* it should be remembered, comes from the pen of an essayist; it represents Goldsmith's first step toward dramatic form. It is the first of the early novels to use an ironic narrator who is a central character of the action as well—both an ironist and the object of dramatic irony.

Dr. Primrose sees more than the people around him and lets the reader, and sometimes the people themselves, know about it. But the reader sees still more than Primrose does. In short, Goldsmith goes one step beyond Fielding, at the same time shedding some of the creaking machinery involved in the omniscient "historian" of Fielding's novels (but stopping far short of the irrational order of *Tristram Shandy*). He has made the irony part of his speaker's temperament, creating a more complex as well as a wittier person while at the same time adding a dramatic irony that was impossible in Fielding's kind of narrative. The situation is still basically a satiric one, focusing on the pretensions to gentility of Mrs. Primrose and her daughters. They are ridiculous; she is unpleasant. The family of a poor parson (he has come down in the world), they try to emulate the gentry with dress, carriage, even a family portrait, and they become prey to the aristocratic wolf who appears in the shape of Squire Thornhill.

Goldsmith duplicates the *Clarissa* situation of seduction, but he treats it in a different way from either Richardson or his satiric equivalent, Smollett. His focus is on the manners of the sheep rather than on the wolf, and it is not a sentimental focus; he studies their aspirations and the Quixotic effects in absurd behavior and in a blindness to the real situation in which a wolf is approaching ever nearer. This emphasis is achieved by placing at the center of the narrative the clever man, the ironist who though he sees through his wife and daughters yet bows to their wishes. He may surreptitiously throw away their face washes, but he allows himself to be guided by them in the posing of the family portrait, the dispatching of the good Burchell, and the encouraging of the evil Squire Thornhill. In fact, although he sees through his wife's values, he unconsciously shares some of them; his contempt of Burchell, the "man of broken fortune," emerges in his fear that his daughter Sophia may in fact fall in love with him:

> but I had too good an opinion of Sophia's understanding, and was too well convinced of her ambition, to be under any uneasiness from a man of broken fortune.
> nor could I conceive how so sensible a girl as my youngest [Sophia], could thus prefer a man of broken fortune to one whose expectations were much greater.[1]

To appreciate the originality of Goldsmith's conception one must look back on the *Vicar* from the vantage point of *Pride and Prejudice*. There the first-person protagonist has been replaced by a guiding intelligence resembling Fielding's ironic "historian," but the central character, Elizabeth Bennet, is an ironist like Dr. Primrose. While observing accurately the pretensions of those around her, she cannot see with complete clarity and is deceived by the manners of both Wickham and Darcy (as Primrose is by Squire Thornhill and Burchell). The theme that emerges from this kind of a central character, however elemental in Dr. Primrose, is self-knowledge and the growth to self-realization. When he recognizes his mistake about the two Thornhills, Dr. Primrose also recognizes something—however rudimentary the treatment as compared with Austen's—about himself.

1. *Collected Works of Goldsmith*, ed. Friedman, 4, 40, 52.

Dr. Primrose is in the position later taken over by Elizabeth Bennet, and he is rather like her in his self-assurance, wit, and limited insight. But he is the head of a family, and his equivalent (if not direct descendant) is Mr. Bennet, a more intelligent version who like Primrose regards his hideous wife and foolish daughters with weary irony but is easygoing; Mr. Bennet has given up the fight and merely observes amusedly. As a result he offers a contrast to his daughter Elizabeth, whose limitation is not withdrawal. Mr. Bennet is ultimately responsible for the fate of Lydia and realizes it, just as Dr. Primrose shares responsibility for the fate of Olivia and at length recognizes his mistake. The whole Primrose family is, in fact, lifted bodily into *Pride and Prejudice:* the ignorant, pretentious, social-climbing mother, the duped Olivia, and the one sensible daughter, Sophia, have their equivalents in Mrs. Bennet, her daughters, and the two sensible sisters, Elizabeth and Jane. The two suitors in the *Vicar* are like Wickham and Darcy—one with surface charm who is actually a Lovelace seducer (Squire Thornhill), the other less prepossessing, in fact somewhat cynical and misanthropic (Burchell).[2] The main question and plot stimulus of the *Vicar*—and of all Austen novels— is how to marry off the daughters. The first thought Dr. Primrose has when he learns that he has lost his fortune is how he will make suitable marriages for his daughters, and this concern drives him (against his better nature) into his wife's camp in his opinion of Burchell. By putting the father in the center, Goldsmith makes marriage the important matter of the novel—but of course from the father's point of view; Austen puts one of the marriageable daughters in the center but gives her some of the detachment of the father in relation to the mating rite.

The first difference between the two novels, as I have noted, is in the protagonist's role. From Fanny Burney's *Evelina* Austen no doubt learned the usefulness and flexibility of the bright young girl's point of view. Her very youth makes the theme more convincingly one of growth and self-knowledge. At the same time, however, by keeping a narrator who more clearly and unambiguously sees

2. Burchell bears the same relation to Primrose as Drybone (the Man in Black) to Lien Chi Altangi, telling his life story, serving as a guide, and allowing him to see beyond appearances. But Primrose dismisses his guide, and this is the beginning of his troubles.

through Elizabeth—though is often parallel to Elizabeth—Austen avoids immersing the reader in Elizabeth's emotions. In this sense Goldsmith is braver than Austen, and like Swift he trusts to his own ability to keep the proper distance between Primrose and the reader without benefit of the omniscient narrator.

All that has been said so far about the *Vicar* applies only to the first seventeen chapters. Goldsmith may have run out of ideas at that point, or he may have picked up his real interest, the myth of Job. Suddenly he has Primrose embark on a journey (talking predictably about life as a journey), and he reverts to an older genre, the picaresque; he loses the wonderfully tight, controlled, and effective microcosm of the family and slips back into the world of the *Chinese Letters* with satiric essays on punishment, liberty, and contemporary drama. While a great part of the originality of the first part comes from its tightness of structure, Goldsmith now accepts Smollett's permissive definition of a novel and gives digressions such as George's account of his life. The romantic and mythic elements emerge to full prominence. Goldsmith makes Primrose a true Job, relies on coincidences (the meetings with Miss Wilmot, George, and Olivia), and builds the disguise imagery that was subordinated to the plot in the first half into a pseudo-unifying force.[3] The ballads and interpolated tales become more frequent. As Frederick A. Hilles has pointed out, these are necessary to make the narrative seem more real by contrast and, with the preposterous reversals and recognitions of the stories, to prepare the reader for the end.[4] But the only blatant romance occurrence in the first half is the fall of Primrose's youngest into a raging stream, from which Burchell rescues her, and I am inclined to suspect that this, as well as the ballad of *Edwin and Angelina,* are interpolations in the light of the second half. The problem of the second half is not, however, germane to my argument, which is only

3. Disguise is a common ground for the two conflicting aspects of the *Vicar*. As a romance motif, it helps to define Burchell's role as the disguised prince and the villainous abductors' role. As a device of the novel of manners, however, disguise runs from the posing of the Primroses above their proper class, to the whores who pose as Lady Blarney and Miss Carolina Wilelmina Amelia Skeggs, to Jenkinson who wears actual disguises as part of his confidence racket (making the connection with criminal biography obvious; cf. above, Chap. 1). For an interesting essay on the motif of disguise in the *Vicar,* see Curtis Dahl, "Patterns of Disguise in 'The Vicar of Wakefield,' " *Journal of English Literary History,* 25 (1958), 90–104.

4. Introduction, *The Vicar,* ed. Everyman (New York, E. P. Dutton, 1951), p. x.

that in the first seventeen chapters of the *Vicar* Goldsmith, starting with an anglicized Lien Chi Altangi, a family setting, and the problem of marriage, produced a new and original form which augmented the picaresque form of Fielding and contributed another stage in the transition from satire to Austen's novel of manners.

The Female Quixote

Before the novel of manners can emerge, however, the focal point must change from the father to the marriageable daughter, whose problem is more central, personal, and intense. Two subjects were available even before Goldsmith wrote—the foolish girl and the intelligent girl, the female Quixote and the Pamela-Clarissa.

Charlotte Lennox' novel, *The Female Quixote* (1752), derives from Marivaux' *Don Quixote Moderne*,[5] in which both male and female Quixotes appear. The fixation of these Quixotes is courtly love with its conventions of the imperious lady, abject servant-lover, and the rest. Mrs. Lennox increases the role of the female (Mlle. Babet), producing her heroine Arabella, and reduces that of the male (Jean Bagnol), until all that remains is the pretended chivalry of Sir George. Arabella contains both aspects of the Quixote syndrome, vice and corrective.

As a villain, Arabella represents the female attitude that Fielding would probably have called prudery—the refusal to recognize her feelings or desires, her very humanity, and the consequent destruction of innocent people because they do not conform to the stereotype she carries in her head. Thus at the end of Book IV Arabella is sufficiently carried away to cry to Lucy (her Sancho-like maid):

> Do you think I have any cause to accuse myself, though five thousand men were to die for me! It is very certain my beauty has produced very deplorable effects; the unhappy Harvey has expiated, by his death, the violence his too-desperate passion forced him to meditate against me: the no less guilty, the noble unknown Edward, is wandering about the world, in a tormenting despair, and stands exposed to the vengeance of my cousin,

5. Written in 1712, published in French in 1737, *Don Quixote Moderne* was translated into English by John Lockman in 1749 as *Pharsamond, or the Knight Errant.*

who has vowed his death. My charms have made another person, whose character ought to be sacred to me, forget all the ties of consanguinity, and become the rival of his son, whose interest he once endeavoured to support: and lastly, the unfortunate Bellmour consumes away in an hopeless passion.[6]

The effect of transplanting the female half of the courtly love code in the eighteenth century is to produce a monster of egotism or self-sufficiency, who can say and believe that "It is impossible to think" that Sir George won't die "since he has not so much as received a command from me to live" (2, 17).

The satire on French romances is less important as a theme than the more general one of form vs. feeling. Quixotism in Arabella means a rigidity of behavior—her favorite word is "questionless"; there is no doubt as to her rightness and everyone else's wrongness. In the central instance of Mr. Glanville, the romance forms stand between Arabella and her feelings and of course thwart Glanville's feelings. Mrs. Lennox' novel demonstrates what happens when a woman is given the Quixote role. There is a great difference between Quixote as a funny-looking old man and as a beautiful young girl. Being female, Arabella has to remain passive: her actions are largely blocking ones rather than the active, questing ones of her male counterpart. Insofar as she remains passive, she appears a prude, wrapped in neuroses; and to the extent that she is an active Quixote, one feels (as in the scene where she makes Glanville read) that if she is not merely atrociously selfish, she is, in fact, out of her mind. In other words, she comes across much more as a character than as a satiric symbol; the reader takes her seriously and asks questions.

There are several reasons for this effect. First, *The Female Quixote* has a small cast of characters and is tightly knit, with unity of place through most of it and few digressions.[7] The episodes are longer and more fully developed than in other Quixotic novels (*The Female Quixote* is closer in this way, as in others, to the Richardsonian novel). So much time is spent on the Glanville courtship, and neces-

6. *The Female Quixote; or, the Adventures of Arabella,* in *The British Novelists* (London, 1810), *I*, 231–32.

7. The one main digression is the mock story of Sir George; the other episodic parts are at least picked up later (e.g. Edward and Miss Groves).

sarily in conversation, that the focus appears to be on the heroine's mind and the way it operates. Second, Glanville and Arabella's father try so hard to understand her that the reader also sees her as demented. The characteristic reaction to her from relations or close friends is sympathy or annoyance. As Sir Charles Glanville says, "I should be sorry to have a daughter-in-law for whom I should blush as often as she opened her mouth" (*1, 83*). Finally, there is no ironic observer like Fielding's narrator to distance Arabella; she is merely described.

However, in Book VII, as if she remembered it was expected of her, Mrs. Lennox takes her characters to Bath and London, introducing Arabella to a wider circle of acquaintance, and it is at this point that the book almost breaks. The intense psychological scrutiny of Arabella made possible by the small circle and the single locale is replaced by a rather clumsy attempt at the rapid satiric survey of society. On the one hand Arabella is presented as the Quixotic fool, and on the other she is the Quixotic observer and ideal. Such scenes as the one in which Arabella and Charlotte Glanville misunderstand each other over the meaning of "adventure" present the positive half of the Quixote syndrome. To Arabella "adventure" is a romantic platonic love; to Charlotte, a sordid affair, probably like Miss Groves' (p. 115). To Charlotte "favors" are kisses or very probably worse, while to Arabella they are offerings of scarves or bracelets as tokens to her "servant." Here Arabella becomes the ideal or, at least, a corrective, and her Quixotism shows how far the world has fallen from the idealism of courtly romance. In "a chapter of the satirical kind" she becomes a satirist of Bath:

> What room, I pray you, does a lady give for high and noble adventures, who consumes her days in dressing, dancing, listening to songs, and ranging the walks with people as thoughtless as herself? How mean and contemptible a figure must a life spent in such idle amusements make in history? (2, 137–38)

"History" is a perspective that shrinks the business of Bath. She goes on to ridicule the effeminate men (vs. her heroes of romance) and the dress- and fashion-conscious men and women (vs. the Service of Love)—all "wholly unworthy of a hero" (2, 139). She concludes (and this applies equally to the scenes with Charlotte): "When actions are a censure upon themselves, the reciter will always be considered as a satirist" (2, 139). Later, apropos of Charlotte, she says, "But with him who is incapable of any violent attraction, and whose heart is chilled by a general indifference, precept or example will have no force." She is opposing indifference to her own strong feelings about what is proper, what is good and evil: "For there is nothing at so great a distance from true and heroic virtue, as that indifference which obliges some people to be pleased with all things or nothing" (2, 7).

Thus if Arabella represents as Quixotic villain the constricting aspect of courtly love conventions, as heroine she represents their liberating aspect. J. M. S. Tompkins is probably correct to include *The Female Quixote* among preromantic novels rather than satiric; Mrs. Lennox does not satirize Arabella's romances as much as use this form as a convenient vehicle for introducing romance into the humdrum life of Arabella and her readers.[8] Nevertheless, *The Female Quixote* is a remote anticipation of the world of manners. In spite of her madness, Arabella has the special quality and beauty of a Harriet Byron, Catherine Morland, or Elizabeth Bennet. Her madness is related to that special quality of imagination that sets Austen's heroines off from the other women in her novels, and the blindness that goes with Arabella's madness is at least analogous to the blind spot in the Elizabeth Bennets and Emma Woodhouses. And then Glanville resembles the Darcys who persevere in the face of the heroine's misunderstanding (and annoying qualities such as arrogance or prejudice), and Charlotte Glanville is the other woman (in *Pride and Prejudice,* Bingley's sister) who is after the man who loves the heroine and who is both jealous and unable to believe that he can really love her rival.

The effect of such scenes as the one with Arabella, Miss Groves, and her woman, Mrs. Norris, is to produce a comic clash of manners —the artificial, book-learned manners of Arabella; the realistic, cynical ones of Mrs. Norris, who thinks she can get money out of Arabella for the information she has to impart; and the shallow city sophistication of Miss Groves (as artificial as Arabella's manners). The scene in which Arabella and Charlotte talk at cross-purposes

8. *The Popular Novel in England, 1770–1800* (London, Constable, 1932; reprinted, Lincoln, University of Nebraska Press, 1961), p. 207.

about the word "adventure" operates in the same way. Manners are, of course, crucial in a man's approach to Arabella. Sir George is *not* rebuffed on his first meeting with Arabella because, with Charlotte pressing all her attentions upon him, he has no opportunity to attempt "a piece of gallantry which could undoubtedly have procured him a banishment from her presence" (*1*, 114). The comedy then arises from misunderstandings: Arabella talks on one level, Charlotte on another (as Don Quixote and Sancho do), much as the representative of one class talks with another, and the resulting misunderstandings make up the fabric of the novel. Mrs. Lennox' novel ultimately comes down to the subject of how the mating ceremony should be carried out: what is decorous, and how much should form give way to feeling?

Harriet Byron: The Courtship

In his last novel, *Sir Charles Grandison* (1754), Richardson went a step beyond *Clarissa* and altered his approach from the dramatization of conflicting forces to the analysis of the "good man" or anti-Tom Jones. Before Sir Charles appears, however, his future mate, Harriet Byron, must reject a series of unworthy suitors. Even after he appears on the scene, Richardson continues to show "the way to the substitution of social embarrassment for tragic conflict, to a light transcription of manners, and to a 'delicacy' which was sometimes silly, but at its best penetrating and subtle."[9] The large number of characters and the leisurely pace have the effect of diffusing the focus to a society rather than narrowing it to a central couple like Clarissa and Lovelace. Richardson's last novel points the way to the novel of feminine manners and sensibility that includes, in a way, *Evelina*.

Richardson also introduces an important locale for satire. His stated aim was to inculcate morality, and his familiarity with female circles, his knowledge of the conduct and letter books—those manuals of social etiquette—led him to use the endless talk and preoccupation with marriage and manners among women as the vehicle for his message. With the conduct book as a model, his approach is inevitably more analytic than in *Clarissa*. Although there is an attempted

9. A. D. McKillop, *Samuel Richardson, Printer and Novelist* (Chapel Hill, University of North Carolina Press, 1936), p. 213.

abduction (which serves to bring Sir Charles onto the stage), the more usual problems are how to rid oneself of a bore or what to do if one spills tea on a petticoat. The emphasis, in fact, is carefully balanced between the punctilio of the correct answer to a social question and the performer's feelings when she makes the error or witnesses it in someone else. As Richardson shows, it is very difficult to present correct and incorrect manners without slipping into satire.

Moreover, Harriet Byron, the letter writer, writes in order to preserve her standards and freedom of choice. Clarissa wrote in order to preserve her integrity or individuality, which was symbolically at least what Lovelace was trying to get away from her. It was a constant struggle to smuggle the letters out and to their recipients, and they were the last signs of her brave will fighting. When she was raped her letters ceased except for those on routine matters. Harriet Byron is as concerned with the preservation and fulfillment of her own nature as was Clarissa, but the threats to her are transferred into a long list of Solmes-like (but harmless) suitors. She says at one point, "I shall have nothing to trouble you with, I think, but scenes of courtship."[10] Her problem, as she explains, is as follows:

> What can a woman do, who is addressed by a man of talents inferior to her own? Must she throw away her talents? Must she hide her light under a bushel, purely to do credit to the man? She cannot pick and choose, as men can. She has only her negative; and, if she is desirous to oblige her friends, not always *that*. Yet it is said, women must not encourage fops and fools. They must encourage men of sense only. And it is *well* said. But what will they do, if their lot be cast among foplings? (2, 1-2)

The satiric attitude is thus built into the situation of courtship in the cold objectivity maintained by the courted girl so long as her affections are not engaged. Mr. Fowler's approach, which from his point of view must have been quite different, from Harriet's shows "every feature of his face working, his hands and knees trembling, and his tongue faltering." "O, Lucy!" she exclaims, "what a disqualifier is love, if such agitation as these are the natural effects of *that* passion!" (*1*, 109). This detachment infuriates her lovers: "Don't smile," cries Greville, "I can't *bear* to see you smile: Why don't you be angry at

10. *Sir Charles Grandison* (London, Chapman and Hall, 1902), *1*, 127.

me?" Her reaction is: "The man is out of his right mind" (*1*, 151).

Thus Harriet is the desirable single woman, the courted girl who can look objectively on all of her suitors because they are focusing attentions upon her which she does not wish to reciprocate. Because of this mild aggression, she can with justification describe them satirically and even parody them at some length. Since the suitors are, finally, harmless, her letters (like Anna Howe's) merely present a witty girl showing off. In her situation, writing of her suitors, showing off becomes one ingredient of the satiric observer. It is also necessary, however, if she is to justify her continued refusals of proposals of marriage, that she find fault and as emphatically as possible demonstrate this fault to her friends and relatives. Her letters, like Bramble's, tend toward the form of satire, and together they produce a list of suitors that is a parade of fools; they assume the form of single professions (Sir Hargrave Pollexfen), debates (Sir Hargrave and Mr. Walden), and group conversations (Sir Rowland, Sir Hargrave, and Mr. Greville at breakfast). Until at length she meets the ideal, Sir Charles Grandison: "What can they mean by their foppery," she exclaims, looking around her, "when Sir Charles Grandison is before them?" (2, 2). At this point the focus moves to Sir Charles; Harriet loves him, loses her objectivity and her satiric raison d'être, passing beyond satire to eulogy. She is transformed by love much as Bramble is by the return of his health in Scotland or as Lismahago is by marriage, and in this sense she is dehumored; thereafter she cannot wait to meet more Grandisons, of which there is a whole family.

Harriet's satire shows how to domesticate satire completely within the form of the novel. Her satiric comments, even her parodies, are psychologically consistent with a girl writing letters, familiar with letter books, and trying to amuse her correspondent: "There, Lucy! —Will this do for Mr. Singleton? It is not much out of character, I assure you" (*1*, 101). She criticizes only certain people and for certain reasons. Compared to her focus on suitors, Bramble's concerns are much more varied, his satiric reference is more external, and his tone is more in need of explanation. Harriet's tone is as quiet and deadly as Mr. Spectator's when she describes the dusty pedant, Mr. Walden, who

not finding himself heard, drew up his mouth as if to a contemptuous whistle, shrugged his shoulders, and sat collected in his own conscious worthiness: his eyes, however, were often cast upon the pictures that hung round the room, as much better objects than the living ones before him. (*1, 78*)

She describes "honest Mr. Singleton" as a man who "had a smile at the serve of every speaker, and a loud laugh always ready at the baronet's" (*1, 83*).

When pressed far enough by a suitor, she can move from the comments of her letters to a direct rebuke, not unlike that of the old stage satirists except that it is controlled (and so made ironic) by the conventions of society. "Is it, interrupted I, a necessary consequence, that the woman who cannot receive the addresses of Sir Hargrave Pollexfen, must be engaged?" (*1, 118*). When Sir Hargrave says, "You are too refined, surely, madam," Harriet thinks, "*Refined!* what meant the man by the word in this place?" But she says, "I believe, sir, we differ very widely in *many* of our sentiments" (*1, 121*).

In a sense, satire is bad manners. Sir Charles Grandison's good manners (or his ease of manners), Richardson emphasizes, enable him to right wrongs—prevent abductions, murders, and lovers' quarrels—with the least possible pain to the people involved. But while the ideal man is totally above satire, other quite decent people upon occasion become satirists; and so, Richardson admits, there are good and bad satirists, depending upon the motive, the tone, and so forth. Satire thus becomes a useful attitude in the social game—either railing or sarcasm, execration or irony.

The explicit discussion of satire in *Grandison* is like that in *Clarissa*. Harriet admits that she is said to have "a satirical vein," but she adds about herself: "she means no ill-nature: she loves every body; but not their faults. . . . Nor wishes to be spared for her own" (*1, 64*). When she is free of the burden of satire, she can chide the "false" satirist of the later volumes, Charlotte Grandison. Charlotte is the irresponsible satirist whose attack has its foundation in an eye to incongruity and a Peregrinish sense of intellectual superiority rather than in a balanced sense of morality and propriety.

The range of Harriet's and Charlotte's letters extends far beyond satire. Satire disappears altogether when Sir Rowland falls on his knees before Harriet: "O, Sir Rowland! said I, you are a good man. How affecting are the visible emotions of a manly heart!" (*1, 131*).

Harriet moves from pity for the harmless, foolish suitors, to detachment from and ridicule for the impertinent and foolish, and to something stronger for the knavish Sir Hargrave Pollexfen. Then she passes into the grotesque and melodramatic in the ultimate in boorish courtships, her abduction by Sir Hargrave. "Two Lucifers" were at the masquerade from which she is abducted (William Wilson and Pollexfen), "but the worst, the very worst Lucifer of all [Pollexfen], appeared in a harlequin dress. He hopped, and skipt, and played the fool about me" (*1*, 220). The clergyman, at whose feet she falls for protection, also turns out to be a masquerader: "The man snuffled his answer through his nose. When he opened his pouched mouth, the tobacco hung about his great yellow teeth" (*1*, 226). Here again is the world of Mrs. Jewkes, Colbrand, and Mrs. Sinclair. "*Dearly beloved*, began to read the snuffling monster—" (*1*, 227).

The critical if not ironic tone remains near the center so long as the situation concerns courtship and the scene is not disturbed by such violent breaches of decorum. As the novel of manners became a genre, it attempted (never with complete success) to strip away the attitudes at either end of the spectrum, the sentimental as well as the melodramatic, leaving the urbane satire or comedy of the central situation. One of Richardson's moods is genuinely satiric, but he was never fully acquainted with the tradition and the forms available to him. The satiric attitude and the juxtaposition of manners in *Grandison* lack the style and the order that characterize later novels of manners.

Evelina: Cinderella and Society

A fourth transitional novel that I would single out is Fanny Burney's *Evelina* (1778), which, as a critic has observed, uses "*Humphry Clinker* as a base for operations in the direction of Jane Austen."[11] Austen was a careful reader of Burney, and Burney owes an obvious debt to Smollett. Although the plot of *Evelina* receives a great deal more emphasis than that of *Humphry Clinker*, both novels are structurally a series of letters describing a series of places visited, an itinerary held together by a conventional sentimental plot. Unacknowl-

---

11. See Edwine Montague and Louis L. Martz, "Fanny Burney's *Evelina*," in *The Age of Johnson*, p. 171.

edged fathers, the lowly who turn out to be highborn, and brothers who find their lost sisters are all ingredients of the sentimental plot in both novels. The themes in both—though different—are conveyed by the cities and country houses visited. *Evelina* goes from the country to London with the acceptable Mirvan family; then back to the country and again to London, this time in the company of the impossible, vulgar Branghtons and Mme. Duval; then back to the country and to Bristol Hot Well with people of quality, the Beaumonts; and finally to Bath with Lord Orville. The effect here is not too different from that of a scene in London or Bath seen through the eyes of Bramble, then Jery, and then Winifred Jenkins and Tabitha. In a more formalized, static way, these letters serve the function of Evelina's different guides, revealing and opposing "different points of view and incompatible ways of meeting the same experience."[12] In this sense *Humphry Clinker* points away from the true-false world of formal verse satire toward the infinitely qualified world of the novel of manners.

The central unit of both novels is the test scene in which the attitudes of various types are brought together and analyzed. *Evelina* is a series of these big scenes—Evelina's first assembly, her first opera, the drawing room of the Beaumonts, and so on. In *Humphry Clinker* the moral discourse in which one satirist attacks an evil is the simplest scene of this sort: Bramble attacks the affectation that makes people desire the fashionable waters of Bath, however disgusting and unhealthy. There are also scenes in which more than one satirist appears, and the object of attack is not so clearly defined. As we move north, away from the blatant folly of London, these scenes increase in number and the distinctions between right and wrong become less clear-cut. The practical jokes and counter practical jokes of the Bulford house party, with their repercussions of hurt pride and endangered health, raise the question of who in a given circumstance is right and who is wrong. And what of Micklewhimmen, the sophisticate who pretends to be an invalid in order to excite compassion from the ladies? The alarm of fire being sounded, he proves himself both wholly sound and a coward, knocking down old ladies in his hurry to save himself; but his good-humored acceptance of the unmasking,

12. Ernest A. Baker, *The History of the English Novel* (London, H. F. and G. Witherley, 1930), 4, 76.

ending in his dancing a jig, leaves one wondering whether he is admirable or not; whether he or Bramble or a clergyman who enters into the argument or Tabby, who refuses to forgive him under any circumstances, is really right. There are also the scenes in which Bramble, Lismahago, Tabby, and others argue, social types mix, manners are tested, and the norm of behavior becomes, almost inevitably, a compromise between two or more partially correct attitudes.

These scenes place the satirist in a larger context. Like Harriet Byron and Charlotte Grandison, Bramble is finally just one more point of view, one more example, in the larger picture of the novel. In *Evelina* Burney presents the characteristic satiric figures common in Smollett's novels—the sharp-tongued Mrs. Selwyn, the practical-satirist Captain Mirvan, and in his way even the fop Lovel. But in every case they are regarded coldly, the moral or public content has gone out of their observations, and they are merely private characters, their particular satiric approach a pattern of manners. Mirvan is a case in point; he is the Smollettian sea dog, as well as the prankster and the Juvenalian whose indignation bubbles over into violent action when confronted with such outrages to his native John Bullishness as the preposterous Mme. Duval. He can be found in any of Smollett's novels, but he has undergone the same metamorphosis as Holder and Bulford in *Humphry Clinker;* he has become a prankster and a boor. The difference appears in the one scene in which Mirvan most resembles the early Smollettian satirists, Random, Pickle, and Cadwallader Crabtree—the incident in which he dresses up a monkey to look like the fop Lovel. The monkey is a commentary on Lovel just as the Pygmalion girl Peregrine creates is a commentary on high society, but the monkey proceeds to emphasize the cruelty beyond satire by biting Lovel's ear. The scene arouses only pity for Lovel, who for a moment becomes a human being as well as a fop. By contrast, the moral function is completely absent in all Mirvan's other pranks, and in the pranks he plays on Mme. Duval he appears simply as a coarse lout, like his counterparts in *Humphry Clinker*.

The chief difference between the two novels, however, lies in the fact that in *Evelina* the places and scenes not only are part of a satiric survey of society, but also are stages in the social climb of a young girl. One difficulty in Smollett's novels up to *Humphry Clinker* was his inability to merge his sentimental plot conventions and his real center of interest (the satiric scene); *Evelina* carries Smollett's work a step further, fitting his psychological form to the logical form of the courtship. For this aspect of her novel, Burney drew upon *Sir Charles Grandison,* omitting the melodramatic end of the spectrum. But the plot Burney follows in *Evelina* is not solely made up of the stages of a courtship; it simultaneously consists of the stages in the social ascent of a young girl. Evelina, the chief letter writer of the novel, has much in common with Harriet Byron, but she has more with Sir Charles Grandison's young ward, Emily Jervois, a naïve observer without Harriet's certainty in her own judgment; Emily's horrible mother becomes Evelina's Mme. Duval, with the implications more fully developed.

Evelina is sharp and critical, and her standards are high; but as Bramble is isolated by his illness, she (like Humphry Clinker) is isolated by her birth. She is outside society, of obscure parentage, and comes from a sheltered life in the country which sets off the vice of London in vivid relief. However, the function of her equivocal position is no longer simply to make her a touchstone or a satirist (though she is a little of both) but to put her outside society—a "nobody" as Lovel calls her—so that she literally does not know who she is; her progression then is not, like Harriet's, toward fulfillment, but toward self-definition and identity.

The same progression is evident in both Bramble and that other "nobody" Humphry. Bramble is shown as a man in search of health, which is finally a knowledge of his own past, achieved by going back over the country of his youth and making an important discovery about himself. But in *Humphry Clinker* searches for self-definition are tangential and subordinate and thus are only other aspects of a larger theme dealing with attitudes toward experience in general. In *Evelina* the satiric aspects, the attitudes toward the world, are subordinated to the protagonist's personal search, which is thus the theme of the novel.

Although Evelina has the satirist's inclination, she is closer to the character of Lydia Melford. What Smollett did not see was the possibility of making the young girl with a finer sensibility than his masculine characters a satirist, perhaps because he knew she lacked the freedom of choice of a man and so could not finally maintain the satirist's standards. Lydia, the naïve, impressionable, sensitive young girl, comes to each new place with wide eyes and (like her uncle and brother) is appalled at what she discovers; pretty soon, however, she recognizes the fashionableness of it and tries to adjust. Lydia is a rough sketch for the figure of a young girl like Evelina, who is an outsider, is sensitive enough to see the wrongness of the society she enters, but still knows she must make common cause with it; she must come to terms with a society she has first seen through.

The obvious source for this aspect of *Evelina,* however, is the French novelist Marivaux' *Vie de Marianne* (1731; Eng. trans., 1736). Burney takes not only the names Duval and Mirvan from Mme. Dutour and Mme. de Miran, and Orville from M. de Valville, but also the situation of the girl in the anomalous position of not knowing her parents but suspecting that they were noble and rich: "If my only Fault," she says, "had been not to be born of rich Parents; had I but a noble extraction without a Fortune; all still would have been safe."[13] But she believes herself to be of a rich, noble family, while her actual status is not above a linen draper's. Her actions soon convince the reader of her quality, but society is not so ready to grant her the place she deserves. She has to bear the middle-class abuse of her linen-draper landlady, an attempted seduction by her "benefactor" M. de Climal, threatened poverty, the jealousy and interference of her potential husband's family, her lover's unfaithfulness, and finally, just when she is on the verge of success, the greedy clutches of the Church which would cheat her out of her recently acquired inheritance.

A brief contrast with *Joseph Andrews* is in order. Fielding may have looked to *Marianne* as a useful example of how Richardson *should* have written; here he found a similar plot (again perhaps one of Richardson's sources) but also detachment, analysis, and criticism of the protagonist as well as a broader and less intense view of experience. The single action of the attempted seduction, which takes up a large part of *Pamela,* is dispatched quickly in *Marianne.* When M. de Climal attempts to seduce Marianne he is scorned and dismissed;

13. *The Life of Marianne: or, The Adventures of the Countess of * * * (London, 1736), *1*, 104.

though she is left temporarily destitute, there is no danger that she will lose her honor. Instead of experiencing one, long, intense trial, Marianne is confronted by a variety of obstacles which bring her into contact with a cross section of French society, from country clerics to tradespeople, from convent nuns to vain young women and gossips. Fielding has Joseph suffer the same persecution and end a scion of a good family. His gentility also shows through as a natural virtue, evident to the perceptive.

The difference between Joseph and Marianne (or Evelina) is notable, however: he is given no awareness of his true status and so never aspires. There is no conflict within him, and his relationship with society is the simple satiric one of virtue persecuted. Fielding merely substitutes charity for chastity as Joseph's main motive force. On the other hand, Marianne (and much more, Jacob in Marivaux' *Paysan parvenu*) acts with a consummate sense of the realities that Joseph blithely ignores. Her virtues are social rather than personal, and her delicate sensibility expresses a happy blending of the ability to respond emotionally and an acuteness in judging the results of a generous and timely action.

In a sense Marivaux has in a single try hit upon the novel of manners that the English slowly evolved over another half-century through the gradual refining of satiric forms and intentions. The two basic situations of the novel of manners illustrate the point. The first is the situation that developed in England as the satirist-satirized was refined into a Dr. Primrose and an Evelina. At the beginning of Part II of Marivaux' novel, Marianne goes to church and observes (as the first-person narrator) all the fashionable folk posing and posturing in their pews. She is a country girl in the great city, and she describes these manners with a fresh style, meditates a bit on them, and then tells how her own simplicity and beauty drew all eyes away from the affected coquettes. For just an instant she sets off the artificial beauty of the others by her own natural beauty, smiling at the psychology of the men (her hand, she says, is what captures them). But almost at once the reader's interest shifts from the coquettes and the beaux looking at Marianne to her own psychology: she is not merely a device for showing up the artifice of the coquettes; she is a character who is becoming vain talking about their vanity.

Her flaw has hardly been fastened upon when the situation is completely overturned by her seeing a handsome young man (Valville) and becoming herself enamored. This leads into the second situation, which could not have taken place with the innocence of Joseph Andrews—the scene of snobbery leading to embarrassment. Marianne has been so smitten by Valville that she walks in front of a horse on her way home and is saved by him. With her apparent gentility she soon has Valville's heart at least partly in her grasp. But only with much difficulty does she keep from him the nature of her lodgings with a linen draper. When the coach takes her from Valville's house to her lodgings, her landlady characteristically attacks the coachman as a highway robber who should be beaten rather than paid. Marianne is horrified to see her lover's footman across the street, taking in the whole, sordid, middle-class scene, which she has tried so hard to keep from Valville. (Significantly, the embarrassment is at the hands of Mme. Dutour, as Evelina's is at the hands of Mme. Duval.)

The scene of embarrassment is more particularly a testing. Embarrassment, for example, is only one of Marianne's reactions. Mme. Dutour exhibits behavior that can be painful only to refined sentiments. The crucial test of this sort comes with M. de Climal's proposition. Assuming that Marianne's virtue corresponds to her social position, he offers her a guaranteed yearly stipend for her consent. Her scornful refusal is a rejection of the moral position of an entire class and demonstrates convincingly her true affiliation with a higher class. Mme. Dutour's middle-class reaction (similar to the one Fielding attributed to Pamela) is to advise Marianne to play Climal for all he is worth—to accept his presents and then let him discover that his money will not buy her virtue. The two elements are constantly in tension—the girl's lack of social status and her actual possession of it. Thus Marianne and Evelina can be shown in scenes in which snobbery leads to embarrassment, in scenes in which embarrassment or indignation is justified (a revelation of their true affiliation with the upper classes), and often in scenes in which both appear simultaneously.

Evelina's struggles to keep the unpleasant Sir Clement Willoughby from seeing her with the Branghtons are very reminiscent of Marianne's efforts to keep Valville from learning where she lives. The important difference is that in the English novel of manners the emphasis is usually on the social blunder and thus on the satire rather than on the sensibility that naturally excludes such as the Branghtons, for Willoughby (unlike Valville), any sensible girl should know, has nothing to offer but his gentility. Even the scenes with the worthy Orville usually put the emphasis on Evelina's error. The novel of manners in England again reveals its derivation from the Quixotic anti-romance in which the aspiring knight in his hopelessly ill-fitting armor but noble heart goes after windmills; he is the ancestor of the girl who does not know her parents but, being a natural aristocrat, half-consciously aspires to social poise and the hand of an earl, committing terrible gaffes, some of which are unpardonable, along the way.

Evelina has too much of the Smollettian character in her to lose all traces of the satiric device. Her embarrassment—the effect of the Branghtons' faux pas on her delicate sensibility—can be taken as another mutation of Bramble's violent reaction to sociomoral corruptions. At any rate, the reactions of cultivated heroines in scenes with boors are gentle cousins to the satiric outburst. In *The Mysteries of Udolpho* Emily reacts thus to the vulgarity of Mme. Cheron: her "countenance, during this coarse speech, varied every instant, and towards its conclusion her distress had so much increased that she was on the point of leaving the room" (Everyman ed., *1, 142*). The embarrassment of Evelina is more personal than Bramble's; her future with an aristocratic husband is at stake, and so, in the celebrated scene at the opera, her enlightened self-importance is caught in the same satiric situation as the Branghtons' stupid self-importance. Both roles are still distinct enough to make her derivation from the English satiric tradition plain, and yet they dramatically merge as they lead her toward abduction at the hands of the proper gentleman Willoughby.

Smollett always stops short of this treatment of the personal problem because, although he reduces his satirical spokesman's attitude to just one way of looking at the world, he still shares with his satirical forebears the assumption that the individual's quest is not as important as the many different endeavors of the people surrounding him. This may offer an explanation for the form of the anatomy he employs, where person after person and scene after scene receive varying but not disproportionate emphasis; the whole human organism is the important consideration, and the satirist feels that a hand or a foot should never make one lose sight of the larger meaning of the whole. In this sense *Evelina* is a careful balance of the old and new: the anatomy of society is still present, and the protagonist is still functioning as a satiric device, but the fictional form given these matters is about to absorb and subordinate them all to the single theme of the protagonist's growing self-awareness.

Jane Austen: Pride and Prejudice

In *Pride and Prejudice* satire has been successfully sublimated. The framework upon which Austen builds still owes much to satire, however, and in her early work her manipulation of the satiric forms of her predecessors can be plainly seen. The result can only be called a novel in which satire is one of the novelist's tools. *Northanger Abbey* (written c. 1797, publ. posthumously, 1818) is the most primitive of the novels, with its forebears almost painfully apparent. The characters are carried over from *Evelina*: Evelina becomes Catherine Morland, the "assiduous" Willoughby (or perhaps Mr. Smith) becomes James Thorpe, the awful Branghtons become the Thorpe family, and Lord Orville becomes Henry Tilney. Evelina's need to prove her cultivation to Orville in spite of the Branghtons and Mme. Duval becomes Catherine's struggle to gain Tilney's respect in spite of the Thorpes. The scenes of Evelina's embarrassment are repeated, but in *Northanger Abbey* they are much more easily circumvented; a short explanation to Elinor or Henry exonerates Catherine from Thorpe's egregious plots. Such scenes are now used less for their own sake; the characters are less obviously types, the scenes less stylized, and the anatomy of society dropped altogether. Society is narrowed to presentable and unpresentable segments, and the focus is clearly on Catherine's adjustment to this world rather than on the world itself.

Northanger Abbey is also, of course, another of the *Don Quixote* descendants. The parody attack on popular fiction (in particular, Gothic romance) connects it at once with the anti-romance and, like Fielding's attack on Pamelian virtue in *Joseph Andrews,* begins in the author's commentary. Catherine, like Joseph, is measured against the standards of popular fiction and found wanting—and so is made a more credible character. The narrator, however, closer to the lover of greatness who recounts the life of Jonathan Wild, tries to bring the protagonist up to the mark, but, as Howard S. Babb has noted, the reader sees "the real difference between the fundamentally honest, good-natured Catherine and the egotistical, exaggeratedly sensitive heroine of the sentimental novel."[14] For example, her father was a clergyman "without being neglected, or poor . . . and he was not in the least addicted to locking up his daughters." Her mother, "instead of dying in bringing . . . [Catherine] into the world, as any body might expect . . . still lived on—lived to have six children more." Catherine herself "had neither a bad heart nor a bad temper; was seldom stubborn, scarcely ever quarrelsome," and so on.[15] The first volume uses this romance-realism contrast as a way to define negatively the realism of the author's fiction.[16] The Gothic is introduced by the ironic Fielding-like narrator as the same sort of alternative reality offered by Fielding in *Jonathan Wild* (moral) or in *Joseph Andrews* (moral and ontological) to define the reality of his characters and situations. The first volume, including the whole of Chapter 5, contains much commentary on the writing of fiction.

Side-by-side with this theme about what is or is not real or novelistic, Austen places the *Evelina* action of the naïve young girl who enters society. Only in the second volume, however, does she connect the two themes, bringing the Gothic parody to bear on the heroine's situation. When Catherine is introduced by her friend Isabella to *The Mysteries of Udolpho,* the point of view of the popular novel becomes more or less lodged in Catherine, and when she reaches Northanger Abbey, she becomes the familiar Quixotic figure who sees reality as romance. Though the Gothic romances she is so fond of do not unhinge her, they make her detect the most sinister and suspicious elements in the most commonplace occurrences and objects. They create her point of view, which is thereafter parallel and, in general, indistinguishable from the narrator's.

14. *Jane Austen's Novels: The Fabric of Dialogue* (Columbus, Ohio State University Press, 1962), pp. 87–88.

15. *The Novels of Jane Austen*, ed. R. W. Chapman (London, Oxford University Press, 1943–59), 5, 13–14. Hereafter referred to as Chapman. Subsequent references are to this edition.

16. See Cynthia Griffin, "The Development of Realism in Jane Austen's Early Novels," *Journal of English Literary History*, 30 (1963), 36–52. See also A. D. McKillop, "Critical Realism in *Northanger Abbey*," in *From Jane Austen to Conrad*, eds. Robert C. Rathburn and Martin Steinmann, Jr. (Minneapolis, University of Minnesota Press, 1958), pp. 35–45.

Catherine is put in the simplest anti-romance situation: her mind full of romance, she goes forth into an unromantic world. But she is also the typical Quixote in that she embodies a double irony: after being proved wrong, she turns out to be in a sense correct.[17] After she has exhibited her Quixotism to the ultimate embarrassment, Henry Tilney, the voice of common sense, shows her how foolish she has been:

> Remember the country and the age in which we live. Remember that we are English, that we are Christians. Consult your own understanding, your own sense of the probable, your own observation of what is passing around you—Does our education prepare us for such atrocities? (p. 197)

However it very soon becomes apparent that she does indeed live in such a world. In the well-mannered General Tilney she sees a sinister Montoni who has done away with his wife. Sure enough, he suddenly and without warning or explanation expels Catherine from Northanger Abbey. When it comes, the explanation for his peremptory, brutal, irrational, and melodramatic action is as commonplace (intentionally so) as those in Mrs. Radcliffe's novels: he has heard from an unreliable source that her family is penniless. (One reason for the episode may have been to satirize this aspect of the Radcliffe-type novel.) But Catherine, whose Quixotism has once again shown itself to be an insight into the truth as well as a folly, concludes "that in suspecting General Tilney of either murdering or shutting up his wife, she had scarcely sinned against his character, or magnified his cruelty" (p. 247). The world of manners and polite society *is* an orderly facade through which the irrational and self-seeking breaks from time to time. Henry Tilney's conventional explanation of society is not finally sufficient.

After the discovery, in General Tilney's action, that romance can be reality, Catherine does in fact become the Gothic heroine, against whom she has been so often measured and found wanting. When she leaves her friend Elinor Tilney, she is urged and agrees to write "by

17. For this aspect of *Northanger Abbey*, see John K. Mathison, "*Northanger Abbey* and Jane Austen's Conception of the Value of Fiction," *Journal of English Literary History*, 24 (1957), 138–52.

every post," a convention which previously had been shown to separate her from the true heroine (cf. pp. 19, 228–29). Once home, she "sunk . . . without knowing it herself, into languor and listlessness"; she has an "absent and dissatisfied look," which her mother considers proof of her "repining spirit"—"so dreadful a malady" (p. 241). The common sense of her mother and Mrs. Allen cannot avail against her "feelings." Then, just in the nick of time, her "fiction" or "dream" comes true: Tilney, the hero, arrives and puts everything to rights. (In both the compact with Elinor and Tilney's arrival, however, Austen does not fail to undercut the romance with unromantic details.)

As the conclusion shows, Austen has not resolved in her own mind whether the book is about reality (or how to write a novel) or about character and manners, her true subject of self-discovery. It turns out to be about both. In terms of the former, the ending proves the point of Chapter 5 in Volume I—that fiction is different from reality, and that reality as well as fiction is not based only on probability and common sense. The second theme, the romanticism of the young girl, is climactic but mixed: Catherine's point of view turns out to be a corrective to both Tilney's and her parents', but she has also *become* the romance heroine and blundered into a few scenes of romance-in-reality. The ending, in that sense, is closer to *The Vicar of Wakefield* than to *Evelina*.

Nevertheless, the association of Gothic and the narrator's mock-heroic tone with the protagonist points toward Elizabeth Bennet in *Pride and Prejudice*. Before turning to that novel, however, we must comment on the character in *Northanger Abbey* who does correspond to the narrator as ironist. Like the narrator, Henry Tilney speaks in ironic opposition to the "novelistic"conventions. As she sets up the clichés of popular novels as contrasts to real behavior, he parodies the commonplaces of Bath social life; after going through the whole catalog of polite inanities with Catherine, he concludes: "Now I must give one smirk, and then we may be rational again." Then turning to the conventions of popular sentimental fiction, he attempts, like the narrator, to define Catherine and himself in terms of them: she must, he says, keep a journal, and he constructs hypothetical pages in the journal to describe her possible reactions to him. When he turns to Mrs. Allen and her fixation on dress, Catherine sees that he is a satirist and fears "that he indulged himself a little too much with the foibles of others" (p. 29); and the reader sees that uncannily (since only he and the narrator have enough evidence to know about Catherine's reading and Mrs. Allen's obsession with dress) Tilney has hit upon the foible of each. He is clearly the Austen mouthpiece, although the author is careful to let him explain his motive—that "nothing in the world advances intimacy so much" as teasing (p. 29). He continues to fulfill the role of authorial surrogate insofar as the author is an advocate of "history" and common sense, and he continues to offer elaborate Gothic alternatives or models for Catherine to the extent that one might well suspect that he stimulates her to her Gothic frenzy (Vol. II, Chap. 5, the equivalent of the chapter in the first volume in which the author discusses the novel as romance and reality). Therefore Tilney is perhaps an even closer ancestor of Elizabeth Bennet than the simpleminded Catherine; like Elizabeth he is an ironist, and like her he sees only a partial truth and is parallel to the authorial irony without being a first-person speaker.

The first thing to be said about Austen's authorial irony in *Pride and Prejudice* (1796–97, published 1813) is that it is not omniscient. It develops Fielding's design in *Tom Jones* of keeping the reader in the dark and creating suspense by giving him only partial answers; it cannot, for example, do more than hint at the truth about Wickham. The way Austen manages this without suggesting any of the manipulation which is occasionally overbearing in *Tom Jones* is to offer a general parallel in her irony to Elizabeth Bennet's point of view, to make her own commentary and degree of awareness (and so omniscience) approximately parallel to that of her protagonist who is in the process of self-education.

Although the irony, as in *Northanger Abbey,* is set in motion before Elizabeth appears, it very soon proves to be an anticipation of her attitude toward the people of her world. The direct statement about her mother in Chapter 1 ("a woman of mean understanding, little information, and uncertain temper")[18] as well as the quiet irony with which her father is regarded express her views of her parents: she feels contempt for her mother and love for her father, but she has a clear recognition of his failings. When Elizabeth appears the irony

18. Chapman, 2, 5.

moves about with a lively insistence, impersonating this or that typical attitude, but always expressing her critical view of society. The irony of the opening chapters, for instance, assumes the point of view of the marriage-eager mother or her equally marriage-eager daughter, who will be Elizabeth's main antagonists as the novel proceeds. The first chapter begins with the generalization upon which the world of *Pride and Prejudice* is built, "that a single man in possession of a good fortune, must be in want of a wife" (p. 3), and it becomes almost Swiftean in the description of Darcy in Chapter 3. Upon his first appearance at the hall everyone is full of admiration for Darcy because of "his fine, tall person, handsome features, noble mien" and because of "the report which was in general circulation within five minutes after his entrance of his having ten thousand a year." In short, he is the ideally eligible husband.

> The gentlemen pronounced him to be a fine figure of a man, the ladies declared he was much handsomer than Mr. Bingley, and he was looked at with great admiration for about half the evening, till his manners gave a disgust which turned the tide of his popularity; for he was discovered to be proud, to be above his company, and above being pleased; and not all his large estate in Derbyshire could then save him from having a most forbidding, disagreeable countenance, and being unworthy to be compared with his friend. (p. 10)

Bingley and Darcy become the ends of a teeter-totter: Darcy is up when his money and figure are seen, but down (and Bingley up) when it becomes evident that he is not offering himself as a marriage prospect (for "proud," read "outside the matchmakers' society"). Unlike Darcy, Bingley "was lively and unreserved, danced every dance, was angry that the ball closed so early, and talked of giving one himself at Netherfield. Such amiable qualities must speak for themselves," the ironic narrator adds, expressing the view of all the anxious mothers, fathers, and daughters (pp. 10–11).

If this is not Elizabeth's detached and critical view of the matchmaking ritual of the ball, it is parallel to it. It is also Elizabeth's view that Catherine and Lydia were fortunate enough never to be without partners, "which was all that they had yet learnt to care for at a ball" (p. 12). Although the verbal irony is turned on the matchmakers a dramatic irony very shortly catches Elizabeth herself. She overhears Darcy's explanation to Bingley for not dancing, which is partly a criticism of the matchmaking ritual and partly an exposure of his feeling that he is above these particular specimens. When he says, "You know how I detest it [dancing], unless I am particularly acquainted with my partner" (p. 11), he is alluding to the arbitrary coupling of dancers that is a preliminary to the arbitrary matching of man and wife. But he also exposes his own mixture of shyness, aloofness, and pride. Elizabeth could be expected to see through his pose, but he turns his eye on her: "tolerable; but not handsome enough to tempt *me*"; after this, she interprets his words and his other speeches as symptoms of pride.

But when she remains "with no very cordial feeling towards" Darcy, one senses the self-awareness that sees herself, the eavesdropper, as part of a comic situation and so tells "the story however with great spirit among her friends" (p. 12). The remainder of the sentence ("for she had a lively, playful disposition, which delighted in any thing ridiculous") is as beautifully ambiguous as Fielding's comments on Lady Booby and Slipslop: it can represent either the fact as reported by the author or Elizabeth's view of herself (not that Austen intends a Jamesian treatment of point of view). Besides the dramatic irony that criticizes Elizabeth, the narrator sometimes detaches her view from Elizabeth's, and the reader is made to see the truth long before Elizabeth does. But often facts are withheld that Elizabeth could not know, and as ironic exposure creeps up on Wickham, in spite of Elizabeth's preference for him, or on Elizabeth herself, the reader tends to interpret these as Elizabeth's unstated suspicions and growing self-knowledge. When, on visiting Pemberley with her aunt and uncle, she thinks that she might have been mistress there but decides that Darcy would never have permitted her to invite her aunt and uncle, Austen adds: "This was a lucky recollection—it saved her from something like regret" (p. 246). This is presumably beyond Elizabeth's awareness, and yet, since she is capable of self-irony and is approaching the point of self-recognition, one may tend to read it as one level of Elizabeth's consciousness. At any rate there is the illusion of being outside Elizabeth and seeing her errors and at the same time seeing the world largely through her ironic intelligence.

Austen has often been said to combine the novels of Richardson and Fielding. I think one can take this to mean that she makes an amalgam of the themes concerning the importance of the self in both novelists (although one must not take this to mean that she ignored the lesser novelists who intervened)—Richardson's obsession with the importance of the unviolated self, combined with Fielding's need to see the self in a social rather than a sexual context. Austen's central figure thus defends her integrity against proposals of marriage, not against physical attack (Elizabeth against Collins rather than Lovelace), and being something of a Fielding character, she is partly wrong. In short, Austen takes the concern with conscience and the inner workings of the heroine's mind from Richardson; the mode of her expression—irony—she takes from Fielding, which allows her to place and judge her characters.

The important element in Austen's amalgam, however, is the theme of self-discovery, perhaps derived from *Evelina* and best seen in her use of point of view. Austen begins with the Fielding narrator and a character and then brings the two points of view together. Fielding never allows this (except perhaps in *Amelia*). In his novels the omniscient narrator and the characters are always radically separate, and so the self-discovery is only in the reader or, in a sense, in the narrator—the only person in the fiction who, by the end, knows the whole truth. Neither Clarissa nor Tom makes as definitive a discovery about himself as the reader's. But in *Pride and Prejudice,* where the narrator's awareness is in general close to the protagonist's, the protagonist comes to self-knowledge: the crucial truth is in a character's realization instead of the reader's. When Elizabeth, after reading Darcy's letter, recognizes the truth about the character of Darcy and Wickham, she sees the truth about herself: "till this moment," she cries, "I never knew myself" (p. 208). The next stage is to recognize that she loves Darcy and to come to terms with this truth.

Fielding's original disagreement with Richardson was based in part on his belief that reality was moral truth, as opposed to Richardson's implication that it was the true workings of a mind, which need be neither true nor false in relation to the world around the character. Austen brings these two concepts together, making reality the clear awareness in a character of relationships and values, of factual and moral truth, as opposed to the deluded, "humourous" views of those others who wear distorting glasses.

Pride and Prejudice is the most brilliant of Austen's novels in part because it is the most polished and stylized. The chapter that stands by itself, the striking satiric portrait, and the symmetry of relationships are at their best here. They represent the fulfillment of the satiric threads followed in Fielding, and in *Pride and Prejudice* they still function as the characters assume new relationships like the dancers of a minuet. A simple example of Fielding's basic touchstone form appears in Mr. Collins' letter to the Bennets in which, recalling that the estate is entailed upon him, he announces his approaching visit. He tells Mr. Bennet that he wishes to "assure you of my readiness to make them [his wife and daughters] every possible amends" for his future possession of the estate. Each member of the family responds in a characteristic way: (1) the tolerant Jane cannot see how he can make amends but "the wish is certainly to his credit." (2) Elizabeth immediately sees through him: "He must be an oddity, I think," she says. "I cannot make him out.—There is something very pompous in his stile.—And what can he mean by apologizing for being next in the entail?—We cannot suppose he would help it, if he could.—Can he be a sensible man, sir?" (3) Mr. Bennet has "great hopes of finding him quite the reverse. There is a mixture of servility and self-importance in his letter, which promises well. I am impatient to see him." (4) Mary, the "literary" sister, sees his letter as not defective "in point of composition." (5) Catherine and Lydia are not interested in anything that does not wear a scarlet coat (Mr. Collins is a clergyman). (6) Mrs. Bennet, however, "was preparing to see him with a degree of composure, which astonished her husband and daughters" (she correctly reads "amends" to mean that Collins wishes to marry one of her daughters).[19]

Such a form, as stylized as Joseph and the coachload of people, seems perfectly appropriate in *Pride and Prejudice* because the novel is about just such artificial forms. The rigid forms connected with the arranging of marriages, dictated by financial considerations only, are opposed by the vitality and common sense of Elizabeth Bennet. The meaning of the above scene or one like the ball at Northerton is concerned with the interplay of levels and kinds of awareness—the limited awareness of the matchmakers and the greater awareness of Jane, Elizabeth, and Mr. Bennet.

19. Ibid., pp. 62–65.

Mr. Bennet, an ironist who lacks the moral fiber of a satirist, stays up late to hear how the ball went: "he had a good deal of curiosity as to the event of an evening which had raised such splendid expectations [in his wife and daughters]. He had rather hoped that all his wife's views on the stranger [Bingley] would be disappointed" (p. 12). He sees through the shams of his family and friends but enjoys their folly. He eagerly awaits Collins' arrival for the diversion a fool will give him and even shows grim pleasure at the end in having the dastardly Wickham for a son-in-law. He is, in fact, a Jery Melford grown old and married to the wrong woman. He married Mrs. Bennet only for her good looks, and when he discovered her folly he merely withdrew into himself and regarded her with an ironic detachment that has become self-indulgent. He is now interested in her only "as her ignorance and folly . . . contributed to his amusement"— which Elizabeth sees as a "continual breach of conjugal obligation and decorum which, in exposing his wife to the contempt of her own children, was . . . highly reprehensible" (p. 236).

Jane's point of view is completely uncritical, a suggestion of her paternal heritage, and a foil to the rigorous mind of her sister. Elizabeth, the clearheaded, satirically inclined critic of her society, inherits the critical part of her father's makeup. Unlike Mr. Bennett, she intends improvement and instruction as the ends of her irony, and so in the Smollettian sense she is a satirist. She first defends herself, saving herself from the sort of relationship to which her father has passively succumbed; then she sees and points to the dangers to her friend Charlotte Lucas and others. Echoing Clarissa's remarks on Anna Howe, she explains to Darcy, for whom she has a satiric reputation: "I hope I never ridicule what is wise or good. Follies and nonsense, whims and inconsistencies *do* divert me, I own, and I laugh at them whenever I can" (p. 57). Austen treats Elizabeth more kindly than Smollett treats his satirists, but like Bramble, Elizabeth is made to represent individualism fighting against the second-rate, the accepted, and the constricting, and, like Bramble, her motive is self-preservation.

Darcy is the other individualist in *Pride and Prejudice*—made so by his great fortune, good looks, and intelligence, as well as by his partial insights into the Bennets' world. In a sense he is above it, in a more aristocratic world, and can look down with detachment. "A lady's imagination," he points out to Miss Bingley, "is very rapid; it jumps from admiration to love, from love to matrimony in a moment" (p. 27). His position and point of view, however, make him too aloof, his ideal too high to reach. If the tone of Elizabeth's speeches is laughingly Horatian, his draws on the sober Juvenalian stance:

> My temper I dare not vouch for.—It is I believe too little yielding —certainly too little for the convenience of the world. I cannot forget the follies and vices of others so soon as I ought, nor their offences against myself. . . . My temper would perhaps be called resentful.—My good opinion once lost is lost for ever. (p. 58)

Darcy is also Juvenalian in that he judges society not by reason or his own vitality so much as by the standards of his ancestors and of tradition. He and Elizabeth are probably drawn to each other because they are the two people who see through this society and act upon their knowledge.

The distinctive Austen subject, then, is the discrepancy between manners and the individual in terms of awareness. It is significant that she should have represented Catherine Morland's adjustment to her world in terms of the Quixote situation. Although we never think of Cervantes as we read her later novels, we cannot miss the fact that they continue to present the same conflict between a conventional and limiting system of values and the freedom and integrity of the individual. But if we do not think of Quixote, we may well think of Tom Jones with his reliance on feeling in a world of petty and often vicious prudence and formalism. (In *Sir Charles Grandison* the satire is on the suitors, never on the system of courtship.) Instead of Jones' instinctive and sometimes confused actions, Austen introduces the author's analytic, ironic intelligence at work commenting, criticizing, and sometimes misunderstanding. The loneliness of a Quixote, a Marianne, or an Evelina is always present, even when the protagonist is among her own family and friends.

Pride and Prejudice as a novel of manners involves a relationship between two sets of values, one ideal and the other real, one free and natural and the other overcodified and unnatural. The protagonist is a young girl who relates these two areas. Initially these are simply individualism and conformity or true love and matchmaking, and so the relationship is between the free individual and a single code of manners. But the situation is complicated by Elizabeth's association with the Darcys against her family, as Evelina associated herself with the Orvilles against the Branghtons and her grandmother. A reaction against one's own original status is implicit, and the typical scenes of embarrassment follow. She "tremble[s] lest her mother should be exposing herself again" (p. 45). When Mary sings before the Bingleys and Darcys, another small touchstone scene is produced around Elizabeth's anxiety:

> Elizabeth was in agonies. She looked at Jane, to see how she bore it; but Jane was very composedly talking to Bingley. She looked at his two sisters, and saw them making signs of derision at each other, and at Darcy, who continued however impenetrably grave. She looked at her father to entreat his interference, lest Mary should be singing all night. (p. 100)

Mary's solo is a small test for everybody there, and everybody reacts accordingly. There is thus a delicate balance—much more delicate than in *Humphry Clinker*—between the observer and the observed, between Elizabeth and the society she sees through. Even the situation of the sensitive young girl hemmed in by the matchmakers is crucially qualified. The image of the matchmaking ball and the husband-hungry mothers builds to the climax of the first volume when Elizabeth experiences, as D. W. Harding has put it, "the fantastic nightmare in which economic and social institutions have such power over the values of personal relationships that the comic monster is nearly able to get her."[20] Collins, the unpleasant young man who happens to be heir to the Bennets' property, is all but forced on Elizabeth. But if Collins is the ogre who brings out the worst aspect of the system, Charlotte Lucas represents the realism of the system, set off against Elizabeth's idealism. She is well aware of all the facts of life in her society, from the knowledge that "a woman had better shew *more* affection than she feels" (p. 22) to the realization that, now "at

---

20. "Regulated Hatred: An Aspect of the Work of Jane Austen," *Scrutiny, 8* (1939–40), 353. This and other useful essays on Austen are reprinted in *Jane Austen,* ed. Ian Watt (New York, Prentice-Hall, 1963).

the age of twenty-seven, without having ever been handsome" (p. 123), her best solution is to marry Collins. Elizabeth is right that Charlotte has sold herself to a fool—ideally such marriages should not be. But in this world they have to be; there is no other place for such as Charlotte Lucas than in Collins' vicarage.

This is, of course, a situation that Austen is satirizing, and Elizabeth's direct criticism is only part of the satire;[21] another part is Charlotte's hopeless realization that for some people this is the only answer. At this point the wife-husband relation has become analogous to the various fool-knave relations of satire. It remains in the background in the false relationships of the Bennets and in almost all of the established marriages in Austen's novels, with always one ideal marriage by which to judge the rest—in *Pride and Prejudice,* the Gardiners'. The foreground is taken up with the process of arriving at the marriage, the courtship's own corruptions and follies, and so usually concerns a mother-daughter relation.

Sometimes the situation can be one of active knavery, involving at least potentially appalling consequences, as when Mrs. Bennet sends Jane to visit the Bingleys on horseback because it looks like rain and she will have to spend the night. The consequence is Jane's cold. Here Mrs. Bennet's machinations have a dangerous physical effect on somebody; Mr. Bennet tells her, "if your daughter should have a dangerous fit of illness, if she should die, it would be a comfort to know that it was all in pursuit of Mr. Bingley, and under your orders" (p. 31). The most notable consequence, of course, is Lydia's elopement, which was caused by Mrs. Bennet and not prevented by Mr. Bennet.

Although Charlotte's realization that one cannot act outside the bounds of social custom (however ridiculous) is criticized, it nevertheless remains the conclusion of the novel. The ending is technically comic in that Wickham, now a member of the Bennet family, is accepted—with varying degrees of enthusiasm—within the family circle (he is, in fact, the final touchstone by which the members of the

---

21. The contrast reaches to the narrator's and the characters' vocabularies, in which words like "fortune," "property," "possession," "establishment," and "business" are juxtaposed with "feelings" and "love." See Van Ghent, p. 102, and Mark Schorer, "Fiction and the Analogical Matrix,' in *Critiques and Essays on Modern Fiction,* ed. John W. Aldridge (New York, Ronald Press, 1952), pp. 83–98.

family are tested). The effect is only partly comic, however. The point that Austen makes—if such a basic assumption can be called a point—is that this is the society one lives in; however badly people behave, however boring or self-indulgent they are, they cannot be excluded from one's awareness (as Mr. Bennet attempts to do). The idealist herself cannot withdraw, though she may marry a man who represents a higher class and a different society. The effect is double—pessimistic in that one can never get rid of the Collinses and Wickhams, let alone the Mrs. Bennets and Lydias. This effect is what Harding refers to as Austen's "regulated hatred," and its satiric implication is "that the ruling standards of our social group leave a perfectly comfortable niche for destestable people and give them sufficient sanction to persist," and so they are "society's embarrassing unconscious comment on itself."[22]

But while this effect is operative, the reader has to withdraw from the book and sit back and see the world as a whole before its full impact reaches him. While he reads the book the effect is different: these people, however awful, are as well known to him as they are to Elizabeth Bennet, and he would no more think of excluding them from his awareness than he would his own neighbors.[23] Their closeness makes him accept their foibles as he does Walter's and Toby Shandy's, but Austen does not force him to believe, as Sterne did, that there is something inherently valuable in foibles. As a result he is given a world in which moral awareness is possible, even emphasized, but not finally acted upon, except in the case of the individual's own salvation. In this sense, it is a more successful performance of the feat Fielding attempted in *Amelia*—to separate the public and the private. Here, for the first time persuasively dramatized, is the "acceptance world" of the novel, which replaces the rigorous moral demarcations of satire. The ending is not satiric because it presents not a hopeless, nightmare world of fallen ideals, but the real world, good mixed with bad, ideals with corruptions of ideals, in which the one cannot realistically withdraw from its relation with the other.

This is quite different from the world of *Tom Jones* in which Fielding shows how mixed people's motives are and how difficult it is to

22. Harding, "Regulated Hatred," pp. 352, 353.
23. Jane Austen's "typical dilemma," Harding writes, is "being intensely critical of people to whom she also has strong emotional attachments" (ibid., p. 355).

judge them. Fielding's world is still essentially a rhetorical one, in which the reader and his application of the story, rather than the creation of a milieu, is the final end; his characters, however, though considerably less convincing as illusions of people, represent a more complex conception of human character than Austen's. Her erring characters in *Pride and Prejudice* seldom suffer from a confusion of motives. What makes her world novelistic is the necessary acceptance of them—not, as with Fielding, because the reader is tolerant and sees the difficulty of judging any human action, but in spite of their unpleasantness.

Here is the center of the realism of Austen's novels. If Fielding sensed that in life judgments of right and wrong are in fact very difficult, Austen sensed that in life—and particularly in domestic situations—one does not feel strongly for longer than a moment about one's acquaintances' failings. They are, after all, one's family or friends, and one has no one else. And so we are made to accept our tolerance for Mr. Bennet, even if intellectually we see that he is bad, because it shows how he *is* accepted—and *must be* accepted by his friends and family—rather than how he *should be* accepted. "Should be" cannot have much of a role in the overall effect of a novel; it may be present but is usually domesticated, absorbed into a larger fiction or qualified out of existence. Even Wickham is accepted because "must be" always wins out over "should be." Charlotte is the spokesman for reality when we are told of her:

> Without thinking highly either of men or of matrimony, marriage had always been her object; it was the only honourable provision for well-educated young women of small fortune, and however uncertain of giving happiness, must be their pleasantest preservative from want. (pp. 122–23)

The fact that the reader nevertheless does not accept Mrs. Bennet or Wickham and suspects that Elizabeth may be gritting her teeth is not only part of the Austen realism but also an indication that satire has not been transformed past recognition.

More important, however, with Austen we arrive through satire at yet another form of realism. Reality has meant successively materialism, illusionism, consciousness, delicate discriminations and judgments, and now with Austen it comes to mean a careful description of how society operates, which has only been glimpsed before in Defoe's interest in how pickpockets or escape artists operated. This is not to suggest that Austen creates a Marxist realism: she does not show the great cause and effect relationships of her age, makes no mention of Napoleon or capitalism, and creates no great types of economic forces. But on her own "little bit (two Inches wide) of Ivory" she does show how her "3 or 4 Families in a Country Village" are motivated and constructed, what forces control them, what happens when a disruption occurs, and how they are then reconstituted. She implies that there is in fact no important connection between her microcosm and the macrocosm; speaking realistically, she might say, the Bennets are independent of and uninfluenced by the great dialectic of history.

Conclusion

Austen's novels not only serve as a sort of destination, containing examples of successful satiric accommodation, but also provide a convenient recapitulation of the incompletely transformed or absorbed conventions that remain a prominent characteristic of the nineteenth-century novel. Inevitably, even in Austen's maturest novels, the satiric convention that retains some of its original meaning creates a jarring effect. Take, for example, Austen's particular version of the Juvenalian convention of the isolated protagonist: in a large family, universally obtuse, there is one member, a moral agent, who is both good and intelligent—in the whole Dashwood clan, only Elinor; and in the even worse Ferrars clan, only Edward. Of all the Bennets Elizabeth is a similar (although more complex) case, and Fanny among the Prices and Bertarms and Anne among the Elliots and Musgroves are even more isolated. The convention of obscure parentage, which is inherited from *Marianne* and *Evelina* (and is perhaps as much a sentimental as a satiric convention), serves to underline the heroine's isolation. Only in *Mansfield Park* is the heroine actually an adopted child; the other heroines carry the impress of the orphan or changeling while being bona fide members of a flourishing family.

Those novels that emphasize only the heroine's isolated and injured integrity lean toward satire, and the bones of the old satiric conventions still show; those novels that emphasize the heroine's error and self-discovery transform the satiric convention beyond recognition into a novel of manners. As seen in the analysis of *Pamela,* whenever the heroine becomes simply passive and representative (the struggle with Mr. B. abating), she becomes the center of a satiric scene in which the rogues' gallery of egoists and snobs is opposed by this one good person isolated in their midst. For this reason, *Sense and Sensibility* (written c. 1797; published 1811), in spite of its balanced title, retains a satiric structure. To some extent the generosity of Marianne Dashwood's sensibility is played off as a corrective against the meanness of John Dashwood's sense. In total effect, however, the novel is not a comedy of manners in which sense is played off against sensibility; rather, every character is carefully fitted into a self-regarding slot, with Austen's emphasis settling solidly on the bad—whether sense *or* sensibility—and the contrasting ideal being expressed in the lonely Elinor, who is "on every occasion mindful of the feelings of others" (p. 62) and lets sense govern her sensibility.

The most extreme case, which has generally been thought to be uncharacteristic of Austen, is *Mansfield Park* (1814), where the heroine, Fanny Price, is not only more right than any other Austen heroine but more isolated and insecure—in an alien family, hemmed in by stupidity, with only Edmund Bertram, himself remarkably obtuse, for a friend. She is not a verbal satirist like Elinor or Elizabeth Bennet, but she is very much a judge and a critic and so normative as to have lost all but the slightest hint of a Tilney-Elizabeth error. *Mansfield Park* is Jane Austen's *Amelia,* her Juvenalian satire. Because of the heroine's near perfection and her role as a persecuted innocent in a strange society, the people around her assume a darker hue than in other Austen novels. Mrs. Norris is surely the most hateful of all Austen's bad characters. Moreover, the worst characters are not allowed back into the society at the end: Maria, Henry, and Mrs. Norris go off to live in exile together, and only with some difficulty are Yates and Julia readmitted.

One could go on listing the more or less successful absorptions of satiric conventions in Austen's novels. Perhaps the best-known is that she never entirely transforms the seductions and abandonments (if not abductions) from the novels of Richardson and Smollett. Their perfunctory, occasionally inexplicable appearance have led critics to raise questions as to Austen's understanding of passion, sex, and the like. It is in this mixed state, however, that satire is most frequently felt in eighteenth- and nineteenth-century novels. Whenever a group of characters assembles, one must ask, are they a representative spectrum of types? Are they all categorized and reduced to a single common vice, or do they in some degree maintain their integrity as characters? The transition can at least partly be perceived as the novelist changes the locus of activity from the coachride, inn, prison, or masquerade ball to the private social occasion—the party or ball to which guests are invited, their presence being directly due to their relationship to each other or to their host rather than to thematic considerations. The larger structure of these novels also wobbles between the anatomy of vice or of society (still the most pervasive form) and the intrigue or romance plot.

Even in the most unsatiric novels such intrusions are commonplace. Critics have complained about the unfairness of George Eliot's treatment of Hetty Sorrel in *Adam Bede,* attributing it to her failure to control her personal feelings. These feelings may have been the ultimate cause, but the immediate cause was the introduction of satiric exposition in the middle of a novel that is otherwise suffused with sympathy. Whenever Hetty appears, satiric irony comes into play. Time after time a description of her angelic expression or Adam's favorable interpretation of her looks is followed by the author's exposure of her self-centered thoughts.

The old and the new, the transformed and the unassimilated, exist side by side. However far Emma Woodhouse—Austen's most complex heroine—deviates from the moral norm in her misunderstandings of her suitors or her attempts to run the lives of others, the reader dogs her steps, and while he recognizes her failings, it is much harder to pass judgment on her than on the motley matchmakers or the helpless suitors who surround her. She is the result of a complex evolution, partly satiric; they are the last remains of satiric conventions that have lost most but not all of their original satiric meaning, at least in the company of such as Emma.

The most tangible result of the satiric tradition in the eighteenth century was, as this chapter has tried to show, the novel of manners of Jane Austen. Our exploration has followed a series of distinctive types of novel as they grew out of the contact with satiric forms, conventions, and impulses; these in turn have been regarded as a kind of evolutionary process culminating in *Pride and Prejudice*.

The Smollettian novel, however, had its own line of evolutionary development, leading to Dickens, and the Fielding-Sterne novels led to Thackeray. These novels must be regarded—as the Austen novel is regarded—to all purposes and intents as individual end products. Our exploration has led to something that can be called the Fielding novel, the Smollett novel, the sentimental-satiric novel, and so on—not to any single or multifold tradition that flows unchecked into the nineteenth or twentieth century. Novels do not grow that way; each corpus of novels and, to a certain extent, each novel is an independent tradition or at least a dead end. (Every great novelist has his *Ulysses* or *Finnegans Wake,* which allegedly brings some tradition, some potentiality, of the novel to a close.)

Without distorting too much, however, we can distinguish three broadly different groups of novels that felt the influence of satire and continue to be written in the twentieth century. The first type consists of the novels containing unassimilated conventions that jar uncomfortably against each other. The conventions either have lost their original meaning while retaining eye-catching formal characteristics or have retained their original meaning but not adjusted to an alien context. The second type is the satiric novel per se, in which satiric conventions tend to transform normative reality into what might be called a satiric vision. This would include not only Smollett and Dickens but, more recently, Evelyn Waugh, Nathanael West, Joseph Heller, and the other lively satirists of our time. The third and most pervasive type is the novel in which satire supports a realism that is nearly parallel to life itself. Whether in the broad epic novel of Fielding or in the novel of manners of Austen, the satire, in commentator or character, is ironic and directed to delicate discriminations and based on very broad and general social and moral assumptions.

Throughout this study we have observed satire adjusting to, rather than being submerged by, the rising "modern" assumptions outlined in our first pages. Satire's eclipse in the later eighteenth century was novelistically inspired only in the sense that the best satirists came to terms with the novel, adjusting its conventions, sometimes modifying their severity, and usually sacrificing either satire's or the novel's autonomy. As it was absorbed by the novel, the satiric judgment was complicated (Fielding) or emotionalized (Smollett) or softened (Sterne); only where it remained firm and unaccommodating, as in the Juvenalian parts of *Amelia* or in many parts of Smollett's novels, does the satiric world remain intact.

Satire maintained enough of its original impulse to preserve the novel from sliding off into the subjectivity that Fielding anticipated from his reading of *Pamela*. In fact, the immersive novel Ortega presupposes never really emerged, certainly not in the great novels of Eliot, James, and Conrad, or in those of the satirically inclined novelists discussed here. Satire has contributed its part as an analytic, critical tool that makes perfectly clear—whether through a commentator or mere juxtaposition—what the reader's attitude should be to Casaubon, Gilbert Osmond, Lord Jim, or Mr. Bennet. The pointing finger that directs the reader back into the real world does finally remain. Satire cannot be said to have given the emergent novel its moral impulse or even confirmed it; this was a sine qua non of realistic fiction, and *Pamela* was as moralistic as one could desire. What satire did do was to show how a realistic work could be moralistic and still realistic.